Profit for Life

Profit for Life

How Capitalism Excels

Case Studies in Living Asset Management

Joseph H. Bragdon

SOCIETY FOR ORGANIZATIONAL LEARNING

Published by SoL, The Society for Organizational Learning, Inc.
25 First Street, Suite 414
Cambridge, MA 02141 USA
1-617-300-9500
publisher@solonline.org

SoL is a nonprofit global membership organization whose purpose is to discover, integrate, and implement theories and practices for the interdependent development of people and their institutions. A
portion of the net proceeds from SoL publishing sales are reinvested in basic research, leading-edge
applied learning projects, and building a global network of learning communites.
For information on membership, professional development opportunities, events, and
other publications—including the e-journal Reflections—please visit www.solonline.org.

Book design: Chris Welch

Library of Congress Control Number: 2006906955

ISBN 10: 0974239038
ISBN 13: 9780974239033

For Jeanne

CONTENTS

Introduction

"The new theory sees the fundamental mission of a business not as profit, but as value creation. It sees profit as a vital consequence of value creation—a means rather than an end, a result as opposed to a purpose . . . . The new theory also makes loyalty a truer litmus test of corporate performance than profits ever were or could be."[1]

"[L]oyalty-based management is about people . . . . It is about motivation and behavior, not marketing or finance or product development . . . . It is about humanistic values and principles of the kind people devote their lives to . . . . People have always been far more motivated to devote energy to organizations with a service goal than to organizations that exist simply to make a buck."[2]

—Frederick F. Reichheld, Director Emeritus,
Bain & Company, *The Loyalty Effect*

Why is it that mature, cyclical firms such as the steel manufacturer Nucor, Southwest Airlines, and Toyota, have returned from 4 to 100+ times the Standard & Poor's 500 Index during the 31 years from 1974 to 2005—a period during which many of their once-giant competitors died or neared bankruptcy?

How did Nokia emerge from its identity as a forest products firm in the nineteenth century to become a giant in radio and electronics for most of the twentieth century, and finally, a global power in wireless communications in the past decade?

What is it about Stora Enso's culture that has enabled it to survive for seven centuries when most publicly traded corporations today live for fewer than 50 years?

How did Canon, Intel, HP, and 3M become the hotbeds of learning and innovation that they are today?

All of these companies have long had stewardship cultures rooted in *systemic caring*. They think and act like living communities that are integral to the larger living systems in which they exist—society, markets, and the biosphere. This conceptual framework is very different from the more traditional, mechanistic view that corporations are moneymaking machines that exist separate from society and the biosphere, both of which conventional economics views as "external" to the legitimate concerns of business.

During the past half-century, as world population and GDP (gross domestic product) have soared, and the Earth's biospheric carrying capacity has declined, these stewardship cultures have become more clearly articulated.[3] Their thought leaders now look more deeply into the connections between the firm, its individual employees, the communities it serves, and Nature. Their quest has been to discover more harmonic and sustainable ways of operating, and more effective ways to leverage one of our few unlimited resources—the human imagination.

Although still outside the corporate mainstream, the stewardship ideas and practices I will describe have made impressive inroads into every major industry and sector. Companies that have pioneered in the evolution of these practices have rolled up huge market share against their traditionally managed competitors.

Interestingly, the shift in management thinking I have observed parallels similar shifts in scientific thinking—away from deterministic theories, such as Newton's laws of physics, and toward theories based on complexity and the interrelatedness of all things, such as those in the newer sciences of quantum mechanics and ecology. We find a similar shift in medicine and psychology as practitioners explore mind-body connections that manifest in consciousness, free will, empathy, spirit, and ethics.

My goal in this volume is to distill the trends I have followed in management practices and other fields into a coherent and unified theory. This effort has been a personal quest that began in the late 1960s when I first saw a connection between corporate ethics and profitability.[4] The depth of that connection largely eluded me so long as I approached the matter in a traditional, linear (Newtonian) manner. However, it became a good deal clearer in the mid-1990s when I began thinking in a more holistic, systemic framework premised on the new sciences.

Living Assets

The most important feature of this new theory is the distinction between living assets (people and Nature) and nonliving assets (capital). I believe that, contrary to the mores of traditional capitalism, *living assets are more important to the productivity and longevity of companies than nonliving, capital assets.* Though this may seem a small matter of emphasis, its policy implications are enormous.

Why are living assets more important? In a word, they are the source of nonliving capital assets. Capital assets could not exist absent the knowledge and productivity of people and Nature. Our most intelligent capital assets, including supercomputers, cannot function without human guidance and natural resources.

I link people and Nature together in my definition of living assets because they are so tightly coupled in the web of life. According to biologist Edward O. Wilson, people have an instinctive reverence for life and Nature, which he calls "biophilia."[5] This instinct became wired into our genes through thousands of generations because people who respected life and Nature were more likely to survive and reproduce than those who did not, and were therefore better able to pass on their DNA to future generations.

If you accept the distinction between living and nonliving assets, then the logic of Living Asset Stewardship (LAS) makes sense. We take care of the things we most value. It's as simple as that. LAS, I believe, is the core of an emergent new theory of management.

Caring for the Things We Most Value

I define Living Asset Stewardship as "caring about people and the things people care about." In the context of Wilson's biophilia thesis, we can further condense the definition to "respect for life."

"Caring," as used in this sense, is not the soft, sentimental variety, but a more-disciplined, systemic caring that looks to the general health of the larger world (society, markets, and the biosphere) in which we operate.

Deep caring exists when we look beyond the end results of our actions to the processes we use to deliver those results. Traditional companies—those that rigorously manage by objectives—generally receive poor LAS ratings, even if their objectives are praiseworthy, because their linear-thinking, mechanistic behaviors inevitably clash with our human sense of individual value and the ways in which we most effectively learn and innovate. Doing "whatever it takes" to produce a number or result is risky because the linear thinker often cannot see beyond the objective to possible unintended consequences.

Alternatively, the best living asset stewards look to the integrity of their management processes by deeply caring for their employees' health and welfare, respecting their values, and serving the growth of their professional competence—trusting that when these things are done, the firm's goals will be met. This has been aptly dubbed "management by means."[6]

According to physicist and management consultant Danah Zohar, when companies operate in such ways (i.e., when their processes reflect our biophilic respect for life), they engage our higher thinking capacities. In such environments, people are more apt to transcend their logical, linear-thinking minds and enter their more intuitive and insightful "quantum" minds. We call this inspiration.

It is no accident that corporate LAS leaders attract and hold the best employees, customers, strategic partners, and investors. Their Living Asset Stewardship inspires us to affiliate with them. Whatever the costs of deep caring may be, they are returned many times over in sales and profit.

The Global LAMP Index®

To test the economic potential of LAS, I constructed a "learning laboratory" of 60 global LAS leaders, collectively called the Global Living Asset Management Performance (LAMP) Index.®[7] Each company in the index was selected for the consistency of its commitment to LAS relative to that of industry peers. To facilitate comparisons, the industry/sector balance of the Global LAMP Index® closely approximates that of the Standard & Poor's 500 Index (S&P 500) and the Morgan Stanley Capital International (MSCI) World Index. A comparison of the investment performance of these indices yields useful feedback on the market's assessment of LAS.

As one might expect, all 60 companies in our LAS learning laboratory are also prominent on global ethics and sustainability indices. But here the similarity to those indices ends. Our system for selecting LAMP companies looks beyond objectives and outcomes (the triple bottom line) to the addi-

Table 1: LAMP Investment Performance

Returns for both LAMP benchmarks*—the 16-company Focus Group and the larger Global LAMP Index®—were consistently superior to the most commonly used benchmarks of global and domestic equity performance.

Index	ANNUALIZED TOTAL RETURNS (AS%) AT YEAR-END 2005			
	1 Year	3 Years	5 Years	10 Years
Focus Group	9.53	17.90	4.98	14.93
Global LAMP Index™	11.63	22.62	8.26	17.37
S&P 500	4.91	14.38	0.54	9.07
MSCI World	9.49	18.69	2.19	7.04

* LAMP returns are based on an equal-weighted back-cast with dividends not reinvested. The S&P 500 and the MSCI World indices are weighted by market capitalization with dividends reinvested. Unlike the benchmark indices, which regularly drop laggard companies and add faster growers, there were no changes in the Global LAMP Index™ for the indicated period.

tional dimensions of means and process. (See Chapter 1 for more on the triple top and bottom lines.) This deeper, more demanding approach to stewardship is more congruent with the ways in which living systems operate. Its authenticity resonates with stakeholders and makes a huge difference in financial returns.

To explore the inner workings of LAS, I have extracted from the learning laboratory 16 companies whose stories we will follow throughout this volume. Notably, these companies, collectively called the Focus Group, are over-represented in mature, cyclical industries that typically operate in traditional, mechanistic ways—the airline, auto, chemicals, forest products, primary metals, and steel industries. The risk in using this configuration was a weakening of the argument for LAS by skewing the Focus Group toward slow-growth industries. However, the benefit is in highlighting the huge gains LAS leaders have earned at the expense of traditionally managed firms in these industries, as illustrated in appendices 2 and 5.

Chapter 5 will discuss in greater detail the selection processes I have used. Table 1 shows how the Global LAMP Index® and the Focus Group have performed; the results are stunning.

The Global LAMP Index® returns of the past decade (1996–2005) were more than double those of its closest proxy (the MSCI World Index) on an annualized basis, and beat the S&P 500 by a large margin, as well. The consistency of the LAMP's performance lead over both benchmarks—in both up and down markets—is extraordinary and can be seen in greater detail in Table 5-1 and Appendix 2. During that 10-year period, the performance of the more cyclical Focus Group was also exceptional, although it lagged behind the larger LAMP index because of its greater exposure to mature, slow-growth industries.

These results defy the conventional Wall Street wisdom that risk and reward are closely linked. By such logic, stocks that outperform in rising markets should underperform in declining markets. Though I do not argue with such reasoning as a general rule of thumb, I think it can be trumped when, as we are now witnessing, a superior strategic model begins to overtake an inferior one.

The results shown in Table 1 are based on back-tests rather than on actual returns. This is appropriate for a learning laboratory, in which our objective is to discover the effects of stewardship best practices. For the sake of consistency, results of the two LAMP averages are based on the same companies—equally weighted at the start of each year—for the entire 10-year test period. We assume no trades that might have heightened performance.

Shared Principles of LAS Leaders

All of the companies in the Global LAMP Index® share core philosophical and organizational principles. These are consistent with the idea that firms are living communities whose primary assets are living assets, and whose existence utterly depends on the health of larger living systems.[8] Because all life and living systems are inherently organized as networks, this mental model sees the optimal corporation as a living network that is closely integrated into the web of living networks in which it exists, where everything is related to everything else.

Although this mindset, or "theory of system," is rarely explicit in the policies of corporate LAS leaders, it is certainly implicit and increasingly expressed in corporate communications.[9] We typically find among LAMP companies:

- corporate mission, vision, and value statements that reflect life-affirming, sustainable ideals;
- operating principles that respect the environment and conserve resources;
- organizations that are decentralized and networked, with localized decision-making authority;
- workplaces where employees are trusted, empowered, and held accountable;
- leaders who mentor and serve the professional growth of employees;
- cultures that support continuous learning, collaboration, and idea sharing;
- fiscal policy designed to sustain the firm for generations and create a legacy for stakeholders; and
- management systems that regard profit primarily as a means to higher-quality service, rather than as an end in itself.

These principles and policies are consistently applied, and are congruent with a theory of system centered on the tight coupling of people and Nature in the web of life. In global LAMP companies we find that theory expressed in cultures that manage primarily by means (symbiosis) rather than by objectives. We also find it expressed in the fast-growing field of "industrial ecology."[10]

Shared Practices of LAS Leaders

Global LAMP companies' management practices are integral to their theories of system, ensuring that LAS principles are implemented at every level. Such consistency and congruency build commitment, trust, and loyalty from within—the foundations of strong relationships throughout the enterprise. Strong "relational equity" is the surest way to build financial equity.

Although the practices of LAMP companies may differ in emphasis or degree, they typically exhibit the following characteristics:

- CEOs and senior leaders continually support LAS in word and deed;
- management and employees are evaluated on their understanding of LAS principles and advancement of stewardship practices;
- sustainability and respect for life are embedded in all strategic thinking and planning;

- IT infrastructure supports ubiquitous networking between employees, customers, suppliers, and other important stakeholders;
- reporting systems are open and transparent, and include robust, balanced scorecard metrics;
- results are continually audited and evaluated to advance learning;
- investments look to long-term synergies rather than quick returns; and
- borrowing is limited and well within the firm's means—even in the worst of circumstances.

In the opening quote of this Introduction we find strong affirmation of the foregoing principles and practices. Bain & Company has built a dynamic franchise on its "loyalty practice." Frederick Reichheld, who led this practice, puts a high premium on "mutual caring, respect, responsibility, accountability . . . and trust" as ways to build loyalty.[11] This is not to say that Bain and Reichheld endorse Living Asset Stewardship, but they do affirm qualities that are deeply embedded in LAS cultures.

Leverage

The operating leverage in corporations comes from *synergies*, not from financial (i.e., mechanistic) gearing. Synergies arise when individual transactions benefit not only the transactors, but also the larger living systems in which they exist. When this happens, the whole becomes more than the sum of its parts. Gearing works differently. It involves a linear and finite *transfer* of energy rather than a continuous and cumulative *cycling* of energy. It also invites risks. Obviously, companies that borrow extensively to leverage their operations must repay the money they borrow.

LAMP companies' aversion to debt is evident in the strength of their balance sheets. More than half of LAMP companies have Moody's credit ratings of A-1 or higher. (See Appendix 3 for credit ratings for the Global LAMP Index® companies.) As seen in Table 3-1, this is almost double the ratio for the global corporate average. Also important, all LAMP companies are rated as investment grade, whereas nearly one-third of the companies comprising the global corporate average are rated below investment grade—a gap that has widened during the past decade. This is not random happenstance, but an integral function of the way the firms operate.

LAMP leaders seek leverage through inspiring employees and nurturing their professional growth. This creates huge synergies, as will be discussed in chapters 1 through 4. These leaders also understand that the carrying costs of debt can overwhelm companies during economic hard times, causing unplanned asset disposals, service interruptions, layoffs, and even bankruptcy. This reality is nowhere more evident than in the auto, steel, and airline industries—a fact that only underscores the outstanding performance of LAS leaders Toyota, Nucor, and Southwest Airlines. All three have been consistent profit and quality leaders in these very industries for more than three decades, with no layoffs. Not surprisingly, they are renowned for the spirit and professionalism of their employees, as well as for their humanistic and caring cultures.

Durability

LAS cultures are more durable than traditional ones because networks are more adaptable than management hierarchies. By engaging all their human resources, rather than just a select few at the top, LAMP companies develop quicker reflexes and deeper insight, which generally feed back to generate superior innovation.

The longevity of our learning laboratory supports this observation. The average and median ages of companies in the Global LAMP Index® exceed 100 years, as shown in Appendix 4. According to a famous study by Royal Dutch/Shell, this is more than double the average life expectancy of exchange-listed corporations, which is in the vicinity of 40 to 50 years.

Successful networking isn't related to company size, as some might imagine, with advantages accruing mainly to smaller, community-based companies. Some of the world's largest companies—Alcoa, Canon, Hewlett-Packard, HSBC Group, Intel, Johnson & Johnson, Royal Dutch/Shell, 3M, and Toyota—are radically decentralized and networked, with authority pushed as far out to the local level as possible. Within each operating unit these companies foster cultures of community, mutual caring, and shared responsibility.

The role of leaders in such organizations is to serve the professional growth of people working within the network—the means of the network's productive capacity—rather than to manage them by "command and control." Robert Greenleaf has called this approach "servant leadership." In his words, "The first order of business is to build a group of people who, under the influence of the institution, grow taller and become healthier, stronger and more autonomous."[12]

The durability of global LAMP companies is further enhanced by an ethic of freely sharing important business information. Employees are closely linked through corporate intranets so people in diverse business units can readily draw on each other's knowledge and experience. They regularly rotate through different business units and functions as a way of building relationships and exchanging skills within the firm. Employees are encouraged to form communities of practice wherein people with similar interests congregate to exchange ideas—both virtually and face-to-face. Those who make significant contributions are quickly recognized and rewarded without regard to their professional status. When business is good, LAMP companies are quick to share their prosperity with employees. When it is bad, they find creative ways to avoid layoffs or to help displaced employees retrain and find new work.[13]

Institutional Investors

Institutional investors today control most of the world's publicly traded shares. As public fiduciaries, they must act prudently and in their customers' best interests. If LAS produces better value and investment returns than traditional business practices do, these investors must favor the winning model. As the relative growth of the Global LAMP Index® attests, they have, indeed, done so.

The more institutional investors come to understand how the dynamics of LAS contribute to profitability, the more active they are likely to become in encouraging better stewardship in portfolio companies. This is already happening on an ad hoc basis among members of the Council of Institutional Investors (CII), a consortium of more than 140 pension funds with approximately $3 trillion under management.[14]

Looking to the future, I believe that institutional investors who learn the ways of LAS and promote it in the marketplace will gain market share. Those who take the opposite course and hold to traditional methods will be left behind. Such incentives will further accelerate the demand for corporations to implement LAS practices.

Ideas That Change the World

A simple shift in thinking—that the world is round instead of flat—gave rise to the sixteenth-century Age of Exploration. The simple act of placing living assets ahead of capital assets on a company's value scale offers analogous opportunities for advancement.

Such ideas usually arise for compelling reasons. The round-world theory emerged at a time when Europeans felt constrained and were looking to find new resources, markets, and trade routes for their expanding commerce. The practice of Living Asset Stewardship arises from a similar sense of constraint. World civilizations today feel hemmed in by the explosive growth of populations and by the decline of Earth's carrying capacity. Commercial thought leaders know we must find ways of producing and trading that are more resource-efficient and harmonious than those now in mainstream use.

Humanity abhors constraint. We want to explore, experiment, learn, and find new ways of living that expand frontiers for generations to come. In today's world of limited physical resources, we know that ideas are our only source of unlimited potential. Increasingly, we recognize that the way forward must be about the primacy of the great web of life. Networked organizations that respect life, that care about people and the things that people care about, inspire us to think and create. Their deep stewardship engages our higher thinking capacities in ways that mechanistic, command-and-control hierarchies could never do.

These realities are so compelling that, once companies get on the LAS path, there is usually no going back. People become wedded to it, will fight fiercely to protect it, and, if they believe they can't protect it, will leave. This kind of passion, as much as the market's validation of LAMP companies, is why Living Asset Stewardship is here to stay.

1

The Value of Living Assets

"Lying at the root of the profound inventions ahead, I believe, will be a slow, gradual process of discovering how the natural world, the living world, operates, and reorienting our institutions to embody this knowledge."[1]

—Peter Senge et al., *The Dance of Change*

This is a tale of two business cultures. One has been the dominant force during the past century. Its operating philosophy, terminology, accounting methods, policies, and practices prevail in most corporations worldwide. The other has been with us far longer, save for occasional periods of dormancy. This "other culture" has recently been reawakened by a group of innovative companies that see it as the best hope for the future of free-market enterprise. The leaders of this renaissance have been winning market share—and winning big.

You might say we are in the midst of a "Copernican Revolution" in conventional business thinking. We are finally waking up to the fact that corporations are not the center of our economic universe, with people and Nature orbiting around them. In fact, the opposite is true. People and Nature are the "sun," the very life source of corporations. Powerful though they are, corporations utterly depend on the living world, the web of life

1

that supports them. Those that weaken the web by treating it as an "externality" weaken themselves from within, while those that try to live in harmony with it are imbued with creative energy. Although mainstream economic and business accounting systems have not caught up with this revolution in business thought, the global markets have begun to shift in this direction.

Business leaders at the vanguard of this revolution—stewardship leaders—create value by reordering their relationships. Rather than assuming they are at the top of a food chain of people and Nature that exists to serve them (an egocentric view), they understand their complete dependence on this chain and take responsibility for ensuring its sustainability (a biocentric view). *This is a huge shift in strategic thinking.* The best corporate stewards see the firm's strength in terms of the living systems that support it, not in terms of their ability to use up those systems. Whereas the egocentric approach assumes the primacy of the corporation, this biocentric approach is a symbiotic one that is congruent with evolution. As we shall see, it engages more of our natural strengths than the corporate-centered approach does because it engages our hearts and, through our hearts, our higher thinking capacities.

To achieve the goals of *this* Copernican Revolution, the leadership companies have adopted organizational strategies radically different from those of traditional business. Rather than centralizing power in the hands of a small core of all-knowing corporate leaders, these companies have decentralized and distributed power through corporate networks. In lieu of scientific management by objectives set by those leaders, emphasis is put on empowerment of employees at the local level to self-organize spontaneously and to make decisions within their areas of competence. H. Thomas Johnson and Anders Broms call this empowerment process "management by means" and I totally endorse it.[2] Such management practices naturally embrace stewardship because they connect with the values and ideals of stakeholders who have a vested interest in the health of their communities and the biospheric resources we all share.

Call this thought model unorthodox or heretical, if you will, but the leading stewardship companies we'll discuss have produced impressive results. As a group, they are more profitable and financially stable than their traditional peers. The value of their shares in world stock markets has outrun all conventional indices for more than three decades. More often than not, they are the innovators who launch the breakthrough products that redefine our markets.

The leading firms of this emergent stewardship revolution have varied histories and backgrounds. They cut across every major industry and sector. Many were founded more than a century ago, and the eldest of the lot is more than 700 years old. But age is not a prerequisite. Some of the best pioneers have emerged only in the past few decades. Their stories, as individual companies and as a group, are compelling.

Two Cultures in Context

The stock market clearly treats the corporate adherents of each of these two cultures differently. Mainstream business and financial analysts can't yet explain why this is so. Critical distinctions between the operating philosophies of the two systems have largely escaped the financial press. This failure to see what is now staring us in the face is a matter of conditioning: conventionally trained managers and analysts don't have the vocabulary and mental models to identify the emerging phenomenon. This book intends to change that.

The clearest line of demarcation between these two systems is their treatment of living assets—broadly defined as people and Nature. Traditionally managed firms generally see themselves as finely calibrated machines: efficient, logically organized, numbers-driven, separate from Nature and society (which are treated as externalities), focused on the bottom line, and driven by a small elite of skilled executives. Their cultures, management, and accounting systems place a higher value on nonliving, or capital, assets than on living assets.

The emergent business culture that is our subject has a worldview radically different from that of the traditional model of business. Companies that embrace this rising culture see themselves as living, organic systems: communities of people with diverse skills, closely integrated with Nature and society, and focused on serving life. They place a higher value on living assets because they know that the health and productivity of people and Nature are inextricably linked, and that the strength of this coupling is the basis of their prosperity. They further understand that living assets are the means by which nonliving capital assets are created. Two of our Focus Group companies demonstrated the point in being the first major global financial institutions to declare their intent to become carbon-neutral operations: HSBC did so in 2004, and Swiss Re in 2003.

Traditional firms that manage by objectives see strength primarily in quantitative terms such as throughput, gross sales, profit, and all too often, executive pay. Firms that manage by means, on the other hand, see strength primarily in qualitative terms—in the integrity of their cultures and processes, and in their speed of learning. To cultivate these qualities, they organize themselves as networks in which energy and information flow spontaneously from all directions to where they are needed.

Philosophically, traditionally managed companies respect power and money, believing these are essential to survival. They see profit as the end, with people and Nature as the means to get to that end. Alternatively, adherents of the living systems model embrace a philosophy that elevates life over wealth, believing that business survival is closely entwined with Nature and society. Such firms see profit as a means to the end of fulfilling their missions and serving their primary stakeholders.

These different philosophies lead to very different ethical approaches. Traditionally managed firms tend to see ethics in terms of obeying the law and optimizing returns on assets. Equity for them is almost exclusively a financial concept. Advanced practitioners of the living systems model view ethics as a respect for life and a way to serve others. Equity to them is mainly relational, and is expressed by the quality of their relationships with people and Nature.[3] In this definition, "people" includes investors as well as employees, customers, strategic partners, and members of the communities in which firms operate.

A Systems Approach

There is a fundamental difference between owning and employing. Owning is *possessing,* a one-way street that entitles the owner to take and give little or nothing in return. Employing is *relational,* a two-way street involving continual give and take, mutual learning, and adaptation. Corporations can *own* nonliving (capital) assets because they are passive, controllable, and amenable to possession. But they must *employ* living assets because people and Nature are self-driven and resist mechanistic control. This makes all the difference in how these assets are managed.

Nonliving assets are easy to manipulate and control because their behavior is highly predictable; they are guided by rational, mechanistic laws such as those of Newtonian physics. We can understand nonliving assets reasonably well using linear cause-and-effect thinking. Rational laws guide the logic of computers, the properties of steel, and the compounding of interest—but they neither direct nor explain people and Nature. If we think of and respond to living assets mechanistically, we overlook their essential qualities and diminish their real value. Because they are continually in flux—networking, learning, adapting, and changing in response to the ebb and flow of life around and within them—we can understand living assets only by taking a holistic, or nonlinear, systems approach.

My use of the word "systems," in the context of systems thinking, refers primarily to living systems such as biosystems, ecosystems, social systems, and free-market systems. Because they are alive, these systems are innately intelligent, adaptive, self-organizing, and connected. They are very different from linear mathematical and computer systems, which deal in abstractions rather than in real life and have no innate abilities or connections other than those conferred on them by humans.

Corporations are living communities—systems that, like bees and flowers, thrive on an intricate web of living relationships. Without the nutrients that feed flowers and the bacteria that make those nutrients available, a bee could not create honey. Corporations, too, rely on a web of relationships with people and Nature to create value. Take away these relationships and the firm, like an isolated bee, will eventually die.

If corporations are living systems, as opposed to mechanical systems, then trying to govern them with mechanistic command-and-control techniques is self-defeating. Any force that tries to overcontrol people or Nature meets resistance. Rather than trying to command living assets and living systems to do what we want, we need to learn what *they* require to be at their productive best. That is what stewardship is all about and why stewardship is the most effective premise of corporate governance.

To create sustainable value, living assets (people and Nature) require just two basic things: the freedom to self-organize in pursuit of their natural interests, and environments that are safe for and supportive of their enterprises. But these they require absolutely. If you provide one without the other, the stability and productivity of any living system will atrophy. To function at full capacity, people must have the freedom to think, question, experiment, discourse, and self-organize. Like that of bees, people's value-added arises from a web or network of symbiotic relationships. When the living systems of society and Nature are offered these freedoms, and the potential for productive relationships, their output is awesome.

Some corporations understand better than others the requirements of living systems. For those that do, the *real* world of business turns on stewarding these systems. These companies are curious about the strategic coupling of people and Nature and the leverage derived from enabling the two to work harmoniously and synergistically. The rapidly growing field of "industrial ecology" is all about this strategic coupling. The corporations and universities engaged in this field are world leaders.

To expand this field of research, however, we must look beyond hard science to understand how Living Asset Stewardship (LAS) inspires us to learn, to innovate, and to transform corporate energy. LAS, in this context, is truly the "heart" of any enterprise.

To Tame or to Tend

The traditional model of the firm sees only chaos in the living systems of society and Nature: raw energy, storms, social conflict, and other "uneconomic" behaviors. The mental model of the corporation that emerged from the nineteenth century looked to impose order on that chaos by mechanistic means—by centralizing authority and scientifically managing by objectives. At a very fundamental level, adherents of this model don't trust the symbiotic, self-organizing, and spontaneous networking capacities of society and Nature. Rather, they seek to overcome natural chaos by trying to control it.

The efforts of traditionally managed companies to control living systems through mechanical means create problems worse than those they are trying to solve. Quite simply, they strip away the best attributes of people and Nature—the symbiotic capacity of living networks to exchange value and knowledge. This capacity is precisely the raw material of innovation. The two systems can work productively only if the control process is reversed, i.e., if corporations use mechanical systems to "tend": to serve people and Nature in appropriate ways.

Soft vs. Hard Management Methods

Although the traditional system can embrace concepts such as eco-efficiency, corporate citizenship, and human rights, and has increasingly done so, these concepts are always framed within a mechanical context and are secondary to its main objectives: to optimize throughput, sales, and profit. If "soft," life-affirming means can serve "hard" ends within a defined time period—perhaps a year or two—they will be used. If they cannot, they are usually dismissed as "nonessential." During business recessions, traditionally managed companies typically drop any activity deemed to be soft, or nonessential, via cost cuts and layoffs.

The organic, living asset model of the firm, by contrast, sees eco-efficiency, corporate citizenship, and human rights as essential to the goal of serving life. Exemplars of this model typically reach beyond these goals to even higher ones in their continual quest for best practices. They take the systemic view that life-affirming behavior inspires loyalty, learning, and innovation among employees, and builds trust with customers.

Three of the most cyclical firms we will follow throughout this book—Nucor, Southwest Airlines, and Toyota—are member companies of the Global Living Asset Management Performance (LAMP) Index.® None of these three has, for several decades, laid off employees for lack of work. Whereas their global competitors regard employees as potential liabilities, and use layoffs during slow economic times to meet short-term financial goals, these three regard employees as precious assets that are essential to growing future customer value. As shown in Appendix 5, there can be no question about which approach is more effective. Each of the three LAMP companies sells at significant premiums to its largest direct competitors in the global equity markets.

The advantages of eco-stewardship are numerous. All of the manufacturing companies referred to in this volume are global leaders in industrial ecology. First, by closing the loops in their diverse manufacturing systems and supply networks, they save billions in materials and energy costs, and generate enormous trust among stakeholders. Product design that uses life cycle assessment (LCA) ensures that customers also will get the benefits of energy efficiency, reliability, and durability, and that at the end of a product's service life it can be reclaimed or recycled to add value for someone else. Our stewardship leaders generate good will and cost savings for their strategic partners by coaching suppliers, shippers, and distributors on stewardship best practices. And, by transparently reporting their environmental impacts and goals, and inviting stakeholder dialogue on these, they build organizational learning capacity and community good will.

Baxter International and Novo Nordisk push the envelope even further. They were among the first corporations to adopt policies on bioethics. Their accounting systems, moreover, merge their financial and environmental agendas so they can forecast future financial gains from environmental improvements.

We consider bioethics as one of our core issues in the environmental, medical and animal spheres. We define bioethics as all ethical issues related to the use of life science technologies for the development and production of biotechnological and pharmaceutical products.[4]

—Novo Nordisk, "Respect for All Life"

These stewardship leaders go the extra distance because they see a spiritual dimension to Living Asset Stewardship that affects the capacity to create and innovate. They cultivate spiritual bonds by caring about the people they serve, and by caring about the things their people care about. Such deep caring, as we shall see, builds trust, commitment, connection, teamwork, and passion. Respecting life has universal appeal.

The relational equity thus achieved by LAS leaders affects the energy, commitment, and innovation of employees, the trust and loyalty of customers, the cooperation of supply network partners, the openness of host communities, and, ultimately, the patience of investors. Over the long term, relational equity is arguably worth more than a corporation's financial equity because it so affects future outcomes.

If the stewardship model has validity, what is traditionally regarded as *hard-fact* management might be more rightly described as *mentally soft* because it destroys so much relational (future) equity. And we now see that the stock market agrees: what has been popularly perceived as the soft path is actually more grounded in hard facts. It is the "traditionalists" who are lost and wandering, and the stewards whose path is leading them to very solid ground.

Inherent Value of Living Assets

To grasp these comparisons more fully, we need to distinguish clearly between the inherent value of living and nonliving assets. People and Nature are uniquely endowed with intelligence (in the sense of reacting to changes in their environments), the capacity to adapt and reproduce, and the ability to self-organize. Over time, as they learn, adapt, and form relationships, living assets become more efficient and generate value, rather than depreciate passively as nonliving assets do. It is worth reiterating: living assets are also the means by which nonliving capital assets are created. These important attributes will be self-evident to many, but are worth reviewing because of one other attribute.

Living assets are keenly aware of their connections to each other and to the larger web of life that contains them. People's innate passion for life and all that is alive has been well documented by psychologists (e.g., Erich Fromm), evolutionary biologists (e.g., Edward O. Wilson), brain scientists (e.g., Joseph LeDoux), physicists (e.g., Fritjof Capra and Danah Zohar), and systems thinkers (e.g., Peter Senge). This reverence is clearly expressed in the legendary credo of Johnson & Johnson, the most consistently profitable U.S. company of the past century. It is central to the kyosei philosophy of Canon, one of Japan's most consistently profitable companies of the post–World War II era. And it is implicit in the culture of Stora Enso, the world's oldest company, founded in Sweden more than 700 years ago.

The corporate stewards profiled in this book are more attuned than their traditional peers to this deeply emotional and spiritual connection that Edward O. Wilson calls "biophilia."[5] This, I believe, is the source of their greatest energy and creativity. People want to be connected and to feel that their livelihoods and professions matter. Serving and enhancing life matter to them because they know their lives depend on other living assets, including the health of their neighborhoods, their market systems, Earth's ecosystems, and the biospheric web of life. When people feel so connected, they are more likely to reach their full potential in terms of their intelligence, adaptability, family life, self-motivation, creativity, and energy (see Table 1-1).

Imagine the energy and enthusiasm of employees at a chemical company that is developing biodegradable enzymes to replace the toxic chemicals used in papermaking. They know paper is essential to modern society and

Table 1-1: Inherent Value Comparison

LIVING ASSETS	NONLIVING ASSETS
Intelligent	Non-intelligent
Adaptive	Non-adaptive
Self-reproducing	Non-self-reproducing
Self-organized	Other-organized
Generative	Depreciating
Active	Passive
Connected	*Disconnected*

that their lives at home or work would be impoverished without it. They also know that the chemicals normally used to produce paper poison the air and water and Earth's critical life systems. They are excited and inspired to search for an environmentally benign solution. In their hearts and minds, they know such a solution will benefit them, their families, and countless communities around the world. They have a transcendent purpose that connects their lives and livelihoods to the larger web of life. If given a chance, they will spontaneously organize themselves into collaborative networks for learning, experimenting, and innovating. They will be naturally cost-conscious because they understand the importance of their mission and the disappointment they would feel if it lost funding. Inspired by the biophilic connections they feel, they eagerly engage their intelligence and adaptive knowledge, their capacities for self-organization and generative learning, and their desire for efficiency. In their hearts they know that if they are successful, they will enable Nature to continue doing what it does best—produce and reproduce the essential goods (raw materials) and services (clean air, water, and recycling systems) that we need for survival. And in their hearts they know that they are helping to nourish future generations.

Biophilia

Biophilia...is the innately emotional affiliation of human beings to other living organisms. Innate means hereditary and hence part of ultimate human nature....

Were there no evidence of biophilia at all, the hypothesis of its existence would still be compelled by pure evolutionary logic. The reason is that human

history . . . began hundreds of thousands or millions of years ago with the origin of the genus *Homo*. For more than 99 percent of human history people have
lived together in hunter-gatherer bands totally and intimately involved with
other organisms. During this period of deep history, and still further back, into
paleohominid times, they depended on an exact and learned knowledge of
crucial aspects of natural history . . . .

  In short, the brain evolved in a biocentric world, not a machine-regulated
world . . . .

  How could biophilia have evolved? The likely answer is biocultural evolution, during which culture was elaborated under the influence of hereditary
learning propensities while the genes prescribing the propensities were
spread by natural selection in a cultural context . . . .

  The constructs of moral reasoning . . . have evolved genetically because
they confer survival and reproduction on human beings.[6]

                                              —Edward O. Wilson, *The Biophilia Hypothesis*

Stewardship companies understand, whether consciously or instinctively, the power of these biophilic urges for connection and serving the quality of life. Consequently, they organize in ways that enhance stakeholder
communication and information feedback. To increase their points of contact, they form networks—optimally, free-forming networks within networks—in which the authority and responsibility of employees are localized. Such forms of organization are quicker to respond to customer needs
than traditional, hierarchical structures because they are closer to the
action. To empower employees further, stewardship leaders invest heavily
in information technology, thereby speeding their access to information,
ideas, and collaborative learning at all critical points of contact. They help
employees self-develop by taking an interest in them, by mentoring them
along their chosen career paths, and by making them partners in the firm's
growth. To ensure the quality of local schools, hospitals, social services, and
other infrastructure, these leaders invest generously in the communities
where employees and customers live. If, by traditional cost accounting, the
total spending of stewardship leaders on these activities seems excessive,
the costs are usually recaptured many times over by gains in relational
equity, operating synergies, and revenue.

  The real cost issue facing most corporations today is not "overspending"
on so-called "nonessentials," but a kind of "underspending"—ignoring biophilic connection and the inherent wealth of living assets. When companies

systematically mistreat people and Nature in their pursuit of short-term profit, they destroy the means of their existence, and undermine the trust and credibility they need to cultivate long-term profit. If they do this long and carelessly enough, eventually their businesses become vulnerable and collapse from within. That is why the average life expectancy of a public corporation is only 40 to 50 years—far shorter than the perpetual life for which it was designed. To paraphrase anthropologist Gregory Bateson, the reason for such failure is not one of strategy execution but one of more fundamental strategic vision: the difference between the way humans think and the way Nature works.

Exemplary Stewardship: 16 Companies

Throughout this book we will explore the practices of 16 companies—collectively called the Focus Group—that are stewardship exemplars. Representing a wide range of global industries, they are subdivided into three categories: high eco-risk, low-impact, and intermediary. The eco-risk category in this sample is deliberately overweighted to make a point—that LAS has the most dramatic impacts in those industries in which it has historically been the most lacking.

The Focus Group was selected from a larger, 60-company "learning laboratory" of stewardship leaders, called the Global Living Asset Management Performance (LAMP) Index.® Although we will look at both groups in terms of their relative investment performance, credit ratings, and longevity, the case studies used to explain LAS will be drawn entirely from the Focus Group. By concentrating on this smaller list, we can explore in greater analytic depth.

To readers who follow sustainability and other socially screened indices such as the Dow Jones Sustainability Index (DJSI), the FTSE-4Good Index, or the Domini Social Index, the names of these 16 companies will be familiar. They are on virtually all the prominent lists of good corporate citizens. In presenting them, I am trying, not to play it safe by hiding within a consensus, but to move beyond consensus analysis into new realms of understanding. In particular, I want to show what makes these exemplars rise above the average performances of their ethically screened peers.

Most socially screened companies fail to pass our more demanding LAMP screens. Their common failing is trying to manage living systems

Table 1-2: LAMP Focus Group Companies in Three Categories

HIGH ECO-RISK	LOW-IMPACT	INTERMEDIARY
Alcoa	Baxter International	HSBC Group
3M	Canon	Swiss Re
Nucor	Hewlett-Packard	
Royal Dutch/Shell	Intel	
Southwest Airlines	Johnson & Johnson	
Stora Enso	Nokia	
Toyota	Novo Nordisk	

mechanistically—by hierarchical command and control. It doesn't work. The result is disconnect and a lack of strategic clarity. In Chapter 13 we will look at some prominent companies that had been anointed by others as "socially responsible" or "sustainable," but have under-performed due to inconsistencies in their corporate cultures.

Living Asset Stewardship

What sets our LAMP exemplars apart from their peers is Living Asset Stewardship (LAS)—the *respect for life* discussed previously. More broadly, LAS describes the mental models, policies, practices, and strategic planning that global stewardship leaders use to nurture living assets. Because we are talking about a concept of corporate management radically different from the mechanistic one that prevails today in the name of profit, I believe we should give it a clear and separate identity. That allows us to think and talk about LAS deliberately, free of the intellectual baggage of traditional man agement thinking.

Living Asset Stewardship is more—much more—than doing a few things right. Companies that practice LAS endeavor to respect life at every turn: in their relationships with employees, customers, host communities, supply net partners, and the environment. This is not an easy road to travel; but it is the only way to be credible, to win the hearts of employees and customers, and to create an atmosphere conducive to spontaneous innovation. Understanding the importance of credibility and trust, LAS leaders care deeply about the professional competence, financial staying power, and openness they bring to their stewardship practices. It's not enough to have good intentions. They must be able to execute them. And to do that they must think systemically, not only about the firm itself, but also about its relationships with the larger living systems that nurture it. These include free markets, society, and Nature.

As a thought process, LAS is radically different from mechanistic business thinking, which is essentially reductionist. Rather than trying to understand things by taking them apart and analyzing their components, LAS focuses instead on whole systems. The most important aspects of living systems and the LAS model described in Chapter 2 are context and relationships—the ways in which the parts of a system or enterprise relate to the whole. As physicist Fritjof Capra tells us, we cannot understand the importance of one component (an atom, for example) by looking at it in isolation. The essential properties of living systems are properties of the whole that no one part can have.

As a model for strategic planning and action, LAS is more about living in harmony with people and Nature than about trying to control them. Without such harmony, living systems cannot be optimally healthy or vibrant. Efforts to control complex systems, to push them beyond their natural limits, usually end in failure because systems inevitably push back. Global warming and the stunning decline of global fishing grounds are examples of living systems pushing back when stressed beyond their limits by human enterprise.[7]

Because the conventional and LAS thought models are so radically different, it is hard to mix and match them. You cannot get good stewardship practices by trying to graft an open, spontaneous LAS culture onto a closed, command-and-control structure. It does not work. The two systems clash and people know it. The market is filled with financial underachievers, such as AT&T, Bristol-Myers Squibb, Ford, JPMorgan Chase, and Xerox, who tried to impose stewardship on their employees via command and control. All of these companies have developed outward trappings of stewardship, but lacked the culture and core competencies to make them work effectively. LAS requires commitment at every level and in every area of corporate enterprise.

One of the clearest signs that stewardship has taken hold in a corporation can be found in its learning behaviors. Is the organization committed to open-book information sharing? Or is information reserved for a select few? Are people encouraged to speak up when they disagree with a policy or practice? Will managers openly admit errors of judgment or execution and then invite dialogue on finding a better way? Are leading and following determined by rank or by expertise?

Many LAMP companies practice open-book management, wherein employees regularly see data on customer satisfaction, order rates, defect rates, financial results, etc. Practitioners reason that the more employees know about a company's business, how they and their teams can affect its productivity, and how, in turn, productivity affects their compensation, the more committed they will become to learning, to teamwork, and to taking initiative to increase productivity.

When advocates of sustainability or corporate social responsibility talk about their research, it is usually in terms of visible environmental and social outcomes plus screening out bad behavior. This is important research that is motivated by stewardship ideals. But, to pass LAS screens, it must go deeper—to how a company defines itself, thinks, learns, and executes—a process I call *deep stewardship*. Because LAS is so deeply process oriented, I refer to it as a "triple top line" approach, as distinct from the more results-oriented "triple bottom line" approach of most sustainability advocates. These important cultural attributes determine whether a company can carry its stewardship practices forward and build on them.

The World's Greatest Manufacturing Company

The auto industry is an excellent setting in which to demonstrate the power of LAS because it has been a bastion of traditional command-and-control management with a poor record on labor relations and eco-stewardship. The industry is also well known for periods of overproduction followed by massive layoffs. North America's two largest automakers, General Motors (GM) and Ford, have been cited for numerous human rights violations. Communities that host their auto plants have often been blighted by environmental degradation, plant closings, and despondency over poor working conditions. Both companies have been reckless acquirers of other auto manufacturers in grabs for global market share, and in those attempts have run their balance sheets down so badly that the companies' credit ratings have devolved to junk-bond status. Beyond that, they have so underfunded their employee pension and retirement benefit plans that their unfunded liabilities either exceed their shareholder equity (GM) or nearly do so

(Ford). If there is a single major industry in which a committed corporate steward has a chance to stand out, this is it.

Toyota is the clear stewardship leader of the auto industry. It meets all of the key criteria for inclusion in the Global LAMP Index®: a highly decentralized and networked organizational structure; an evolved system of management by means; product leadership in terms of design for environment (DfE) and life cycle assessment (LCA); a logistics management system that projects its values and production methods down its supply chain; progressive ways of connecting with and serving the communities in which it operates; and a highly evolved systems thinking capacity. These criteria will be discussed in greater depth; the main point is the consistency and congruency of Toyota's processes, in both its structure as a living enterprise and its commitment to contribute to the communities it serves, as stated in its "Guiding Principles."[8]

Toyota's specific accomplishments and how they were achieved are best understood in that "service to life" framework. It was the first automaker to introduce an energy-efficient, hybrid gas/electric engine vehicle (the Prius in 1998), for which it was named a "laureate" by the United Nations (U.N.) Environment Programme in 1999. Toyota is currently far ahead of other manufacturers in developing an eco-efficient hydrogen-fuel-cell car. The company treats employees as valuable assets, rather than as costs and potential liabilities, and has been consistently profitable with no layoffs in more than four decades. Its environmental, health, and safety (EHS) standards are the highest in its industry. Its Aaa credit rating is far above that of industry peers. This is only the beginning of a remarkable story that saw Toyota emerge from the wreckage of World War II, with negligible financial resources, to become the world's greatest manufacturing company.

In the decade after the war, Toyota realized it could not compete with its larger, capital-intensive rivals by playing the game according to their rules. It had to develop an alternative strategy suited to the means it had available—the skills, dedication, and learning capacity of its employees. The solution the company developed is a classic example of Living Asset Stewardship. Toyota's production would be based on natural processes rather than mechanistic ones. The aspects of natural systems that most interested its chief engineer, Taiichi Ohno, were those of *continuous flow, learning,* and *adaptive improvement,* so he devised a production system around these principles. The community of people at Toyota would operate as an ecosystem in which diverse, highly networked individuals could symbiotically self-organize in pursuit of common goals. Each production team would be connected to all others and ultimately to the final customer via a system of value exchanges. The company would run by cybernetic principles, using a continually recursive process of learning and adaptation that would deliver what was needed when it was needed with the least amount of effort and energy.

Whereas GM and Ford operated under quantitative targets imposed by management, Toyota decided to let the flow of work in its plants relate to the qualitative means of employees and their working environment—their process knowledge, the infrastructure for learning and communicating, and their responsiveness to customers. Toyota based the *rate* of flow through its plants on changeover times (the intervals needed to customize each vehicle). To improve the rate of flow, employees were given incentives to connect, self-organize, and exchange knowledge so they could learn as they worked to devise a better system. Production teams knew exactly what materials they would need and when, thus enabling just-in-time delivery and reducing the need for inventories. As this system became more efficient from within, employees learned to change tool dies in three minutes—versus three days at GM and Ford—making it possible to do more with less effort and expense.

If we look deeper into Toyota's production system, we see an organization held together by a culture of caring. When orders are slow, rather than laying off production workers, Toyota finds other work for them—shifting some from "volume" to "newness" work focused on new products and processes, and sending others out in teams to help suppliers learn the famed Toyota Production System (TPS).

Toyota's workplace is also renowned for its culture of employee mentoring, trust, and continual learning, or *kaizen.* Because employees feel valued, respected, and vested in the company's success, they offer thousands of ideas each year for improving product quality and plant efficiency, most of which get adopted.[9]

By showing employees and customers that it cares about the things they care about—especially the social and environmental impacts of its products and processes—Toyota gets additional streams of useful feedback. The company's transcendent vision of "Greener Cars, Greener Factories, Greener Planet" resonates with the biophilic instincts of stakeholders.

Their suggestions and feedback have helped make Toyota's cars progressively safer, more energy efficient, and more recyclable.

We need to strive for "zero emissions" at all stages of the automobile life cycle from production through use and disposal . . . . [We] are determined to lead the world in firmly establishing the use of environmental technology.[10]

—Fujio Cho, President, Toyota

Toyota also bases its "order line" accounting system on stewardship principles. Johnson and Broms tell how it allocates costs to one of three basic purposes: supporting the *volume* of ongoing business, maintaining existing *structures* (systems) needed to operate the business, and conducting extra work caused by *newness*, based on living system principles. "These three purposes," they explain, "are analogous to those all living systems must fulfill if they are to survive, adapt, and evolve."[11] Volume costs contribute to metabolic sustenance. Structure costs support natural refurbishment of the living system (analogous to cell replacement). Newness costs are an investment in adaptation. "Viewing costs, revenues, and profitability in the context of these purposes recognizes that a business, like any life system, must maintain continuing and effective relationships with the world around it. Nurturing the relationships implicit in these purposes, not cutting costs, leads to improved levels of performance."[12]

Other automakers have a difficult time justifying the order-line costs that Toyota incurs because their accounting systems are based on quantitative targets rather than on nurturance of relationships implicit in the business. Where others see money being spent suboptimally or inefficiently on Living Asset Stewardship, Toyota sees synergies. One can debate the merits of these accounting systems forever, but the market understands results and has rendered its verdict. As this book goes to press, the value of Toyota's stock is four times that of Ford's and GM's combined, though its annual sales are lower. Toyota's profits per vehicle are at the upper end of the auto industry scale—in spite of having some of the world's best-paid and cared-for employees. These are impressive affirmations.

Toyota has become one of the world's preeminent manufacturers by creating, in the words of former CEO Fujio Cho, a "global human network" based on "respect for people" and high ethical standards. It is totally committed to LAS from the inside out—from the way it organizes its production and accounts for its effort to the way it connects with stakeholders. Toyota's skill in networking and managing by means is a prime example of effective industrial ecology because it yields continuously improved products, with a minimum of waste, that are tailored to its customers' exact needs. Based on these strengths, Toyota leads the world's major auto manufacturers in repeat business and market-share growth. With good reason *Fortune* Magazine has declared: "Indeed, by nearly every measure, Toyota is the world's best auto manufacturer. It may be the world's best manufacturer, period."[13]

The World's Oldest Company

Stora—renamed Stora Enso in 1998—is the world's oldest company. It has survived for 700-plus years because from the beginning, its owners (initially a religious diocese) and managers cared about employees and the community in which it operated. Stora's governance became decentralized in the mid-fourteenth century due to a royal charter and a mining statute that dispersed power among a group of master miners and established fair wages and work sequencing. Since then the company has survived and grown, thanks to an open, tolerant culture that learns and adapts from the bottom up. Like Toyota, Stora's Living Asset Stewardship has endowed it with strong relational equity.

Arie de Geus summarizes Stora's extraordinary history "from the Middle Ages through the Reformation, into the wars of the 1600s, the Industrial Revolution, and two world wars in the twentieth century . . . . [Through the centuries,] while it coped with shifting social and political forces, the company continually shifted its business, moving from copper to forest exploitation, to iron smelting, to hydropower, and eventually to paper, wood pulp, and chemicals. Its production techniques also shifted— from steam to internal combustion, then to electricity, and ultimately to the microchip."[14]

Stora could not have adjusted to these huge changes had it not been a cohesive community or open to new ideas. No amount of financial equity could have saved it had it chosen to be a world unto itself and face these challenges alone. During its lifetime, the company's leadership has probably changed more than 50 times. The likelihood of having 50 or more prescient leaders, back to back, defies all reasonable odds. The only plausible explanation for its survival is that it has been a living community with a strong base of relational equity created by open and tolerant dialogue with employees and other stakeholders.

Today Stora Enso is a global corporation with more than $16 billion in annual sales. As the world's largest paper company, it continues to build relational equity by caring for the living assets it draws upon—the biodiversity of its timberland, the well-being of its employees, and the health of its host communities. Stora's tolerance for open dialogue and new ideas continues unabated. To promote the broadest possible outreach, the company transparently reports its financial, social, and environmental objectives, and its progress in attaining this "triple bottom line." Then it welcomes stakeholder feedback. It also regularly polls employees concerning their job satisfaction and ideas for improvement.

If we decide to . . . construct a paper mill, we are ready to found a school for teaching up to the upper secondary level and to improve the hospital services already offered there. This would mean additions to the social infrastructure to the benefit of the whole local community.[15]
—Bjorn Hagglund, Deputy CEO, Stora Enso

As at Toyota, Stora Enso's employees are given substantial local authority. The company is decentralized into nearly 50 business units, based on geography and product offers, each of which has considerable autonomy. Employees are treated like partners with a wide variety of self-help training programs, global job opportunities through Stora's Internal Job Market System, and performance-based compensation. Nonmanagerial employees, most of whom are unionized, can earn salary bonuses of up to 7 percent of salary plus profit sharing. The success of creating strong relational equity among employees is reflected in Stora's low voluntary turnover rates (2.2 percent in 2003). Since 1998, turnover among the top 200 managers has been only 2 percent. Such low employee turnover reduces costs, boosts profitability, and improves the odds of longevity because it allows intellectual capital to accumulate and compound.

Few companies in the world can match Stora's long-standing commitments to community and environment. Few within the forest products industry can match its productivity, profitability, and financial strength. It is a company built on relational equity.

Opening the Quantum Mind

How did Toyota become such a manufacturing leader and Stora such a long-lived enterprise? Their successes can be explained in terms of organization, accounting systems, methods of value creation, or specific actions, but in the final analysis these are all variations on a central theme. The deeply caring cultures of these companies create spiritual bonds among employees and others engaged in the value-creation process. These connections engage their hearts—a proven pathway to higher thinking capacities.

People and Nature are linked in the definition of living assets for two reasons. At a practical level, they—we—are obviously tightly coupled. Humanity cannot survive without the support of a healthy biosphere. But at a more spiritual level, where higher consciousness resides, we know we are more than a physical arrangement of atoms. We have an extra dimension that ultimately defines us—a consciousness, a desire for meaning, a vision of perfection, a feeling of oneness with Nature or God. When we feel this unity, this spiritual connection, we feel more whole, coherent, and creative for reasons we shall explore more fully in Chapter 3. I believe Toyota and Stora have evolved to what they are today by honoring our need for such connection.

When we experience this spiritual pull, this biophilic connection or wholeness, we open ourselves to visions of a different world—one that is harmonic, expansive, and whole rather than fragmented, alienated, and narrowly ego-driven. Our minds crackle with energy. When we merge our *beings* with this larger vision of well-being, we feel an urge to learn, explore, and discover new ways. We become passionate about the meaning of our work and creating some universal good in our enterprise.

Management consultant and physicist Danah Zohar says such passion activates whole-brain thinking, in which our mental, emotional, and spiritual selves merge. We sense the larger web of life that contains our habit-bound lives. When this happens we begin to think outside of the box, to see new patterns in chaotic market conditions, or to envision new paradigms. We see things in whole new dimensions, just as quantum physics has

helped us reopen our awareness of the physical world. Because of this like-
ness, she calls passionate whole-brain thinking "quantum thinking."

Edward O. Wilson puts it succinctly: "Humanity needs a vision of an
expanding and unending future."[16] This biophilic urge is the emotional
juice behind LAS. Companies that consistently and congruently honor this
urge release incredible energy and insight from within. They also become
more trustworthy and believable to external stakeholders. The benefits to
corporate image, brand names, employee morale, teamwork, and innovation are considerable.

Quantum Thinking

The Brain's Spirit

Quantum thinking issues from a different part of the brain than Newtonian
thinking (p. xvi) .... [It is] rooted in and motivated by our deep sense of meaning and value. It is our spiritual thinking and our vision thinking. (p. 26)

Associative, habit-bound thinking gives us pattern-recognizing abilities
that are very similar to the Newtonian wave paradigm (p. 26).... Creative, rule-
breaking, and rule-making thinking behaves very much like the emergent
structures found in the quantum paradigm. (p. 27)

Quantum thinking is holistic. It unifies and integrates and sees the whole
picture. It integrates the thinking processes of the brain's serial and associative systems, and it unifies all the millions of data impinging on the brain at
every moment into a field of experience with which we can deal. (p. 37)

This third kind of thinking gives us our "spiritual intelligence," our intelligence rooted in meaning, vision and value. It allows us to use our whole brains
.... Organizations need it (need infrastructures that make it possible) to use
their whole brains. We need it to rewire the corporate brain. (p. 120)

Creative thinking, the thinking that originates crucially from the spiritual
self, issues from a brain dynamic that functions very like the processes and systems described by quantum physics and the other new sciences. (p. 20)

[H]uman creativity is so similar to the creativity of quantum processes that
I find it useful to call creative thinking *quantum thinking*. For similar reasons,
I often refer to the spiritual level of the self as the *quantum self.* This allows us
to find a language, a set of images, and even an organizational model for nurturing creativity and creative leadership in the existing language, imagery,
and organization of quantum and chaotic systems and the quantum brain.
(pp. 20–21)

The essence of quantum thinking is that it is the thinking that precedes categories, structures, and accepted patterns of thought or mind-sets. It is with

quantum thinking that we create our categories, change our structures, and transform our patterns of thought. (p. 21)

—Danah Zohar, *Rewiring the Corporate Brain*[17]

Companies with the most consistent access to these higher thinking capacities have cultures that reach beyond the mental intelligence of employees to their emotional (caring) and spiritual (deep caring) intelligences, as well. This cannot be done by hierarchical command and control. It requires the respectful listening, dialogue, and collaboration that typically exist in highly networked LAS cultures. There are, as we shall see, many ways to evoke this kind of involvement.

The companies in our Focus Group use diverse methods to engage the biophilic passions and quantum minds of employees. Each has a meaning unique to the company and its industry. At research-intensive firms, such as Baxter International and Novo Nordisk, employees are inspired by corporate commitments to bioethics. At manufacturing firms, such as Alcoa, Canon, Nucor, Stora Enso, and Toyota, they are inspired by concerns for environment, health, and safety (EHS) that extend from the workplace out to host communities and beyond, to the world at large.

The energy and passion that propel quantum thinking in stewardship companies can be described as a reinforcing cycle between Living Asset Stewardship (LAS) and organizational learning (OL.) As LAS inspires people about their work, it increases their desire to learn; as learning increases, so does a company's capacity to innovate; and as innovative capacity increases, so does the likelihood of profit. The cycle then repeats as profit reinforces LAS, as shown in Figure 1-1.

The cycle is "reinforcing" because LAS catalyzes both cause and effect. As a cause, LAS inspires quantum thinking, organizational learning, and innovation. As an effect, it is fed by the profit it generates. If there is a single way to describe the energy and creativity of global LAMP companies, this is it.

The internal workings of the cycle are entirely natural. The reinforcing cycle of LAS + OL leverages an unlimited human resource, intelligence, and conserves those that are scarcest and most vulnerable: Earth's physical resources. By starting with a vision of an expanding and unending future, it is guided by Nature's laws—laws that have worked for billions of years.

Figure 1-1: The Reinforcing Cycle of LAS and OL

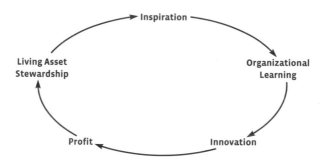

LAS inspires employees to learn because it triggers their biophilic instincts and excites their imaginations. As organizational learning increases, so do the possibilities of innovation and profit. This is called a reinforcing cycle because profit strengthens the possibilities of stewardship, thus keeping the cycle running onward and upward.

Conclusion

Corporations are living systems or communities that exist within the larger living systems of the free market, society, and the biosphere. Living assets—people and Nature—are the source of nonliving, or capital, assets. They are inherently more intelligent, adaptive, efficient, self-regenerating, and connected than are nonliving assets, and therefore have greater value-added capacity. It is one of the anomalies of traditional business theory that nonliving assets are held to be more precious than living ones. By reversing this order—by placing a higher value on living assets than on nonliving ones—we come up with a far more durable and productive model of the firm.

A small but growing list of global corporations is now adopting this more productive model—a deep stewardship process I call Living Asset Stewardship (LAS). These companies are different from their traditionally managed peers in two other respects: they are more decentralized and networked; and they manage more by qualitative means (e.g., building learning capacity) than by quantitative ends.

When companies do this with professional competence, they become innovation leaders in their respective industries/sectors. I have tracked 60 global stewardship leaders, collectively called the Global Living Asset Management Performance (LAMP) Index,® that broadly replicate the industry/sector exposure of the Morgan Stanley Capital International (MSCI) World Index, and find that the stewardship group consistently outperforms. In the following chapters we will take an in-depth look at 16 of those companies, collectively called the Focus Group.

The connectedness of living assets is the key to their magic. People have a natural reverence for life (biophilia). When corporations respect people and Nature in their policies and practices, and when that respect is a consistent factor in all corporate relationships, they earn relational equity. Unlike financial equity, which is a reflection of past accomplishments, relational equity is the key to future accomplishments. In the long run, it is far more valuable than financial equity, as exemplified in the cases of Toyota and Stora Enso.

Companies build relational equity by engaging the quantum minds of employees and others within their value-creating networks. The quantum mind is stimulated when our activities are congruent with our deepest beliefs and values. Quantum thinking is a whole-brain activity that connects us to the larger web of life in which we exist. The magic of global LAMP companies resides in their ability to inspire a reinforcing cycle wherein Living Asset Stewardship (LAS) begets organizational learning (OL), OL begets innovation, innovation begets profit, and profitability feeds back to reinforce LAS.

The power of LAS, relational equity, and quantum thinking ultimately resides in the human spirit. People want harmonious relationships not only for the tangible benefits they yield, but also because such relationships are spiritually meaningful. Stewardship leaders understand this. They rise above their peers because they generally attract the best employees, the most loyal customers, the most patient investors, and the most creative partners.

In the final analysis, LAS is an adaptive behavior that has spontaneously emerged in the marketplace. It is an evolutionary answer to the failures of the traditional, mechanistic business model—e.g., global warming, environmental degradation, workplace stress, and the breakdown of community life—that emerged from the industrial age under the protection of limited-liability laws. LAS is in the mainstream of evolution. The traditional model of business is an evolutionary dead-end.

LAS uses intelligence the way it should be used: to affirm life and healthy growth. It represents a rebirth, a renaissance of business thinking that offers hope as well as results. It also plays well in the marketplace.

The LAS Model

"[T]he idea that companies can build shareowner value by striving to make both a profit and a contribution is not just a cornerstone of good corporate citizenship; it is still the foundation of everything we do at HP. Whether it's upholding high standards of transparency and accountability, vigorously managing our performance in environmental sustainability and human rights, or using technology to provide opportunity in underserved markets, it is our goal to build trust by leaving each community in which we do business better for our presence."[1]

—HP Global Citizenship Report 2005

The HP Way

David Packard, cofounder of Hewlett-Packard, was once asked to describe the company's greatest inventions. With barely a pause, he replied, "The HP Way." It was not one of HP's many technology breakthroughs, as the questioner assumed, but a deeply humanistic mental model of the company that enabled those breakthroughs. The HP Way, originally publicized in January 1957, has always been a topic of lively discussion within Hewlett-Packard. Since then, through a process of dialogue and consensus building, it has been updated to include new topics, such as the environment, while its core mission of service to humanity has been kept intact.

Mental models make a huge difference to a firm's innovative capacity, longevity, and profitability. This is one of the strongest themes to arise from my study of global stewardship leaders. The best models are formulated as responses to simple existential questions—"Why do we exist?" or "What is our purpose in life?"—and develop from there. They are infused with values, often fiercely held, concerning "what we stand for" and "how we treat people."

Of course, different companies in different industries will offer widely varying answers to these questions. But in global LAMP companies the answers inevitably distill down to a *respect for life*. HP's purpose in life is innovation "for the advancement and welfare of humanity" and its values include sensitivity to "the needs and interests of the community" and "protecting the physical environment."

At HP, as in most LAMP companies, discussions that go to the core of corporate purpose occur continually and in virtually every context. In 1998 HP held a company-wide dialogue on what it would take to be the "world's best industrial research lab." It was exciting because it engaged people at every level and with multiple backgrounds and viewpoints. Employees, used to the idea of HP being a technology leader, believed the goal of being best was attainable. But that goal didn't become tangible until someone asked, "Why not also aim to be best *for* the world?" This touched on HP's sacred mission of innovation "for the advancement and welfare of humanity." From then on, talk turned to radical new ideas, including breakthrough technologies for education, remote medical care for third world nations, and a sensor net for global environmental issues.

In September 2002, HP Labs announced a breakthrough in molecular electronics that has multiple applications toward "the advancement and welfare of society." It was the highest-density electronic memory ever invented—a 64-bit memory that had a bit density more than 10 times greater than anything in the market and used molecular switches so tiny that more than 1,000 could fit on the end of a human hair. As was true of all prior HP products, this innovation was a learning tool, a device for leveraging the human mind. It was also an affirmation to employees and customers, discouraged by a prolonged global recession, that HP Labs was fulfilling its promise.

This breakthrough was well timed for another reason. HP had just completed a merger with Compaq that caused a serious rift within the company about the meaning of the HP Way itself—a rift so serious that Walter Hewlett, son of the cofounder, resigned from the board in protest. During the period of internal strife that followed, HP needed affirmations that its culture and humanistic mission were intact. Though employees openly debated the merger's merits—a dialogue that, incidentally, affirmed the vitality of HP's culture—they needed to know that HP mattered to the world. The molecular electronics breakthrough gave them that affirmation.

The merger with Compaq was the brainchild of HP's newly appointed CEO, Carley Fiorina, who saw it as a way to achieve economies of scale in core technologies. The danger in this thinking, one which later proved to be the case, is that a quest for scale pulls companies in the direction of centralized authority and management by objectives—a trajectory antithetical to the aims of networked firms that manage by means. Fiorina was eventually fired (in January 2005) because, in fact, she had tried to centralize too much authority in her own office and in so doing threatened the culture that had produced HP's greatness. In the week following her firing, the market's response was positive: HP stock rallied with a gain of more than 10 percent.

People don't easily let go of transcendent ideals and values once they have lived and worked with them. In the course of history, all such ideals are challenged, or even pushed to the brink, by events. Just as some of the principles of the young U.S. democracy, as shaped in the Declaration of Independence, were mightily challenged during the Civil War, so too has the HP Way encountered its own trials. But the people who love its culture have clung to it and defended it in ways that suggest it will be around for decades or centuries to come. I would not write off HP because of the events of some strategic missteps during the first five years of the twenty-first century. It may need some time to recover, but its culture performed heroically.

The ideals that suffuse HP's business model, that give it this enduring quality, are unusual in today's business world because they focus on service to humanity and on processes that respect life, rather than on profit alone. "Profit," as Packard once said, "is not the proper aim of management; it is what makes all of the proper ends and aims possible."[2] Greg Merten, who led much of the post-merger effort to conserve the HP Way, agrees. To him, HP's ideals are about *connecting* as much as they are about *contributing* to the welfare of humanity. At the individual level, Merten says, we connect through openness, trust, tolerance, humility, and above all, through appreciative listening; at the corporate level we connect by creating a "compelling idea of the future that inspires people to self-align around the company's mission."[3] This is powerful stuff because it engages all the inherent strengths of living assets (see Table 1-1).

I think many people assume, wrongly, that a company exists simply to make money. While this is an important result of a company's existence, we have to go deeper and find the real reasons for our being. As we investigate this, we inevitably come to the conclusion that a group of people get together and exist as . . . a company so they are able to accomplish something collectively they could not accomplish separately—they make a contribution to society, a phrase that sounds trite but is fundamental . . .[4]

—David Packard, HP cofounder

The ideals that underpin the HP business model and corporate strategy have been in place for nearly five decades. They have survived for this long because they are consistent with the true nature of the firm (living community), the life-affirming (biophilic) values of employees, and the desire of people everywhere to find a higher meaning in their enterprise.

The passions expressed during HP's internal debates about the Compaq merger and Carley Fiorina's attempts to centralize power clearly show us where employees stood on LAS versus the traditional business model of the firm. HP people did not want to work under the spiritually numbing conditions of a model in which mechanical thinking was imposed on organic systems and people were required to work for abstract numbers (sales, profits, etc.) without any sense of meaning and self-fulfillment. Fortunately, HP's board of directors agreed.

A Major Change in Thinking

Hewlett-Packard's corporate philosophy and governance represent a major change in thinking from the traditional business model that emerged out of the nineteenth century's fascination with mechanics. In spite of recent setbacks, no one can quarrel with HP's long-term success. Since 1970— during which time the company reinvented itself many times—HP stock has returned roughly five times the benchmark S&P 500 rate.

Using HP as a point of departure, we'll examine the fundamental differences between the LAS model and the traditional one that pervades today. These distinctions are organized into three categories: existential (why do we exist?), functional (how do we operate?), and values-based (what do we stand for?). Once these differences are understood it should not be difficult to appreciate why the deep stewardship practices of HP and the Global LAMP Index® have had such natural advantages over their traditionally managed peers.

Existential: Why Do We Exist?

The LAS model assumes that a company is an organic living system whose defining elements are living assets; that it exists within the larger web of life, on which it utterly depends; and that its "reason for being" is to serve humanity in sustainable ways that don't harm the web. These underlying assumptions could not be more different from those of the traditional model, which posit the opposite: a company is mechanical; its defining assets are nonliving (capital); its existence is separate from Nature and society, which are viewed as externalities; and its sole reason for being is to return a profit to its owners and managers.

Consistent with their opposing paradigms, LAS and traditionally managed companies have vastly different corporate cultures. Stewardship companies are organized principally as flexible, self-organizing, emergent networks dedicated to co-learning and co-adapting (means), as distinct from the more rigid and ordered structures, dedicated to financial returns (ends), of traditional firms. The word "emergent" in this context refers to the capacity of a culture for spontaneous generation of new ideas and innovations from within. In the most advanced LAS cultures—such as those we have seen at Toyota, Stora Enso, and Hewlett-Packard—ideas and innovation emerge at every level, not just at the top, because employees are respected as intelligent beings and allowed to self-organize locally. It is no wonder, then, that HP employees resisted so strenuously any suggestion that the firm might become more centralized, ordered, and mechanistic.

The humanism and self-organizing dynamics of LAS companies may sound unfocused and chaotic to a traditionalist, but they are not. The glue that holds stewardship companies together comprises a common cause, a transcendental, life-affirming reason for being, and a spiritual quest that engages our biophilic longing for oneness with Nature and for an infinite vision of humanity. Edward O. Wilson calls this "an expanding and unending future." People would far rather commit to such a culture than to one whose primary reason for being is the finite one of enriching owners and managers. These are enormous and fundamental differences, and they lead to equally large differences in the functional attributes and values of a company, as described in Table 2-1.

Functional: How Do We Operate?

Corporate authority under the LAS model is more decentralized and localized, and governance more diffused, with responsibility existing at every level. This reflects the intelligent, adaptive, and self-organizing attributes of living assets. Consequently, stewardship workplaces are more open and interactive, rather than closed and bureaucratic, and information flows more freely and is transparently shared at every level.

Employee and organizational learning at stewardship companies are likewise more spontaneous and collegial. People are mentored, counseled, given "stretch" assignments, cross-trained, and provided with tools to educate themselves on the job as the need or motivation arises. This approach is far more effective than traditional "one-size-fits-all" training courses because it is more connected to employee interests and priorities. Employees become more inspired and passionate when they can follow their own interests, particularly when these converge with a firm's own mission or reason for being.

Strategic thinking is another area in which clear distinctions can be made between the old model and the LAS model. LAS leaders naturally lean toward holism, inclusiveness, and organic structures. They have an innate sense that the whole is synergistically worth more than the sum of its parts and that one can never understand a part of the whole outside of its context. (Imagine, for example, the value of a human hand detached from its owner.) This systemic perspective explains why Toyota, Nucor, and Southwest Airlines have never laid off an employee for lack of work. It also reveals why LAMP companies have broadened their goals from a narrow focus on profits to the well-being of the communities they serve, broadly defined to include, in most cases, the biosphere.

Each year we meet with our stakeholders—including the people in our communities, employees, socially responsible investors, environmental/sustainability groups and other industry leaders—to ask them how we can continually improve . . . .[5]

—Craig R. Barrett, President and CEO, Intel

Table 2-1: Mental Model of the Firm

	LAS	TRADITIONAL
Existential Attributes		
Paradigm:	Organic, living system	Mechanical, nonliving system
Context:	Integral to web of life	Separate, web is an "externality"
Culture:	Networked, emergent	Structured, ordered
Defining elements:	Living assets	Nonliving capital assets
Dynamics:	Self-organizing, humanistic	Directed, materialistic
Reason for being:	Serve humanity/life (infinite)	Serve owners/managers (finite)
Functional Attributes		
Authority:	Decentralized, localized	Centralized, hierarchical
Governance:	Diffused responsibility	Command and control
Workplace:	Open, interactive	Closed, bureaucratic
Communication:	Transparent, shared access	Restricted, limited access
Learning:	Self-directed, spontaneous	Prescribed, formulaic
Strategic thinking:	Holistic, inclusive, organic	Analytic, reductive, acquisitive
Leverage:	Inspired employees	Financial engineering
Key Metrics:	Balanced scorecard*	Financial indicators
Values-Based Attributes		
Mission:	Quality of life, service	Quantity of profit, financial wealth
Vision:	Sustainability, harmony	Control of resources, markets
Organizational:	Eco-centric, collaborative	Anthropocentric, competitive
Employees:	Value generators, assets	Costs, potential liabilities
Leadership:	Serves, mentors, teaches	Dominates, orders
Financial:	Low debt, self-financing	Higher debt, frequent borrowing
Profit:	Means to fulfill mission	End in itself

* A balanced scorecard uses both relational (leading) and financial (lagging) indicators.

Traditional companies, by contrast, are characteristically more analytic, reductive, and structurally acquisitive. In their world visible size counts for more than invisible synergy, and it is common practice to buy and sell business units or to lay off employees as if they were so many disconnected parts.

When stewardship companies seek strategic leverage, they are naturally more inclined to do it by focusing on means—such as stakeholder dialogue and organizational learning—rather than on ends. This works brilliantly, as is evident in the experience of Toyota (see Chapter 1). It is far less risky than the financial engineering approaches used by Ford and General Motors, which are focused on economies of scale and throughput. To achieve those supposed numerical ends, Ford and GM took on mountains of debt—the carrying costs of which now threaten their very existence.

Debt leverage is not the mechanical advantage we are often led to believe it is. During the past quarter-century, it has been used too frequently to prop up sick, traditionally managed companies that systematically ignore living system principles. Such reliance on debt creates multiple problems because it weakens the corporate borrower, puts investors at risk, harms credit markets, and ultimately threatens all who depend on orderly credit markets. Thus, the *Financial Times* reports: "In 1980, two-thirds of S&P's corporate ratings were at the investment grade level, but by the end of the decade the balance had shifted and two-thirds were high-yield or junk status. Since 1980 there have been only two years when rating upgrades outnumbered downgrades, and today the biggest concentration of companies is in the B category—at most only three notches above an extremely speculative CCC rating."[6]

To avoid such pitfalls, LAS leaders use a "balanced scorecard" system—one that focuses as much on their forward-looking relational equity as it does on their backward-looking financial equity. It is a far more effective approach to learning and planning because it implicitly embraces life.

Values-Based: What Do We Stand For?

The third area of clear differentiation between the LAS and traditional models is that of corporate values. In their classic book, *Built to Last*, Collins and Porras affirm the centrality of values, although they don't say these have to be life affirming.[7] Their main requirement is that a firm's values authentically arise from within the organization and reflect the organization's character. That's good enough for our purposes. Life-affirming values authentically arise out of LAS cultures and, once in place, are ferociously guarded by managers and employees alike.

When a firm's core values inspire employees and are congruent with corporate culture, they catalyze productivity and innovation from the front lines to the front office. The spectacular revival of Nucor is a good example of this. The company emerged from bankruptcy in the 1970s determined to be the most employee- and community-friendly steel company in the nation. Today Nucor not only has achieved those goals, but also is the nation's largest (by market capitalization) and most environmentally progressive steelmaker, is a global productivity leader, and carries a solid A1 credit rating. Its once-formidable domestic competitors, by contrast, have been in and out of bankruptcy and have steadily lost market share. At year-end 2005, for example, U.S. Steel's credit rating was Ba2 (junk). In 2003 Bethlehem Steel was swallowed up by the International Steel Group for a fraction of its former value.

> Core values are the organization's essential and enduring tenets . . . a small set of general guiding principles . . . not to be compromised for financial gain or short-term expediency.[8]
>
> —James C. Collins and Jerry I. Porras, *Built to Last*

Because the "reasons for being" of stewardship companies coalesce around serving humanity in sustainable ways, it naturally follows that their values would embrace life. The corporate missions of our global LAMP companies and their visions of the future all echo variations on themes concerning service, quality of life, sustainability, and systemic harmony. Their organizational values are palpably biocentric and collaborative—as distinct from the more egocentric and competitive leanings of traditionally managed firms. Employees are seen as assets and value generators, rather than costs or potential liabilities. Leaders at every level reinforce this perception by mentoring, teaching, and serving the professional growth of employees—and trusting that these caring behaviors will then be projected outward by employees to customers and host communities. In all these ways the LAS model operates like an ecosystem, a symbiotic community of individuals whose energy and talents generate a whole that is worth more than the sum of its parts.

To maintain the integrity of that whole, global LAMP companies are financially conservative. Because they intend to serve in perpetuity rather than make quick returns for owners and managers, they typically carry less debt in relation to their equity than do their traditionally managed peers. By concentrating on their core competencies, as Toyota and Nucor have done, and avoiding the temptation to over-expand via acquisition, LAS leaders also tend to enjoy more-consistent free cash flows. As a result of such firmly held financial values, the Global LAMP Index® has average and median credit ratings that are four to five points higher than the Moody's Investors Service (Moody's) average for all corporations. At year-end 2005, Toyota's credit rating (Aaa) was 13 notches above GM's (B1), and 12 above Ford's (Ba3), both of which now carry deep junk bond ratings.

An additional distinction between LAS and the traditional model of the firm centers on the role of profit. Stewardship companies treat profit as a means to achieve their transcendent goals rather than as a discrete end in itself. This proposition is heresy to traditionalists. Yet it works for precisely the reason David Packard cited: when employees are inspired and trusted to self-organize in pursuit of shared life-affirming goals, they work more effectively. The result is a reinforcing cycle of Living Asset Stewardship and organizational learning that accelerates innovation and profit (see Figure 1-1). Contrary to the worst fears of traditionalists, the costs of maintaining stewardship cultures are not unrecoverable. They are returned many times over in cash flow and profit.

The Power of Inspiration

Inspiration is the principal lever of Living Asset Stewardship. People are more effective when they work with their hearts as well as their minds. When companies look beyond the immediate physical needs of constituents to their values, beliefs, and emotional needs, they win people's hearts. We shall explore this further in the next chapter, but it is so integral to the LAS model that it must be briefly introduced here.

Few companies are more articulate in addressing the human spirit than Canon. Its corporate philosophy, kyosei, looks to the "common good" of all "communities, nations, the environment and the natural world." Although it lacks the clarifying concept of living assets as distinct from nonliving capital assets, it touches on virtually every attribute of LAS, starting with the notion of the firm as a living community.

Ryuzaburo Kaku, an ordained Zen Buddhist monk and honorary chairman, coined the term "kyosei" in the late 1980s. In doing so, he made explicit a vision and values that had long been implicit in Canon's culture and traditions. From his spiritual training, he understood the power of a clear call to respect life and to serve a higher purpose.

It is my belief that . . . kyosei should occupy a central position in the personal ethics of each individual. I also believe it should be a creed that all corporations and nations follow, and that it should be the guiding principle for the new world order that is currently emerging.[9]

—Ryuzaburo Kaku, Honorary Chairman, Canon

In addition to the kyosei philosophy itself, Kaku gives us an important four-stage progression that aptly describes the evolutionary path of LAS. This progression recognizes that stewardship rarely emerges full blown at the founding of most companies. During the first stage, when companies are simply trying to survive, those most inclined toward stewardship learn the value of caring for employees. Later, as these companies become a local presence, then a national presence, and finally a global presence (second through fourth stages), they expand the scope of their caring and seek harmony in increasingly large systems.

When a kyosei company becomes truly global, Kaku says, its social responsibilities transcend national boundaries. It begins to address "global imbalances" that will ultimately affect everyone everywhere—the economic imbalances between rich and poor, technological imbalances symbolized by the digital divide, and environmental imbalances that threaten the well-being of future generations.

To many, Canon's kyosei agenda will appear burdened with extra costs, yet it has recaptured these many times over by inspiring its employees and stakeholders. Few companies in the world can match its eco-stewardship, innovation, consistent free cash flow, balance sheet strength (Aa2), or shareholder returns. Canon is an LAS exemplar.

Understanding Cycles

By definition, all living systems and life processes are cyclical. We are most familiar with cycles of birth and death, the changing of seasons, weather patterns, economic and market fluctuations, and the diurnal pattern of day and night. But these are only small aspects of the cyclical "big picture." To understand the LAS model fully, one must understand that we live in a world defined by networks within networks and cycles within cycles—all continually in flux. It is hard to imagine how linear thinking or reductive analysis could make sense of these multilayered cycles, which continually feed back on one another. In a purely practical sense, we don't need to engage in that mental exercise because linear, mechanistic thinking has made a mess of the natural world, including the world of business. The only way we can understand the firm as a living entity, and the living systems within which it exists, is to understand the cycles that affect its livelihood.

The study of cycles can quickly become very complex, but we can make do here by understanding three basic principles of Nature. The first of these is the power of each individual to self-organize as it strives to sustain itself and actualize its potential. Though this implies the potential to grow without limit, we know that does not happen. Trees don't grow to the sky. If they did, they would ultimately command such a large share of Earth's resources that there would be nothing left for the other species on which they depend for their existence. This leads us to the second precept—the balancing principle of interdependence. A healthy forest has thousands of species, all of which collectively support the tree culture and each other in ways that prevent any one of them from dominating. Some of these species, in fact, kill trees. But that is not all bad because dead trees become food for other species and, through them, compost for more trees. This "recycling of resources" is why trees and other species have life cycles.

The symbiotic interdependence of the forest species example leads to the third principle of Nature—the need for diversity. To be healthy, a forest needs not just a few species, but thousands. Ecosystems that contain fewer species are less stable because they are more vulnerable in the event of the loss of any one. The interplay of all species within a healthy forest creates many layers of cycles—all converging toward greater diversity and complexity as species evolve into subspecies, thereby continually generating newness at every level.

Taken together, these three principles describe the relentless urge of life. When that urge can freely operate, the web of life provides abundantly. But when that urge is blocked, Nature and society push back. This is an important point because it explains why traditional business practices today generate so many layers of systemic resistance. This resistance shows up in the guise of, to name a few examples, employee stress, absenteeism, turnover, customer defections, government regulation, class action lawsuits, rising insurance premiums, resource depletion, and global warming. Such "push-back" or negative feedback drives what systems thinkers call a balancing cycle.

The practical consequence of balancing cycles is restraint on the growth of activities that harm the web of life, as we shall see in Chapter 4. The purpose of balancing cycles is to drive life forward successfully. If we are astute, we will observe the feedback these cycles offer about what works and what doesn't, and thus learn, adapt, and live in closer alignment with natural principles. LAS leaders are far better than their traditional peers at reading these cycles and profiting from them.

A Descriptive Framework

Because there are so many changing relationships, information events, and cyclical energy flows embedded in a large corporation and its operating environment, one could never precisely map the whole system. We can, however, create a generalized diagram that outlines the way these systems operate within the firm, as shown in Figure 2-1. If magnified and pushed to its limits, this type of diagram is capable of immense complexity.

Figure 2-1 is a map of key constituent relationships that affect the firm's daily operations. At the center of the diagram is a general description of healthy LAS culture. Between the center and the inner core of stakeholders—employees, customers, investors, and the public—are a series of loops or channels, along which flow the information, services, money, and energy required to keep a corporation healthy. There is another, more-complex, system of loops that connect these stakeholders to one another. These transactional loops operate more efficiently in stewardship companies than in traditional ones because there are fewer hierarchical and bureaucratic blockages.

The power of the LAS model resides in its networking capacity and the freedom with which information feedback cycles can operate. In following the relational lines you will see conceptually the potential for connections, rapid feedback, learning, innovation, and profit. The model operates like any ecosystem. There are exchanges of value between individuals in the system and between the system itself and its constituents. The most energetic systems are clearly those that provide the most benefits to the broadest range of constituents because they generate the most effective exchanges of value.

Figure 2-1: The LAS Model

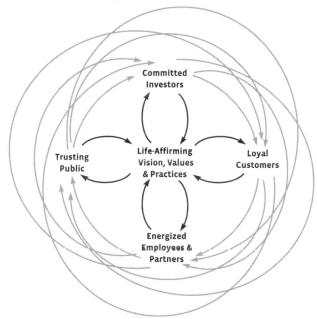

The energy of the LAS model arises from the life-affirming vision, values, and practices at its core. These inspire employees and strategic partners to buy into the firm's mission with their hearts as well as their minds. They build customer loyalty and public trust. The synergies of this system—the increased potentials for collaborative learning, innovation, and profit—attract investors willing to commit for the long term.

The model diagram touches all the firm's essential constituent relationships. In the center we see how each constituent group is motivated by the firm's core vision, values, and practices to engage in a continual exchange of value. Stewardship firms welcome such exchanges by openly discussing their proximate business goals as well as their goals for the larger living systems that support them (the free market, society, and the biosphere). Such transparency invites feedback from all directions, helping the firm to learn and adapt more effectively as the world around it changes.

The outer rings of the diagram describe feedback channels between the firm's constituents. For example, inspired employees build public trust, which reinforces commitments to the firm by investors, customers, and partners. Loyal customers and committed investors validate the firm to all constituent groups. In these ways, each constituent builds on the enthusiasm of others, opening channels of communication and value exchange.

Toyota's famed production system works in this way. Its creator, chief engineer Taiichi Ohno, studied work and information flows to find key leverage points at which output could be raised with minimum effort and waste. The symbiotic networks he devised during the 1960s—which lowered Toyota's break-even point by an order of magnitude—are today models of manufacturing efficiency because they have so many built-in feedback loops.

The story of Shell's recent (1993–1998) strategic transformation shows how a multinational giant with more than 100,000 employees became more entrepreneurial and inspiring to employees by organizing along the lines shown in Figure 2-1. Shell's purpose was to remove hierarchical and bureaucratic blockages in its organization and to vest more authority and responsibility in frontline employees who were in closer contact with the firm's ultimate customers. In doing so it followed a principle called "subsidiarity." Practically speaking, this meant managers who were used to giving orders had to trust employees to do the right thing and hold them personally accountable for results. Each leader was required to find his or her individual ways of making subsidiarity work. Many had to undergo personal transformations themselves in order to become more open individuals, better listeners, and leaders more sensitive to the subtle fields of thought and emotion that affect team energy and spirit.

Steve Miller, the group managing director who led much of the transformation process, said the cultural shakeup was worth it. Rather than throwing Shell into confusion, it actually gave the company more control over its operations than ever before. "You get more feedback than before," Miller said. "You learn more than before. You know more through your own people about what's going on in the marketplace and with customers than before . . . . [Employees execute better because they have] a common understanding of where they are going and a common understanding of the business."[10]

The magic of the LAS model, and the reason its basic concepts have worked so well at Toyota and Shell, is its fluid networking capacity. People are social beings. They naturally collaborate with one another to learn, experiment, innovate, and optimize their value-added capacities. When companies trust employees, value their expertise, and give them greater flexibility to self-organize, they become energized. When they can also work toward shared goals and visions that affirm their values and beliefs, they become passionate.

Careful readers will note that Figure 2-1 makes no specific reference to the larger living systems on which all companies depend; that topic will be addressed in Chapter 4. For present purposes it is enough to know how LAS works conceptually—that it incorporates all the fundamental principles of living systems.

The LAS model acknowledges that in business, as in Nature, everything is related to everything else. To be effective, corporations need continual feedback from all living assets and systems on which they depend. This does not need to be a daunting exercise in information overload, but a matter of extracting the most important information about a company's essential relationships and getting things approximately right. Because natural systems are inherently adaptive and self-correcting, this is usually good enough.

As in natural ecosystems, information and energy in stewardship firms flow easily in all directions: from the center to key constituents and back, as well as among key constituents. The idea is to optimize points of contact with vital sources of information and to learn quickly from them. In this way, if a corporation creates social, environmental, or financial stresses that threaten its business prospects, the warning signals get sent back quickly, enabling it to refine vision and strategy appropriately.

The LAS model, in short, is all about building and maintaining *relational equity* where it most counts. This is the mark of true leadership. More than past financial results can, forward-looking relational equity based on LAS principles will tell us whether a company has the "right stuff."

The Balanced Scorecard

The balanced scorecard offers a way to track forward-looking relational equity and backward-looking financial results simultaneously. Introduced in the early 1990s by Robert Kaplan and David Norton,[11] it helps corporate leaders monitor current constituent relationships as well as the corporate learning and innovation that hold the key to future relationships. As such, it offers a way to manage LAS with the same professional competence companies bring to other important functions.

Forward-looking relational feedback typically focuses on employee morale, customer satisfaction, investor loyalty, and professional respect. At the business-process level, it also looks to customer response times, speed to market, key-process cycle times, R&D productivity, and competitor innovations. Toyota has developed additional metrics for employee learning. Every year LAMP companies find new ways to use the balanced scorecard as they dig deeper into the dynamics of constituent relationships along the inner loop of Figure 2-1. This evolving art is a boon to corporate learning and planning, and evidence of humanity's capacity to adapt and profit from the feedback of living systems.

The strategic value of the balanced scorecard has been demonstrated by three Harvard Business School professors who evaluated the service-profit chains of successful corporations based on relational networks much like those in Figure 2-1.[12] Working backward, we see how profit emerges from a caring stewardship culture:

- Profit and growth flow from customer loyalty.
- Customer loyalty arises from customer satisfaction.
- Customer satisfaction arises from the value of services provided.
- Service value is created by satisfied, loyal, and productive employees.
- Productivity arises from employee satisfaction and loyalty.
- Employee satisfaction arises from a corporate culture that serves employee growth.
- Corporate culture reflects the internal quality of an organization.
- Internal quality arises from leadership that understands the importance of care and relational equity.

Although not specifically referenced to relational equity, the service-profit chain does, in fact, value it by focusing on the needs and satisfaction of the people it serves—customers and employees. Companies that benchmark important relationships along their product and service chains, and find ways to measure their progress in developing these relationships, are generally better prepared than those that don't. Not surprisingly, the above-mentioned study of service-profit chains included many LAMP companies.

Increasingly, relational metrics look to the systemic conditions within which companies exist. Many firms now report on their greenhouse gas emissions and on the environmental and human health impacts of their products and processes. Shell, for example, publishes data on its greenhouse gas emissions even though it operates in an industry that accounts for a disproportionate share of those emissions worldwide. Novo Nordisk and Baxter, understanding the value of biodiversity to their customers and themselves, have been developing metrics to measure their systemic effects.

The efforts of stewardship companies to understand their systemic impacts, however bad they may be, has brought them important public credibility. When they regularly measure and report on those impacts, people get the message that these companies are serious about reforming their practices and becoming more harmonious. If global LAMP organizations enjoy extraordinary loyalty from employees, customers, investors, and other constituents, this is a key reason why.

An LAS Evaluation Tool

We have seen why the organic LAS model of the firm is more connected and emergent than the traditional mechanistic one (Table 2-1), and how the synergies inherent in LAS cultures play out (Figure 2-1). We have also briefly looked at the dynamics of LAS cultures in terms of their inspirational qualities, cyclical information feedback, and measurement systems (the balanced scorecard).

Now let's turn to a tool I have developed to map a company's Living Asset Stewardship (Figure 2-2). It is a diagram on which a company or analyst can score a firm's respect for life using six variables, each measured by a line that originates at the center. Each line is scaled so the highest score is at the periphery. When scoring on each variable is done, the scale points are connected to form a perimeter. The larger the perimeter, the larger the frontier for potential learning and adaptation—the very attributes companies need to sustain themselves into the future.

At the top of the diagram, companies are scored on their respect for individuals and at the bottom on their respect for living systems. The north-south axis at the center of the diagram reveals how a company respects living assets (people and Nature) in its culture, a vision of the future, transparency, and strategic planning. The northwest-southeast axis tells us how it respects the people that add value to its offers (employees, suppliers, and strategic partners) in the way it is organized, financed, and operated. The southwest-northeast axis tells us how responsive a company is to the long-term needs of customers and host communities, including how well it listens to their concerns.

Figure 2-2: LAS As an Indicator of Learning Capacity

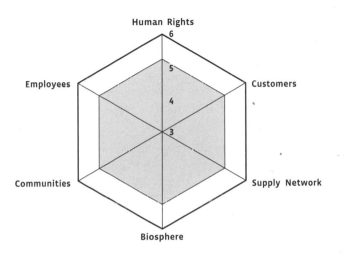

This illustrates the connection between Living Asset Stewardship (LAS) and a company's learning capacity. People are more motivated to learn and exchange ideas when companies care about them and the things they care about. Companies that respect their employees, customers, suppliers, and host communities get more helpful feedback than those that don't. Companies that place high values on human rights and limiting their biospheric impacts are more inspirational.

Corporate culture is graded on a 6-point scale ranging from 0 (lowest) to 6 (highest), with 3 being average. To be included in the Global LAMP Index,™ companies must score higher than 4 in each category. Most LAMP companies score between 4.8 and 5.2. Those with the highest combined scores in an industry/sector tend to be the learning leaders. The shaded area inside the diagram connects a company's scores on each variable, and its perimeter represents a hypothetical learning interface.

Figure 2-2 shows the profile for Toyota, the LAS and learning leader of the auto industry. Its two largest global rivals—Ford and GM—would barely show up on this diagram because their scores hover between 2 (below average) and 3 (average) on most variables.

This diagram implicitly recognizes the previously discussed fundamental principles of all living systems: (1) the *interdependence* of individual constituents on each other (relationships) and on the system itself (context); (2) the *diversity* of the individuals within the system (potential feedback loops) that enables it to learn and flexibly adapt to changing conditions (resiliency); and (3) the capacity of individuals to *self-organize* (innovate), a recursive process that enables species and systems to grow continually and generate newness (evolution).

Metaphorically, the exterior of the diagram operates like a cell's membrane system—a semipermeable interface between the corporate system and its supporting environment, as well as a physical barrier that holds the organism together. It is always active, opening and closing to let certain substances in (information, energy, or materials) while voiding its wastes in forms that provide food for other organic processes (recycling). These activities maintain a company's metabolic function and preserve its unique identity. They also help the company continually to regenerate itself—a process biologist Humberto Maturana calls "autopoeisis" (self-making).[13] This autopoeitic capacity is what makes the corporation a living system as distinct from a nonliving machine.

When companies operate in ways that are appropriate to their living environments, they experience less cognitive dissonance and stress. Employees are free of mental abstractions that conflict with the realities of their living world—abstractions that treat Nature and society as "externalities," and define the firm in terms of profit rather than in terms of learning, adapting, creating newness, and customer value.

For corporate planners, the LAS evaluation tool (Figure 2-2) is a visual way to present balanced scorecard results, and to assess potential leverage points for improving performance. The LAS tool should help the well-informed securities analyst to grade companies on their capacity to learn and adapt. In this way, it can improve the accuracy of forecasting and stock picking, and enable analysts to give more constructive feedback to the corporations they follow.

Conclusion: We've Only Just Begun

The LAS model is based on principles of Nature that have existed for billions of years. Its central metaphor is a network of self-organizing individuals that continually learns and adapts both from within itself and in relation to the world around it. The energy of this network derives from the symbiotic relationships within it—networks within networks and cycles within cycles, constantly evolving toward improving systemic quality, stability, and longevity. This metaphor works whether we are talking about the subatomic particles of a single-celled organism, the culture of a corporation, or the larger context of the Earth itself. Whenever we see life we see networks, and whenever we see networks we see the possibilities of evolution.

The LAS model is a map of relationships, energy flows, and information feedback based on common attributes of all global LAMP companies. Some, of course, fit better than others; but all fit better than their non-LAMP industry peers. My sole contribution to the model has been to notice these behavior patterns and to show how they connect.

The framework I have sketched out is a guide for further research and inquiry, and is purposely general because there is no one-size-fits-all stewardship formula. Every company must chart its own stewardship course based on the resources it uses, the markets it addresses, and the skills it has at its disposal.

The stewardship leaders in the Global LAMP Index,® however imperfect, suggest that this framework has merit. Once committed to LAS, few companies stray far from it. When people get used to a good thing, they usually want more of it, not less. As in Nature, highly adaptive systems out-produce and outlive those that are slow or unable to adapt. If capitalism is to have a future, it is in Living Asset Stewardship.

3

The Heart of Enterprise

"Humanity needs a vision of an expanding and unending future."[1]
—Edward O. Wilson, *The Biophilia Hypothesis*

A bank is the last place most people would look for a culture of heart, especially following the 2002 revelation of the self-serving and misleading business practices of Citigroup, JPMorgan Chase, and so many others. But HSBC Group never allowed voracity to overrule its humanity and ethics. Rather than pursuing mega-deals negotiated by a small, highly compensated, elite group of senior managers, HSBC has favored ethical lending by local bankers and teams who deeply know their customers. The bank's primary focus is the welfare of ordinary people, employees and customers alike.

HSBC expresses its heart through a culture of servant leadership that cascades through the bank and out to its customers. People at every level are mentored and served by their leaders and fellow team members. They, in turn, bring this spirit of service to clients, whose loyalty and referrals have made HSBC one of the world's fastest-growing banks.

HSBC's growth and financial stability can also be traced to its tradition of thrift. This is modeled from the executive suite on down. HSBC leaders are paid a fraction of what their counterparts at Citigroup and JPMorgan Chase earn. In 2001 Sir John Bond received $2.8 million in total compensation—a figure far below the $26.7 million, excluding stock options, that Citigroup chairman Sanford Weil pulled in.[2] In 2002 Bond's compensation was about 16 percent of that of Donald Layton, a division head at JPMorgan Chase. Bond, now retired, traveled to work by train, flew economy class on short trips, and made a point of switching off the lights each time he left his office.

Bond's successor as chairman was HSBC's CEO Stephen Green—an Anglican lay minister who wrote a book on faith and business that embodies the bank's ethical principles.[3] In keeping with its teamwork values and tradition of thrift, Green famously cut out all executive bonuses for 2001 and 2002. "We took the view," he said, "that a business that had not performed for the shareholder couldn't expect to receive bonuses."[4] As a result of these cuts, some younger bankers and research analysts left HSBC in protest. But more important, Green's action affirmed the bank's culture of fairness, which was crucial to its reputation in the world. Sir John Bond later told the *Institutional Investor*, "We had corporate clients come up to us and say, 'Thank God you've taken a stand.'"[5] Interestingly, the bonus cuts did not cause an exodus at the top. In 2003 HSBC's top 35 executives had more than 850 years of experience between them—an average of nearly 25 years—even though their peers at other banks had for years been more highly paid.

HSBC calls itself "The World's Local Bank" and does everything it can to make a reality of what could easily be just another empty slogan. Its staff reflects the cultures it serves: Caucasians are a minority; one out of seven employees is Chinese; and one in seven is Latin American. To strengthen the communities it serves, HSBC generously supports education and gives staff paid time to volunteer at local charities. It also supports global environmental issues that affect local living conditions and public health. In 2004 it publicly declared its intention to become "carbon neutral" by reducing business travel, buying renewable energy, trading carbon credits, and planting trees.

Commenting on HSBC's 2000 acquisition of Credit Commercial de France (CCF), France's seventh largest bank, the *Economist* noted, "[CEO

Sir John] Bond spent more time on the humanities of the deal than on price."[6] Stephen Saali, President of Republic National Bank, made a similar comment on why he favored an acquisition by HSBC: "HSBC has a very humane way of dealing with employees, and that is an important part of this for us."[7]

Does this "humane" approach to business work? Many would think it soft—featuring too much caring and too little hard-nosed competition. But they should think again. Since 1970, HSBC has grown from a large regional base in Hong Kong to the world's third-largest bank by market capitalization. A dollar invested in HSBC shares during this time span, with dividends reinvested, would have generated an average return of approximately 20 percent per year—nearly double the average annual returns on the S&P 500 and far ahead of its major global competitors.

HSBC's magic is deceptively simple. The respect and caring they invest in employees and customers is returned to them many times over in loyalty, trust, and repeat business. It's a self-feeding, self-reinforcing process that emanates from the heart.

The heart is a powerful force. It, more than the brain, is the organ that produces our biophilic instinct and intuition, our passion to create, our insights, our energy and determination, and our heroic deeds. Corporations that honor the centrality of the heart in human behavior have natural advantages over those that don't. When the time comes to deal with adversity and change, they are better prepared, more resilient, and surprisingly resourceful.

[A] business is not some legal abstract entity. Companies are composed of people with feelings and aspirations just like everybody else. And most people want to do something they are proud of . . . . Most of all, we need to make the connection between people's every day lives and business.[8]

—Sir John Bond, CEO, HSBC

The Day Southwest Was Challenged

Southwest Airlines dramatically proved the value of heart on 9/11—the tragic day in 2001 when al Qaeda terrorists flew fully loaded commercial airliners into the World Trade Center towers and the Pentagon. In contrast to other domestic carriers that quickly cut service, laid off employees, and appealed to the government for multi-billion-dollar bailouts, Southwest maintained its service, made no layoffs, and contributed $1.5 billion to the company profit-sharing plan as a gesture of confidence in employees. In the days and weeks that followed, executives and employees made spontaneous gestures of concern for each other that strengthened Southwest's culture of family loyalty and spirit. The top three executives quietly discontinued receiving pay for the remainder of the year. Employees volunteered to work longer hours, covered for each other at work and at home, and raised $1.3 million through donated pay as a contribution to the company.

The response at Southwest was not something that could be created on command. Employees spontaneously reciprocated with heart because such response is integral to their culture. The gestures of Southwest employees in the wake of the 9/11 tragedy were not unprecedented. During the fuel crisis that accompanied the 1991 Gulf War, employees donated, on average, $20,000 per month to help buy fuel. Why would this happen?

The company has a long history of servant leadership—a collegial system wherein leaders at every level serve the career growth and well-being of employees—rather than a hierarchical system in which leaders tell employees what to do via command and control. Southwest also fosters an informal, but consistently applied "no layoff" policy. It hires for attitude, rather than credentials or appearance, believing that motivated, caring people can be taught the skills they need. It is an open, sharing culture whose members are well informed and personally cared for as family members and employees. They share in the company's profit and are encouraged to have fun. Company leaders continually reinforce this culture in word and deed: then CEO Herb Kelleher and his executive team once rushed to help short-handed baggage handlers at Love Field in Dallas, Texas.

Southwest's management further reinforces its culture of respectful care by keeping the company financially strong. Contrary to the advice of investment bankers to borrow aggressively so Southwest could buy more planes and fly more routes, management has opted to maintain a strong balance sheet and to expand only when the company is operationally ready to do so. Consequently, on the day of the terrorist attack, Southwest's debt-equity ratio was only one-fifth of the airline industry average, and it had nearly a billion dollars in cash on hand.

Southwest's financial policy consciously connects financial stewardship with care for employees and other stakeholders. One of the company's ubiquitous tag lines is: "We manage in good times so that we will do well in bad times." Largely for this reason, Southwest did not have to resort to layoffs or cut service after the 9/11 tragedy. In fact, as a heartfelt gesture to customers, it quickly advertised full refunds on all returned tickets, saying, *"We gave you the freedom to fly. Now we give you the freedom NOT to fly."*

By respecting both employees' needs for job security and customers' fears about flying in an extreme situation, Southwest added to its solid core of relational equity. How can the value of this equity be measured? It cannot be isolated or precisely counted for a balance sheet appraisal, which explains why Southwest's major competitors neglect it. But there are ways to connect, empirically, Southwest's relational equity to its financial success. The net present value (NPV) of employee and customer loyalty—money earned by higher levels of employee productivity and repeat business, or money saved through lower rates of employee and customer defection—can be measured.[9] A more holistic approach is to compare the trend of Southwest's stock market capitalization with that of industry peers who have harmed their relational equity by putting their financial goals (ends) ahead of their relationships with employees and customers (means). As this book goes to press, the stock market capitalization of Southwest is greater than that of its four largest domestic competitors *combined*.

An important addition to this story about Southwest's heart in the face of adversity is the fact that it has been the most profitable airline in the U.S. for well more than a decade. Its servant leadership style and stewardship culture have been evident since its founding in 1971. The employee and customer goodwill Southwest gained on 9/11 is therefore part of an ongoing story. If accountants and equity analysts can't measure the precise effects of these practices using conventional accounting tools, they can at least generally connect them to Southwest's success via its share appreciation.

Real Leverage

The most salient point that emerges from the Southwest story—indeed, from the stories of all Focus Group and LAMP companies—is the power of inspiration. That is what LAS produces. When people feel emotionally

bonded to a company, they are naturally more coherent, enthusiastic, willing to learn, eager to serve, and inspired to innovate. In fact, *the human
heart is the most powerful operating lever a company has*—far more powerful and effective than the more commonly used lever of financial debt.

I emphasize this statement because it is so contrary to conventional
business theory. Yet there is considerable empirical evidence to support it.
LAMP companies generally produce higher returns on equity (ROE) in
spite of carrying substantially less debt leverage than their traditionally
managed peers. This is supported by both their stock market performance,
as we have seen, and their bond ratings.

Table 3-1 shows how Global LAMP companies are clustered at the top
end of Moody's ratings—far higher than their global corporate peers. No
LAMP companies carry speculative "junk" bond ratings, whereas roughly
one-third of the companies that comprise the global corporate average are
rated in this speculative category. A more detailed breakdown of LAMP
credit ratings appears in Appendix 3, and a closer look at Focus Group
financials can be found in Table 11-1.

An important point missing from Table 3-1 is the continual erosion of
corporate credit ratings since 1980. During this time, while traditionally
managed companies took on increasing amounts of debt to leverage up
their returns on equity, companies in the Focus Group and Global LAMP
Index® maintained their financial integrity and high credit ratings in the
vicinity of Aa3/A1.

In all cases the reasons for this financial prudence are clear. LAMP companies want to be responsible stewards in difficult times as well as in good
times. They refuse to gamble their relational equity with customers,
employees, strategic partners, investors, and other stakeholders by overextending themselves in pursuit of growth. Given their organic, systemic
mental models (see Chapter 2), which place a high value on relationships
and continual service, this is not surprising.

The reinforcing cycle of Living Asset Stewardship and organizational
learning (LAS + OL) also plays a role in the financial stability of LAMP
companies. Inspirational cultures that seek to serve ends beyond profit
alone tend to be more innovative than those focused solely on profit. This
lean toward innovation increases the probability that their products and
services will enjoy robust demand and gross margins. With such advan-

Table 3-1: Credit Ratings of LAMP Companies vs. Global Corporate Average at Year-End 2005

DISTRIBUTION OF MOODY'S CREDIT RATINGS

Rating	Global LAMP No.	Index® % Total	Corporate Average as %*	
Aaa	4	6.67	2.33	Top Grade
Aa1	5	8.33	2.41	
Aa2	4	6.67	4.33	Very Strong
Aa3	11	18.34	8.97	
A1	10	16.67	8.82	
A2	10	16.67	8.99	Strong
A3	4	6.67	9.89	
Baa1	7	11.67	8.33	
Baa2	4	6.67	8.39	Medium Grade
Baa3	1	1.67	6.94	
Ba1	0	0.00	3.46	
Ba2	0	0.00	3.74	Speculative ("Junk")
Ba3	0	0.00	3.95	
B1	0	0.00	4.85	
>B1	0	0.00	14.62	Deep Junk
Totals:	60	100.00	100.00	

* The corporate average is based on the number of global companies rated by Moody's.

Note: More than half of LAMP companies fall into the five highest Moody's rating categories (A1 and higher), versus fewer than 26 percent for the average rated corporation. All LAMP companies are rated as investment grade (Baa3 or higher). By contrast, 31 percent of the global corporate average (companies) are rated as speculative (Ba1 or lower), with nearly half that number rated in the bottom tiers (B1 and lower). Source: Moody's Investor Services, Inc.

tages, it is not surprising that LAS leaders also produce more consistently positive free cash flow, as discussed in Chapter 5.

With this compelling evidence in mind, let's look further at the proposition that LAS is the heart of enterprise. In particular, why do people respond more positively to LAS cultures than to traditional ones? What governs the strong emotional responses we have to these cultures?

Why the Heart?

Most people associate the heart with soft feelings that cloud the clear, hard thinking needed for business decisions. But nothing could be further from the truth. In fact, the heart is an intuitive, fast-thinking guide to the methodical, slower-thinking rational brain. It has its own independent nervous system—a neural network that is the source of our emotional and intuitive intelligence. The heart's intelligence is embedded in approximately 40,000 neurons (nerve cells)—as many as are found in various subcortical centers of the brain.[10] These neurons are directly linked to the amygdala, the emotional center of the brain that quickly tells us whether or not we are in danger and whether we can trust that a person or activity will be good for us.

This powerful linkage to the emotional center of the brain evolved more than 100 million years earlier than did the "rational" centers of the brain. It protected our mammalian forebears from imminent danger and helped them forge long-term bonds (of family and community) to ensure the survival and continuation of our species. It is this survival circuitry that underlies and defines the heart's intelligence and wisdom.

The Institute of HeartMath, out of Boulder Creek, California, has done extensive research into the heart-brain connection. The organization's work makes an important distinction between *coherence* and *stress* in today's corporate world. Coherence is a state in which people are mentally, emotionally, and physically connected to what they are doing. Stress occurs when there are serious disconnects. When people are in a coherent state, they are healthier, more effective, and innovative. No energy is wasted. Alternately, when they feel psychological stress their efficiency drops off, they become mentally blocked, and they develop health problems such as depression, high blood pressure, heart attack, ulcers, substance abuse, etc. According to the American Institute of Stress, in 2001 U.S. companies paid out approximately $300 billion for stress-related lost time, healthcare, worker's compensation, and training of replacement workers.[11]

According to HeartMath research, companies create stress when the heart's wisdom is overridden—typically, when they ask or force workers to do something that conflicts with their ethics and beliefs. When that happens, the heart's rhythm becomes distressed, disharmonic, and incoherent. This incoherence is radiated to every cell of the body by the heart's electromagnetic field. Spectral analysis of electrocardiograms reveals resulting changes in the heart's rhythm and electromagnetic field. The heart sends distress signals to all the vital systems, including the immune system, through the autonomic nervous system. When these distress signals become a constant in our lives, "our sensitivities to feeling get shut down . . . and constant low-grade anxiety or depression sets in."[12]

The feedback effects of such anxiety and depression weigh heavily on traditionally managed companies. Their internal malaise, as we have seen with Ford and General Motors, stifles innovation from within and drives them to seek regeneration via acquisition. This, of course, adds to their debt levels without doing anything to solve their fundamental problems. Companies can't do this for long—particularly when faced with competitors, such as Toyota, that are deeply committed to LAS. It is no wonder that traditionally managed companies have such short lives.

As we have seen, cardiac coherence is the opposite of stress. It is a product of positive emotions that arise when people feel appreciated, cared for, and inspired by their work. Such coherence can be measured biomedically by monitoring the electrical synchronization of brain and heart to determine whether the nervous system is operating efficiently in support of health, mental clarity, and productivity.[13] One of the secrets of LAS companies' success lies in their ability to create environments that minimize stress and, therefore, support cardiac coherence.

Such information is obviously of great interest to corporations, in terms of both managing costs and optimizing efficiency. Not surprisingly, three members of the Focus Group—Hewlett-Packard, Johnson & Johnson (LifeScan division), and Shell—are among HeartMath's corporate clients.

Emotion, not intellect, is the fuel that drives business. Intellect provides the direction, but not the fuel.[14]
    —Doc Childre and Bruce Cryer, Institute of HeartMath, *From Chaos to Coherence*

We don't really need to read deeply into the science of heart-brain physiology to understand the linkages summarized here. We all know them from personal experience. How often, for example, have we formed a quick impression of a person or situation that we later changed only to regret it? We may then have thought, "I should have trusted my instinct!" Have we felt stressed or upset when an employer or colleague has done something we consider unethical, or worse, if we have been asked to participate in an unethical act? Alternately, how energized did we feel the last time we did something that affirmed our beliefs and values and made us want to participate? How were we feeling the last time we had a deep insight? Were we connected and congruent with the life around us, or disconnected and separate? In all these cases, our hearts give us feedback and guidance, and we usually function best when we heed that guidance.

The advantages we get from following our hearts, and that companies get from engaging our hearts, arise from the deeply human, biophilic urge that makes us want to work and behave in ways that support life. It is wired into the neurology of our hearts and the parts of our brain that are most connected to the heart. Evolutionary biologists say this urge entered the human gene pool because, through thousands of generations, those who respected life lived longer than those who didn't and were therefore better able to pass on their DNA.[15] During the past decade, advances in heart and brain imaging have helped us understand better the power of this biophilic urge and the related emotions of love, appreciation, respect, empathy, and caring. As Daniel Goleman tells us in *Emotional Intelligence,* these behaviors get us what we want more efficiently than behaviors that arise out of their opposites: fear, disrespect, intimidation, and control. "Intellect," he says, "cannot work at its best without emotional intelligence . . . . [E]ach is a full partner in mental life."[16]"[O]ur deepest feelings, our passions and longings, are essential guides, and . . . our species owes much of its existence to their power in human affairs."[17]

When I calculated the ratio of technical skills, IQ, and emotional intelligence as ingredients of excellent performance, emotional intelligence was twice as important as the others for jobs at all levels. [*commenting on competency tests from 188 companies*][18]

—Daniel Goleman, "What Makes a Leader"

Toward Sustainable Leverage

The reinforcing cycle of LAS + OL offers a more powerful and sustainable form of leverage than the financial leverage preferred by traditional, mechanistically managed firms. Why? Because inspired, hopeful people learn faster and retain more than uninspired, despairing people. Also, inspired employees tend to generate more consistent free cash flows as a result of their superior innovation.

Companies rarely get into trouble by over-inspiring employees. But the consequences of taking on too much debt can be harmful in multiple ways. Financially stressed companies put employees under continual pressure to produce numbers (ends) at the expense of customer, supplier, and other stakeholder relationships (means) or face the prospect of layoffs. This adds to workplace stress and increases the probabilities of negative feedback.

LAMP companies maintain sound finances precisely because they don't want to put their employees and other stakeholders at risk. Consider the case of Nucor, possibly the world's most productive steelmaker. Since 1995, except for brief periods, its cash holdings have exceeded its total debt. But what makes Nucor an interesting case is the way the company has turned around since 1966, when it was the Vulcraft division of the near-bankrupt Nuclear Corporation of America. In that year Vulcraft had balance sheet equity of only $2.3 million. Since then, the successor company (Nucor) has increased this equity every year without interruption, largely by empowering its employees and by staying out of debt.

Today, Nucor runs more than 30 independently operated mini-mills, virtually all from recycled scrap steel. It is now the largest domestic steelmaker, both by tonnage produced and by stock market capitalization. Its credit rating is A1, the steel industry's highest.

Ken Iverson turned Nucor around by following a simple plan based on five stewardship principles that came straight from the heart.

First, commit to employees. Today Nucor employees are the highest paid, best cared for, and most independent thinking in the steel industry and they respond by being the most productive.

The second—strive for world-class innovation—derives from the first. Nucor employees are encouraged to observe, learn, and innovate as they work, and are paid according to what they produce. With such financial incentives, ideas fly off the plant floor. There is no corporate R&D or engineering department, nor a chief technology officer. Decisions regarding the adoption of technology are made collaboratively by teams composed of mill managers, engineers, and machine operators—people who do the work.

Third, locate in small rural communities. Because Nucor does this, it can be close to its employees and their families, and can make qualitative differences in people's lives. Beyond bringing high-paying jobs to these communities, Nucor gives generously to local charities and offers college scholarships to employees' children (up to almost $3,000 per year for each child).

Fourth, be an environmental leader. Nucor is by far the largest recycler (by weight) in the country and the most energy-efficient steel company. It was the first steelmaker to monitor emissions at each mill continually—24 hours a day. It aims to make every plant compliant with ISO 14001 guidelines and progress toward that goal is monitored monthly.

The fifth principle—keep management lean—is based on trust. There are only four layers of management between the CEO and the floor worker and only 66 people in the head office. Nucor's divisions are all independently run at the local level and employees work in teams that are largely self-directed. To remove barriers to communication, everyone is treated the same. There are no executive perks and privileges.

These five principles are not just words at Nucor. They are the way the company lives. Since Nucor began pouring steel in 1969, no employee has ever been laid off for lack of work. Its egalitarian burden-sharing program avoids layoffs during hard times by making a percentage cut in all workers' compensation, starting with the CEO (who, during the recession of 1982, took a 75-percent reduction). When times are more robust, employees get special bonuses in addition to their weekly incentive pay. Nucor's profit-sharing plan (for employees below the officer level) distributes at least 10 percent of pre-tax profit each year. Beyond that, Nucor subsidizes employee purchases of company stock and gives employees free shares on five-year anniversary dates. To emphasize its concern for environment and community, Nucor looks beyond the immediate environs of its mills, which are clean and safe, to the areas in which its employees live and play. In Berkeley, South Carolina, where it operates two mills, Nucor funds a trust that protects a local 5,000-acre land preserve. In other areas Nucor has sponsored waterfowl protection and wetlands preservation projects far beyond the scope of its competitors' gestures.

Here's my pecking order: You take care of your employees first. If you have loyal, dedicated, hard-working employees, they'll take care of the customers.[19]

—John Correnti, CEO (1996–1999), Nucor

Nucor is an organic community of people who are conscious of their purpose: to serve and innovate. Moreover, they are trusted to organize themselves spontaneously. Because they are entrusted to do the right thing, individual employees and team members rise to the occasion. They are active and inspired, and use their collective talents intelligently. Nucor builds enthusiasm that is self-sustaining and generative by consistently respecting the lives of employees and community members, and the surrounding environments. Nucor's credibility as a long-term partner with its stakeholders is strengthened by its strong balance sheet. By optimizing "heart leverage," it has been, for the past quarter-century, the most adaptive, emergent, and productive company in its industry. Since 1980, while other U.S. steel companies have either shrunk or sunk into bankruptcy, it has grown sales and earnings at double-digit rates.

Toward Quantum Thinking

Quantum thinking is thinking inspired by the heart. It is different from the rational, linear thinking we employ in most activities because it departs from established paths of cause and effect to find new solutions. It happens when we feel coherent and connected with our ideals and values. During such times we create our greatest works of art and our greatest innovations. We feel passionate in our quest, and open to information and feedback from all directions.

Physicist and management consultant Danah Zohar puts it this way: "commitment, involvement, and love" are natural expressions of consciousness that draw people into "quantum systems" (e.g., biosystems, social systems, etc.).[20] Such expressions arise from a biophilic "quantum understanding" that each individual needs to be connected to the whole. "Crudely put," Zohar says, "mind is relationship and matter is that which it relates. Neither, on its own, could evolve or express anything; together, they give us ourselves and the world."[21] "[D]ynamic relationship is the basis of all that is . . . . It gives us a view of the human self that is free and responsible, responsive to others and to its environment, essentially related and naturally committed, and at every moment creative."[22]

Nucor's culture inspires quantum thinking in its employees by treating them as heroes, and by nurturing their aspirations to be the best they can be and to do good works. Warren Bennis has described its culture as one of "lofty aspirations" in which "creative dissent is welcomed" and management is sensitive to "the views of everyone who has a stake in the company." He also finds at Nucor an atmosphere conducive to dialogue: one in which leaders are also good followers, and both leaders and followers "share certain characteristics such as listening, collaborating, and working out competitive issues with peers."[23] If quantum thinking requires being connected, having open minds, feeling free to explore new ideas, and pursuing ideals and values, Nucor is clearly the champion of its industry. The spontaneous flow of ideas off the floor of a typical Nucor mill is prodigious. Virtually every process improvement the company has made, from finding simple ways to save money to designing whole systems, has come from the people doing the work.

Nucor's humanistic culture bonds employees to the company and makes them want to participate in its evolution. The company's ethics center on care for the individual, families, communities, and the environment that embraces them all. It is a populist ethics that people understand in their hearts, not an ethereal one that requires deep knowledge of ecology or a sophisticated worldview. "Heart" is Nucor's most powerful lever in its quest to be the "safest, highest quality" steel company in the world.

Behaving ethically in business can be very hard work. But it is work you must take on.[24]

—Ken Iverson, Chairman (1998), Nucor

We don't need to be ethicists to see that our higher thinking capacities are grounded in morality and ethics. Whatever the motivation is called— inspiration, right-mindedness, trust, or morality—ethical behavior calls forth the best in us. Edward O. Wilson notes that people have an "instinct to behave ethically" that is hard-wired into our genes. When we harmonize the rational thinking capacity of our brains with our hearts' more holistic wisdom, we become energized with a passion to learn and to explore. Global LAMP companies know this and have better access to quantum thinking because of it.

Quantum learning begins with the heart and with a hope that we can live in closer harmony with each other and with Nature. It cannot be programmed or force-fed to employees via formal training sessions and learning manuals. Nor can corporations alter the genetically based wisdom of our hearts by asking us to accept abstractions of a mechanistic reality—numbers and profits—that conflict with the biological world in which we live. Our biophilic wiring is too deeply embedded. If companies want the best from us, they must care about us, and about the things we care about that embody our values and beliefs. When we work with our hearts as well as our minds, employers get our best efforts. When companies order us to override our ideals for the sake of the company, they get only a fraction of our capacities.

We can now understand better the leverage companies get from the reinforcing cycle of Living Asset Stewardship and organizational learning (LAS + OL). It arises from the heart and the ability of people in a state of heart-brain coherence to access their higher (quantum) thinking capacities. This is the key energy source of global LAMP companies. It doesn't take a lot of capital to set this LAS + OL cycle in motion—just authenticity and heart. Twenty-five years ago, Nucor and Southwest Airlines were virtual start-ups in the U.S. steel and airline industries. Fifty years ago Toyota emerged from the wreckage of World War II with practically no capital except for the energy, determination, and dreams of its employees. Today, all three companies are profit leaders in capital-intensive industries in which borrowing capacity and debt leverage were presumed to be critical strategic advantages. The common denominator in their successes has been engaging the hearts of employees and other stakeholders to catalyze the reinforcing cycle of LAS + OL.

Strategic Vision

Global LAMP companies have a natural advantage in strategic planning because their corporate cultures, mental models, and thought processes are more coherent. They have a clearer sense of their real identities (see Table 2-1), and understand the extraordinary leverage in caring about people and the things people care about. They are more adept at utilizing the insight and capacities of employees on the front lines. And they are extraordinary networkers.

The network is the central metaphor of all living systems and the central organizing principle of LAS cultures. Global LAMP companies create networks that nurture and utilize the collective insights, wisdom, and talents

of all constituents, rather than those of a select few at the top of a hierarchy. This alone predisposes them to be better at strategic visioning. The
best corporate stewards find ways to make these networks continually self-
replenishing, as Nokia does by engaging the hearts of all constituents.

Nokia is in every way an open, inclusive, and vibrantly interactive network. This is evident in its organization, in interactions with suppliers and
customers, in the open architecture of its products, in the transparency and
relevance of its public reporting, and in its biophilic ideals. Every year all
employees participate in an annual visioning process through a series of
meetings, called "Listening to You," that brings ideas up from the front lines
and distills them into a strategic vision. These ideas then percolate back
down through the ranks by means of numerous presentations that generate additional feedback. Because everyone gets to participate, when Nokia
decides to "go all out" in pursuit of a goal, there is already in place a high
degree of consensus and commitment.

Our strategies and goals need to be inspirational and easily understandable,
but the drive to achieve can only start from within each of us. Everyone at
Nokia should genuinely say: "I care!"[25]

—The Nokia Way

Nokia sees its employees, suppliers, and customers as important constituents in a large, interconnected ecosystem. Nokia's stated mission is *to
connect people*, and it does. Its interactive supply net, which electronically
links all suppliers into a single coordinated network, is essential to the
ecosystem's health, which in turn feeds back to support the health of all its
constituents. Nokia freely shares information on its goals and processes,
believing that the synergies of the network's collective insights and contributions will outweigh the ability of competitors to copy its products freely.
This belief that a well-integrated network can out-think and out-produce
traditional competitors required a strategic leap of faith. So far, it has
worked brilliantly.

Nokia's strategy is inherently ecological because it sees its own value and
that of its partners in terms of the value of the whole ecosystem in which it
operates. Every participant has a voice. Implicit in this process is a faith that
all participants are inherently predisposed toward life and that people, act-

ing on their shared beliefs and values, will ultimately move the company in the right direction.

Such cultures have what Danah Zohar calls a collective "sense of identity . . . aspirations . . . deeper, motivating core values and long-term strategies" that coalesce into a spiritual core.[26] When this core is respectful and coherent, employees care more about their work, inquire more deeply into its meaning, think more creatively, and become more innovative. In short, they enter the reinforcing cycle of LAS + OL that is the heart and continually emergent energy of global stewardship leaders.

Nokia's strategy is strikingly different from the mechanical worldview and multiple tradeoffs of traditional capitalism. In Danah Zohar's mind, the mechanical view fails "because it does not work towards a greater ordered coherence. It reflects neither the intuitions nor the personal needs of most people, nor the simple, quite classical fact that we . . . are all interdependent and that our human lives are inseparably intertwined with the world of Nature."[27]

[A] change of heart occurs when people look beyond themselves to others, and then to the rest of life. It is strengthened when they also expand their view of landscape, from parish to nation and beyond, and their sweep of time from their own life spans to multiple generations and finally to the extended future history of humankind.[28]

—Edward O. Wilson, *The Future of Life*

How to Recognize a Company with Heart

I am often asked how one can recognize a company with heart—one that appeals to the biophilic instincts of its employees and stakeholders, and inspires their quantum minds. There is no pat formula, but stewardship companies in the Global LAMP Index® have some strikingly similar attributes:

- an authentic mission, vision, and values that arose spontaneously from within the firm and that strongly appeal to the heart;
- a decentralized, networked organization, based on the principle of subsidiarity, in which employees are trusted to self-organize in their areas of competence and are held accountable;

- a culture of servant leadership, wherein the role of leaders is to serve the professional growth of employees, and employees are treated as precious assets rather than potential costs and liabilities;
- a commitment to continual learning that gives employees permission to experiment and fail in their quest for innovation; and
- a history of prudent fiscal management that reflects an intention to serve humanity in sustainable ways for generations to come.

Even if stewardship leaders don't openly talk about touching the hearts of stakeholders, they do it instinctively in these five ways. Their respect for life is palpable, visible, and highly contagious. It touches our hearts and inspires us to reciprocate by being loyal customers, investors, and supporters. As the saying goes, what goes around comes around.

The Transcendent Truth

Ultimately, the whole case for heart leverage rests on biophilia, Wilson's term for our innate reverence for life. This is an expression of our heart's wisdom, a deep knowing that everything we do in business is ultimately connected back to the web of life that sustains us. We are all constituents in a larger organic whole and our health depends on the health of the whole. When we come to this realization, when we begin to define ourselves as constituents within the web of life rather than as autonomous individuals, we enter a spiritual realm that is at once nourishing and creative.

The spiritual or biophilic connection between people and other life forms is the highest achievement of evolution to date because it connects everything from the distant past through the present and far into the future. Our ability to connect across huge expanses of biological time, and even physical space, is part of our unique genetic heritage. We alone, among all species, have this capacity. Our connective instincts are, in part, wired into the higher cortical functions of our brains. But they also arise from our hearts, which are linked directly to the more primitive and instinctive parts of our brains and central nervous systems. These connective instincts have evolved within us through thousands of generations and are deeply spiritual, insightful, and creative. Heart instincts are capable of taking immense conceptual leaps. They caused our ancestors to wonder about the stars, life, and the origin and order of things, and to create language so we might share our insights. If the seat of this spiritual inquiry is the human heart, and the heart governs our intuition and creative thinking, then it is a powerful tool that we minimize at our peril.

To those who may question the biophilic premise of LAS and its underlying message of managing from the heart, I refer again to Wilson: "Were there no evidence of biophilia at all, the hypothesis of its existence would still be compelled by pure evolutionary logic. The reason is that human history . . . began hundreds of thousands or millions of years ago with the origin of the genus *Homo*. For more than 99 percent of human history people have lived together in hunter-gatherer bands totally and intimately involved with other organisms. During this period of deep history, and still further back, into paleohominid times, they depended on an exact and learned knowledge of crucial aspects of natural history . . . . In short, the brain evolved in a biocentric world, not a machine-regulated world."[29]

The genetic argument reaches further back in time. Wilson continues, "All higher eukaryotic organisms, from flowering plants to insects and humanity itself, are thought to have descended from a single ancestral population that lived about 1.8 billion years ago . . . . All this distant kinship is stamped by a common genetic code and elementary features of cell structure."[30] Although this kinship is not part of the ordinary person's consciousness, it is deeply embedded in our vital systems, including our hearts.

Conclusion

The proposition that Living Asset Stewardship is the heart of enterprise— that heart-based LAS cultures leverage returns on equity more effectively than does borrowing—is virtual heresy in the cultures of Wall Street and traditionally managed companies. It is nevertheless validated by empirical operating and financial evidence, by our knowledge of heart-brain communication, by the dynamics of all living systems, and ultimately by the logic of our own human evolution.

All living systems operate as networks with broadly distributed intelligence, resources, and energy. The more open and inclusive the network, the stronger the system. Companies that operate on this principle have natural advantages over isolated hierarchies. No amount of financial engineering or investment banking advice can change this.

Global LAMP companies may not always be at the top of their game, for they have product cycles and bad years as all companies do. But they all have an uncanny ability to learn, adapt, and move on to new heights of discovery, mastery, and profit. The secret of their longevity and success lies in recognizing that they are, fundamentally, living communities with brains, heart, and spirit, and in using these limitless resources to their best advantage.

The brain is a remarkable instrument for memory, pattern recognition, and logical thinking. But it needs the heart's wisdom for guidance and spirit for the energy to persist. When all three capacities are simultaneously engaged, companies become highly charged and innovative.

As we accept more readily our hearts' wisdom, our insight and capacity to act intelligently grow. Our respect, appreciation, and reverence for life— when engaged in a reinforcing cycle of LAS + OL—catalyze constructive growth. We are not talking about sentimental love here, but the practical, bottom-line type of love and compassion that understand what is in our long-term best interests. This is precisely where global LAMP companies find their greatest leverage. And a powerful lever it is.

We are entering a new era of existentialism . . . [based on] the concept that only unified learning, universally shared, makes accurate foresight and wise choice possible. In the course of it all, we are learning that ethics is everything. Human social existence, unlike animal sociality, is based on the genetic propensity to form long-term contracts that evolve by culture into moral precepts and law. The rules of contract formation were not given to humanity from above, nor did they emerge randomly in the mechanics of the brain. They evolved over tens or hundreds of millennia because they conferred upon the genes prescribing them survival and the opportunity to be represented in future generations.[31]

—Edward O. Wilson, *Consilience*

4

Optimizing Synergies

"[We] found that investor loyalty was heavily dependent on
customer and employee loyalty, and we understood that we were
dealing not with tactical issues but with a strategic system."[1]
—Frederick Reichheld, *The Loyalty Effect*

"The more the mind is fathomed in its own right, as an organ of
survival, the greater will be the reverence for life for purely rational
reasons."[2]
— Edward O. Wilson, *Biophilia*

The strength of the LAS model lies in the synergies stewardship creates both inside and outside the firm. It optimizes the intelligence, adaptability, and creativity of people by connecting them to each other and to Nature in ways the traditional model cannot. Its energy arises from within rather than from the top down, as employees at all levels find their common interests and channel them into the firm's core activities. Top-line managers serve this process by mentoring employees, listening to their ideas, and offering them as much local authority as they can handle. Employees respond by self-organizing in ways that leverage their individual skills and interests.

As people find their interests and values more integrated into the firm's activities, they work with their hearts *and* minds, and are inspired to reach beyond themselves and their immediate responsibilities to express their biophilic urges to serve a higher good. As the firm affiliates with and enables these urges, employees become more loyal and more committed to—even passionate about—the common interests of the group. They want to be there to co-create a better world for themselves, their families, and their ever-widening communities of interest. Resultant decreases in employee turnover and improvements in customer service lead to increased orders and lower defection rates. Reichheld shows how such employee commitment strengthens customer net present value (NPV), returns on equity (ROE), and shareholder loyalty.[3] As a consequence, the firm's economic value-added (EVA) is leveraged up.[4] Its economic performance improves (relative to that of its peers), and this is usually reflected in its share price. We've glimpsed this process in the three previous chapters, and will now see how it works in terms of systems dynamics.

A Systems Perspective

Systems dynamics offers a way to visualize how living systems work and relate to one another—from both the bottom up and the top down. It does this by mapping feedback circuits within the firm (the micro level), and between the firm and the larger systems that support it (the macro level). When these are mainly positive, we say they are *synergistic,* as is typical for LAS companies. The conceptual maps we use to show these synergies are called causal loop diagrams. These are easy to follow because they concentrate on the big picture and stay within the bounds of common sense. Readers who wish to pursue systems dynamics at a more detailed level (at which thousands of feedback cycles can be mapped) may consult the Bibliography for useful sources.

The big picture of LAS begins with the firm in the context of the larger systems that contain it: the free market, society, and the biosphere. In assessing these relationships we need to ask, "Is the firm compatible with those systems or at odds?" As a general rule, the more compatibility or harmony we find, the more synergism we are likely to see; conversely, the more dissonance or incompatibility within the firm, the greater the risk of failure. These simple rules are usually borne out over time via stock market returns. The Global LAMP Index® supports this thesis, as is discussed in Chapter 5. When LAS is pursued as a strategic imperative—with the same professional discipline as marketing, R&D, or customer service—companies tend to gain a performance edge.

Table 4-1: Functions of Causal Loops

CAUSAL LOOP	DESCRIBES	SERVES
Primary reinforcing cycle	Growth	Self-actualization of individual
Balancing cycle	Resistance	Interdependence Health of whole system
New reinforcing cycle	Learning Adaptation	Diversity Evolution of new life

The relationships described by the causal loop diagrams explain three universal attributes of all living systems—those of *self-actualization* (growth), *interdependence* (competing systemic demands that limit growth), and *diversity* (learning, adaptation, and evolution.)[5] The drive of an individual or corporation to grow is described as a primary reinforcing cycle. Obstacles to unlimited growth of the individual or corporation include the competing demands for energy and resources by other entities—corporations, people, etc.—that also need to survive. Because each ultimately depends on another, there is a need for systemic balance. Laws that regulate corporate pollution, workplace conditions, product safety, and monopolistic practices are conscious efforts to maintain systemic balance. Global warming is a biospheric expression of the need for restoration of balance. Such systemic push-back, or resistance, limits growth and is described by balancing cycles. As a result of the continuing interplay of growth and resistance, action and reaction, living systems learn and adapt. This produces new life and ever-expanding diversity. The energy of this emerging life then drives new reinforcing cycles of growth, which meet new resistance, and so on. Nothing stands still.

Figure 4-1 describes the growth of the limited-liability corporation as a primary reinforcing (R) cycle, followed by the delayed resistance of two balancing cycles. The R cycle at the upper left of the diagram started in 1896 when corporations first gained limited-liability status.[6] This event enabled anyone to invest in a corporation without being personally liable for adverse impacts that corporation might have on people or Nature. This protection from liability opened the floodgates of investment that built more enterprise, thereby lifting the economy and releasing an unprece-

Figure 4-1: The Dysfunctions of the Capital Investment Model

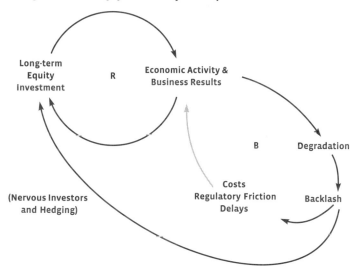

Long-term equity investment fuels a reinforcing spiral of growing economic activity. But, growth brings issues: environmental degradation brings costly backlash, and investors become nervous.

dented torrent of growth, profit, and investment. As the R cycle gained momentum, the larger systems that supported the corporation pushed back. The two balancing loops shown on this diagram reflect public concern over environmental and public health degradation produced by unchecked corporate growth. As this degradation grew, from the 1960s onward, it produced a backlash of consumer resistance followed by public resistance in the form of new laws and regulations. It also produced an investor backlash expressed by increased hedging and nervous short-term trading.

There is nothing pernicious about balancing cycles in the marketplace or anywhere else. Their purpose is to maintain the general health, diversity, and balance of a living system. By resisting growth that would harm the whole, they force us continually to adapt. Balancing cycles are evident today in shortages of clean water, desertification, soil contamination, the decline of Earth's rainforests and fisheries, the breakdown of human immune systems, financial crises (e.g., debt defaults, and currency crises), political backlash, and in many other contexts. There can be no doubt that these systemic push-backs exist—they are the stuff of daily news. The value of systems thinking is in seeing these push-backs for what they are: valid systemic warning signals rather than random events, lack of human enterprise, or political mischief. They give us an opportunity to see into the future and plan ahead.

The severity of these balancing cycle push-backs reflects decades of systemic abuse. Laws limiting investor and corporate liability, combined with laws limiting disclosure of important public information, have allowed firms to ignore their social and environmental impacts. These laws and their outcomes have made companies slow learners and resistant to adaptive change. Although shifts in regulatory law eventually forced companies to be more accountable for their effects, as those impacts became more adverse there were spontaneous push-backs on other important fronts as well. Employees, customers, and investors took matters into their own hands. Companies' operating costs increased due to rising employee turnover rates, critical commodity bottlenecks (e.g., clean energy, water, etc.), regulatory friction, customer defection, and eventually, weather-related calamities.[7] Social push-backs included work stoppages, consumer boycotts, and shareholder lawsuits. As these instances of negative feedback gained strength, the protective wall of limited legal liability lost its effectiveness. Companies were compelled to find new ways of learning and adapting or risk extinction.

Awakening to New Solutions

One of the miracles of Nature and humanity is our mutual capacity to learn from experience and adapt. This is what Living Asset Stewardship is all about. Reinforcing cycles of growth and self-actualization ultimately meet resistance from balancing cycles that protect systemic health and the diversity of interdependent species. This continual interplay of action and reaction drives evolution through learning and adaptation, and is represented as two additional reinforcing cycles in Figure 4-2 (R-2 and R-3).

This new reinforcing cycle (R-2) is a constructive response to the balancing cycle of degradation and cost escalation. Earlier described as the reinforcing cycle of LAS + OL, it inspires inquiry, experimentation, and the pursuit of knowledge, which in turn feed back to innovation, profit, investment, and regeneration. Meanwhile, the solutions that arise from R-2 drive a third reinforcing cycle of economic, social, and environmental remedia-

Figure 4-2: The New Reinforcing Cycle of LAS + OL

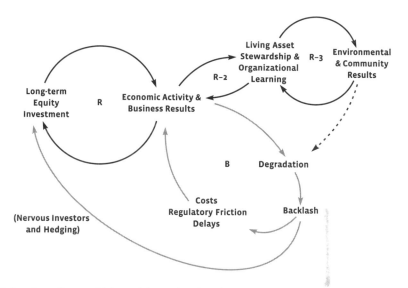

Living Asset Stewardship and Organizational Learning can improve business results and environmental/community results, thus weakening the degradation loop.

tion (R-3) that begins to reverse some of the damage done by the first reinforcing cycle (R), thereby slowing some balancing cycle push-backs.

The 16 companies in the LAMP Focus Group are all extraordinary because early on they recognized many of these systemic actions and reactions. Whether by conscious choice, intuition, or long tradition, they became living asset stewards. As the competition for global resources with traditional firms heated up, rather than abandoning their long-term systemic perspectives and stewardship practices to jump on the bandwagon of short-term profit, they became more professional in their application of LAS. They devised new metrics and information-exchange networks that would enhance systemic feedback and learning. Taking the long view, they realized that success would ultimately hinge on the speed of their learning and adaptation, and that pursuing short-term profit to the detriment of larger living systems was a blind alley and the road to ultimate destruction. LAMP companies read the writing on the wall: as people became more savvy about systemic impacts, they simply would not tolerate abusive behavior.

The messages contained in Figures 4-1 and 4-2 are clearly ascendant. During the past two decades the corporate tide has shifted toward LAS concepts and cultures.[8] The success of the Global LAMP Index® affirms this.

The recent greening of General Electric and its new emphasis on "Ecomagination" (May 2005) suggests the trend is gaining a powerful following. Although the traditional model of the firm continues to dominate, the systemic degradation and balancing cycle push-backs it generates number its days. Given the demonstrable successes of the LAS model, the corporate walk in its direction will soon turn to a jog and then a run.

For this reason, LAMP companies cannot be complacent. At best, they have a head start on a long evolutionary path. As more companies adopt the LAS model, there will be a rush toward more effective stewardship practices. What might those look like? That's as yet unclear, and a question perhaps more for scenario planners, but the best practices of LAMP companies offer some clues (see Table 4-2).

Perceptions That Drive the Balancing Cycle

How managers and society perceive corporations matters greatly because deeply held perceptions affect corporate cultures and governance. Most people see companies in the traditional mold as described in the left-hand column of Table 4-2. Until recently, few have seen the firm's potential as the organic entity described in the right-hand column—a community of interest that thrives on Living Asset Stewardship and organizational learning. Holding such limited expectations, and failing to see the potential, society too often acquiesces in the worst behavior of corporations.

Similarly, the mental models of traditional corporations limit their choices and predispose them to poor decisions. Believing their world is governed primarily by laws of *physics* rather than by *biological* laws, they tend to see resource supplies as relatively fixed and therefore scarce. Such beliefs are rooted in fear and expressed via an obsession with control—the faster we can control scarce resources, to the exclusion of others, the wealthier and more powerful we will become.

This model recognizes mainly tradeoffs—not synergy. If workers get paid more, then profits and shareholder returns will suffer. If companies invest in social capital such as community education, environment, and health and safety, they will have less to spend on "productive" capital such as facilities and equipment. This line of reasoning led to the popular view that the "business of business is business" and nothing more. Milton Friedman, the Nobel laureate in economics, once said the only responsibility of a business was to turn a profit. It was commonly believed that corpo-

Table 4-2: Two Approaches to Management

TRADITIONAL MODEL	STEWARDSHIP MODEL

Mental Model

Top-down perspective	Bottom-up perspective
Focus on capital assets	Focus on living assets
Newtonian physics/predictability	Biology/randomness
Firm as isolated machine	Firm as integral to the web of life
Self-centered orientation	Symbiosis/collaboration
Limited resources (fixed pie)	Intelligence as unlimited
Competition as primary	Cooperation as primary

Principles

Finite game of quick returns	Infinite game of sustainability
The firm as solely important	Living relationships matter
Profit as the primary "end"	Profit as means to higher end
Financial success	Mission to "serve"
Employees as replaceable	Employees as precious assets
Employees caring about paycheck	Employees caring about "web"
Employees as passive	Employees as wanting to make a difference
Employees as needing direction	Employees as self-organizing

Policies

Learning ordered by management	Learning served by management
Learning prescribed	Learning self-directed
Learning as focused	Learning as contextual
Learning as a cost	Learning as opportunity
Employees to be programmed	Employees to be mentored

Unwritten Rules

Wait until you are told	Experiment/take initiative
Must add value now	It's OK to think long-term
Don't screw up	Mistakes are part of learning
We're watching you	We trust you
Hoard information (power)	Share information (power)
Defend your turf/get ahead	Use teamwork/share

Practices

Minimum training	Continuous training
Periodic reviews	Continuous feedback
Focused training	Open-ended training

Measured output	Measured learning
Progress monitored	Progress inspired
Your ideas owned by us	Your ideas recognized by us
Outcomes	
Passive employees	Inspired employees
Noncaring customers	Loyal customers/repeat sales
Impatient investors/traders	Patient investor-partners

rations could be responsible citizens only through charity, giving back to the community a small portion of their profits.

With this perspective, each stakeholder group—employees, customers, Nature, shareholders, community—assumes an adversarial relationship to the others. Because each decision a firm makes is seen as zero-sum, resolution of differences is almost always achieved through a dynamic of power. This dreary view dampens the only corporate resource that is truly infinite—creativity.

This physical, fixed-pie view of business has become so prevalent that very few people question it. Peer pressure and inertia keep the mechanical/industrial model of the firm alive, even though its weaknesses have been exposed and new, more successful conceptual models of the firm have been successfully tested. Entrenched beliefs, no matter how unfounded, die hard.

The New Symbiotic Reinforcing Cycle

The symbiotic stewardship model described in the right-hand column of Table 4-2 presents the firm as a tightly coupled biological system comprising humans and Nature. As partners in the web of life, we share a common biological heritage, continually exchange information, and cooperate to ensure our mutual survival. These exchanges—which occur randomly, instinctively, and consciously in countless ways—have enabled Nature, through more than 4.5 billion years, to create ever-greater diversity, complexity, and value from a fixed base of physical matter. The LAS model is simply a human adaptation of this natural model.

The microprocessor, a symbiotic amalgam of human ingenuity and silica, both is a product of the LAS model and reinforces it. Although made from one of Nature's cheapest and most abundant materials, it is a valuable learning tool. It enables us to produce more with less impact on Nature, to think more systemically about the feedback from commercial activity, and to remedy some of the damage done.

The reinforcing cycle of LAS + OL is much more powerful than the predecessor cycle of capital flows and investment in industrial capacity, as we saw in Figure 4-2. Rather than leveraging the finite capacities of nonliving (capital) assets, Living Asset Stewardship leverages the infinite learning and adaptive capacities of people and other living assets. Like the microprocessor, LAS catalyzes quantum efficiency gains.

Evolutionary science reveals that complex systems are more adaptable and stable than simple ones because they are more diversified. The tight coupling of humans and Nature via LAS strengthens companies because it inspires both innovation and diversity. When corporations see themselves as integral parts of a larger biological system, they tend to become better stewards of their living assets.

Synergies Within the Firm

Consider how Living Asset Stewardship works within the firm. Figure 4-3 shows relationships between three of its most important living assets: employees, customers, and shareholders. Each link is a causal connection, and together they explain the mutually reinforcing nature of employee value, customer value, and shareholder value. The rationale of the linkages is straightforward. *Employee value creates customer value* because customers are drawn to happy, engaged employees. *Customer value creates shareholder value* because satisfied customers buy more, are less price sensitive, and spread good will by word of mouth. *Shareholder value creates additional customer and employee value* because firms with high shareholder value have more financial options and higher esprit. *Customer value also adds to employee value* because employees feel more fulfilled and inspired when working with happy customers.

In companies whose employees are also shareholders, via stock option plans, retirement plans, etc., increased shareholder value creates additional employee value because employees can share the wealth and the ownership. Even in companies in which most employees are not shareholders, increased shareholder value gives employees more security and opportunity for advancement.

Figure 4-3: Stakeholders Have Mutually Reinforcing Interests

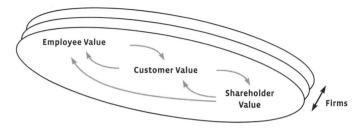

Each link is a causal connection. Together the links explain the mutually reinforcing nature of employee value (EV), customer value (CV), and shareholder value (SV). Each link has a rationale. EV creates CV because customers respond to happier employees. CV creates SV because customers buy more and are less price sensitive. SV creates CV because the firm with high SV has more options for investment to create additional CV. CV creates EV because employees are more satisfied when dealing with happy customers. SV creates CV because in the modern firm employees are often themselves shareholders. Even if they are not shareholders they have more security and opportunity for advancement. These links, and the mutually reinforcing nature of the system, depend on the stewardship demonstrated. Effective stewardship makes all these links strong, increasing the success and value for all the participants at the same time. Weak or ineffective stewardship weakens the links, creating a "zero-sum game" with tradeoffs. The overall result is firm value which accrues to all three stakeholder groups. What about society and Nature?

The strength of these links depends on the stewardship demonstrated. Effective stewardship, shown by respecting the lives and needs of all three stakeholder groups, strengthens these links while increasing the value of the firm for all its participants. As in Nature, such synergies within the firm compound to make the whole more than the sum of its parts.

Synergies with Society and Nature

The partnership between a firm and its living assets strengthens as it reaches out to embrace Nature and host communities. As Figure 4-4 demonstrates, each link is a causal connection; together the links explain the mutually reinforcing nature of values for the firm, the community, and the eco-sphere. In this network of relationships, the rationale for each link derives from the premise that value for the firm can create value for the community and Nature, and vice versa. Stewardship is the catalyst that

Figure 4-4: Living Asset Stewardship Drives a Reinforcing Cycle That Benefits the Firm, Society, and Nature

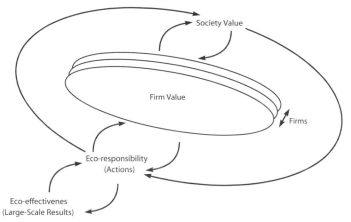

Again, each link is a causal connection. Together the links explain the mutually reinforcing nature of values for the firm, for the community, and for the ecosphere. Each link has a rational of the form, "Value for the firm creates value for the community because . . ." Again there is a question of stewardship: these links and the reinforcing nature of the system depend on the stewardship demonstrated. Without stewardship, the links are weak, the reinforcing possibility is overshadowed by the "zero-sum" nature, and it's an impossible tradeoff.

enables these positive feedback links, and the reinforcing nature of the system depends on the vitality of the stewardship.

Firms contribute to Nature only as they remediate their damage to it and learn to live in harmony with the web of life. They can't improve natural systems because they don't control them. Nature is the universe in which the firm, and everything else, function. Nature can live without companies, but companies cannot live without Nature.

In Figure 4-4, from top to bottom, the potentially reinforcing linkages between the firm and society can be seen. What's described is a composite model based on corporate best practices; no single corporation satisfies all the model's requirements.

Firm value creates value for society both because healthier employees create a healthier society, and because a healthy, successful firm has the flexibility to support the community. The word "health" in this context broadly encompasses personal happiness, growth, and fulfillment, and includes the feeling of connection between people's work lives and their most deeply held beliefs and values. This type of health enables people to open their hearts and minds to learning, to constructive problem solving, and to strengthening the ties between the firm and its stakeholders. Such healthy, reinforcing behavior feeds success. It is generative because it strengthens the partnership between humans and Nature.

Increasing value for society cycles back to firm value. A prosperous firm and its employees feed the community's tax base, support opportunities for better education and health, improve infrastructure, and enhance civic engagement. Stewardship firms encounter less crime and regulatory friction, and benefit from greater trust, a stronger social-economic infrastructure, and a rising income tide—the building blocks of strong franchises.

Farther down Figure 4-4 are illustrated more synergies between the firm and Nature. Eco-responsible firms are more aligned with the values of their stakeholders, generate less waste, and are usually more innovative than are their peers. Corporations that recognize the inextricable union of humanity and Nature—and thus respect life by striving to emulate waste-free natural systems—tend to be more profitable than those that continue to view themselves as disassociated from Nature. Employees feel inspired to learn, share ideas, and innovate because their values are honored. Customers are more eager to buy because they welcome solutions that are friendly to Nature and the environments in which they live. Distributors and others who add value to a firm's offers are encouraged to collaborate and add further value because they want to be connected with companies that are productive, respected, and trusted. Their reputations are enhanced in doing so.

As the eco-responsible firm's value grows, so does its potential for deeper eco-effectiveness and partnering with Nature. "Eco-effectiveness" is a measure of a company's ability to have no adverse effects on Nature through its products and processes. "Partnering with Nature" is a concept introduced by Novo Nordisk: a company tries to enhance Nature's carrying capacity and diversity via its products and processes. Such a company has both the financial resources to invest in more-evolved solutions and the innovative spirit to make those investments pay. In short, it enjoys a virtuous cycle of innovation, trust, and financial return that continually feeds its eco-effectiveness.

As this cycle of eco-effectiveness becomes a more dominant feature of corporate strategy, and as the synergies of ecologically responsible firms become more apparent and emulated, the adverse impacts of corporations on Nature should begin to diminish. It will, of course, take a long time to restore damage already done to the web of life due to the long-term effects of past and present environmental degradation. Leadership companies know this, and understand they have a lot to learn about harmonious coexistence with Nature. This knowledge adds urgency to their organizational learning programs, and gives them further opportunities to assert their leadership and win public confidence.

The outer rim of Figure 4-4 shows the mutual benefits of a healthier society and eco-sphere. When the interaction between firms and citizens becomes more aligned, respectful, and trusting, perceptions and expectations will shift. The virtuous cycle of inspiration, trust, innovation, and profit will grow. Companies will move beyond individual stewardship to more active collaboration, as demonstrated in Denmark's Kalundborg eco-industrial park.[9]

The dialogue that arises from these healthier relationships—between citizens and companies, among companies, and among all members of society—will be more inclusive and insightful than it is today. People want to learn when they feel engaged and when they believe their participation counts for something.

In sum, the LAS model is a powerful tool because it produces so many positive feedback opportunities both within and outside the firm. It is synergistic because it builds strength on strength. Employees become happier, healthier, and more productive. Customers get better value. Corporations enjoy more sustainable profit. Shareholders benefit from better performance. Society and the environment become healthier and more supportive of corporations. The feedback events are generative because each is mutually reinforcing with one or more others. The beneficial effects are compounded.

The Limits for Any Reinforcing Loop

This conceptual blueprint for synergistic growth nevertheless runs into two constraints: (1) limits on how quickly the average corporation is willing and able to adapt, and (2) limits to the Earth's ability to keep up with a growing population's demand for more resources. The first is a problem of inertia and lack of strategic vision. Most companies still believe that stewardship costs more than it provides in benefits—a belief this book refutes. The second addresses the more intractable problem of Earth's carrying capacity and is harder to solve. For example, if we double the fuel efficiency of cars, but triple production of them, the environmental impact can only worsen.

The best we can do in such a world is to move rapidly to dematerialize production—to increase the amount of recycled, reusable, and renewable materials utilized; to increase the usefulness of these materials through better design; and to eliminate the need for nonrenewable energy to produce, market, operate, and dispose of them. This is well within our intellectual and learning capacities, and it is where the corporate world is heading.

To some, the previous paragraph will appear speculative. Yet such adaptation is happening now. The impetus comes from within corporations as they learn more about the synergy (and limits) of natural systems, and from citizens as they learn how corporations can become more harmonious with the living systems that embrace them. Peter Senge describes the success of this co-learning and co-evolution process as generative learning.[10]

Generative learning is powerful because it continually reinforces itself. It is passionate because it flows from our deepest beliefs and values. It is connected and relevant because it responds to real-world challenges. It is cumulative because we can store it and reuse it in books and databases, and it compounds because we continually build on it. These attributes enable us to adapt quickly when we see a clear need to do so.

In companies that encourage generative learning and allow it to flourish, it becomes deeply insightful and innovative. This kind of thinking leads to quantum jumps in efficiency and utility with decreasing material input—what Paul Hawken, Amory B. Lovins, and L. Hunter Lovins call "factor efficiencies."[11] The Internet and fiber-optic cable are good examples of such efficiencies.

Conclusion

The LAS model is more synergistic than the traditional model of the firm because it focuses on releasing the infinite potential of human ingenuity rather than trying to control finite resources and human behavior. The engine of this learning process is the reinforcing cycle of Living Asset Stewardship and organizational learning (LAS + OL). Corporations that pioneered this strategic shift have gained financial strength and market share as their stewardship practices have evolved. Although they still have a long way to go on the road to sustainability, LAMP companies now have distinct advantages. They are the fastest learners in a world in which rapid adaptation and innovation constitute the only path to survival. Chapter 5 examines how the enhanced learning and adaptive capacities of LAMP companies have also produced above-average stock market performance.

We cannot overemphasize the notion of survival. Corporations, and the global markets in which they operate, are at a crossroads as Nature's carrying capacity nears its limits. The reinforcing cycles of Living Asset Stewardship offer solutions to the lagged balancing cycle of environmental and social degradation that increasingly threatens our markets today. It is a powerful solution because it leverages our limitless resource: human potential.

5

The Global LAMP Index®

"A sustainable future, we are convinced, lies within the grasp of those
people who can imagine it, forge strong and enduring relationships,
learn from each other, and act boldly in the light of knowledge and
integrity. We can already imagine zero injuries, zero emissions, and
zero waste. That is our 'true north.'"[1]

—Alain Belda, CEO, Alcoa

The Global Living Asset Management Performance (LAMP) Index®
was conceived with three purposes in mind:

- to explore more broadly themes arising from my learning laboratory
that suggested the emergence of a new conceptual model of the firm;
- to be a performance benchmark that was better than traditional indices
at defining value, and that would guide more-informed investor decision
making in both stocks and bonds; and
- to serve as an efficient investment vehicle for long-term investors.

The idea of exploring a new mental model of the firm came to me in
1996 after reading Peter Senge's classic on systems thinking, *The Fifth
Discipline.*[2] At the time I had spent more than 30 years researching stewardship companies for my private clients and had assembled a useful bank

of information and impressions. Looking back on that experience, I remember feeling encouraged that stewardship research had entered the financial mainstream, first through socially responsible investing (SRI) and later as part of a more-holistic sustainability agenda.[3] But I was also dismayed by the fragmentation of SRI/sustainability research and the inability of its leading proponents to break away from corporate behavior patterns that worked against real Living Asset Stewardship. As long as SRI and sustainability investors embraced companies that were predominantly hierarchical in their organization, and that managed primarily by numerical objectives (ends) rather than by relational means, I saw those well-intended stewardship efforts creating more problems than they solved. I did not see how companies could authentically pursue a triple bottom line of economic, social, and environmental return unless they operated under a triple top line agenda.

Living Asset Stewardship is a triple top line approach because it is premised on respecting life throughout a company's operations, and on becoming progressively more harmonious with the living systems that support and are the context for the firm (the biosphere, society, and the free market). It does not look to make mechanistic corporate cultures more Earth- and people-friendly, but to change those cultures so as to make them more integral with the web of life.

There are two main problems with the early, though still prominent, SRI and sustainability approaches. First is their use of negative screening, and second is their focus on outcomes, as distinct from the culture and processes that yield those outcomes. Socially responsible investment researchers and investors sought, in the main, to avoid offensive companies. "Offensive" companies usually had egregious environmental and workplace practices; offered products deemed dangerous (e.g., alcohol, tobacco, weapons, nuclear power), sinful (gambling), or shoddy; condoned or participated in human rights violations; and/or tested the health effects of their products on animals. Though they also favored companies with good practices, SRI researcher evaluations tended to focus on specific issues (e.g., ratios of women and minorities employed, or tons of emissions reduced) rather than on the means by which these practices were accomplished. Such over-specialization, however helpful in surfacing specific risks, missed the big picture that LAS addresses. In effect, it spent so much time looking at specific trees that it failed to see the forest and evaluate its capacity for sustainable growth.

Today's sustainability movement, with its focus on the "triple bottom line" of economic, environmental, and social return, goes a step beyond SRI by offering a more systemic view of corporate performance. Its second-generation approach recognizes that all three aspects are ultimately related. However, its bottom line focus on outcomes often misses the critical importance of culture and process. Consequently, a company like Bristol-Myers Squibb could get top ratings from sustainability researchers (AAA from Innovest) and asset managers (#1 pharmaceutical in the Dow Jones Sustainability Index) in spite of its hierarchical culture that is driven by numbers (profit) rather than shared ideals and a sense of community (see Chapter 13).

Using the triple bottom line approach, first-generation SRI and second-generation sustainability researchers have made valuable contributions. They have, in fact, identified some excellent stewardship companies—every company in the Global LAMP Index® is qualified by such research—but they have yet to discover why certain of their favored companies perform better than others. That is the essential virtue of LAS. By focusing on the cultures and processes that most consistently produce a sustainable triple bottom line, LAS offers a more unified and productive approach.

Imagine two companies that have made similar reductions in their environmental impacts: one does it via top-down edict and the other uses group-wide dialogue and consensus. I submit that the means by which they make those reductions "count" more than the initial reductions themselves. The company that achieves those reductions by engaging employees in dialogue and affiliating with their biophilic instincts and their desires to contribute to a higher cause (all attributes of a sound systemic approach) is more likely to continue making progress than the one that does it by command and control. Employees are more inclined to buy into a policy and to contribute to its implementation if they are consulted than if they are ordered.

In the final analysis, business and commerce are all about living systems. Corporations and the markets they serve are living communities of people who, by virtue of their genetic coding, care about life. The most valuable and productive assets of these communities are living assets. When the production and consumption patterns of these communities harm the global web of life, corporations and their stakeholders drain communities' most precious resources. Alternatively, when these patterns become more harmonious with the web, corporations and their stakeholders become more resourceful and productive via the reinforcing cycle of LAS + OL.

Global LAMP Index® Performance

Traditional capitalist theory and interest groups committed to modifying that theory are fundamentally handicapped. Modification can't work if the theory it is trying to modify is conceptually unsound. In such cases the best way forward is a new theory that is more congruent and harmonious with the real world. LAS offers such congruency and the Global LAMP Index® validates it. As Table 5-1 shows, LAMP not only outperforms its peer benchmarks, but also does so by a wide margin.

The 10-year test represented in Table 5-1 takes us through a diverse range of conditions: four years of a record bull market (1996–1999); three years of a sharp bear market correction (2000–2002); and three years of recovery (2003–2005). These variations are enough to test the mettle of any portfolio and make the results shown above more credible than had they been attained in a more placid market environment.

It should be remembered that during this 10-year period, the Global LAMP Index® was a hypothetical learning laboratory constructed with the benefit of considerable hindsight. That said, I did not use this advantage to create hypothetical trades to improve performance. The performance shown in Table 5-1 is for the same 60 companies through the entire 10-year period.[4]

Compared to its closest peer index—the Morgan Stanley Capital International (MSCI) World Index—the average return of the LAMP 60 was substantially higher in every year. Table 5-1 shows a pattern of "higher highs" during up years and relative steadiness during down years. The annual excess returns on the Global LAMPIndex® run from a low of 2.06 percentage points to a high of 22.72 points. Were we to remove the LAMP 60 companies from the MSCI World Index in making our comparisons the numbers would likely be even more convincing.

Much the same picture emerges in a comparison of the LAMP 60 and the S&P 500. In all 10 years shown on the following page in Table 5-1, LAMP led the S&P, often by significant margins. This was especially true during the most volatile five-year period (1999–2004), wherein the S&P 500 formed its bull market top, crashed, and then partially recov-

Table 5-1: Performance Comparisons (1996–2005)

GLOBAL LAMP INDEX® VS. MSCI WORLD

AND S&P 500 INDICES

Year	*Total Returns: Principal + Dividends (as %)*			*LAMP Excess (% pts.) vs.*	
	LAMP	MSCI	S&P 500	MSCI	S&P 500
1996	27.72	13.47	22.94	14.25	4.78
1997	33.91	15.76	33.35	18.15	0.56
1998	29.23	24.31	28.57	4.92	0.66
1999	47.66	24.94	21.04	22.72	26.62
2000	2.02	(13.19)	(9.10)	15.21	11.12
2001	(6.02)	(16.80)	(11.88)	10.78	5.86
2002	(13.80)	(19.88)	(22.09)	6.08	8.29
2003	40.61	33.10	28.67	7.51	11.94
2004	16.78	14.72	10.88	2.06	5.90
2005	11.63	9.49	4.91	2.14	6.72
Totals as %:					
Cumulative:	394.42	97.37	138.31		
Annualized:	17.33	7.04	9.07		

Returns for the Global LAMP Index® are back casts based on equally weighting each LAMP company at the start of each year. The foregoing LAMP results assume dividends are taken rather than reinvested. Returns for the S&P 500 and the MSCI World indices are weighted by market capitalization and assume reinvestment of dividends as earned. There can be no assurance that any of the performances or performance patterns indicated in this chart will continue into the future. Source of MCSI data: Morningstar

ered. In the two years when LAMP's performance margin was narrowest (1997 and 1998), the S&P 500 had an advantage over most other countries' indices because the global technology boom that defined the bull market was centered mainly in the U.S. In spite of this, and of LAMP's underweighting in U.S. companies (35 of the 60 reside outside the U.S.), the Global LAMP Index® did exceptionally well.

During the 10-year period shown in Table 5-1, the average annual return on LAMP was 17.37 percent, compared to 7.04 percent for the MSCI World Index and 9.07 percent for the S&P 500. The comparable return for the Domini 400 Social Index was 8.45 percent—slightly above the S&P 500. Because the Dow Jones Sustainability Index (DJSI) was not operable in

1996 we cannot compare it to the MSCI World Index for the 10-year period; however it has generally lagged the MSCI World Index during the past
seven years (1999–2005). Annual investment returns for the Domini 400
and the DJSI are shown in Appendix 7.

Based on these results it is hard to say whether the SRI or sustainability
approaches as they are currently practiced add significant investment
value. I think these alternative approaches can, at best, add value by limiting environmental and other systemic risks. However, this potential is too
often eroded by their failure to see the risks in hierarchically managed companies that manage by objectives.

To sum up these findings: the Global LAMP Index® produced significantly better returns in all market phases—bull, bear, and recovery. In
doing so, it led the S&P 500, the MSCI World, the Domini 400, and the
DJSI in each year since 1996. This defies the conventional logic that equates
reward with risk. In fact, LAMP's greatest performance lead relative to its
comparators came when the market was in its riskiest phase (1999–2002).

Risk/Reward Attributes

Volatility is an important element of risk. Following the three-year bear
market (2000–2002), LAMP recovered its modest 17.2-percent loss in less
than a year. In fact, by year-end 2003, it showed a 16-percent gain for the
four-year period. By comparison, at year-end 2005, the MSCI World and
the S&P 500 indices were still struggling to recover their deeper losses.
LAMP's lower volatility during the market's weak years, of course,
increased the leverage it had in its strong years. This explains, in large part,
why LAMP's cumulative returns for the 10-year period were nearly three
times those of the S&P 500 and four times the MSCI World's returns.

The risk/reward attributes of individual LAMP companies and the index
as a whole benefit from two things: (1) the reinforcing cycle of LAS + OL,
which builds intellectual capital, drives innovation, and continually replenishes the firm through free cash flow, and (2) consistently strong balance
sheets, which confer an ability to survive hard times.

These advantages, however, don't protect LAMP companies and their
investors from all risks. Quite a few LAMP companies had volatile periods
between 1996 and 2005. But their capacities for recovery were superior and
as a group they balanced out each other's cyclical ups and downs.

LAMP's performance, as earlier mentioned, defies the conventional logic that there are tradeoffs between risk and reward. Stocks and portfolios that excel in up markets are expected to underperform during bear markets. Under perfectly efficient market conditions this theory holds up, but that is not what we have today. We are in transition between two market systems: companies operating on the emergent LAS model are taking market share from those operating under the traditional one. This reduces the cyclicality of the LAMP gainers and increases that of the losers.

Investors see the difference even if they don't yet think in terms of the LAS model. They therefore tend to exercise more patience toward LAMP shares—in effect treating them as core holdings. As more investors do this, a rising demand floor under LAMP shares is created, and that translates into a stewardship premium, as is discussed later in this chapter.

Creating the Global LAMP Index®

The 60-company Global LAMP Index® has seen a number of changes since I first conceived it in 1997. There are two reasons for these changes: (1) to achieve a sector diversification comparable to that of the MSCI World and S&P 500 indices, and (2) to reflect the evolving definition of LAS itself. These were natural changes because the index was initially designed to be a learning laboratory and a benchmark of LAS best practices across a broad spectrum of industry sectors. We needed to go through a number of iterations before we could properly define the index. It is noteworthy that more than two-thirds of the companies in the first iteration of the index, including all 16 of the Focus Group, remained in the index when it was finalized in 2002.

The process of defining LAS took approximately five years, from the spring of 1997 to the summer of 2002. It was a time of intense research during which I became more familiar with systems theory; reprocessed, from the perspective of these theories, information on companies I had long known; got feedback from colleagues in associated fields; and redefined, retested, and so on. My information sources varied broadly, and included organizations committed to systems thinking,[5] commercially available research on corporate responsibility, academic research and case studies, business publications, and data freely available on the Internet from non-governmental organizations. These third parties provided a composite of

information that was then used to validate information from the corporations themselves.

The only investment research I used was credit rating histories by
Moody's and Standard & Poor's. These gave important insights into the
commitment of stewardship companies to their idealistic missions and to
the long-term trust of stakeholders. The best corporate stewards are as fis-
cally responsible as they are environmentally and socially responsible
because they intend to serve and lead for generations. The credit histories of
global LAMP companies are remarkably stable, as is shown in Appendix 3.

After my first draft of the LAMP index, I published a paper in 1998 titled,
"The Value of Living Assets," which drew the distinctions between living and
nonliving assets shown in Table 1-1.[6] The paper, which included sections on
systems thinking and quantum learning, ended with a sketchy diagram on
the feedback effects of Living Asset Stewardship that was the forerunner of
the current LAS model fully described in Chapter 2. Once the idea was
launched, I had no trouble finding research partners and collaborators.

As I dug deeper into corporate research during the next several years, it
became apparent that there was a unifying concept of LAS that could be
expressed in three simple words: respect for life. If living assets were people
and Nature, and these were the source of nonliving capital assets, then
respect for life was the only sustainable way forward. Once stated as such,
it seemed obvious. Companies had to respect life to become more than the
sum of their parts. Only then could they attain the synergies and extraordinary efficiency of living ecosystems, wherein nothing is wasted and adaptive learning is continuous. This single insight was tremendously clarifying.
It framed a cogent, new general theory of the firm that was truly and ele-
gantly distinct from the prevailing machine model, and it allowed me to be
more deliberate in evaluating stewardship cultures.

As my knowledge of systems thinking and Living Asset Stewardship
grew, I gained a second insight: a reinforcing cycle exists between LAS and
organizational learning and it is the chief energy source of stewardship
companies. This important insight explained the "magic" of stewardship
companies in practical, logical terms. LAS was grounded in evolutionary
biology, human genetics, brain science, and psychology. People are more
effective when they engage their natural biophilic urges. Inspired people
produce better value and profit than uninspired people. Suddenly all the
pieces began to fit together.

From this point forward, finding candidates for the Global LAMP Index® became easier. Screening companies was still a detailed and painstaking process, but I now knew what I was looking for. My candidate list grew to more than 100 companies. To shorten the list to a more manageable number, I raised the bar for entry in many industries, often dropping companies widely considered to be strong environmental stewards.

This move toward more demanding industry screens was revealing because it focused the index on companies that were most consistent and congruent in their LAS practices. It was one thing to have a corporate culture and long-term business strategy that respected life, but quite another to execute this strategy professionally on a consistent basis.

The three most common causes of disqualification from the Global LAMP Index® have been entrenched hierarchies, obsessive management by objectives, and excessive debt leverage. Living systems are networks, not hierarchies. The well-being of all constituents, even the least powerful, is tightly interwoven with the well-being of the whole system. Entrenched hierarchies—with their bureaucratic chains of command and isolation from the natural world—reflect a lack of respect for lower-placed employees and Nature that subverts systemic well-being. Companies that manage by setting high objectives for sales and profits without attending to the means of achieving those objectives (relationships and organizational learning) too often stress employees and get results the opposite of those intended. Excessive debt leverage puts at risk the whole system and all its constituents—often for the sake of short-term profit and self-serving management bonuses.

After five years or so of research and testing, I had a list of strong global stewardship pioneers—companies that had become stewardship leaders in their industries by sticking to their core values through multiple business cycles. All of them understood, explicitly or implicitly, that LAS was the heart of enterprise, and set out to be the best they could be at keeping alive the reinforcing cycle of LAS + OL.

Other Criteria for LAMP Selection

The Global LAMP Index® of 60 companies is exactly double the size of the Dow Jones Industrial Index (DJII) of 30 companies. The LAMP is oriented to companies with large stock market capitalizations for two reasons: (1)

they have credibility as change agents that smaller, less-known companies lack, and (2) it is important to show that stewardship cultures can operate effectively in large as well as small organizations. The number 60 was determined by a selection process that had two overarching priorities: (1) achieving a broadly representative industry/sector diversification while also (2) maintaining high quality standards for index inclusion. After extensive testing, I realized that using a smaller number of index companies would have compromised diversification, and using a larger one would have diluted standards.

To be included in the index, companies had to have at least 20 years of operating history. This would allow us to look at the evolution of stewardship practices through a variety of political-economic, business, and market conditions—including economic recessions and expansions, as well as swings in investor sentiment from extreme optimism to pessimism. LAMP's age requirement quickly weeded out "fair weather stewards." It also allowed us to see how the best stewards handled hard times—a revealing test of their commitment to best practices.

For industry/sector diversification we used the 10-sector Global Industry Classification Standard (GICS) format that had been jointly developed by Morgan Stanley and Standard & Poor's. This common classification system, effective March 2002, allowed us to align LAMP sectors so the Global LAMP Index® would represent a fair cross section of the global economy. We also sought diversity within each sector so that no major industry group was left out. Thus, LAMP has exposure to older smokestack industries such as autos, chemicals, energy, primary metals, and steel as well as newer, more knowledge-intensive industries such as healthcare, finance, media, and information technology. The industry/sector diversity of LAMP is summarized in Appendix 6.

If the index is overweighted in one direction, it is toward companies operating in information technology, which was the most volatile GICS sector during the 10-year period described in Table 5-1.[7] One might expect this would make index performance more cyclical and risky, but that has not been the case. As earlier noted, LAMP companies have gained global market share and these gains have mitigated their cyclicality.

Finally, all index companies had to have publicly traded shares because the purpose of the index was to track share performance. It is easier to gather data on publicly traded companies—especially those traded on the world's major stock markets—because they are required by law to disclose information to shareholders.

LAS Criteria for Index Selection

Companies screened for the Global LAMP Index® were tested on eight closely related LAS criteria that collectively manifest a corporation's respect for life. The first three deal with corporate culture. The final five are more specific tests of LAS. In brief, we look for the following attributes:

1. **A commitment to "systems" or "holistic" thinking:** The critical variables are the way a company defines itself and its primary assets, how it evaluates its impacts on the larger living systems that support it (the free market, society, and the biosphere), and how these variables are reflected in the firm's strategic planning. Companies that excel at systems thinking are highly focused on relationships. To assess the quality and evolution of their relationships, they use a balanced scorecard approach that combines backward-looking financial metrics with more forward-looking relational ones focused on LAS.

2. **A commitment to human rights:** People are living assets. The only unlimited resource to which companies have access is the human imagination. Companies that promote human rights and diversity in their workplaces and communities are magnets for creative people. The best corporate stewards endorse human rights internally in their codes of conduct and externally by supporting international agreements such as the U.N. Universal Declaration of Human Rights.[8]

3. **A clear sense of "why we exist" as a company:** This is typically expressed in a vision, core values, shared beliefs, and a code of conduct that, together, unify purpose and inspire employees to excel. Companies that do best on this screen have life-affirming goals that transcend profit. For them, profit is a means to achieving these goals rather than an end in itself.

4. **Respect for employees:** We look for companies that treat employees as assets and partners rather than as costs or potential liabilities. Such companies are highly networked. They mentor and guide employee growth, invest heavily in their education, respect individuals' opinions, openly share information at all levels, localize decision-making authority, freely

recognize and reward contributions, vest employees in company profits, and more. The best ones trust employees' judgment and capacity to self-organize rather than tell them what to do via bureaucratic chains of command.

5. **Respect for Nature:** We seek companies that look beyond the easy cost savings of eco-efficiency to actually mimicking Nature in the ways they operate. Such companies typically use life cycle assessments (LCA) to minimize adverse environmental impacts—from production through product use to eventual disposal and recycling or reuse. They continuously try to close the manufacturing loop so nothing is wasted. Companies that do best on this screen openly discuss their environmental risks with employees, customers, and other stakeholders in an effort to learn and evolve best practices.

6. **Respect for customers:** We look for companies that deeply listen to their customers, and connect with their values and beliefs as well as their more overt needs. Companies that do best on this screen achieve a high level of customer intimacy through frequent contact and dialogue. Some directly engage customers in their creative processes.

7. **Respect for strategic partners:** We seek companies that treat suppliers and others who add value to their offers as strategic partners. They coach their partners in stewardship best practices and engage them in co-learning, believing that the synergies thus created will lift the whole supply network to a higher level.

8. **Respect for host communities:** We look for companies that care, as a matter of course, for the local and global communities in which they operate. They understand that these communities are part of the living network that sustains them, so they symbiotically contribute to the health of that network. The best ones use their core skills to support health, education, and community welfare. They also partner with local suppliers and subcontractors, and support human rights.

In global LAMP companies these eight attributes are closely interwoven. Although few get top grades in all categories, all score well above comparable industry peers. These 60 companies have an evolving sense that over the long term their economic health is closely tied to the health of the living systems in which they operate and the well-being of the living assets they engage in their enterprises.

The more you think in decades rather than in quarters, the more you realize that economic, ecological and social interests in a company are no longer in conflict.[9]

—Bjorn Hagglund, Deputy CEO, Stora Enso

The Stewardship Premium

Waste not, want not. We do not waste what we respect. Companies that respect living assets do not waste them. These are the fundamental principles of stewardship and the market values them.

Stewardship leaders understand the risks of depleting precious social and natural equity through neglect or overuse. Within the firm they strive to eliminate waste by becoming more eco-efficient and by using the intellectual resources of all their employees, not just those at the top, in this quest. They understand the value of respect toward the larger external systems that support them, and husband the resources within these systems. And finally, they recognize how such stewardship affects employee morale, customer trust, resource availability, and regulatory friction. When they behave in these ways, the market puts a premium on their equity.

Although the Global LAMP Index® contains only 60 companies—fewer than 4 percent of the number in the MSCI World Index—the combined value of their shares at year-end 2005 was more than $3.8 trillion, or approximately 20 percent of the value of the MSCI World Index's comparable market capitalization. This, of course, reflects the past success of their stewardship strategies. But more important, it reflects investors' expectations of the future. Those expectations are manifest in the share price premiums LAMP companies command per dollar of sales, cash flow, or earnings.

Consider the market capitalizations of Toyota and Southwest Airlines. Although not the largest companies in their industries in terms of sales, their equity shares at year-end 2005 were worth more than those of their three largest direct competitors combined. The market clearly sees greater value in their business practices over the long run.

In most industries and sectors, LAMP companies have market capitalizations that would place them in the global top three. As for Toyota and Southwest, this is less a function of their sales volumes or the value of their capital assets, than of the leverage inherent in their stewardship, generated by the reinforcing cycle of LAS + OL. Some analysts refer to this premium as intellectual capital, which indeed it is. But to label it as such without also recognizing its linkage to LAS would be to miss the point. Stewardship is a powerful generator of intellectual capital.

The stewardship premium is usually largest where it is systemically most needed, for instance, in high eco-risk industries such as airlines, autos, chemicals, forest products, primary metals, and steel (see Appendix 5.) "Eco-risk" is used here in its broadest sense: derived from the ancient Greek, meaning *the house or space in which we live.* Costs associated with eco-risk therefore include those of social friction within the workplace or the community, as well as the more obvious costs of environmental degradation, global warming, and disease. The market increasingly understands these risks and incorporates them into securities prices.

The stewardship premium, however, reflects more than simple risk avoidance or the absence of systemic abuse. It also demonstrates the growth in value-added capacity that stewardship leaders get by inspiring employees, business partners, and customers. In every industry sector, we find the stewardship leaders to be innovation powerhouses. They tend to be quick adapters and champions at reinventing themselves to meet emerging market needs.

This capacity for reinvention often makes peer comparisons difficult, and this in turn complicates the process of computing a stewardship premium. Canon, for example, migrated from cameras (1960s), to copiers (1970s), to office equipment (1980s), to computer peripherals (1990s), to multi-media (at present). In the process it has moved from the consumer sector to office equipment and now to information technology. During the past century Nokia moved from forestry to radio to electronics, and only since 1986, into the global telecommunications sector, of which it is today a leader. 3M aims to derive at least 30 percent of sales from products invented in the past four years and usually exceeds that target.

We can categorize such companies for brief periods, but their intellectual, adaptive, and product development skills defy longer-term sector classifications. Canon long ago outran its global competitors in cameras (Kodak and Fuji Photo) and office equipment (Xerox and Pitney Bowes). Where it will be five or 10 years from now is anyone's guess. In evaluation of this company, market share analyses and peer earnings comparisons are of limited value. Calculating a stewardship premium on Canon shares is difficult because it is virtually in a class by itself.

Not all LAMP companies trade at stewardship premiums all the time. A well-earned premium may descend into a discount, but in most cases the disappearance of a stewardship premium simply reflects short-term swings in investor preferences—typically toward companies engaging in deals and short-term trading strategies rather than more long-sighted LAS ones. These episodes rarely last very long because growth from homegrown ideas is usually more durable than growth through trading and deal-making.

A company can also lose its stewardship premium by violating its ethical standards as Royal Dutch/Shell did by overstating oil and gas reserves in 2002–2003. In such a case, the offending company must quickly fire the wrongdoers, conduct a thorough investigation, transparently report the findings and the lessons learned from the investigation, and take steps to ensure that similar violations don't happen again. Shell did all of this because its core values had been violated and its corporate spirit was in jeopardy. Consistent with its passionate learning culture, Shell also treated the ethical breach as a mission-critical learning experience to be discussed at every level throughout the company. Seeing this rapid and thoughtful response, investors were relatively uncritical. In the future, Shell's stewardship premium will likely be determined by its leadership "renewable energy" initiatives, which will become more valuable as global oil supplies become more depleted. (This will make a fascinating case for future business historians.)

The tendency of steward-led companies' shares to trade at a premium is, of course, a huge advantage. Investors are attracted to companies that can sustain superior long-term growth with less volatility (see Table 5-1). This makes it easier for stewardship leaders to raise capital in the equity and bond markets. It also gives them a more stable currency for employee stock options and more time to manage their businesses—as distinct from managing investor perceptions about their businesses.

[W]ith pressure on natural resources and whole eco-systems rising, the nature of risk is shifting: these trends potentially threaten the very foundation of society and business. Sustainability—the preservation not just of economic but natural and social capital—has thus become a key concern.[10]
—John R. Coomber, CEO, and Bruno Porrer, Chief Risk Officer, Swiss Re

---

The Reinforcing Cycle of Capital Formation

The advantage of lower-cost capital is hard to overstate. It reduces the threshold of economic profit and feeds a powerful reinforcing cycle of capital formation. This reinforcing cycle of capital formation supercharges the reinforcing cycle of LAS + OL. Figure 5-1 illustrates how it works: lower-cost capital strengthens financial resources; better financial resources support more vigorous capital spending and R&D; higher rates of internal investment and research spending improve possibilities of future revenue growth and profit; more profit feeds back to stewardship premium and so forth.

Capital is naturally attracted to opportunity. Stewardship companies sell their debt and equity at a premium, thereby lowering their financing costs, because they are perceived to be less risky and more vital. The reinforcing cycle of capital formation reinforces the cycle of LAS + OL and vice versa. The synergies are powerful and appear to be gaining influence in the marketplace.

The Bond Market

It is worth looking beyond the stock market's valuation of global LAMP companies to their creditworthiness. Although these companies tend to be under-leveraged and self-financing, their capacity to borrow is a strategic asset—especially during difficult economic times. It is much easier to raise capital with a Moody's credit rating in the range of A1–Aa3 (the LAMP average) than with a Baa3 or lower rating (the global corporate average).

Long-term bond investors consider a variety of risks in deciding whether to buy a bond. These include the cyclical risk of interest-rate volatility, the liquidity risk of being able to buy and sell without significantly shifting market prices, and the credit risk that a bond will be downgraded to a less-desirable credit rating. Investors are naturally attracted to companies with strong records of financial stewardship because the bonds of these companies tend to pose less credit and liquidity risk. Knowing this, both Moody's and Standard & Poor's now include some stewardship screening in their credit evaluations.

The value LAS offers to credit analysts is a capacity to look deeper into a company's business practices and the quality of its stakeholder relation-

Figure 5-1: LAS and the Reinforcing Cycle of Capital Formation

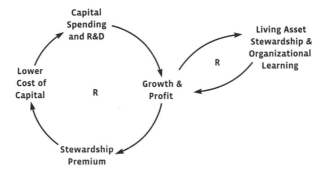

The reinforcing cycle of LAS + OL by itself generates extraordinary profit and growth. It also supports a second reinforcing cycle of R&D plus capital spending, which further accelerates profit and growth. This second cycle is enabled by the "stewardship premium" on a company's stock, which lowers its cost of capital, making it easier to finance R&D and capital spending. The two cycles clearly reinforce one another.

ships (relational equity). To begin with, LAS poses lower systemic risks to the environment, public health, and social well-being. It also limits specific risks of employee turnover, customer defection, regulatory backlash, insurance costs, etc. Both of these areas have impact on longer term credit and liquidity risks. On the income side of the ledger, the enthusiasm and innovation we find in LAS cultures adds an extra margin of safety.

To optimize returns on their bond portfolios credit analysts must know how to evaluate an LAS culture. They should also know how to map that culture (see Figure 2-2), because this offers insight into a company's capacity for learning and innovation. As staple investments in most pension funds and endowments, bonds are priced largely on the basis of perceived credit risk during the life or duration of the bond. The larger the perceived risk, the more interest investors will seek as inducement to buy the bond.

Because bonds are longer-term assets than are stocks, they are often bought and held to maturity, which may be five, 10, or more years into the future. Their credit ratings and market prices, therefore, offer us an important second opinion—one focused on a company's longer-term prospects, as distinct from the intermediate term of the next 12–18 months. I have greater confidence in the staying power of LAMP stocks and the Global

LAMP Index® knowing credit analysts support my favorable opinion of these 60 companies.

Investors often favor bonds over stocks when they are uncertain about their economic futures. If LAMP companies have top credit ratings and the capacity to hold those ratings, that information is worth knowing. During equity bear markets one often sees a flight to high-grade bonds. Selecting the right bonds is especially important during such times.

Conclusion

We are a society obsessed with numbers and empirical proof. Global LAMP companies have many ways to measure the value-added of their individual stewardship initiatives. But for now there is only one credible way to measure LAS in the aggregate as a model for business: stock prices. They are the best holistic measurement tool we have because they quickly adapt to changes in market conditions, just as living organisms do when their natural environments change. They distill into a single number everything that is known at a given time by interested global buyers and sellers. Although such numbers may from time to time become distorted, over long periods of time they form a useful composite picture.

The evidence collected from the stewardship leaders of the Global LAMP Index® supports the proposition that the LAS model is superior to the traditional model of the firm. The stewardship premium affirms this. So does the consistency of the Global LAMP's performance lead in rising and falling markets.

Why is this so? Why is the LAS model now so productive relative to the more widely accepted traditional model? One answer is that the world has changed. In relative terms, it is much smaller today than it was a decade or two ago. Since then, world population and living standards have grown immensely in relation to Earth's biotic carrying capacity. Perhaps a more basic answer is that we lost our biophilic compass during the Industrial Revolution when we disconnected the firm from the living systems that support it. We are now rediscovering that compass, and LAS is part of a much larger global trend toward realignment with our very ancient and human orientation toward life.

The ultimate power of LAS resides in its respect for life. If corporations are living systems or communities that exist within the much-larger living systems of the free market, society and Nature, this must be so. If living assets are the source of nonliving capital assets, this must be so. There is really no way around it. The traditional model of the firm, protected as it is by limited-liability laws and accounting principles that largely ignore living assets, cannot compete with the LAS model. The traditional model of the firm is an end game because it denies the primacy of life. The superior performance of the Global LAMP Index® affirms this.

In the future, the Global LAMP Index® should be a better barometer of corporate success than the MSCI World, the S&P 500, the DJII, or any industrial equivalent because it reflects more accurately what makes companies thrive in the new millennium: synergism, intelligence, networking, inspiration, and innovation.

Toward a More Effective General Theory of Business

"The time has come for economists and business leaders . . . to acknowledge the existence of the real real world."[1]
—Edward O. Wilson, *Consilience*

The *Real* Real World

The world desperately needs a new general theory of business that recognizes the real real world of which Wilson speaks. Such a theory would be in harmony, rather than at odds, with our larger living systems. The perceived "real world" of the Industrial Revolution is not real in any lasting sense, but a grand experiment in the mechanical leveraging of living systems. Although that experiment has temporarily succeeded in producing monetary wealth, it has frayed and destabilized the larger living systems from which that wealth is derived. No amount of financial hedging or tinkering at the margins will ameliorate the systemic challenges now before us—the decline of Earth's carrying capacity, the breakdown of community values, and eroding public confidence in the free market's pricing efficiency.[2] The risks before us today are not at the margins, but at the core of the traditional model of business. Only fundamental change in the ways business is conceived and operated will restore the systemic health we so urgently need. That change must be predicated on the deep truths of Living Asset Stewardship, which are inherent in all living systems, large and small—the *real* real world.

Economists often use the word "real" to strip away the illusory effects of inflation or deliberate overstatement. Real national income and real corporate earnings are supposed to get us closer to the truth of our economic progress than the income and earnings we normally see from raw data. But even economic reality described in these terms is a limited truth—at best, a truth upon an artificial stage. Incomes and earnings have little meaning if the living systems that hold up the economic stage are threatened.

There has to be a better way. And there is. The essential attributes of the LAS model have been around for centuries. My role has been simply to classify them as parts of a symbiotically connected, theoretical whole—one that allows us to see more clearly what is working and what is not.

My general theory of business begins by acknowledging a heretofore-unrecognized asset class—living assets. The theory holds that living assets (people and Nature) are inherently more valuable than nonliving (capital) assets because they are the very source of capital itself. As was noted previously, this is the opposite of what is assumed under generally accepted accounting practices (GAAP). In building from this first (living assets) principle, we get a general theory of the firm radically different from the one that predominates today. The conceptual model of Living Asset Stewardship sees the corporation as a living system (community) that is *integral* to the larger living systems of society and Nature. The traditional model, by contrast, sees the corporation as a mechanical device that is largely *separate from* society and Nature. These opposing models naturally see costs very differently. To a traditional company, stewardship generates irretrievable costs; to a global LAMP company, stewardship is a synergistic process whose costs are returned many times over in revenue and profit.

Underlying Assumptions

This chapter aims to move us *toward* a more internally consistent and compelling theory, but not to elaborate it fully. By exploring the assumptions that underlie our two opposing models, I hope to reveal their inherent

Table 6-1: Comparing Assumptions

FOR ALTERNATIVE THEORIES OF THE FIRM

LAS Model		*Traditional Model*
A living community	**Who are we?**	A mechanical wealth generator
Integral to Nature and society	**And why do**	Separate from Nature and society
We exist to serve	**we exist?**	We exist to generate profit
Living assets (people and Nature)	**What do we**	Nonliving (capital) assets
Relationships (relational equity)	**value?**	Transactions (financial equity)
Living Asset Stewardship	**How do we**	Command and control
Focus on means (capacity	**manage?**	Focus on ends
to serve)		(objectives)
Hierarchy of values		Hierarchy of managerial authority
Balanced (relational and financial)	**How do we**	Primarily financial
Holistic perspective	**measure?**	Linear (cause/effect) perspective
Optimizing value to customers	**What is**	Optimizing profit
Systemic harmony (infinite view)	**success?**	Systemic control (finite view)
Stable finances (for better LAS)		Leveraged finances (for
		M&A/mergers and acquisitions)

strengths and weaknesses, and consistencies and inconsistencies. If I succeed, the apparent performance advantages of the LAS model—as demonstrated by the Global LAMP Index® and Focus Group companies—should become clearer.

Table 6-1 compares the basic assumptions underlying each model in five set areas. These sets define directional leanings rather than absolutes, and give us an opportunity to see contrasts amid shades of gray. No firm fits either side perfectly. It's good enough for our purposes that LAMP companies generally "fit" in the left column of the table and traditional companies in the right.

The first set in Table 6-1 is existential. These questions examine how the firm sees itself in relation to the larger world and why it exists. The second set is focused on values—what the firm holds to be most precious. The third set considers management style—processes that make the firm run.

The fourth set deals with metrics—how firms identify and measure what's important. Finally, the fifth set is about definitions of success—how the firm defines things such as growth, progress, and the ability to carry on.

After evaluating these assumptions in the context of their impacts on corporate results and the living systems that support corporate enterprise, we must finally ask, *Which approach, which theory of the firm, leaves humanity with the most options?* If we accept that the purposes of corporations are to thrive in service to humanity and to help us toward our goal of an "expanding and unending future," this is the most important question we can ask. It captures at once our needs for both near-term results—goods, services, employment, profits, etc.—and long-term systemic health.

Edward O. Wilson gives this question a sense of urgency. By his reckoning, humanity faces a critical bottleneck. If the rest of the world were to come up to a North American living standard, as business and commerce are now conducted, we'd need the resources of "four more planet earths" to sustain it.[3] And this is a projection based only on the present picture. In an extrapolation out to the year 2050, the situation becomes even more perilous.

World population, now 6.1 billion people, is expected to double by 2050.[4] Living standards are rising in China (with a population of 1.2 billion) and in other developing nations. Meanwhile, essential natural systems that support our lives on Earth—climate, oceans, rivers, forests, croplands—are in decline. People everywhere are stressed by overcrowding, disease, poverty, and the fraying of underfunded social safety nets. Religious fundamentalists, political extremists, and terrorists exploit these situations in ways that shock us. Even in countries presumed to be the safest and most prosperous, there is a growing awareness that our options are narrowing. I believe these trends have now come to a tipping point. We are mentally and emotionally primed for new mental models.

Albert Einstein famously said, "We can't solve problems by using the same kind of thinking we used when we created them."[5] It seems, therefore, that the traditional model of business must at least be deeply questioned. If we live in a world where every living being is ultimately connected to every other, going it alone isn't an option. Every company is adversely affected by the impacts of poverty, disease, global warming, and social unrest. Bacteria, terrorism, and catastrophic weather events don't recognize geopolitical boundaries. If business wants healthy employees and markets, it cannot ignore the health of our air, water, and soil. To grow and prosper sustainably, companies must advance beyond the traditional thinking that got them where they are today.

Global LAMP companies have considered these realities and decided to search for harmonious new ways. Although not as far along on the learning curve of sustainability as they need to be, they are at least leaning in the right directions. They want a more durable global prosperity. They see the benefits of Living Asset Stewardship. Their employees, customers, host communities, and other stakeholders appreciate their desire to transform and become more integrated with the living systems around them. They express this appreciation in higher levels of trust and loyalty. The extraordinary performance of the Global LAMP Index® is not random happenstance. It is grounded in a more congruent general theory of the firm.

Exposing Assumptions

The contrasts we see in Table 6-1 are significant and fundamental. It is extremely difficult to mix and match the two systems—as many SRI and sustainability proponents wish were possible—because the goals of each are profoundly incompatible. Living Asset Stewardship can't be bolted onto a machine model. Corporate managers must choose a paradigm. By exposing the assumptions of both models, I hope to clarify the choices they must face.

Who are we? And why do we exist? The answers to these corporate identity questions set the tone for corporate culture. In the Living Asset Stewardship (LAS) model, the firm is perceived as a living community of people that is integral to society and Nature, and focused on serving life. This mental framework is unified and consistent. It recognizes our human aspiration for "an expanding and unending future." It is wired into our genes. We do not work to destroy our neighborhoods and children's futures. We work to improve them.

Gradually, I have come to see a whole new model for my role as a CEO. Perhaps my real job is to be the ecologist for the organization. We must learn how to see the company as a living system and to see it as a system within the context of the larger systems of which it is a part. Only then, will our vision reliably include return for our shareholders, a productive environment for our employees, and a social vision for the company as a whole.[6]

—Philip Carroll, CEO (1993–1998), Shell Oil

The "who are we?" of traditionally managed firms is very different. Arising from the linear scientific reasoning of Sir Isaac Newton, and the nineteenth-century fascination with mechanics, the "machine model's" answer to that question still holds the firm to be a mechanical wealth generator that is separate from Nature and society and focused solely on profit. This model deems employees and Nature to be replaceable (disposable) parts, and therefore sees layoffs, resource depletion, and hazardous waste dumping as normal, cost-effective behaviors. Its symbol of efficiency is the factory assembly line, which is still the way much corporate work is organized even in high-tech, knowledge-age companies. The machine model's separation from Nature and society is enshrined in the notion that its impacts on these larger living systems are "externalities" to be ignored by generally accepted accounting practices.

Were we to stop here and ask which culture and set of assumptions leave humanity with the most options, and which we'd rather work in, the answer should be self-evident. The stewardship culture wins. So why in the world aren't we choosing that right now? Why don't we "just do it?" Sadly, the choice is not that simple. When the question is posed abstractly in terms of future options, as I have just done, people easily see the big picture. But when it's framed in concrete terms—what we can personally do today to effect systemic change—many opt for the familiar status quo: "I have other things to worry about . . . . Just give me my paycheck and let someone else make the decisions." Psychological inertia and fear of change keep the traditional hierarchical approach going in spite of its obvious and alarming flaws.

Given the stakes involved, there is little question that the life-affirming LAS model will ultimately prevail simply because it must. The alternative is unthinkable. The important question is how long it will take to transform the present dysfunctional system wherein the firm is at odds with the living systems that support it.

The gradual—and slow—path of reform is the riskiest because it prolongs the breakdown of the biosphere and increases our exposure to global catastrophes. This view is supported by the world's leading reinsurance companies, which underwrite catastrophic risks. Munich Re estimates that by 2050 the effects of climate change could cost companies $300 billion annually in weather damage, pollution harm, and industrial and agricultural losses. That is big money and, if corporations choose the slow path, it will get a lot bigger because such damages usually have compounding effects. Swiss Re, believing an ounce of prevention is worth a pound of cure, does what it can to preempt future hazards by engaging in public education and convening high-level dialogue at its Ruschlikon Center. Its message is similar to that of Munich Re: business as usual is a bad option. The only sustainable way forward is corporate stewardship.

> In spite of huge annual fluctuations, a clear trend becomes apparent from looking at natural catastrophes over the last 30 years, indicating that insurance losses caused by natural catastrophes have risen dramatically. This increase mainly reflects higher population densities . . . and the high vulnerability of some modern materials and technologies. Furthermore, this is a consistent trend: losses caused by natural catastrophes will continue to rise.[7]
> —Swiss Re, *Natural Catastrophes and Reinsurance*

> Terrorism risk in many ways closely parallels natural catastrophe risks such as earthquakes, storms and floods. In both cases, enormous inherent loss potentials make diversification difficult to achieve; individual events can affect entire economies.[8]
> —Swiss Re, *Terrorism—Dealing With the New Spectre*

What do we value? This question is framed in terms of assets and equity because it offers a familiar context to corporate readers, as well as a useful platform for discussion of the ethical roots of LAS, which are grounded in *respect for life*. Stewardship companies understand that because living assets are the source of nonliving assets, weakening the source makes no sense. Traditional companies lean in the opposite direction. When forced to choose, they "do whatever is necessary" to protect capital and cash flow. If that means laying people off and harming the biosphere, so be it.

Toyota is an interesting study in this context because it operates in an industry renowned for poor labor relations, polluting factories, and environmentally unfriendly products. More than do its peers, Toyota strives to respect life in everything it does—from the design of its autos to factory-floor operations to the customer experience. As previously mentioned, Toyota has been continually profitable since 1960 with no layoffs, while also becoming the world leader in eco-friendly auto manufacturing.

The ways in which Toyota treats people and Nature are absolutely critical to its success. Its employees, suppliers, and dealers know they are valued. They are energized by Toyota's environmental leadership and eager to reinforce it. They like being on a winning team that does well by doing the right thing; and so they work with their hearts as well as their minds. Their combined success, of course, attracts customers and investors. It all flows.

How companies manage their equity reflects the values they place on their assets. Both stewardship and traditional companies see value in financial (shareholder) equity, but there the similarity ends. Whereas traditional companies tend to see financial equity, like earnings, as an end in itself, stewardship companies see it as a means to the higher end of building strong relationships (relational equity). They believe, as does Novo Nordisk, that the future is entwined in their relationships within the living systems that support them.

If we distill these different approaches to assets and equity down to their essences, we see that stewardship companies value lastingness. They want lasting relationships with the people who produce for them and buy from them, as well as those who finance and supply their operations. They want to be productive for generations, to build legacies for the future. It is a conservation ethic that leaves them and all living systems with virtually open-ended options. The traditional model, which focuses primarily on next quarter's profit, offers no such prospect. As described in Chapter 4 and Figure 4-1, people and Nature increasingly resist it because this model continually threatens them.

Our values are expressed in all our actions . . . . Decency is what counts . . . . Every day we try to find the right balance between compassion and competitiveness, the short and the long term, self and commitment to colleagues, and society, work and family life . . . . We shall all over the world conduct our business as socially and environmentally responsible neighbors, and contribute to the enrichment of our communities.[9]

—Novo Nordisk, Corporate Vision Statement

How do we manage? The fundamental difference between owning and employing is about give and take between the parties. Owners possess: they receive benefits and give nothing in return. Employers engage in a transactional arrangement that involves negotiation of terms of exchange, mutual learning, and adaptation. Though corporations can own nonliving assets (capital) because they are intrinsically controllable, living assets (people and Nature) will, ultimately, have none of that. They have intelligence, free will, and a survival instinct that resists harm to themselves and to the planetary web of life. Living and working with a view to mutually advantageous, long-term relationships makes all the difference in how these assets are managed.

The critical attributes of living assets—their connectedness, their continual learning and adaptation, their self-organized and generative striving for efficiency—are essential to prosperity in our global economy, which faces serious systemic risks. The stolid, "straight ahead" attributes of traditional command-and-control structures cannot adjust quickly enough to changes in the world about them. Living systems cannot be managed with mechanical devices. If we are to realize the full economic potential of people and Nature, they must be nurtured and stewarded. That is the essence of management by means.

It is of course more difficult to manage by diverse means (stewardship) than it is to pursue a single end (profit). To do so requires maturity, patience, humility, wisdom, and moral courage—assets not readily found in cultures attuned to on-demand results. *But the issues at hand are the future health, safety, and prosperity of human civilization,* not some nicety or abstraction. The world moved from monarchy and the divine right of kings, to democracy and the rule of law *because it was the only practical way forward for civilization.* Living Asset Stewardship is now gaining ground in the corporate world for the very same reasons.

Just as democracy makes political systems more flexible and adaptive, LAS does the same for commerce. It does so by creating a hierarchy of values—as distinct from a hierarchy of absolute managerial authority—that optimizes our human potentials. Good manager-stewards let employees take responsibility for decisions in their areas of primary competence: they understand that people on the front lines usually know the most about what is working and what is not. Rather than micromanaging, manager-stewards enable employees to build expertise, and appeal to their higher values as a way to build commitment. Such managers would rather have active employees who question procedures and spontaneously innovate than passive ones who grudgingly take orders.

Core value statements—such as Canon's kyosei, the HP Way, Johnson & Johnson's credo, and Shell's "Profits and Principles"[10]—carry enormous weight in LAMP companies. Baxter International puts a premium on caring and empathizing with the patients they ultimately serve. Managers and employees at its Hyland Immuno Division use "visualization" as a way of building customer intimacy, trust, and loyalty as well as team morale and commitment to service. Employees are encouraged to come face-to-face with patients to understand their needs more fully. Several hundred Baxter employees have helped to run summer camps for children with hemophilia. This has given employees intellectual and emotional knowledge of their customers that is hard to match, and a passion to serve that generates its own momentum. In such a culture, workers don't need to be told what to do by a hierarchical chain of command. They instinctively know. And in turn, they feed back information that is critical to the company's future success.

Our environment is one of continuous learning in which all employees, regardless of cultural background, gender, level or position can develop their full potential.... Decisions are made as close to the customer as possible so that we can act quickly to assure total customer satisfaction.... We work openly and supportively in teams, aiming towards common goals.... Individuals and teams have the responsibility, authority, resources, and support to make decisions and take actions.... We value and reward creativity, diverse thinking styles and intelligent risk-taking.... We act to maximize potential success, rather than to minimize potential failure.[11]

—Baxter International, "Shared Values"

What do we measure? And how do we measure it? Corporations measure what is important to them. A corporation's metrics can reveal a lot about its culture. Traditionally managed firms, for example, tend to be linearly focused on financial cause and effect. They are interested primarily in present activities (e.g., throughput or sales) or those in the recent past (e.g., profit). Stewardship companies go a step further. Important as past and present performance indicators may be, their metrics look more to the future. The evaluative methods they use to get this balanced approach are generically called the balanced scorecard.

Forward-looking metrics are concerned primarily with the quality of a firm's relationships with key constituents—employees, customers, suppliers, distributors, investors, citizen groups, and regulators. Stewardship companies use these new metrics as strategic indicators of future value-added capacity, profitability, and financial strength. Metrics that indicate future value-added capacity address employee morale (via questionnaire results) and turnover, the quality of relationships with suppliers, and the ability to engage others in new product innovations, as well as feedback from distributors and customers regarding market trends. Those that assess future profitability deal with customer satisfaction, repeat business and referral trends, feedback from citizen groups regarding product safety and environmental impacts, and regulatory trends. Metrics that look at future financial strength would also address investor loyalty. These examples only scratch the surface of the potential of forward-looking relational data. Stewardship companies have taken the state of this art into individually customized areas that are beyond the scope of this discussion.

The short-term orientations of traditional accounting metrics not only are incomplete, but also often subvert the forward-looking initiatives that stewardship companies try to cultivate. Companies that measure only the costs of employee benefits and education, and not the benefits they derive from happy, loyal employees, for example, often undermine employee morale and commitment and thereby sabotage customer relationships. Likewise, companies that skimp on maintaining close relationships with suppliers and other constituents generally generate fewer new ideas and less-productive market feedback.

The important rule to remember is this: *everything in a living system is linked to everything else over time.* Cause and effect may not be immediate. The interval between a customer visit and a new order may be several months long. The period between toxic releases into the workplace and employee health claims may be a matter of years. The lag between reckless burning of carbon-based fuels and our recognition of global warming was decades long. *But in the end, everything gets counted.* Companies can and should build such knowledge into their metrics systems. Those that do are far better prepared for stability and success in the long run than those that don't.

Accounting for the many complex feedback circuits of interdependent living systems is not an easy thing to do. It requires a holistic perspective on business rather than a single-minded focus on sales and profits. There are no set rules or one-size-fits-all methods. The most innovative firms in balanced scorecard accounting—such as Baxter International, Novo Nordisk, and Shell—approach the task by setting priorities and then challenging business unit leaders to come up with their own customized metrics. They also work closely with their auditors, specialized consulting firms, and citizen groups, such as the Global Reporting Initiative, in seeking best practices.[12]

Shell's Business Case for a Balanced Scorecard[13]
- attracting and motivating top talent
- reducing costs through eco-efficiency
- reducing risk
- influencing options and evolving portfolios
- influencing product and service innovation
- attracting more loyal customers and enhancing the brand
- enhancing reputation

Shell's balanced scorecard metrics evolved from an exhaustive self-audit during the mid-1990s. The review tackled large issues, such as human rights and global warming, and addressed the need to improve dialogue with broad groups of opinion generators. To implement its balanced scorecard, Shell also introduced new, integrated management systems that addressed its financial, environmental, and social performance. For the company and its employees, this self-audit and review was cathartic. It was an opportunity to engage in discussion of important issues—and yielded what CEO Mark Moody-Stuart described as "emotional enthusiasm."

Shell's new internal metrics told employees what was important, and it was a message employees wanted to hear. As they gained confidence that Shell had its priorities right and that they could make a difference, their commitment grew.

Which approach to metrics leaves us with the most options? The answer is, again, clear. For most corporations, the future is far more important than the past. Traditional accounting methods don't reveal much about the future. Only the balanced scorecard approach does. From a broad, systemic viewpoint, the balanced scorecard also legitimizes caring and points to a future with fewer adverse impacts on society and the biosphere. Employees like this and want to build on it. Their emotional enthusiasm drives the reinforcing cycle of LAS + OL, which, as we have seen, feeds back into greater innovation and (ultimately) higher sales and profits.

What is success? How do we know we're succeeding? Profit is a common denominator of both the LAS and traditional models because it is a prerequisite for corporate survival. But the similarity ends there. To traditionally managed companies, profit is the *end* that justifies all enterprise. To stewardship companies, by contrast, it is a *means* toward the higher ends of customer service, systemic harmony, financial stability, and creation of a legacy for future generations. These higher ends look past the finite present to an infinite future.

Which definition of success has been most effective? If the superior stock market performance, credit ratings, and average longevity of the Global LAMP Index® are any indication, there should be little doubt: the LAS approach wins hands down. A review of some paired comparisons will clarify the picture.

Johnson & Johnson and Bristol-Myers Squibb have both been global powers in the healthcare industry and prominent on SRI and sustainability approved lists; but otherwise, these two firms are cultural opposites. Johnson & Johnson puts service to customers, employees, and host communities ahead of shareholder returns—an approach embodied in its corporate credo. Bristol-Myers Squibb follows the more traditional management-by-numbers approach, asking business units to do whatever it takes to hit preset sales and profit growth targets.

Because people (especially creative employees in the healthcare business) find it harder to affiliate with abstract numbers than with life-affirming ideals, the shortcomings of managing by the numbers began to hurt Bristol-Myers during the 1990s (see Chapter 13 for the fuller story). With its new-product pipeline running dry, the company began to manufacture its earnings to create the appearance of success. This, of course, backfired. In 2002 Bristol-Myers was investigated by the U.S. Justice Department and the Securities and Exchange Commission (SEC) for misleading accounting practices, and later forced to restate its earnings for the prior three years as lower—by more than $2 billion. Investor confidence in the company was badly shaken. For the decade ending December 2005 the cumulative return on Bristol-Myers stock was less than a fifth that of Johnson & Johnson.

Canon and Xerox depict much the same story. Both have been global powers in the office copier market, as well as SRI and sustainability favorites, but otherwise cultural opposites. Canon's kyosei philosophy, which looks to an infinite future of shared global prosperity and ecological harmony, has spawned a profusion of innovative products. Xerox, by contrast, has been so obsessed by its market share in the copier market that it left many of its most promising futuristic ideas on the lab bench.[14] As the global copier market gave way to paperless electronic data systems, many of which were introduced by Canon, Xerox too began to misrepresent its results. In a settlement reached with the SEC in 2002, it was forced to restate equipment sales (lower by $6.4 billion) and pretax profits (lower by $1.4 billion) for the five-year period between 1997 and 2001. Just as for Bristol-Myers Squibb, Xerox's overconcentration on sales and profit, and lack of stable ethical values cost them dearly. For the 10 years ending in 2005, Canon's share return was more than six times that of Xerox.

Because stewardship companies are concerned with building stakeholder trust (relational equity) and creating legacies for future generations, they put a higher value on balance sheet strength than do traditional companies. LAMP companies tend to err on the side of financial stability, believing a strong balance sheet is essential to carrying out their goals of service, whereas traditional companies tend to err on the side of leverage as a means of acquiring other companies and boosting returns on equity. Because of these differences, companies in the Global LAMP Index® have, on average, much lower debt-equity ratios than do their peers and significantly higher ratings on their senior unsecured debt.

The relative strength of global LAMP balance sheets is not entirely due to fiscal caution, however. It also reflects the stronger cash flows that accrue to stewardship companies (as a result of the reinforcing cycle of LAS + OL), as well as the damage that traditional companies inflict on themselves by their mechanistic, numbers-oriented management practices. Moody's gives Johnson & Johnson its highest credit rating (Aaa) and has upgraded Canon (Aa2) since 1999 while downgrading Bristol-Myers Squibb by four grades (Aaa to A1) and Xerox by five grades (A2 to Ba1).

This review of the assumptions that underlie the two theories of the firm—and how these assumptions translate in the real world—shows undeniably which model leaves humanity with the most options. The LAS model offers far more potential for learning, adaptation, and sustainable prosperity than the bottom-line view of the traditional model because it is more stable, more inspirational, and more profitable.

If we consider the psychologies underlying both the LAS and traditional models (as described in Table 6-1), we are struck by another sharp contrast. Living Asset Stewardship embraces the natural chaos of humanity and living systems as part of our collective learning experience and responds by being open and interactive. Traditionally managed companies, on the other hand, distrust these chaotic behaviors and try to control them. Unlike LAMP companies, which are driven by spirit and hope, traditionally managed firms' view of the world is palpably more pessimistic and fearful. To traditionalists, resources are scarce and must be hoarded. To stewards, the most precious resource is the human imagination. And that is limitless.

When these worldviews play out, they naturally lead to different behaviors. For these reasons, I believe LAS today is in *a state of becoming,* while the traditional model is unraveling in a survival endgame. In this situation, more often than not the *end* becomes a self-fulfilling prophecy. It was earlier noted that the average life expectancy of an S&P 500 company is shy of 50 years—*less than half* the average age of Global LAMP Index® companies. From this time forward, life expectancies for traditionally managed companies are likely to shorten further.

Centrality of the Corporation

The failures of the traditional model should not blind us to the promise of the stewardship model. The problematic issue is not capitalism, but how capitalism is practiced. We don't judge Nature solely on the basis of its first, colonizing species. We take a more holistic, evolutionary view. We must do the same with corporations.

Corporations today are the most adaptive, innovative large institutions yet invented. As agents for change, they have a decisive edge. Unlike our great deliberative organizations (educational institutions and governments) and meditative bodies (established religions), they live on the margin under continual and unrelenting pressure to learn and adapt. Failure to do so can result in bankruptcy or takeover. If survival means that corporations must become more integrated with the larger systems that support them—and, as this book attempts to show, it inarguably is—then that's the direction corporations must ultimately take. Their *real* real world is: adapt or die.

The economist Joseph Schumpeter called capitalism a process of "creative destruction." This is another way of saying "adapt or die." If LAMP companies are gaining market share over traditional ones, as we have demonstrated, it's because they are better at adapting. The 60 companies that comprise the Global LAMP Index® represent approximately 4 percent of the number in the MSCI World Index, yet the LAMP companies' market capitalization is nearly one-fifth that of the MSCI World Index firms. The superior growth of LAMP companies during the past two decades, in relation to both the MSCI World and the S&P 500 indices, affirms the growth of their market share and influence.

Some people are uncomfortable with the notion of creative destruction. But look around. What do you see in Nature? Like Nature, the global marketplace is a place of continual flow, exchange of value, adaptation, and evolution. These activities are expressed through consumer spending, employee demand, capital investment, community action, government regulation, boardroom reflection, and a host of other activities at both the local and global levels. People in the marketplace, like natural organisms, will almost always choose what's best for them. If products and processes destroy more value than they create, or overtax the living systems that support them, they will get replaced, though the replacement can take a while because the repercussions are not always felt immediately, or even directly, until they work their way through the biosphere.

This process of creative destruction and continual adaptation is what drives corporations. As socioeconomic institutions, they now command the lion's share of the world's wealth and resources. How they govern themselves and relate to the living systems of the free market, society, and Nature is therefore vitally important to us.

This is not to dismiss the effectiveness of thoughtful government policy and regulation, and the contributions of universities, the media, citizens groups, or global nongovernmental organizations (NGOs). They all have important roles to play in the ongoing processes of corporate learning and adaptation, and in creating an agenda for a more harmonious world order. The best stewardship companies understand this and enlist the intellectual resources of such groups for critical feedback. In some cases these networks spin off permanent public-private alliances, such as the Forest Stewardship Council and the Marine Stewardship Council. In other cases, they address ad hoc issues as Royal Dutch/Shell did with Greenpeace in 1995 concerning the decommissioning of its Brent Spar ocean drilling platform.

To facilitate stakeholder dialogue, most LAMP companies publish annual reports on their environmental and social impacts. The strategic value of these reports is the dialogue and learning they promote.

The centrality of corporations is not a function of their wealth alone. They are the most adaptive organizations we have. They collect and process information everywhere. The best ones—those now growing the most rapidly—want to know the real real world. They go to great lengths to discover how its vital systems operate so that they can likewise operate more harmoniously and synergistically. They want to become legacies, to pass on the intellectual and process DNA for future generations. For them, LAS is not a discretionary matter, but a strategic imperative.

To achieve progress in science and technology we must first appreciate the wonders hidden in the world around us. Then we must pursue technologies for the future by attaining an understanding of the scientific principles behind these wonders.[15]

—Canon Science Lab, "What Is Light?"

The reinforcing cycle of Living Asset Stewardship and organizational learning (LAS + OL) embodies a powerful force for innovation and profit. This force is like electricity was a century ago. Companies that harness its natural strengths thrive. Those that resist change risk obsolescence.

Conclusion

We have explored two models of capitalism: one that works in harmony with the living systems that support it and one that operates in conflict with those systems. Under the LAS model, corporations identify value in terms of the whole—using synergistic, multiple-win strategies that benefit employees, customers, investors, society, and Nature. Traditionalists see value more narrowly in terms of profit to the firm, even if it comes at the expense of society and Nature—which it usually does.

We have, unfortunately, little time and few resources to waste in shifting from the world of traditional capitalism to stewardship capitalism. The carrying capacity of ecosystems we depend on for food, water, and clean air is diminishing. According to Wilson, "The ecological footprint—the average amount of productive land and shallow sea appropriated by each person in bits and pieces from around the world for food, water, housing, energy, transportation, commerce and waste absorption—is about one hectare (2.5 acres) in developing nations" and about 2.1 hectares (5.2 acres) for the total human population.xvi If world population doubles by 2050, these hectare totals will be halved. That leaves too little space to accommodate the living standards to which people in China and other developing countries aspire, much less to increase the living standards in North America, Europe, and Japan.

Which management approach leaves us with the most options? More of the same guarantees a train wreck. We can manage sustainably only if we proceed from a hierarchy of values that puts life ahead of profit. The Global LAMP Index,® imperfect as it is, affirms that when we do this, when we take this leap of faith, profits naturally follow.

Productivity of the Open Workplace

"The first order of business is to build a group of people who, under the influence of the institution, grow taller and become healthier, stronger, more autonomous."[1]

—Robert K. Greenleaf, "The Servant as Leader"

Companies are living communities of people dedicated to a common purpose. Their primary assets are living (people and Nature) and intimately connected through the biospheric web of life. Living assets are the means by which companies create nonliving capital assets. This creative process works best when companies function as open networks in which people can spontaneously self-organize as conditions about them change. Networks are the common structure of all life and living systems.[2] Highly networked companies are usually quicker and smarter than traditionally managed hierarchical companies.

Living Asset Stewardship (LAS) is a mental model that recognizes these fundamental truths. It is premised on respect for life because companies cannot exist without the support of living assets and living systems. Companies that practice LAS maintain the vitality of the living assets they employ by stewarding them. Such companies care for employees and help them to be the best they can be. Further, they care about the things their employees care about—the well-being of host communities, the environment, and the people with whom their employees interact. Such caring builds relational equity, which is the foundation of financial equity. It also generates, on the part of individuals and teams within the company, a desire to learn that becomes a means of fulfilling company mission. For these reasons I say LAS is a process of managing by means. To LAMP companies, "means" are simply ends in the making.

These are the dominant themes we've explored thus far. They are very different from the ways in which most people think about business, but they work. And they work brilliantly. We know this from the performances of the Global LAMP Index® and the Focus Group. This chapter will examine how Focus Group companies use networking and management by means to empower employees—to make them "healthier, stronger, [and] more autonomous."

Robert Greenleaf saw immense leverage in such an approach and he was right. Employees are part of a company's connective tissue—linking it with the larger living systems that sustain it (the biosphere, society, and free markets). By empowering workers to engage their eyes, ears, hearts, and minds in an enterprise, the company gains knowledge, insight, and motivation. These are the attributes it needs to drive the reinforcing cycle of LAS + OL, wherein LAMP companies find their greatest leverage.

Why Openness?

If companies are living communities of people interacting with each other and Nature, they cannot be efficient unless they are open. Networks need openness to refresh themselves and adapt in a continuous way. As a rule, the more open a system is, the more diverse it is likely to be; and the more diverse it becomes, the stronger it gets. Diversity brings new skills, new knowledge, and adaptive capacity—and hence, more options.

To operate effectively, networks need to be open at many levels. Having a diversity of people is not enough. To become optimally efficient, corporate networks also need to share information openly, be open to the ideas and insights their employees and other stakeholders bring, and welcome dialogue with them. They must be open to questions, challenge old assumptions, and experiment with new ideas. And they must be responsive to the real needs of employees, recognizing that the health of the network depends largely on the health of its constituent parts. All these attributes are core characteristics of LAMP companies.

Such openness is hard, if not impossible, to achieve in hierarchical companies that treat executives like royalty and employees like servants, and manage by command and control. This level of openness threatens the very premises of their cultures: that management knows best, that all employees need to know are procedures and how to follow orders, and that employees are therefore expendable. People working under such constrained conditions can't grow as quickly as those in open workplace companies because they don't have the means or motivation to do so. In a knowledge-based economy this is a huge liability and a major reason why LAMP companies so consistently outperform traditionally managed ones.

How It Works

There is no simple formula that describes an open workplace because all living systems are different and are continually evolving. Table 7-1 expands on the short list of general attributes. It presents a conceptual view of the company itself and then moves on to a practical description of the policies and practices that affect employees. To emphasize the differences between the open workplace model of LAS and the more traditional workplace model, I have juxtaposed the qualities of each.

These distinctions are qualitative   describing patterns of organization, relationships, and values—rather than quantitative. They describe how a system works in multi-dimensional ways, as distinct from the one-dimensional perspective of numbers (e.g., people employed, output generated, sales, profit, etc.). The very human qualities of openness, caring, listening, and inspiration, for example, cannot be precisely measured. But they can tell more about a company's capacity for learning, adaptation, and innovation than abstract numbers ever could.

There is no ideal open organizational structure; what works at one company at one moment in time may not work at another because individuals and relationships change. Nevertheless, we can say that companies whose qualities, on the whole, are most aligned with those in the "Open Workplace" column in Table 7-1 have advantages over those whose qualities are most aligned with those in the "Traditional Workplace" column.

Table 7-1: Characteristics of the Open Workplace

OPEN WORKPLACE	TRADITIONAL WORKPLACE
View of Company	
A living network dedicated to service	A mechanical system dedicated to profit
Integral to society and Nature	Separate from society and Nature
Operating on cybernetic principles[ii]	Operating by command and control
Managed by qualitative means	Managed by quantitative objectives/ends
Energized by shared ideals, values	Energized by money, power
View of Employees	
Employees as precious assets	Employees as costs, potential liabilities
Employees as growing when cared for	Most employees as limited
Employees as trustworthy	Employees as needing direction
Employees' health, safety as priorities	Company needs as priorities
Guiding Principles	
Emphasis on ethics (what we stand for)	Emphasis on compliance with laws/regs
Human rights as fundamental	Human rights as political
Diversity as a strength	Sameness as a strength
Authority as decentralized, localized	Authority as centralized, hierarchical
Leaders as mentors and guides	Leaders as dominant
Empowering employees to self-organize	Keeping employees in their place/niche
Valuing intuitive insight of employees	Valuing reasoned insight of top executives
Information as freely shared	Vital information for management only

Of course, all companies have management hierarchies, are energized by money, set quantitative objectives, and direct employees about what to do. But in comparison with traditional companies, open workplace companies have fewer layers of management, more idealistic cultures, more holistic vision, and more empowered employees. In addition, managers at open workplace companies spend more time mentoring and coaching employees—helping them to be more expert, professional, and authoritative—rather than simply telling them what to do. The value of Table 7-1 is the clear distinctions between workplace cultures that allow us to determine more easily which way a company is leaning, and how consistently and congruently it operates as an open, networked culture.

It is hard to overstate the importance of consistency and congruency in creating an open workplace, given that traditional management practices are antithetical to openness. The two cultures clash. Many of today's fallen corporate angels—among them AT&T, Ford, and Xerox—tried to adopt the outward appearances of living networked systems but failed because their managements were too bureaucratically isolated, too fond of their own ideas, too dismissive of frontline employees, and too focused on quantitative objectives. Although the leaders of all three companies have made extraordinary efforts to be diverse, employee friendly, and environmentally responsible, their workplace cultures utterly undermine these efforts. Employees instinctively know when market share and profit count more than ethics and citizenship. They have a hard time getting inspired and energized when managers talk down to them, withhold vital information, and treat them as potential costs.

The main advantages of open workplaces are the speed, responsiveness, and learning capacity of their human networks. Knowledge, competence, value creation, and the capacity to influence others create power in networks. Dominion over others, by contrast, usually causes unnecessary blockages and reduces the power of networks. This comparison explains the edge LAMP companies tend to have in learning, innovation, and profit.

Human Rights

Respect for human rights is absolutely essential to an open workplace. LAMP companies tend to look beyond the obvious case for diversity—the benefits of having diverse perspectives and skills among their employees—to a more spiritual case that resides within the human psyche. They see human rights as an expression of our shared humanity. Most of us don't accept the notion that there are ethnic hierarchies, or that some people deserve more rights than others by accident of birth. In the words of President Lincoln, denying "the common right of humanity" amounts to "blowing out the moral lights around us . . . eradicating the light of reason and the love of liberty."[3] Human rights cannot be denied or slighted by an ethical, values-based community if it is to be credible to its stakeholders. So long as one of us is denied such rights, Lincoln said, we all must live in doubt about our own rights.

Even though there are hierarchies within ecosystems, in Nature no living being is inherently more valuable than another or has superior rights of self-determination. Single-cell organisms are as important as more evolved plants and animals because ecosystems can't function without them. Bacteria maintain systemic health and food supplies for all life. Even this simplest microorganism is self-governing in the minimal sense of determining what to eat, where to go, and how to exchange its DNA.

The open workplace, like the intricately networked ecosystem, can't self-organize and optimize the collective skills of its constituents if some individuals are systematically devalued and mistreated. People who are mistreated become apathetic, detached, minimally productive, and sometimes hostile to the company and fellow employees. Those who witness mistreatment, even if they haven't suffered it themselves, feel stressed.

Companies that actively value and promote human rights have more secure and inspired employees than those that don't. Employees of LAMP companies generally have higher morale and lower turnover rates than do their peers in companies not proactive on human rights. The positive feedbacks from this are immense. With less turnover, employees have more time to connect, to know each other's skills, to exchange ideas, and to co-learn. The energy and inspiration they derive from these interactions—especially when focused on life-affirming goals—feed their desire to experiment and innovate. The reinforcing cycle of LAS + OL derives much of its strength from honoring human rights. I believe the strong correlations between the human rights practices of LAMP companies and their creative energy and profitability are more than pure coincidence.

Global LAMP companies clearly understand human rights dynamics:

- 100 percent have high ethical standards that encompass human rights, equal opportunity, employee health and safety, and respect for the individual.
- 98 percent explicitly address these ethical standards in their corporate values and internal codes of conduct.
- 63 percent have signed or endorsed international framework agreements—such as the U.N. Universal Declaration of Human Rights, the U.N. Global Compact, the Global Sullivan Principles, and core conventions of the International Labor Organization (ILO)—that further affirm these values.

- 60 percent have adopted Global Reporting Initiative guidelines that use Social Accountability (SA 8000) standards to benchmark human rights.

These strong commitments typically transcend mere compliance with the law. They express "who we are and how we want to be perceived." Alcoa's "Guide to Business Conduct," for instance, says the company's human rights and workplace standards must always be upheld "even if these are higher than those required by local law."[4] To ensure compliance across all business units, Alcoa audits its performance against set goals and then has the results independently verified. Alcoa also expects its suppliers and subcontractors to report on their human rights policies and performance, letting them know that substandard performance is grounds for termination.

As a lending institution, HSBC goes a step further. Its code of conduct requires that due diligence procedures on project loans consider "human rights impacts" and "the risks of repression." In 2003 the bank co-authored the Equator Principles, which specifically include due-diligence considerations of "human health . . . involuntary resettlement . . . and impacts on indigenous people."[5]

Like HSBC and Alcoa, most LAMP companies extend their human rights agendas beyond their corporate boundaries. Virtually all have set standards for their suppliers and business partners. Baxter International offers suppliers an *EthicsKit*[6] and guidance on how to meet the company's expectations. Hewlett-Packard works to raise human rights standards in developing countries where it does considerable outsourcing, and in 2002 co-organized a 25-company Global Compact Learning Forum to share experiences and potential solutions on a range of issues, including human rights.

In the final analysis, human rights cannot be separated from the notion of the corporation as a living system. A living system cannot be healthy if whole groups of people in and around it are discriminated against. This is not to say that corporations must hire and promote based on ethnicity, religion, or some other notion of diversity because that, too, is contrived and inauthentic. The point is that all employees must be treated fairly and with respect, or the very notion of service—and particularly, service to life—is undermined.

A t Intel . . . our goal is to attract, welcome and retain the most talented people worldwide. To do this, we must foster an environment where everyone can
be comfortable. The wide-ranging perspectives, abilities and experiences of
our workforce are key to the success of our company and our people, and fundamental to our role as a technology leader and a global citizen.[7]
                        —Intel Global Citizenship Report 2002: "Diversity and Opportunity"

Caring for Employees

LAMP companies know that in an open networked culture everything is
ultimately related to everything else. The health of a network depends on
the health of its individual constituents and the synergies they create when
working together. The individual and the network are inseparable. They
have a shared destiny.

Open organizations, knowing that the health of their individual constituents is vital, care about people's needs. People generally respond by
caring, in turn, for the organization and its mission. Such mutuality breeds
cooperation and collaboration, which are essential to organizational learning and capacity building. The reinforcing cycle of LAS + OL runs on the
power of caring. Caring begets caring.

LAMP companies don't just theorize about all this. They actually operate in these ways. In keeping with their open networked approach to organization, they treat employees as whole individuals, not as isolated factors of
production that check in and out of their workplaces at regular intervals.
They serve the growth of employees within the context of their real lives—
by caring about their health and safety, their opportunities for professional growth and learning, and their families and communities—and trust
that all of this effort will circle back in ways that ultimately strengthen the
network. A brief summary of best caring practices follows.

Employee health and safety constitute a vitally important indicator of
caring, particularly in manufacturing where there is often exposure to
injury and harmful substances. When Paul O'Neill became CEO of Alcoa
in 1987 he decided to make this issue the company's highest priority—one
that would be addressed in top-level meetings even ahead of profit. So
embedded has this objective become that today Alcoa reports its lost work-
day (LWD) accident rate to all employees and stakeholders in real time. The

rate hovers near 0.1—significantly better than the national average for all manufacturers of 2.2.

Both O'Neill and his successor, Alain Belda, see employee health and safety as a practical ethic—ethical in the sense of caring for employees' lives, and practical in the sense of lowering costs. To accomplish this goal, they needed the cooperation of workers; and to get that cooperation, Alcoa had to show it deeply cared about everyone's well-being. Because Alcoa plant workers were routinely exposed to the dangers of molten metal and heavy machinery, the best way to care was to make elimination of *all* job-related injuries the company's top priority. To show its seriousness, Alcoa developed environment, health, and safety (EHS) metrics that it uses to audit all business units. Executive bonuses are based, in part, on EHS improvements.

Around Alcoa, O'Neill liked to say he was less focused on the bottom line or on the company's stock price (ends) than on the factors that led to the bottom line (means). If employees were to believe in Alcoa's respect for life and be inspired by it, stewardship had to be palpable in everything the company did that affected employees' lives—from conditions within the workplace to its wider impacts on Nature and society. To advance that agenda, in 1997 Alcoa launched the *Life!* program, a collaboration with Yale's School of Occupational and Environmental Medicine.[8]

Both O'Neill and Belda saw the challenge of zero lost workdays as a metaphor for taking on other large challenges, and they were right. Doing so won employee loyalty and inspired workers to contribute their best efforts and ideas—a boost to revenues. It also reduced the costs of lost production time and workers' compensation claims.

Alcoa's caring approach to employee health and safety is typical of LAMP manufacturing companies. Intel's injury and illness rate is the lowest in the semiconductor industry—approximately 40 times better than the average U.S. manufacturer's. Johnson & Johnson has a reputation as one of the safest U.S. companies for workers. Nucor is the safety leader in the steel industry, as is Toyota in the auto industry.

We have to go beyond zero injuries .... We have to send employees home healthier than when they came into work. We do that through wellness and fitness programs that give them physical, emotional and work life support.[9]
—William J. O'Rourke, VP, Alcoa, Environment, Health & Safety Audit 2002

Servant leadership is another common attribute of companies that deeply care for their employees. According to Robert Greenleaf, who coined the term, the purpose of servant leadership is "to build a group of people who, under the influence of the institution, grow taller and become healthier, stronger, more autonomous."[10] In most LAMP companies, executive compensation is based, in part, on skill at developing the competence and professional skills of employees.

Southwest Airlines helps employees to grow by actively engaging them in problem solving and group learning at all levels. This serves a dual purpose: using the insights of those who do the work and giving employees a sense of control over their lives. At the local level, Southwest uses cross-functional employee teams—baggage handlers, gate attendants, pilots, mechanics, and others—to discuss practical workplace issues that affect their performance. These range from covering for one another at times of peak demand to "the power of caring and compassion" in serving customers and the ideals of "day-by-day doing the right thing" without having to be told. At the corporate level, Southwest has a Culture Committee whose mission is to keep Southwest's spirit alive. Like the cross-functional teams, this committee comprises primarily the "people who do the work." It meets several times a year to gain their collective insights on issues that affect corporate morale, and to solve system-wide problems, such as handling late arrivals while maintaining adequate security vigilance. Both approaches—the cross-functional teams and the Culture Committee—involve employees in strategic thinking and help them see the importance of their work as members of the Southwest team.

Nucor serves employees by giving them a sense of empowerment over their work lives, creating a team environment in which people freely exchange ideas and coaching, and maintaining an open-door policy to division leaders. At Nucor steel mills there are no employee time clocks—there is only a work ethic that arises from within each individual team as it strives to surpass its production goals. Employees write their own job descriptions and are given wide latitude to self-organize around tasks as they see fit. The presumption behind this system is that plant workers closest to the action care about the collective welfare of their teams, are intelligent, and can therefore be trusted to do the right thing. What makes this system work is a culture of mutual accountability. People understand that their teams and divisions will stand or fall on their own merits. In the words of former CEO Ken Iverson, "There's no cavalry waiting to ride to the rescue . . . . There's just you and the people working with you."[11]

Nokia is one of the most networked companies in the Global LAMP Index.® Employees are coached, mentored, and encouraged to experiment and "have fun" so they can grow as individuals and become more insightful. They are also given rich opportunities to improve their competencies via lateral transfers. Everything of importance is done by self-organizing teams and a system of "distributed decision making" that implicitly recognizes the value of those closest to the action. Nokia continually seeks employee feedback on important issues via surveys, focus group discussions, and an intranet that invites comments and suggestions. Every year, all personnel join in a company-wide "visioning" process that invites each to imagine better ways of "connecting people" inside and outside the company. By nurturing and serving everyone in the system, the system itself gets stronger, more innovative, and productive.

Like Southwest and Nucor, Nokia's workplace operates on servant leadership principles whose design means that everyone has a vested interest in helping one another be the best they can be. The result: each is the lowest-cost producer and the most profitable company in its industry.

The servant-leader is functionally superior because he is closer to the ground—he hears things, sees things, knows things, and his intuitive insight is exceptional.[12]

—Robert K. Greenleaf, "The Servant as Leader"

Work/life balance is an important element of the open workplace because it enables more people to participate and because it shows employees that the company respects their time. The benefits of work/life programs generally pay back quickly in terms of reduced employee stress, increased loyalty, and productivity. As Intel sees it, helping to balance people's lives "reduces barriers to effectiveness" and "maximizes employee contributions over the course of their careers."[13]

The range of options offered by Intel includes flexible and alternate work schedules; telecommuting (45 percent of employees do this some of the time); job sharing; childcare assistance and nursing-mother rooms; health and wellness benefits; fitness centers; counseling; and paid sabbaticals. Intel University is an in-house training organization offering more than 7,000 self-help career development courses, many of which are available online and accessible at employees' convenience. The quality and accessibility of these work/life programs is such that Intel has been consistently rated by *Fortune* Magazine as one of the best companies to work for in the U.S. and one of the top 10 in Europe.

Intel knows that in a company with 80,000 skilled employees, it is hard to predict the source of the next innovation breakthrough. By embracing all employees, rather than a privileged few, Intel optimizes the possibilities of connection and increases the odds that it will survive and thrive for future generations.

Hewlett-Packard, one of the pioneers of work/life balance, has surveyed employees about its program since 1995. By 1999 it found that employee satisfaction with the fit of work and "regular' life had jumped an average of 10 points, and attrition rates were stable or down at most worksites. Given that it cost the equivalent of a year's salary to replace an employee, retention—especially of technology workers—was a bottom line issue.

Profit and burden sharing are critical features of the open workplace because they foster partnership with employees. It is notable that as a result of such sharing, Nucor, Southwest, and Toyota, all of which operate in highly cyclical industries, have operated profitably for decades without laying off employees for lack of work. All three also enjoy the highest credit ratings of their industry peer groups.

At Nucor, when steel orders recede for long periods, everyone in the company takes a pay cut so all employees can stay on the job, and senior management takes the deepest cuts of all. Conversely, when business is good every employee is eligible for production bonuses that are issued every pay period. The fairness and equity of this system bond employees to the company. To them, efficiency is not only a corporate matter, but also a personal one. Because of their efficiencies, Nucor's employees are the highest paid in the steel industry even while the company has the lowest employee costs per ton of steel produced.

The story at Southwest is similar. Although heavily unionized, it has earned enormous employee loyalty and productivity because the team's interests are always put ahead of those of its executives. In 1973, it became the first airline to offer a profit-sharing plan to employees. Virtually all employees are stockholders. When airline traffic plummeted in the aftermath of the 9/11 terrorist attacks on the U.S., Southwest's top three executives quietly went without pay until profitability was restored. The company also contributed to employee profit-sharing plans just a few weeks after the attack while other airlines were appealing to their governments for financial assistance. Southwest executives don't mind being the lowest paid in the airline industry because their company stock has grown to more than 1,000 times its 1974 value. That performance has also been a big win for employees.

When orders are slack at Toyota, employees are reassigned within the firm or sent out as missionaries to coach suppliers in the Toyota Production System (TPS). The company uses such periods to focus on learning—learning to produce more with less—rather than on cutting payroll as its major global competitors do. As a result of the employee commitment and efficiencies gained, Toyota has been consistently profitable since 1960 without layoffs, and has a coveted Aaa bond rating. During both recessionary years of 2001 and 2002, each of Toyota's U.S. employees received annual profit-sharing checks in the vicinity of $8,500 while its big three rivals announced layoffs and skimpy bonuses of approximately $100 for each worker.[14]

Appreciative inquiry is a way of drawing employees into the strategic visioning processes of the firm—a form of caring that yields both good information and employee commitment. Although the name for this practice is relatively new, the practice itself has been around for centuries. Stora, the world's oldest continually operating company, has persisted since the thirteenth century because it has had a sense of community that fostered consultation. Nokia's annual company-wide "visioning" process, mentioned above, is another example. One of the best-documented cases of appreciative inquiry is Hewlett-Packard's 1998 inquiry into what it would mean to be the world's best industrial research lab.

The WBIRL project, as it came to be known, put this question to the entire global employee network of HP Labs, rather than to a select group of executives on retreat. Barbara Waugh, the project leader and worldwide personnel director of HP Labs, created a variety of venues for dialogue. Lab workers presented their views as "voices of the organization." Senior managers met in strategic sessions to "consider core technologies that might be needed for multiple future scenarios at HP Labs to unfold." Weekly "chalk talks" for engineers, "coffee talks" (administrative assistant forums), and a community forum created additional opportunities for dialogue, listening, and learning. A grants program was set up to give small stipends for innovative ideas, enabling people to act at the corporate grassroots level and take personal responsibility for work in which they believed.

In all these efforts, the leader spent most of her time "helping the parts to see the whole" and linking together people with complementary ideas. After several months of dialogue, she put forth the related question: "What would it mean for HP Labs to be the best both in and *for* the world?" This galvanized employees and refocused them on HP's original ideals of "first and foremost making a contribution to society." From then on, talk turned to radical new ideas on breakthrough technologies to serve humanity and the planet.[15]

David Cooperrider, who coined the term, says appreciative inquiry asks us to pay special attention to "the best of the past and present" in order to "ignite the collective imagination of what might be." It seeks to "amplify what's working" and to "focus on life-giving forces"—the very essence of Living Asset Stewardship.[16]

Recognizing employees for their contributions is a way of caring that is incredibly powerful, yet too often overlooked in traditionally managed companies. At LAMP manufacturing companies employees' ideas are often the source of their greatest innovations. Both Canon and Toyota have built their success by harvesting thousands of employee suggestions each year—each of which is specifically recognized. Employee innovations are so effective at Nucor that the company doesn't have an R&D or engineering department.

At 3M, regarded by many as the preeminent corporate innovator, employees are trusted to follow their dreams and instincts. Those who develop new ideas, technologies, and business ventures are recognized with a variety of awards and honors, and their success stories are published for all to see on the company's website. To encourage free thinking among its technical people, 3M allows them to spend up to 15 percent of their time on projects of their own choosing. Every year, several employees who have made outstanding contributions are elected by their peers to 3M's Carlton Society, an honor the rough equivalent of an internal Nobel prize.

One of the ways 3M encourages innovators and early adopters is by offering employees with good ideas "Genesis Grants" from an in-house venture capital fund. To obtain a grant, the employee must first convince a team of peers from different parts of the company—marketing, finance, engineering, production—of the innovation's potential. Then, together, they present it to a new-venture team. If the project is selected for development the initiator/champion and all team members get promoted as it moves along. Should any executive along the way wish to stop the project, the burden of proof rests on the nay-sayer. Projects that get turned down may be appealed and reinstated.

By generously recognizing the accomplishments of employees and giving them a chance to prosper from their ideas, 3M consistently generates successful new product offerings. Thirty percent or more of their sales in any given year are generated from products developed during the prior four years.

Compared to 3M and its LAMP peers, traditionally managed companies are handicapped. They have a difficult time accessing employees' ideas because they assume that the only meaningful intelligence in a company resides at the top or in specialized groups. Praising employees, of course, challenges that myth. The pity of this mind-set is that it creates employee resentment as well as an unnecessary wall to innovation. Such resentment intensifies when executives steal or take credit for the ideas of others—an all-too-common occurrence in hierarchical cultures.

The positive feedbacks obtained by caring for employees are far too numerous to detail here. Yet the case for such caring is pretty simple. The health of a living system resides largely in the health of its living parts. Traditionally managed companies handicap themselves when they treat employees like disposable machine parts with limited capacity and intelligence, and when they subordinate employee needs to the goal of next quarter's profits.

Subsidiarity

The strategic premise of subsidiarity is very different from that of a bureaucratic chain of command. It assumes people are real assets rather than potential liabilities or costs. It gives employees authority to make decisions in their areas of competence without managerial intervention. The term gets its name by delegating power for most business decisions to the local or subsidiary level. Under the principles of subsidiarity, senior managers intervene only in decisions that have major impacts on the welfare of the firm. Otherwise, it is assumed that employees are intelligent, that they know best what needs to be done at the local level, and that they can be trusted to serve well when properly mentored and trained. Companies that act on these principles tend to have better vision and strategic execution than those that don't because they use their network capacity more effectively.

Most global LAMP companies would be considered radically decentralized by traditional standards. They have small, nimble home office staffs. Their business units tend to be autonomous, with few management layers. These units typically have small-to-medium-sized staffs (50 to 400 employees) so that people at the local level can get to know each other's competences and skills. The role of the home office is to serve local business units, whose managers in turn serve the professional development of frontline employees. The glue that holds such companies together is not centralized authority but a shared vision of where the firm is going, as well as deeply shared values rooted in LAS.

Alcoa employs only 400 people at corporate headquarters—a small staff for a company with 131,000 employees and more than 400 operating locations in 43 countries. Nucor's home office staff of 66 serves 11,500 employees in 50 operating facilities in 17 states. In both companies there are four layers between business unit managers and frontline workers. There are no closed offices. Manufacturing employees work in teams that give each individual a great deal of autonomy to self-organize for tasks.

HSBC Group calls itself "the world's local bank." With more than 60 autonomous subsidiary companies and 9,800 offices in 77 countries and territories, it is as localized as a global bank can get. Unlike other banks of its size, HSBC makes most of its lending and investment decisions at the local level with local people, rather than trying to create mega-deals by superstar managers from the home office. Intel lets its individual fabricating plants (fabs) run as if they were separate, autonomous businesses. Royal Dutch/Shell's transformation (1993–1998), discussed elsewhere in this book, was specifically modeled on the principles of subsidiarity.

What makes subsidiarity work at these companies is a principle that Charles Handy calls "type two accountability." If type one is simply avoiding mistakes, type two turns on the ideas of "seizing every opportunity" and "making all possible improvements."[17] Employees at LAMP companies generally feel confident about taking type two accountability because their authority is clearly established in company rules and practice. Furthermore, they are served by data systems that give them the information they need to make good decisions on the spot.

Trusting the Wisdom of the Network

For a company that deals in ideas and innovation, Intel's open workplace is greatly enriched by the diversity of its employees' cultural backgrounds, perspectives, and viewpoints. There are no barriers to entry other than competence and a desire to be on a team that seeks to revolutionize the ways in which civilization learns, adapts, and evolves. The possibilities for catalyzing constructive change and serving life at Intel are infinite. Intel's openness, multicultural composition, and tolerance for new and different ideas strengthen its ability to pursue those possibilities. Employees believe they are special, not simply because they are meticulously cared for, but because they believe their combined efforts can make a difference. Intel's diversity and intellectual ferment excites them. It resonates everywhere. It is one of the main reasons why Intel has, in the few decades since its founding in 1968, become a world leader in innovation.

HSBC, founded in 1865 to finance commercial development in China, has a more long-standing open workplace history than does Intel. Although now based in London, the company's management and employees reflect the diverse global markets it serves. People of Anglo-Saxon heritage are a minority within management. (For more on the demographics of HSBC's workforce, see the discussion in the beginning of Chapter 3.)

HSBC has thrived by listening to these different voices and by trying to make the world a better place wherever it serves. To affirm the humanistic principles that underpin its culture, the bank openly supports and promotes initiatives that acknowledge the worth of people everywhere, such as the U.N.'s Universal Declaration of Human Rights, the U.N. Global Compact, and the Global Sullivan Principles. Knowing that its lending and other commercial activities affect the lives of employees and customers alike, HSBC will not lend to borrowers that violate its ethical standards. It supports environmental and education initiatives that improve living conditions in all its markets. And it offers people in the 77 countries and territories it serves opportunities for advancement that many would otherwise lack. Collectively, these activities strengthen

HSBC's employee network by strengthening the commitment of individuals within the network.

HSBC is renowned for its attention to human networks. During its 2000 acquisition of another bank, CEO John Bond was said to have invested more time on the humanities of the deal than on the price. To many, that might seem old fashioned. But it speaks volumes about the culture and values that have made HSBC one of the world's fastest-growing banks during the past 30 years (1972–2002).

[A] business is not some legal abstract entity. Companies are composed of people with feelings and aspirations just like everybody else. And most people want to do something they are proud of .... Most of all, we need to make the connection between people's everyday lives and business.[18]

—Sir John Bond, Chairman and CEO (1998–2006), HSBC

Productivity

Employees at Nokia's flagship plant in Salo, Finland are paid 30 times the wages workers receive in low-cost Asian factories, yet their productivity is so high that Nokia's cost (of making and selling an average phone) in the third quarter of 2002 was only $114—almost 20 percent less than the $139 average cost for its closest rival.[19] Nucor, in spite of paying the highest wages in the steel industry, has the lowest labor costs per ton of steel produced in the U.S.

Toyota's manufacturing costs per vehicle are thousands of dollars below those of its direct competitors even though its wage rates are comparable. By the late 1980s its cybernetic production methods produced vehicles with one-third the defects of mass-produced cars, using half the factory space, half the capital, and half the engineering time. Alcoa, which has adopted many practices of the Toyota Production System, is by far the most profitable company in the metals industry.

Southwest Airlines has been consistently profitable for more than three decades, during which time most airlines lost as much as they made. The diverse, humanistic, and brainy cultures of HSBC and Intel have been equally outstanding. During the past 30 years (1975–2005) shares of all three companies have outperformed the S&P 500 by huge multiples.

When organizations concentrate on nurturing relationships rather than on achieving quantitative targets, they will spontaneously generate financial results consonant with healthy long-term survival.[20]

—H. Thomas Johnson and Anders Broms, *Profit Beyond Measure*

MBA Preferences

In 2003 researchers from the Stanford Business School and the University of California, Santa Barbara published a survey of more than 800 people with MBA degrees from 11 leading North American and European business schools. The researchers found that most of the MBAs sought employers with stewardship cultures.[21] Ninety-seven percent of respondents said they would take a 14-percent pay cut to work for an "ethical" company—a contradiction of the traditional culture's supposition that money is what ultimately counts.

The survey results supported LAS cultures on other counts as well: intellectual challenge topped the list as the most important attribute for MBAs in their job-choice decision. The financial package was only 80 percent as important as intellectual challenge. Ethics and caring about employees were also top-tier attributes—approximately 77 percent as important as the top criterion of intellectual challenge.

According to the researchers, MBA preferences have been increasingly leaning toward stewardship companies—especially since the Enron and WorldCom scandals of 2001 and 2002. These findings reflect sound economic thinking as well as ethical principles. The performance gap between stewardship companies and traditionally managed ones—proved by the Global LAMP Index®—has become increasingly obvious. The best new MBAs clearly prefer teams with winning records over those that are in decline. If this trend in MBA preferences continues, the flow of talent to stewardship companies will further increase their performance edge. Correspondingly, it will hasten the demise of traditionally managed corporations.

Conclusion

The ultimate measure of all commercial enterprise is productivity—deriving the most value at the least cost. Open workplace companies approach this goal by embracing diversity and making employee well-being a higher priority than profits. Their rationale is simple: employees are the means by which they achieve profit. Emotionally secure, happy employees are more loyal and productive than unhappy ones.

If it costs extra to care thoughtfully for employees—to give them individualized coaching and training, work/life balance, healthy and safe working conditions, and the stimulation of an open, interactive workplace— these costs are recaptured many times over in increased productivity.

Great ideas, the driving force of great companies, are most likely to emerge in open cultures because they welcome the intellectual ferment of questioning, challenging assumptions, and experimenting. Appreciative inquiry, however it occurs, engages the heart as well as the mind. People with different backgrounds, cultures, beliefs, and perspectives, who are free to express themselves, make open workplace cultures vibrate with energy.

It is not easy to build and sustain such an open workplace. Although its humanity, empathy, and trust sound soft, in practice an open workplace is tough and professionally disciplined. Charles Handy puts it well: "Organizations based on trust have, on occasion, to be ruthless. If someone can no longer be trusted, he or she cannot be given an empty space. To keep the spirit of subsidiarity [and openness] intact, those who don't merit trust must go elsewhere, quickly."[22] Just as there are no guarantees of individual longevity in Nature, there can be no guarantee of lifetime employment in corporations.

The open networked companies of the Global LAMP Index® succeed not only because they empower and care for their employees but because they also hold them accountable. They treat employees as responsible, intelligent, and caring adults and what they get in return is just that.

8

Transcending Eco-efficiency

"We can generate wealth that can improve quality of life and not
jeopardize the planet."[1]
—Lars Rebien Sorensen, CEO, Novo Nordisk

The global economy is an open system that draws raw materials from
the environment and returns approximately 94 percent of these
material flows back to the biosphere in the form of waste and pollution.[2] Companies that learn how to convert this pollution and waste back
into usable resources have huge productivity advantages. With a little ingenuity they convert these hidden resources into real value and profit while
reducing adverse impacts on Nature that could become a serious drag on
earnings.

Most large corporations have learned to be more *eco-efficient* by making incremental improvements, in material and energy use, that reduce
operating costs and environmental impact. But they have barely begun to
tap the synergies of *eco-effective* design and processes, pioneered by some
of the more advanced global LAMP companies, that *partner with Nature.*
This chapter will take us beyond the low-hanging fruit of eco-efficiency

to the more advanced eco-stewardship methods of our Focus Group exemplars.

The best eco-stewards strive to reduce their total impact on Nature through becoming more eco-effective by, in effect, mimicking Nature's own processes. Their ultimate aim is "zero adverse impact." To accomplish this, they use a life cycle assessment (LCA) technique that tracks the environmental impacts of their products and services along a continuous path from initial product design through production, resource use, supply chain effects, packaging, shipping, retailing, purchase, use, and ultimate disposal. Their goal is to replicate the dynamics of natural systems so that the waste from a product or process becomes "food" for another, or is sequestered within a closed-loop system until it can be rendered back into "food."

One of the recurring themes in this book is the consistency and congruency with which LAMP companies respect life in pursuit of their businesses. They not only model themselves on living ecosystems, but also strive to mimic the eco-effectiveness of those systems. Few companies do this better than Novo Nordisk, the Danish manufacturer of industrial enzymes and pharmaceuticals. It is a highly networked organization that manages by means. Environmental costs, benefits, and impacts, along with productivity and quality, are integrated into everything it does.

Novo's accounting system tracks every effluent and waste stream from every plant in its system, as well as those of its suppliers and shippers. From these data Novo can calculate its total systemic impacts on global warming, ozone depletion, acidification, and eutrophication. Novo then publishes the data collected by its eco-accounting system on its website and in annual sustainability reports.[3] This affirms to employees the importance of its environmental agenda, a matter of corporate pride. It also stimulates organizational learning. Novo uses these reports to enrich discourse on its processes and their impacts—both inside the firm and at "stakeholder forums." The knowledge it gains from these feedback sessions is then invested back into improving its processes.

Participants at these forums include prominent environmental activists and others whose knowledge of the natural world can help Novo to become more harmonious and integrated with Nature. Bioethics, a prominent topic in these stakeholder forums, reaches into every corner of Novo's business—from genetic engineering to Novo's management of the biotic materials it collects in remote areas. The company is willing to discuss anything and everything that could advance its ecological knowledge. Novo's research budget typically runs at 20 percent of sales.

Much of Novo's business is based on its knowledge of enzymes—natural catalysts that speed up chemical reactions. Enzymes are biodegradable, and their use requires up to one-third less energy than do synthetic chemicals to produce an equivalent result. The pharmaceuticals Novo manufactures are based on these biological materials found in Nature.

Novo's philosophy is one of "partnering with Nature." This means more than just finding and extracting value from biota it finds in the natural world. Such partnering also means respecting the biological systems that produce these substances (bioethics), and helping indigenous people, in whose tribal lands these resources are often found, to share in the benefits of their development.

Novo was the first multinational corporation to have a formal bioethics policy. To ensure that this policy remains at the center of corporate strategic planning, Novo has a Committee on Environment and Bioethics, comprising seven corporate vice presidents, that continually reviews the company's impacts and potential impacts.

Novo's internal accounting practices include a series of eco-productivity indices that measure its efficiency in using energy, water, raw materials, and packaging. Marc Epstein and Bill Birchard, co-authors of *Counting What Counts*, say that "these indices also happen to be proxies for normally ultra-sensitive figures on manufacturing efficiency."[4]

At Novo Nordisk, bioethics encompasses all ethical issues related to the use of life science technologies for the development and production of biotechnological and pharmaceutical products, including access to genetic resources, conservation of biodiversity, patenting, labeling, animal welfare, and the safe use of biotechnology.[5]
—Henrik Gurtler, Chairman, Novo Nordisk's Committee on Environment and Bioethics

---

Novo is also well known for its pioneering work in *industrial ecology* at Kalundborg, a small industrial city on Denmark's seacoast. Since the early 1970s it has partnered with other companies to create the world's first eco-industrial park. The Kalundborg model reduces waste through a system of reformulating and selling effluents so the unwanted byproducts of one company become the inputs of others. Novo has proven that by making economic use of their byproducts, companies can generate extra revenues, save on material and disposal costs, and minimize the burden of compliance with increasingly stringent environmental regulations.

The initial participants in the eco-industrial park were a Novo pharmaceutical plant, a coal-fired utility (Asnaes), an oil refinery (Statoil), and a wallboard plant (Gyproc). Instead of dumping its thermal waste into a nearby lake, Asnaes exports steam for heat and power to Novo, Statoil, and 3,500 nearby homes. Scrubber sludge from the cleaning of Asnaes's flue gases is sold to Gyproc, and its fly ash is sold to a company that makes cement and road aggregate. Asnaes's cooling water is piped to fish farms that produce approximately 250 tons of sea trout and turbot each year. The fermentation tanks that Novo uses to produce insulin and enzymes generate a nitrogen-rich slurry that the company delivers as fertilizer (Novogro) free to local farmers, whose crops in turn feed the bacteria in Novo's fermentation tanks. The oil refinery sells to the power station its treated wastewater for steam and its desulfurized waste gas for fuel, and sells its molten sulfur to a nearby chemical plant. There are more exchanges within the system, but the point is made without listing them all: reprocessing and selling waste is more economic than dumping it.

As Novo has learned from its pioneering experiments, eco-data collection, and stakeholder dialogue, it has become more adept at designing plants that optimize the value of its material resources in partnership with Nature. There can be little doubt that these efforts have paid off: Novo is a financial powerhouse. During the past quarter-century (1981–2004), its stock has returned more than double the S&P 500. Novo's gross margin usually exceeds 70 percent. Its return on invested capital (ROIC) consistently tops 20 percent and generates a substantial free cash flow. Consequently, Novo has little need to borrow. Its balance sheet at year-end 2005, as for most years, showed no net debt, because cash and equivalents exceeded debt from all forms of borrowing.

The Systemic Challenge

Companies that think and behave holistically, as Novo does, have advantages in a world that is running down its resources. These advantages are likely to grow as global resource depletion becomes more extreme. In addition to maintaining superior profitability and balance sheet strength, Novo and its LAMP counterparts have developed knowledge and skills the rest of the business world will need to survive in this increasingly stressed environment.

The systemic challenge is so huge it boggles the mind. In order to explain the challenge in "condensed" form, I've borrowed from a few authors who know far more than I about human demands on the biosphere and the rate at which we are weakening the web of life on which we all depend.

Consider, for example, what it takes to sustain the average middle-class U.S. family for a year. According to Hawken, Lovins, and Lovins, to provide for their needs, industry "moves, mines, extracts, shovels, burns, wastes, pumps and disposes of . . . one million pounds of material." Based on 1995 data, the total annual flow of waste in the U.S. industrial system—excluding wastewater—is 50 trillion pounds, of which less than 2 percent is recycled. Thus, over the course of a decade, "500 trillion pounds of American resources will have been transformed into non-productive solids and gases."[6] We clearly can't go on doing this. Many parts of the country are running out of water, soils are becoming depleted, and accumulations of toxic substances threaten our health. Global warming is another problem about which we are only beginning to learn.

Edward O. Wilson puts the systemic challenge into a global biologic perspective. He notes that the accounting systems we use to compute GDP largely ignore Earth's biotic balance sheet and therefore give us a false sense of security. Ecosystems that determine climate and thereby much resource availability, such as the great rainforests and oceans, are being overharvested, polluted, and run down. He describes the convergence of Earth's declining carrying capacity with the rapid growth of population as a bottleneck. Writing in 2001, Wilson summarized the bottleneck as follows:

> Consider that with the global population past six billion and on its way to eight billion or more by mid-century, per-capita fresh water and arable land are descending to levels resource experts agree are risky. The ecological footprint—the average amount of productive land and shallow sea appropriated by each person for food, water, housing, energy, transportation, commerce and waste absorption—is about one hectare (2.5 acres) in developing nations but about 9.6 hectares (24 acres) in

the United States. The footprint for the total human population is 2.1 hectares (5.2 acres). For every person in the world to reach present U.S. levels of consumption with existing technology would require four more planet earths.[7]

With this as a base assumption, projected increases in consumption around the globe—especially in fast-growing countries such as China—on top of estimated population increases, would seem likely to demand the resources of seven or more planet Earths within the next half-century. This, of course, is impossible. Thus, we are compelled to make better use of the resources we now have and to stop running down the biosphere that makes those resources available to us.

Incrementalism Won't Work

The incremental approach of eco-efficiency is insufficient to extract the resources of four more planet Earths, much less seven. To achieve that, *we must radically redesign the way business is done and the products and services it delivers.* We must learn to produce what we consume with Factor Ten effectiveness—making the same goods with only 10 percent of the energy and materials formerly used.[8] This goal has been endorsed by the World Business Council for Sustainable Development (WBCSD), which includes many global LAMP companies. Eco-effectiveness is viewed by most of those companies as a strategic imperative.

Although most people don't know the breadth and depth of the systemic challenges as presented here, they are nevertheless aware of the world gone awry in a general sense. People experience it physically and emotionally as heart and respiratory diseases, cancer, stress, depression, substance abuse, and the decline of civility. They feel it viscerally in urban sprawl, over-crowding, traffic jams, trashed public places, polluted waterways, and the shrinking of our forests and farms. They respond to it by buying bottled water, organic foods, and goods made from certified forest products; by flocking to parks, zoos, and eco-tourism destinations; by choosing to work for organizations that are pushing the frontiers of eco-stewardship; and by surrounding themselves at home and work with plants and aquariums. Collectively, these experiences and responses are like the gathering of a giant wave. Particle by particle they may be indiscernible. But collectively, their direction is unmistakable, their force unstoppable, and their momentum accelerating.

Companies that understand the strategic challenge and aim for eco-effective factor productivity gains, as Novo has done, have huge advantages over those that deny the challenge exists or that try to resist the oncoming wave. Yet, as advanced as Novo and other LAMP companies may be in comparison with their peers, given the immense scale of the challenge, they have only scratched the surface.

Letting the present situation continue "as is" is not a viable option. The traditional, mechanistic approach to running a business does not work in a tightly connected and interdependent biological world. Global LAMP companies are successful because they recognize they are living communities whose primary assets are living assets (people and Nature) and because they are skilled at symbiotically leveraging those assets. When they take this path, they arouse our spirits and our biophilic instincts. Even though these companies, in their operations, are far from the solutions we ultimately need, people want to affiliate with them. If nothing else, theirs is a gesture of hope.

Nature is ours to explore forever; it is our crucible and our refuge; it is our natural home; It Is all these things.[9]

— Edward O. Wilson, *The Future of Life*

The Business Challenge

The economic and systemic challenges described cannot be met by orthodox methods. Generally accepted accounting principles that favor nonliving assets over living assets are blind to the bottlenecks forming within the global economy and mislead corporations into self-destructive behaviors.

Seeing this, LAMP companies have created a new set of rules within the framework of free-market capitalism that coalesce around Living Asset Stewardship. The pioneers of LAS long ago decided they could not wait for accountants and governments to sanctify a new conceptual model of enterprise. They had to deal. For them it was either adapt or die.

The eco-challenges for corporations are huge and press on five fronts, each of which impacts productivity and profitability:

- cost competitiveness
- employee morale
- customer trust and loyalty
- license to operate
- survival of the corporation

The eco-stewardship of Focus Group companies, although expressed in different ways, has given them economic advantages. Samples of some best practices follow.

Cost competitiveness. 3M reports that it has prevented the generation of 1.6 billion pounds of pollution and saved $810 million through its "Pollution Prevention Pays" (3P) program.[10] (Because these numbers include only first-year savings, rather than cumulative savings, they are very conservative.) The 3P program was introduced in 1975 to eliminate pollution at the source rather than remove it after the fact.

The program integrates industrial ecology principles into 3M's product formulations, equipment and process designs, and recycling/reuse programs. The company's managers use homegrown sustainability metrics to monitor wastes and develop new solutions. Managers of all business units are evaluated, in part, by a "waste ratio"—with a red line separating those who achieve goals from those who do not. Those whose activities fall below the line must justify the fact in writing.

Because many of 3M's products are chemical-based (coatings and adhesives), the company has devoted a large portion of its R&D budget since 1990 to reducing the toxicity and adverse impacts of its products and processes. In 1994, it completed development of a closed-loop system, called the Brayton Cycle, to capture and recycle solvents. In 1997 3M developed hydrofluoroethers (HFEs) as a replacement for ozone-depleting chlorofluorocarbons (CFCs), opening a huge potential market. In 2000, on the day 3M announced the phaseout of its "Scotchguard" line of water-repellent products (due to environmental concerns about fluorocarbons), and the end of its production of perfluorooctanyl sulphonate and perfluorooctanoic acid, its stock rose by 5 percent. In spite of the $200 million projected cost of the phaseout, it was clear to investors that the long-term benefits of eliminating toxic chemical exposure far outweighed phaseout costs.

Today, in support of the global quest for cheap, clean energy, 3M supplies membrane electrode assemblies (MEAs) for processing materials used in making fuel cells. As they have done so many times before, 3M scientists saw MEAs as a way to leverage their expertise into an area that would make the company and its customers more eco-effective. To support such long-lead initiatives, 3M has an in-house venture capital system. This system has been invaluable not only for the breakthroughs it has produced, but because it continually affirms to employees 3M's commitment to eco-stewardship and the hope of better things to come.

When 3M designs new products or redesigns old ones, it uses proactive life cycle analysis (LCA) and design for environment (DfE) techniques that consider the total systemic impacts and costs of a product from cradle-to-grave (inception to disposal) and from cradle-to-cradle (inception to reformulation into something new). It is a far more comprehensive approach than the traditional one of looking at manufacturing and delivery costs only. It has created countless positive feedback effects in terms of innovation, customer loyalty, employee morale, and lower legal and regulatory costs.

Since the 1975 introduction of the 3P program, 3M stock has regularly outperformed the S&P 500 Index. Its pioneering efforts in eco-effectiveness have created a learning organization that is transforming the way we use chemistry—a vital contribution to a world now suffocating in toxic waste.

Pollution (waste materials) + *Knowledge* (technology) = *Potential Resources*
—Rationale behind 3M's Pollution Prevention Pays (3P) program

---

Employee morale and productivity. Canon employees are inspired by the company's respect for life, as expressed in its kyosei philosophy, Environmental Charter, and organic management approach. The ideals of the charter appeal to the hearts and biophilic instincts of employees "to harmonize environmental and economic interests in all business activities, products and services . . . . offer products with lower environmental burden through innovative improvements in resource efficiency, and eliminate anti-social activities that threaten the health and safety of mankind and the environment."[11]

These ideals are highly integrated into Canon's networked organization. Employees have extraordinary personal freedom to pursue insights that might lead to eco-effective solutions, and they respond with hundreds of thousands of ideas and innovations each year.[12]Included among these are technologies—such as amorphous silicon solar panels developed at its Environment Engineering Center—that either save or create the energy needed to operate Canon's products. According to the U.S. Patent Office, Canon has been consistently among the top three recipients (by number of patents) since the early 1990s.[13]

By modeling Nature in its organization, Canon's goals of living in harmony with Nature take on added meaning to employees. The firm's networked organization is totally consistent and congruent with its life-affirming kyosei philosophy. The principle of subsidiarity operates everywhere.

Canon's integrated approach to environmental management inspires employees and gives them the support they need to innovate. Its environmental accounting system, introduced in 1983, discloses data for all operating facilities individually and in the aggregate. Environmental and economic goals are integrated in all corporate activities. Company-wide, Canon is committed to Factor Ten innovation. Its Design for Manufacturing Center employs DfE and LCA on all products. Its Global Environment Information Network, introduced in 1999, is an intranet that allows all 184 consolidated subsidiary companies in the Canon Group to "collect and share environmental information." The network also helps in green procurement and in managing chemicals and industrial wastes. Canon's advanced monitoring systems seek recycling and waste elimination possibilities on more than 230 emissions, and register some 9,000 chemicals used in production, assigning a registration number and a risk evaluation to each. The most hazardous chemicals are targeted for elimination. Canon's annual environmental report gives detailed breakdowns of emissions and sets detailed goals. Like Novo, Canon uses this report as a means of reaching out to the public for critical feedback that could enhance its organizational learning.

Canon's EQCD Concept—Environment, Quality, Cost, Delivery—sets a standard of excellence that constructively challenges employees to think in terms of factor efficiencies. It says "Companies are not qualified to manufacture goods if they cannot provide environment assurance . . . .

Companies are not qualified to market goods if they cannot produce quality goods . . . . Companies are not qualified to compete if they cannot meet cost and delivery requirements."[14] One can imagine a day when Canon's "environmental assurance activities" will include not only energy-saving information technologies (IT), but also the solar energy capacity to run them cheaply and independently.

Inspired employees have made Canon a global productivity leader. During the past three decades (1975–2005), return on the company's stock has been more than 10 times that of the S&P 500 Index. In that time, Canon has vaulted past its once-dominant U.S. rivals Kodak (cameras) and Xerox (copiers). At year-end 2005 Canon's market capitalization ($53 billion) was worth more than twice as much as Kodak ($7 billion) and Xerox ($14 billion) combined.

Canon's Environmental Assurance

In the interest of world prosperity and the happiness of humankind, pursue maximization of resource efficiency, and contribute to the creation of a society that practices sustainable development.

—from the Canon Environmental Charter

Customer trust and loyalty. Johnson & Johnson's credo, which has become its corporate "trustmark," puts a higher priority on environmental protection than on profit. Design for environment (DfE), computer-based tools create safer, less resource-intensive products with less waste, less cost, and with shorter cycle times. Johnson & Johnson (J&J) earns trust by making its products healthful and safe not only for people, but also, increasingly, for the environment. Responding to customer concerns, J&J has virtually eliminated animal testing from nonmedicinal products and has significantly reduced it in pharmaceuticals. In 1998, the company became a lead sponsor of the Johns Hopkins University Center for Alternatives to Animal Testing. These programs strengthen J&J's already-strong reputation for integrity, and have made it the most trusted U.S. company.[15]

Johnson & Johnson knows that deep customer trust and loyalty can be earned only through the integrity of its products and processes. The company's DfE tools do this by cataloging the regulatory, health, and environmental aspects of thousands of reagents and materials it uses in research and manufacturing. This database of knowledge helps product designers to reduce development costs by "getting it right the first time," and to lower material costs by eliminating wasteful use of resources. Using DfE, a Swiss affiliate's (Cilag AG) production of an asthma treatment and a thrombin inhibitor required only half the number of synthesis steps of a typical product-development process. According to the company, "the asthma treatment saw a 65% increase in yield with an 82% reduction in solvents, while the thrombin inhibitor yield increased by a factor of five with a 44% reduction in solvent use."[16] DfE reduced Cilag's waste streams, made its manufacturing processes safer, improved product quality, cut material costs, and improved speed to market. It was a win for consumers, employees, the company, and the environment.

Johnson & Johnson expresses its concern for life in its environmental motto: "Healthy People, Healthy Planet, Healthy Futures." Like the J&J credo itself—which puts care for patients, nurses, doctors, employees, communities, and the environment ahead of profits—the motto is a clear and uplifting statement of intent. It looks beyond the bottom line to the health of the total web of life. This kind of symbiotic thinking forms the foundation of J&J's trust.

During the past 30 years (1975–2005), J&J stock has tallied nearly five times the return of the S&P 500 Index. The company today is by far the world's largest healthcare business. Whatever sum it has spent to build the public trust it now enjoys has returned many times over in profit.

J&J ranks first or second on every one of the eight key [reputation] measures— the hallmark of a true industry leader.[17]

—Jeffrey T. Resnik, "A Matter of Reputation," *Pharmaceutical Executive*

License to operate. Hewlett-Packard believes that "Good citizenship is good business." Like all LAMP companies, HP considers eco-stewardship part of its license to operate. This "license" is based mainly on public trust and acceptance, although it is also written into laws governing the environment and public safety. To HP, it means being welcome in host communities and having access to the employees, resources, and markets it needs to grow.

An important part of HP's citizenship initiative is a new, 100-percent recycling system for used computer equipment based in Nashville,

Tennessee. When such equipment is buried in landfills, rather than recycled, it presents a high risk that hazardous materials—such as heavy metals and other toxic substances in batteries, mercury lamps, switches, solder lead, and other items—will leach into the ground and ultimately, into community water supplies. This poses major risks to public health, local ecosystems, and community quality of life. Given the rapid obsolescence and disposal of much computer equipment, this is already an immense problem. HP's Nashville plant recycles used equipment from both the U.S. and Canada, creating a multiple-win solution that benefits communities, Nature, customers, and the company alike.

Recycling has long been central to HP product design. In 1988 it created a Product Recycling Solutions (PRS) team to help design equipment for easy recycling and to create cost-effective recycling methods. HP's Nashville recycling system was designed by this team in collaboration with Micro Metallics, a subsidiary of Noranda. Product that cannot be harvested for parts or reused, moves through a plant where it is shredded, granulated, separated, and sorted for remanufacturing. The system allows HP to recover everything, including precious metals. To make future recycling more cost-effective, HP also redesigns its computers, learning from one generation to the next, so they can be more easily stripped for parts before recycling. Products are now designed for end-of-life as well as lifetime performance. Solutions include, for example, reducing the number of plastics used from 15 to 2, and placing all hazardous materials in one corner of a circuit board to make them easier to remove.

The final piece of the puzzle involves getting the materials back into our own products. This should reduce the cost of the supply chain for all materials, increasing our competitive advantage and reducing the environmental impact."[18]

— Renee St. Denis, PRS Manager, Hewlett-Packard

For HP, the advantages of this proactive approach are considerable: lower material costs, increased customer satisfaction, higher employee morale, and greater public trust. Beyond securing its license to operate in the communities it serves, HP's experience affects future legislation on product take-back and recycling, which will confer a significant competitive advantage on it and other competent recyclers.

Taking the high road and serving community has been integral to HP's culture since its founding in 1939. The innovations inspired by HP's idealism have far exceeded the costs of its citizenship initiatives. HP shares have outrun the S&P 500 by approximately five to one during the last 30 years (1975–2005). The $8.7 billion excess of cash over debt on HP's balance sheet at the end of fiscal 2005 affirms the company's seriousness about maintaining its idealistic culture and retaining its license to operate.

Survival of the corporation. Stora Enso's culture of "shared responsibility" has much to do with its unrivaled longevity. Having arisen from a small rural community in Sweden, and from a mining enterprise in which the lives of workers were continually in each other's hands, it developed a symbiotic culture of respecting life, working for the common good, and planning ahead for the next generation. It is remarkable that this culture has endured for 700+ years—through multiple ownership and management changes, and through episodes of war, plague, economic depression, technology change, and resource depletion. That it has is testament to its inherent strength.

The notion of shared responsibility is deeply familial, conveying a sense of shared destiny, mutual caring, and trust. People long for these experiences in their hearts and, finding them in an organization, will do their utmost to perpetuate the enterprise. In a very general sense, that is why I think Stora has lived so long.

Shared responsibility is also deeply ecological. It is the way living networks operate: the parts serve the whole and vice versa. Like ecosystems, businesses that work this way continually refresh themselves from within and so, are able to live long lives.

When shared responsibility becomes a reality rather than a slogan in an organization, people naturally want to affiliate with it. That is why LAMP companies tend to attract the best employees, customers, strategic partners, and investors. This power of attraction, combined with the inner integrity of Living Asset Stewardship, drives a reinforcing cycle of affirmation and strength that works much like the reinforcing cycle of LAS + OL.

Stora strengthens its enterprise and ensures its longevity by minimizing waste. In 2003, its waste-utilization rate, expressed as the percentage of residuals being used for beneficial purposes, was 96 percent. Its Imatra mills on the southern coast of Finland generate 90 percent of the power they need by burning dried, fibrous sludge from their landfills. They also pipe methane gas from the landfills to microturbine power plants that generate electricity for sale back to the grid. By increasing its use of biofuels rather than oil, Stora's mills have improved their energy efficiency and significantly reduced greenhouse gas emissions.

In collaboration with the World Wildlife Fund and other stakeholder groups, Stora has also been a leader in protecting old-growth forests whose biodiversity is an important genetic resource for future generations. Virtually all Stora's own forest land, as well as that leased for harvesting, is certified by the Forest Stewardship Council or equivalent authorities as being responsibly managed, and most of the wood fiber it buys from third parties must also be thus certified. Stora uses a "chain-of-custody" audit system to verify the integrity of these fiber supplies. Its target is "that all fiber sources be fully sustainable and recognized as such by all stakeholders."[19]

Stora Enso clearly understands that the quality of its stewardship is the best assurance of its longevity. When it enters a community, it considers the total impacts of its operations and invests in social infrastructure as part of its license to operate. Helping communities build roads, schools, and hospitals involves extra expense, but the payoff in good will and employee commitment is huge.

Within its industry, Stora is the sustainability leader[20] and by far the most financially secure. At year-end 2005, its debt-equity ratio (56 percent) was less than half that of its largest global competitor, International Paper (132 percent), in spite of its more conservative accounting procedures. Also noteworthy, Stora has grown its capacity during the five years ending in 2005, while International Paper has been forced to shed billions of dollars in assets by selling forest land and closing mills in order to reduce debt and tighten financial operations. In a world of overstressed forest resources, I believe Stora's market share gains speak to the coherence of its culture of shared responsibility, which is based on ecological values, community care, and fiscal prudence. People want to affiliate with it because they trust its values and believe it is headed in the right direction.

Maintaining Discipline

To achieve cost effectiveness, high employee morale, customer loyalty, community trust (license to operate), and longevity, companies must manage their eco-stewardship as professionally as they do their production and marketing. This requires creating meaningful goals and information feedback systems that keep the company continually moving toward those goals. Novo Nordisk's eco-productivity indices and Canon's Global Environment Information Network are examples of such systems; Baxter International also belongs in this elite group.

Baxter uses a balanced scorecard metric system that applies dollar-based measures to merge the agendas of its environmental and financial managers. Its 2003 sustainability report offers a summary "Environmental Financial Statement" that matches environmental savings against costs for projects initiated in the past year. It also shows aggregate savings from projects initiated in prior years that impact current-year results. Total income, savings, and cost avoidance for 2004 totaled $82 million, up from $59 million in the prior year. Because of its experience and skill with environmental accounting, Baxter can now confidently forecast the future financial impacts of environmental product and process improvements. Confident forecasting allows them to design products that are more eco-effective and generate new environmental consulting services to client hospitals.

Baxter's experience with environmental accounting goes back to the early 1980s when it started measuring its scrap rate. As a result of its learning since then, Baxter recycles or reuses virtually everything that can be recovered. Its annual sustainability report details the tonnage of materials saved and the effect on company finances. It also reports on its usage of water and energy in relation to set goals, and the savings accomplished as they near or attain those goals.

Between 1996 and 2004 Baxter achieved a 22-percent improvement in energy efficiency and a 35-percent reduction in greenhouse gas (GHG) emissions per unit of production. Baxter estimates that the investments it has made in these areas from 2000–2005 yielded $80 million in savings and cost avoidance in 2004, with $9 million of that from energy savings alone. According to Ron Meissen, senior director of worldwide Environmental, Health, and Safety (EHS) resources at Baxter, "The benefits go far beyond cost avoidance and energy or raw material savings . . . . Many of the initiatives we have put in place have yielded higher quality levels, greater production output and flexibility, [and] reduced waste, as well as improvements in workplace safety."[21]

As part of its strategy to put an economic value on its GHG emissions, in January 2003 Baxter became a charter member of the Chicago Climate Exchange—a voluntary consortium whose members are committed either to reduce emissions by 1 percent per year during a four-year period, or to purchase sufficient carbon credits to meet their program commitments. To ensure accuracy, each company works with external GHG auditors in establishing baseline emissions and annual target levels. The two main benefits of this exercise are deeper insight into the company's production processes and clarity of purpose. The message to all business units is clear: GHG emissions are costs that must be contained and managers will be accountable for containing them.

Baxter is the leading company on climate change in the healthcare arena and it takes action with goals that suit its corporate purpose as a healthcare company.[22]   —Richard L. Sandor, CEO, Chicago Climate Exchange

---

From an economic perspective, Baxter is one of the most interesting cases in this book because it is currently recovering from a period of global oversupply in plasma products—its main profit earner and a product line in which it is the global quality leader. Unlike the other Focus Group companies, it did not outrun the S&P 500 during the past 30 years (1975–2005). Baxter's stock dropped by approximately 70 percent between March 2002 and March 2003, a precipitous fall that caused it to fall marginally behind that index.

Baxter closed marginal facilities and laid off 3,500 people, or 7 percent of its workforce—moves that called into question its humanistic culture and capacity for strategic planning. In May 2004 Moody's lowered Baxter's long-held credit rating (A3) one notch to Baa1, which was a delayed and relatively mild reaction to the company's difficulties.

Moody's restraint reflects, in large part, its belief in Baxter's integrity and the strength of its core competencies. Although still too early to tell how the company will emerge from its stumble, it has held to its ethical principles, balanced scorecard disciplines, and fastidious eco-accounting standards. Rather than throw these principles and practices aside, or worse, blame its recent difficulties on them, it remains at the vanguard of the stewardship movement. By proving itself to be fully committed—or conversely, not a "fair weather steward"—Baxter has maintained the confidence of employees. These are grounds for hope.

In the meantime, though it took some large write-downs in 2002, Baxter has maintained a strong stream of free cash flow, supported by some innovative product introductions in its primary markets.[23] It has also been rebuilding its balance sheet by reducing debt and stockpiling cash. In doing so, Baxter is assuring stakeholders that it intends to remain an innovative force both in medical technology and in its stewardship practices.

Baxter's experience raises a crucial point about LAMP companies. Their cultures are resilient and self-healing *because they maintain their stewardship disciplines during difficult times.* They do this with the confidence that LAS is not an ethical luxury, but a business stance that strengthens a company from within. Thus, when LAMP companies make mistakes, as all companies do, their odds of returning to robust health are far better than average.

Industrial Metabolism

Companies are living systems—communities of interacting elements or organisms (such as people and Nature)—that use resources in their metabolic activities. The metabolisms of the healthiest ones use resources and energy most effectively, whereas the least healthy dissipate their strength by wasting energy and resources (aka entropy), and eventually self-destruct.

This analysis fits with the previous observation that LAMP companies are longer lived on average than traditionally managed ones. The LAMP 60 have average and median lives exceeding 100 years—more than double the average age of S&P 500 and MSCI companies. LAMP companies are not perfect: even the best of them, like human beings, have metabolisms that are dissipative. But, like humans and all other living systems, they have a capacity to self-heal and regenerate that traditional companies lack. It is for this reason that so many LAMP companies measure their ages in centuries.

This chapter began with a discussion of the enormous amounts of waste generated by the U.S. and world economies. Such waste is entropic, and a sign of poor health. But within this waste stream lies an opportunity that is potentially very large. If 94 percent of the energy and materials used each year is wasted, and a mere 6 percent actually adds to our quality of life, then mining that waste stream is a good opportunity for profit. Framed this way, the picture for Factor Ten (or greater) efficiencies seems positive, indeed.

Who will realize these profits remains to be seen. But it is a good bet that LAMP companies will be in the vanguard because they have such a head start.

Conclusion

It is astonishing that our industrial metabolism converts so little of the energy and materials it consumes into product, and that so much of our waste poisons the biospheric web of life. If corporations and mankind want to survive and thrive into the indefinite future, we must rebalance this ratio of product to waste, and ensure that whatever waste is generated becomes food for Nature or another industrial process via recycling.

The best corporations understand this and strive for Factor Ten efficiencies—a 90-percent reduction in energy and materials used to make the same goods. Like Novo Nordisk, they look for natural processes or substances (e.g., enzymes) to replace artificial ones that are toxic to the environment (i.e., most synthetic chemicals). Like 3M and Canon, they use DfE and LCA to squeeze waste out of products and processes while simultaneously working on alternative energy offers (e.g., fuel cells at 3M or solar cells at Canon). Like HP, the best companies push the frontiers of recycling and public service to maintain their licenses to operate. Like Baxter International, they develop disciplined eco-accounting systems that guide corporate strategy. And like Johnson & Johnson, they are so consistent in their eco-effectiveness that they become magnets to the very people they need to propel them forward.

What is the magnetic appeal of eco-stewardship leaders? Why do they attract the best people and, like Stora Enso does, hold their loyalty? I believe it is because we humans know we are linked completely and inseparably to Nature. When corporations run down the biosphere and their own metabolic sustainability, we sense it and are repelled. Alternately, when corporations try to do the right thing, even if they fail in their efforts, we are attracted and become attached to them. Our biophilic instincts—an expression of our quantum knowing about the web of life—tell us they are worthy of our trust and loyalty.

If we react more passionately to corporate bioethics today than we did 10 years ago, it is because we intuitively know that we *must act*. We will not stand idly by and watch the web of life unravel. Our survival instincts compel us to take a stand. That is why our growing awareness of the environmental stakes is accompanied by a desire to affiliate with companies that are eco-stewardship leaders. As employees, consumers, and investors, our preferences shift, and that conveys economic advantages on stewardship companies. The Global LAMP Index® merely reveals the results.

Customer Intimacy

"[T]he only possible source of sustainable competitive advantage in
the new economy will be the bonds of loyalty you generate . . . . The
bottom line is this: a 5 percent increase in customer retention rates
increases profits by 25 percent to 95 percent."[1]
—Frederick F. Reichheld, Director Emeritus, Bain & Company

Baxter International trimmed executive bonuses for 2001 because its
dialysis filters had played a role in the deaths of 53 patients in seven
countries, including the U.S. Baxter executives had met all of their
2001 performance goals for sales, income, and cash flow, and the company's
stock outperformed most of its rivals in the drug and medical-products
industries. Under normal circumstances, hitting or exceeding operational
performance targets would mean the top 20 Baxter executives would
receive 100 percent or more of their target bonuses. Instead, every top-line
executive, including CEO Harry Kraemer, was cut back. Meanwhile, Baxter
recalled all of its outstanding filters and budgeted $150 million for plant
closures and compensation to victims' families.

To Kraemer, there was no alternative. Baxter's reputation for quality and
safety, and its close relationships with hospitals and patients, were among
its most important assets. The company had to reaffirm its total commit-

ment to patient safety—not only to its hospital customers, but also to all its worldwide employees. I talked with Jenni Cawein, a member of Baxter's Sustainable Development Team, shortly after the bonus cutback announcement. She spoke of the sadness she and other employees had felt on learning of the patient deaths, and how they later felt uplifted and inspired by Baxter's quick and decisive remedial actions.

Why would Baxter's employees feel such a personal affinity with high-risk patients and such sadness at the deaths of some? Employees at many companies would have blocked out the human tragedy or accepted that such deaths were less attributable to them than to the hospital or the patients' original condition. But that was not Baxter's culture. There, employees at every level are taught to empathize with patients and to feel personally involved.

At Baxter's Hyland Immuno Division—which operates in the difficult and exacting market of hemophilia and HIV therapies—employees are trained in visualization as a way of building empathy for patients and team commitment to service. The process begins by "embedding a powerful and true vision of the customer . . . and manifesting that vision in all the activities of the company."[2] Hyland invites employees to participate in programs that bring them face-to-face with patients. Peter O'Malley, VP sales, explains: "Our philosophy is to make the customer come alive every way we can . . . . The customer is always present in our minds and in the culture and in the feelings of this organization. We talk about customers all the time—not only at national sales or quarterly meetings."[3] Baxter salespeople often accompany doctors on grand rounds in order to become more familiar with patients' needs. Managers help hospitals and clinics solve expense and logistical problems along the entire service chain through frequent consultation and total supply solutions. Back office and sales support workers volunteer to help run summer hemophilia camps for children. Writing in the *Gallup Management Journal,* Guido de Koning notes, "After 14 years of camp visits by employees, there are several hundred in the organization who share this experience and thereby collectively understand how their work affects the ability of the entire organization to deliver value to customers . . . . [A]ll the members of an organization [should] face the customer . . . [to gain] intellectual and emotional knowledge of the customer [and have] a picture of . . . the customer waiting there for [them]."[4]

Baxter sees patient care and hospital care as integral. Through their meticulous care of supply needs along the entire hospital service chain—from nurses to doctors to technical support teams—the company saves millions in health-delivery costs and frees caregivers to devote more time and energy to patient well-being. One service provides virtually all the supplies needed for a surgical procedure in one customized package, thus saving huge amounts of expensive hospital time, labor, and inventory management.

Baxter's deep attention to the needs of its customers transcends profit and executive compensation. It probably could have settled the problems surrounding its dialysis filters for much less than $150 million. At a time when other healthcare companies with lesser safety records were richly rewarding executives, it could have topped up executive bonuses. But it didn't. And that mattered. Harry Kraemer opted instead to reaffirm Baxter's mission: *"We are in the business of saving and enhancing lives."* He knew instinctively that without a total dedication to that mission of deep customer care, the company would lose its spirit; and if it lost its spirit, it would eventually lose its capacities to serve, innovate, and generate repeat business.

Deep customer knowledge and breakthrough insights about the client's underlying processes are the backbone of every customer-intimate organization today . . . . Baxter International knows more about the use and management of supplies in a hospital than any of its clients . . .[5]
—Michael Treacy and Fred Wiersema, *The Discipline of Market Leaders*

Respect for Life

If we look further into Baxter's organization, we see that the respect it shows for patients and hospitals is part of a larger culture of respect for life. This culture makes their commitment to customer intimacy more congruent and believable. Within the Global LAMP Index,® few companies can match Baxter's respect for Nature and eco-effectiveness. Like Novo, it has a corporate policy on bioethics, its environmental accounting systems and public disclosure reflect global "best practices," and it is committed to the triple bottom line of economic, environmental, and social performance.[6]

Baxter is effective in conveying its respect for life inside the company because it uses a balanced scorecard to assess not only its financial results (lagging indicators), but also, its impacts on the larger living systems that sustain it (leading indicators of public trust). In language all employees can understand, it measures and communicates the company's various environmental impacts; it shows workers the cost savings on pollution controls and reduced packaging, as well as revenues derived from recycling. This allows employees at every level to participate more fully in contributing to solutions. Baxter also tracks the environmental practices of suppliers and coaches them in improving their performance. In 1999, it agreed to phase out PVC (polyvinyl chloride) materials in its IV (intravenous) healthcare products because it was convinced that their manufacturing and disposal used and released chemicals that were harmful to human health and the environment

Baxter's respect for life also touches employees. OSHA (the federal Occupational Safety and Health Administration) consistently rates Baxter as an exemplar in safety and health management. *BusinessWeek* has named Baxter one of the top 30 "family friendly" companies in the U.S., and the firm is continually rated at the top of "best workplace" surveys for its care of employees. Baxter treats employees like partners—keeping them informed about balanced scorecard priorities via a real-time intranet system, and offering all stock options via a Global Stock Option Plan. And, knowing how critical they are to morale and performance, Baxter's office of business ethics also helps employees deal with ethical questions as they come up.

Baxter's respect for life also extends out to the communities in which it operates. At the local level, it encourages employees to get involved with community activities, backs their volunteerism with matching grants, and supports healthcare for children and the poor. Globally, it supports the U.N. Global Compact, the Kyoto Protocol, and the U.N. Universal Declaration of Human Rights.

In sum, Baxter's holistic respect for life arises from awareness that in all living systems, everything is connected to everything else. Congruence matters. In order to achieve customer intimacy and excellent service, the company must be a leader in serving life.

What It Takes

The term "customer intimacy" emerged from the Harvard Business School in the late 1970s. I have expanded on that definition, based on our Living Asset Stewardship research, and contrasted it in Table 9-1 with the definition of the more-traditional approach.

Table 9-1: Defining Customer Intimacy

CUSTOMER-INTIMATE APPROACH	TRADITIONAL APPROACH
Philosophy and Purpose	
Emphasizes customer needs (results)	Emphasizes company wants (profit)
Seeks total solution: qualitative approach	Seeks quick sale: quantitative approach
Respects customer values (emotional bonding)	Is values-neutral
Seeks to improve customer value continually	Seeks greatest sales with least effort
Serves employees, like customers, by listening	Tells employees what to do
Approach to Customer	
Desire for relationship (infinite approach)	Desire for transactions (finite approach)
Spirit of caring and trust (win-win)	"Get what you can" (win-lose)
Listening, empathy (How can we help you?)	Hard sell (What can we sell you?)
Open communication at all levels	Set channels of communication (bureaucratic)
Brainstorming with/on the side of customer	One-size-fits-all customer surveys
Seeking unexpressed/unmet needs (proactive)	Responding to visible demand (reactive)
Continual readiness to serve	Service at seller's convenience
Value Proposition	
Benefits (effectiveness, ease of use)	Product or service
Getting what customer wants when it's needed	Getting what the "market" wants
Total product responsibility (DfE + take-back)	Limited warranty
Competitive cost through life cycle	Competitive initial cost
Quality, durable goods	Planned obsolescence

Companies that deeply respect their customers understand how people's emotional needs are often as important as their economic needs. Customers are usually looking for more than simple physical goods or finite services. They want solutions that answer their psychic needs as well—for ethics, caring, empathy, trust, loyalty, responsiveness, and commitment.

Consumer research shows that customers buy with their hearts as well as their wallets, and they generally prefer to trade with companies that practice good stewardship. RoperASW, which has been tracking Americans' preferences for green products since 1990, affirms this. Its 2002 "Green Gauge Report" stated: "Consumers are trading out of what is unimportant (products and services that don't fit into the future) and trading into the future (the life that I want for me and my family)." In terms of buying preferences, it noted that 9 percent of Americans are committed "green" buyers; another 6 percent are "greenback greens" who buy green when price, quality, and convenience meet their standards; and a further 31 percent are "sprouts," who go back and forth on green issues. Most important, the 15 percent who are the most committed green buyers come from educated, upper-income households whose buying tends to influence others.[7] Consumers in Europe and Japan are even more environmentally conscious.[8]

We also know from corporate environmental and sustainability reports that companies increasingly look to a vendor's ethics and social responsibility in making purchasing decisions. Every manufacturer in the Global LAMP Index,[®] for example, manages its supply chain with a view toward some greater good. Most have guidelines that favor ethical vendors with compatible LAS values. The best ones, like Baxter, partner with vendors to discover more eco-effective and socially constructive solutions. If you want a LAMP company to buy from you these days, you had better know its corporate values and be prepared to think of tailored, synergistic, multiple-win solutions. If you don't, someone who does these things is likely to take your place.

Customer-intimate service focuses on relationships rather than on the next transaction. It is built on a spirit of caring and trust: the company doesn't win unless the customer wins. To build this level of caring and trust, customer-intimate companies are good and empathic listeners. They try to put themselves in the customer's place, anticipate unexpressed or unmet needs, and are continually ready to serve.

Southwest Airlines, for example, offers people the "freedom to fly" rather than a finite segment of air travel. Its goal is to "Meet customers' short-haul travel needs . . . make fares competitive with the automobile . . . and minimize total travel time, including ticketing and boarding."[9] Southwest offers further benefits by addressing the total travel needs of customers—including auto rentals and hotels—via its website. Most customers find using this service more efficient, convenient, and responsive than using conventional travel agents. This service also provides an incremental source of commission revenues to Southwest. Unlike other airlines, when load factors in a market rise, rather than boosting fares, Southwest adds flights—another customer-friendly gesture.

As a result of Southwest's rapid turnaround times at the gate combined with their fuel-efficient Boeing 737 jets, the airline's fuel-efficiency ratings are the highest in its peer group. The savings that Southwest achieves as a result of its efficiency get passed on to customers in lower fares.

According to a 2001 study by the federal Department of Transportation, Southwest saves travelers more than $6 billion a year through its low fares and the competitive response it forces from other airlines. Employees take pride in this because it affirms the value of their work. They care that customers get what they want when they want it— low everyday fares and cheerful service—because they, too, are treated with respect and heart throughout the company.

Respect Everywhere

If companies want caring, cheerful people who are eager to serve customers, they must model that behavior in everything they do. This means fostering respect everywhere. When executives respect and serve employees, the spirit of caring cascades through the organization and out to customers. This is the leverage in servant leadership discussed in Chapter 7.

Southwest Airlines shows its respect for employees by meticulously serving them in their professional and family lives.[10] In 1973 it became the first airline to offer a profit sharing plan to employees. Virtually all employees are stockholders. Although heavily unionized, Southwest has excellent labor relations because it puts the team's interests ahead of those of executives. Chairman and founder, Herb Kelleher, goes without perks that would separate him from frontline employees. He and other executives have joined employees to handle baggage or hand out peanuts during heavy traffic periods—gestures that reinforce Southwest's culture of service. On occasion, Kelleher and other executives have also gone without pay to show their willingness to sacrifice for the sake of the team.

We are committed to provide our Employees a stable work environment with equal opportunity for learning and personal growth . . . . Above all, Employees will be provided the same concern, respect, and caring attitude within the organization that they are expected to share externally with every Southwest Customer.[11]

—The Mission of Southwest Airlines (January 1988)

When Southwest hires, it looks for attitude—friendly people who want to help others and have fun in the process. This goal is so important to Southwest's culture and customer service that the airline hires fewer than 5 percent of all job applicants. Though employees never let their spirit of fun dilute their professionalism, they know their fun-loving attitude goes a long way toward reducing the stress of travel and helping customers to relax. Southwest's Culture Committee sees to that by bringing together employees from all over the company to brainstorm about ways to help or serve one another in performing their jobs, thereby making the customer's experience more enjoyable. The committee's mission is to foster care and respect throughout the company by "attending to matters of the heart."

All the important elements of Southwest's business model distill down to this one: respect for people. The company serves communities that are underserved by the major hub carriers. Rather than force customers to travel through expensive, congested areas, Southwest respects their time and pocketbooks by coming to them. This strategy respects employees, as well, because the operating advantages of smaller airports—where passengers, planes, and baggage can be serviced more quickly—reduce work stress. Employees spend less time commuting and more time with their families.

The business outcomes of Southwest's respectful model are impressive. It is consistently ranked as the nation's best-managed and most-profitable airline. It regularly wins the "triple crown" award for having the fewest delays, the lowest level of lost baggage, and the fewest customer complaints. Southwest gives people "the freedom to fly" by respecting their time, their finances, and their peace of mind, and by respecting the needs of employees who, in turn, serve customers with care, humor, and heart.

Making Customers Feel Valued

Southwest succeeds in its consumer-oriented business because it makes customers feel valued. It delivers on its promises by consistently being there when customers need them with pleasant, affordable service. But what about serving corporate customers who have more complex needs? Customer-intimate companies approach them in the same spirit—by making them feel valued and cared for.

HSBC, which calls itself "the World's Local Bank," makes its corporate customers feel valued by "being there for them" wherever they operate. Customers get quick, knowledgeable attention because they are served at the local level by expert people who care about their success. It is a partnership approach: each business customer is served by a team led by a senior relationship manager, who is responsible for total service, plus appropriate product specialists. These specialists understand a spectrum of risks that may affect the customer's business performance, including environmental and employee health and safety risks. Multinational corporate clients are served by a Global Relationship Manager, who is supported by regional and local relationship managers with special knowledge of local conditions, and by an Advisory Relationship Manager (from HSBC's Investment Bank), who helps develop flexible financial solutions. The expertise and global knowledge these people bring often allow them to see problems or opportunities of which the customer is unaware.

The composition and responsibilities of these teams affirm that HSBC wants to be more than a bank. It wants to be a partner and co-creator of innovative solutions. It knows that if it helps customers grow and prosper, they will become more loyal. And if it can see deeper into a customer's operations, it is likely to identify more lending or financial management opportunities. This intimate, hands-on relationship strategy is very different from the transactions-based strategy of mega-lending and deal syndications pursued by most global competitors. HSBC doesn't over-concentrate on mega-deals or aspire to be in the top tier of global deal-makers. It simply wants to be there for customers with what they need, when they need it, and where they need it.

HSBC's symbiotic relationship strategy won the bank many friends during the Asian financial crisis of 1997 and 1998. It quickly dispatched to troubled markets an elite group of 370 international officers, handpicked and groomed by top management, to help customers stay out of trouble. These bankers, drawing on team resources, helped many companies stay in business by restructuring their operations and selling off money-losing units. While these were not world headline–grabbing operations that showered the bank with glory, they quietly built customer loyalty and future business opportunities.

Specialty services include a Continuously Linked Settlement system that HSBC co-created to help clients settle transactions involving multiple foreign currencies. In a world market in which most goods incorporate parts from diverse countries, this system is essential. HSBC specialists tailor it to the back-office needs of clients, and then pass on to them the volume discounts the bank receives as a major global currency trader. By leveraging HSBC currency trading expertise and its intimate knowledge of customer operations, it creates a tailored win-win solution to the benefit of all.

HSBC is also meticulous in the care it gives to retail customers. It does not treat them like second-class citizens as most other big banks do, but extends to them the same ethic of service and personal attention. This spirit permeates HSBC because it is embedded in the bank's culture. Evidently HSBC's retail customers agree. A 2002 independent survey among Canadian bank customers revealed that HSBC Bank Canada had the highest percentage of customers who would recommend the bank to friends and family, and the highest percentage of customers rating overall customer service as excellent.[12]

Largely because of the customer loyalty and repeat business that HSBC's customer-intimate approach generates, The Banker magazine has rated HSBC as "Global Bank of the Year" for three consecutive years (2003–2005). In terms of sustainable investment return, a January 2004 Financial Times/PricewaterhouseCoopers poll rated HSBC as the 25th-most-respected global company for creating shareholder value.

Made to Order

One of the most important expressions of customer respect is giving people exactly what they want—when they want it and in a way that minimizes adverse impacts on the world in which they live. This is easier done in industries that sell knowledge-based services, such as banking or insurance, than it is in heavy manufacturing. But Toyota has shown that autos, too, can be made to order quickly, efficiently, and with continually diminishing stress on the environment. The secret is in humanizing its plants by nurturing employees and empowering them to learn and network in pursuit of innovative insights, as described in Chapter 1.

Virtually every car Toyota produces is built to the specifications of an individual customer or dealer. Toyota can make infinite variety from a limited pool of resources because it has the built-in adaptability of an open, living system. That, in fact, is the magic of the Toyota Production System (TPS). To meet customer specifications, each factory workstation acts as a proxy for the ultimate customer. As production moves forward, A produces for B, B for C, C for D, and so on. The factory floor becomes an intricate network of symbiotic relationships along a giant food chain. Although workers never come in contact with the ultimate, real-world customer, they are responsible to "internal" customers—the people in the next operation or the next step in the food chain. Here's how Johnson and Broms describe it:

> Those hundreds and thousands of internal connections satisfy the overall relationship between the company and the final customer. They do so because the company links all internal connections in a continuous flow and because standards that each person sets for his or her work insure that serving the needs of the internal customer ultimately fulfills the final customer's needs.[13]

When a car rolls off a Toyota production line—whether in Japan, North America, or Europe—it is completely tailored. It is also designed to meet pressing public demands for environmentally safer products. Hazardous materials used in production, such as arsenic, cadmium, mercury, and lead are being replaced by more-benign materials. Newer models can be easily stripped and recycled rather than sent to landfills. Toyota's goal is to achieve a 95-percent recovery rate for vehicle materials.

Toyota also offers customers the satisfaction of operating the world's cleanest, most-efficient auto engines. In 2004 it had the world's best fleet efficiency ratings and its hybrid Prius swept four major awards: North

American Car of the Year, Motor Trend Car of the Year, the Society of Automotive Engineer's (SAE) Best Engineered Vehicle, and International Engine of the Year. Looking to the future, Toyota also leads in fuel cell research. In 2004, after three years of testing fuel cell cars in the U.S., it started leasing prototypes to universities and companies that agree to partner in refining the technology, and it joined a five-year partnership to co-develop a hydrogen-based public transportation infrastructure in California.

As one might expect from its environmental initiatives, Toyota is very good at creating *perceived value:* anticipating and creating shifts in customer demand by listening carefully to car buyers' practical and emotional needs. As people react to market-changing events—such as global warming, toxic waste accumulations, fragile petroleum sourcing systems, urban traffic congestion, and shifting demographics—they inevitably look for new solutions. Toyota quickly perceives and creates new value-added opportunities because it operates as an open system—one that continually weighs new information that could impact its markets—rather than as a closed one wedded to a particular worldview. This largely explains why, through the years, Toyota has gained market share over its closed-system competitors (especially Ford and GM), and why it has developed such exceptional customer loyalty.

Toyota's open system and skill in creating perceived value are connected to another important attribute of customer-intimate companies—the quest for continual improvement as the world around it changes. Toyota calls this learning and innovation process "kaizen," and enables the process to develop spontaneously on the factory floor by giving employees incentives to improve quality and production methods continually. Kaizen is based on the premise that effective learning is self-induced, not imposed from above, and that employees will be inspired to learn if they believe in the value of their work. The key to kaizen, then, is employee inspiration and commitment, and the key to that is treating employees with respect.

The number of global LAMP companies that repeat this theme is amazing. Respect your employees and they will respect your customers. Respect your employees' values and biophilic instincts and they will continuously strive for greater insight, learning, and adaptive innovation. That is what drives the reinforcing cycle of LAS + OL.

Continual Improvement

Nothing in Nature stands still. Ecosystems and species continually adapt and evolve as the world about them changes. The more efficiently organisms collect and process information and exchange services with others in their networks, the more likely is their survival. Simply stated: they must adapt or die. The same holds true for corporations. Companies cannot be customer intimate by standing still. They must continually anticipate and address new customer needs.

Few companies are better at utilizing their networks for continual improvement than Nokia. Nokia engages employees, strategic partners, and customers by "visioning" with them. Each year it invites all employees into this process as a way of boosting group dialogue, learning, and innovation. It continually seeks the best ideas of strategic partners through its "value net"—an open, interactive IT network. And it engages customers by constantly asking what they would want in an ideal world and then delivering it to them quickly.

Nokia's networking strategy succeeds because it is consistent and congruent with the company's vision of itself as a highly networked living system. It consciously builds in features that increase network efficiency—openness, inclusiveness, and responsiveness to individual needs. Nokia's products and services are zealously committed to open standards and inter-operability in wireless communications, often signing deals with other companies, even competitors, to develop shared operating systems and standards.

Nokia's "value net" strategy is a classic example of its capacity to achieve continual improvement via networking. Its idea is to move goods to customers quickly and seamlessly "through one Nokia window" by electronically linking everybody on the supply chain into a single net. This means they have to be very transparent to suppliers and share a wide spectrum of information about goals and processes. In adopting this strategy, Nokia is less concerned about exposing some of its best ideas to competitors than it is about failing to adapt quickly enough in a market that is evolving at lightning speed. This collaborative strategy has enabled Nokia to be the innovation leader in its industry.

Nokia's ultimate vision is to enable mobile phones to work like computers, cameras, PDAs and televisions—essentially "bringing the Internet to everybody's pocket." Nokia calls this "digital convergence." This vision is further expressed in Nokia's motto, "connecting people," and in its overarching goal to "build a sustainable mobile information society." To accomplish this, it is reaching deeper into developing markets in China, India, Russia, Latin America, and Africa with products tailored to the needs and pocketbooks of its customers. Nokia's business model is premised on the idea that the easier it is to use mobile phones and the better they work together, the more people will want to buy them and use them to improve the quality of life.

We have been working closely with [a United Nations] task force on the theme of enabling . . . universal access. We believe the fastest, most cost-effective way to achieve an inclusive society, where people have easy access to information, is through mobile communications.[14]

—Veli Sundback, SVP, Nokia

Nokia got its start in the telecommunications business in 1986. Yet by year-end 2005—20 years later—it had surpassed all direct competitors in market share, and it had become one of the world's largest companies by sales ($36 billion) and market capitalization ($81 billion). It achieved these kinds of results largely through its skill in connecting with people and then developing customer-intimate solutions to their needs.

Promises

Promises are an expression of our very human desire to bond—to form lasting relationships based on mutual caring and trust. All businesses are based on promises, explicit or implicit, that they will provide value to us, in exchange for which they hope to gain our loyalty, repeat business, and referrals. Companies that keep their promises generally far outperform those that don't.

Few industries rely on future promises more than do insurers of catastrophic risk. We hope we'll never need them, but we want to know that if and when we do, they absolutely, positively will be there for us. Swiss Re is such a company.

Swiss Re's promise to customers is clear and simple: to provide expert advice on risk and capital management, and absolute security when disaster strikes. Clients believe these promises because Swiss Re has the in-house knowledge and capital strength to back them up. That knowledge and strength, in turn, are supported by Swiss Re's stewardship culture and commitment to organizational learning. Few companies, anywhere, make better use of the reinforcing cycle of LAS + OL in delivering value to customers.

In a broad sense, Swiss Re's expertise is focused on the behaviors of large living systems—ecosystems and social systems—that are stressed by human negligence. It needs to know how these living systems work and how they connect to our lives in order to assess the risks associated with global warming, water shortages, threats to human health, and terrorism. Having considered the complexity of these issues and their obvious impacts on our quality of life against the limits of its own resources, Swiss Re has engaged in a global, networked strategy to build its expertise and raise public awareness. It was, for example, a leader in launching the 1995 Insurance Industry Initiative under the United Nations Environment Programme (UNEP);[15] it has been an outspoken advocate of the Kyoto Protocol on reducing global warming; it regularly convenes global dialogue and teaching on sustainability at its Ruschlikon Center near Zurich; and it publishes, as a public service, numerous studies on managing systemic risks. Beyond these public efforts, Swiss Re has integrated principles of sustainable development into its own operations and investment practices.

The depth of Swiss Re's expertise and its continual quest for knowledge are important attributes in building customer intimacy and delivering on its promises because they build trust and confidence. Swiss Re also draws clients in by partnering with them—coaching them on sustainability best practices and offering financial incentives for better performance. These incentives and consultations go beyond saving clients money and reducing Swiss Re's claims exposure. They look to better systemic health—a goal that transcends the fiscal realm. This reaching for a higher good inspires greater employee and customer loyalty, and engages the higher thinking capacities of Swiss Re client-service teams.

Clients also appreciate Swiss Re's candor. The company doesn't hide the truth, for fear of offending clients or contradicting the false promises of others, about global climate change, toxic waste hazards, or any other risks. Clients trust Swiss Re because it sees the big picture coherently, explains each institution's policy options intelligently, and has the financial strength to back up its promises.

Swiss Re is more interested in being the best underwriter of catastrophic risks than in being the biggest. It will not write policies simply to generate revenue because careless underwriting can result in huge claims losses. Swiss Re knows that to serve customers it must have strong finances and an unshakeable ability to deliver on its promises. Although its balance sheet has weakened since the catastrophic claims of 9/11, it still carries a coveted Aa2/AA credit rating—one notch above that of its largest competitor, Munich Re—and is striving to regain its former Aaa/AAA rating.

> Swiss Re does not necessarily have to be the biggest global player, but it must be number one in terms of quality.... Selling the product is no longer first and foremost. Our teams are now putting much more energy into developing and offering customized solutions...[16]
>
> —Ulrich Bremi, Chairman, Swiss Re (1999)

Value Proposition

Above all, customer-intimate companies want to deliver real value to their customers. Nokia does this by offering feature-rich products that are easy to use and answer real customer needs. Toyota does it by manufacturing cars to customers' exact specifications. Southwest does it by giving passengers the service they need, when they need it, at a price they can afford. HSBC does it by being a local banking partner anywhere in the world. And Swiss Re does it by offering customers unparalleled risk-management tools. As do all LAMP companies, these exemplars take immense pride in the quality of their products and services.

Beyond the practicality of their offers, they understand the basic message of Roper's 2002 Green Gauge Report, previously cited: "Consumers are trading out of what is unimportant (products and services that don't fit into the future) and trading into the future (the life that I want for me and my family)."[17]

LAMP companies also find rich markets in sister LAS companies that extend their stewardship practices into their supply chains, as described in the following chapter. For these companies, the fuel efficiency of traveling on Southwest lowers their corporate greenhouse gas emissions. The systemic perspectives and holistic risk management services of HSBC and Swiss Re help them to manage their costs better over extended periods.

Governments, too, are becoming more interested in the total value proposition of corporate vendors—the "external" as well as the market costs and benefits of their offers—for the simple reason that they are often left footing the bill for corporate layoffs, pollution, and employee stress.[18] The more deeply a company's value proposition touches a customer's needs, the more loyalty that company generates. Beyond the appeals of price and performance, household, corporate, and government consumers increasingly want to know how the goods and services they buy ultimately affect society and Nature. This is a mega-trend that will not go away so long as the web of life that supports us all is threatened.

Relational Equity

Customer-intimate companies build what management consultant John Dalla Costa calls "relational equity" when they attend to the total needs of a customer—including those of the heart and spirit. Traditionalists may scoff at this, but LAMP companies prove, time and again, that customers respond favorably when companies look beyond the practical aspects of a transaction (e.g., air transport, a loan, a cell phone) to the higher human needs for meaning.

Customers trust ethical companies and bond with them because they feel these companies share their values. Emotional bonds are forged when a product or service reflects respect and care for the customer. Spiritual bonds are forged when that respect and care extend out to the biosphere and society—the context in which the customer lives. LAMP companies generally enjoy greater customer loyalty than do their traditional peers because they seek this level of customer intimacy. They also garner extra profit opportunity because products and services that respect the living systems from which they are derived often cost less to produce. And in many cases, people are willing to pay more for the emotional and spiritual value-added, as is demonstrated by the fast-growing markets for organic food.

Dalla Costa rightly says, "Relational equity is not a replacement for shareholder equity, but rather works as its constructive complement."[19] Although less easily measured than financial net worth, relational equity generates profit because loyal customers are worth so much more than occasional ones. Companies spend billions on advertising to develop customer trust and loyalty, and ensure a steady stream of repeat business.

LAMP companies know that good stewardship does this inherently, and that advertising is no substitute for poor relational equity.

The reality of today's markets is that customers have many options. Not only are they willing to switch for better product or service value, but they also will do so quickly if they believe a practical alternative is more congruent with their beliefs and values. And that is no small thing.

[R]elational equity recognizes that value increasingly involves a return on a relationship. Management of customers, employees, suppliers, strategic partners and global brand reputation are but some of the relations that are now of critical strategic importance to managers. These relationships are growing in complexity and now involve satisfactions that are not just functional but also emotional and moral. Since the worth of companies depends more and more on its varied relationships, the point is no longer that ethics must provide an ROI, but that ROI without ethics is much riskier and often unachievable.[20]

—John Dalla Costa, President, Center for Ethical Orientation

Conclusion

Customer-intimate companies build customer relationships around two strong bonds: (1) a total product/service solution, and (2) an emotional connection that enables customers to express their needs fully and holistically. Employees of such companies approach this bond-building process as they would a good neighbor—with a sincere willingness to help.

If you want employees to respect and care for customers, you must first respect and care for your employees; and if you want to show respect for your employees, you must honor their values. Respect breeds respect and caring begets caring. There are no shortcuts. Nothing turns a customer off more quickly than an employee who acts as if he or she does not want to be at work, or who refuses to connect or empathize with a need. Conversely, nothing creates stronger bonds than employees who deeply and genuinely care.

For every 5% increase in employee satisfaction, there is a resultant 2% increase in customer satisfaction, returning up to 1.8% in net profit.[21]

—Michael Treacy and Fred Wiersema, *Harvard Business Review*

Caring becomes a cultural norm and a catalyst to customer-intimate relationships only when it is commonplace throughout a company. That is a fundamental premise of Living Asset Stewardship and why LAS is the heart of enterprise. Customers long for real connection. During the past decade, companies that connect and bond with customers have garnered hundreds of billions of dollars' worth of new business from defectors from traditional companies. That is the story behind the stellar performance of the Global LAMP Index.[®]

Inspired Supply Network Management

"Nokia has altered the playing field with . . . a 'global supply web'
that links Nokia suppliers and plants and also supports vendor-man-
aged inventory and collaborative planning. These capabilities have
contributed to 20 percent margins, a 35 percent market share, and an
average cost to make and sell phones that is 18 percent lower than
[those of] its rivals."[1]

—William C. Capacino et al., "A Global Study of Supply Chain Leadership
and Its Impact on Business Performance"

The operating leverage in Living Asset Stewardship comes from inspiring people to work with their hearts as well as their minds. Companies that care about people and their concerns generally prosper more than those who care only about the bottom line. Chapter 7 discussed how leading corporate stewards leverage the interests, skills, and passions of employees. In this chapter we will see how they do the same with suppliers and other strategic partners.

Supply *network*, rather than the more common supply *chain*, is more congruent with the notion of the corporation as a living system—a human environment that operates much like an ecosystem. All living systems, whether human or otherwise, are genetically wired to operate as networks. When companies organize themselves and their supply systems as networks, they become healthier and more efficient.

In Nature, networks evolved over the course of billions of years precisely because they served the health and efficiency of living beings. Healthy bodies rely on healthy cellular networks just as healthy ecosystems rely on healthy organismic networks. Supply nets are no different. The intelligence, strength, and adaptability of living networks arise from the diversity of their individual constituents and from their capacity to self-organize. Large corporate supply nets encompass thousands of companies in multiple tiers and millions of people with specialized knowledge. Very few companies use these immense resources effectively.

To understand the dynamics of a living network, think of a free-trade zone. Within such a zone people can exchange information, goods, and services as freely as they want so long as they don't harm others or the network itself. This symbiotic behavior recognizes the interdependence of the system and its constituent parts. In the natural world the interdependence of network constituents is maintained by their diversity and capacity to self-organize. There is no central command post in an ecosystem because none is needed. The network processes new information and adapts far more quickly than a command post ever could.

For this very reason supply networks don't respond well to centralized control. No matter how ardently they disbelieve it, or how hard they try, corporate leaders cannot change this dynamic. The urge to self-organize is embedded in all individuals and living systems, and it is the only way they can operate at full capacity. The people in a corporate supply net who know best what is needed to make it run are those closest to the action. When they can communicate and transact freely, the network hums.

Like the stock market, networks have a collective intelligence that transcends that of any one constituent, because they are "plugged in" to so many entities. Part of the collective intelligence of supply networks is the spontaneous desire of people within them to add to the quality of life. This is natural because the network and all its constituents want to live and continue life into future generations. Of course, not every individual has the network's well-being in mind—there are, after all, cancer cells with their own proliferative agenda—but it holds for most constituent elements as a matter of instinct. We are genetically and logistically wedded to the web of life. As Edward O. Wilson says, we have an affinity for life that has been bred into us through thousands of generations.

When people within a supply network are free to self-organize within their areas of competence, they are naturally inclined toward LAS. If companies encourage them to seek life-affirming solutions, they become inspired to learn and innovate. Thus, the reinforcing cycle of LAS + OL operates. Conversely, when companies tell people to make, buy, and sell things that harm life, they are inclined to withdraw their energies, and productivity then suffers.

LAS-Driven Supply Nets

The fastest-growing supply systems today are networked and operate on LAS principles. They and their constituents are gaining market share at the expense of traditionally managed, sequential supply chains.

Consider the case of Hewlett-Packard, which has one of the largest supply networks in the world. In 2003 it spent $52 billion (approximately 71 percent of gross revenues) on buying materials, components, and services from thousands of suppliers worldwide. Because many of HP's suppliers are, themselves, large multinationals with extensive supply chains of their own, and because HP requires them to model its social and environmental responsibility (SER) program as a condition of doing business, its procurement policies will ultimately ripple out to two, three, or more tiers, creating an SER domino effect.[2]

HP's goal is to spread the influence of its SER program, modeled on the U.N. Global Compact, so that it becomes an industry standard supplier code of conduct.[3] HP has published a roadmap and intends to follow it on the SER journey. In a pragmatic, day-to-day sense, this roadmap affirms HP's confidence in the synergies of its own stewardship. In a longer-term visionary sense, HP's effort should strengthen its corporate ecosystem— the area of its widest economic influence—by creating a chain reaction of inspired learning, innovation, and profit. The SER roadmap, in effect, multiplies the reinforcing cycle of LAS + OL.

The IT industry recognizes the growing promise of LAS-inspired networks, both within the operations of its most competitive companies and in the demands of its fastest-growing customers.[4] Because IT people make corporate networks operate faster and more efficiently, they are well aware of the immense leverage operating within networks. Companies that achieve this leverage will overwhelm those that don't.

A Total Systems Approach

Canon clearly sees itself and its suppliers as interlocking living networks operating within the larger living networks of Nature and society. This is inherent in its kyosei philosophy of "working for the common good," adopted in 1988, and its "green procurement standards," introduced in 1997. The evolution of these standards, which have been twice upgraded (in 2002 and 2003), is due largely to Canon's aggressive use of IT. Their technology enables them to take a total systems approach to managing their supply net. Therefore, they are able to focus simultaneously on economic value-added (EVA),[5] environmental sustainability, employee well-being, and human rights. Because each of these systemic attributes is connected to the health of the total supply system, gains in one area feed back to the others, creating a compounding effect. In this way the total system becomes, synergistically, more than the sum of its parts.

Canon enjoys the added advantage of being an early adopter of LAS principles. Its tradition of stewardship goes back to its founding more than six decades ago. Its *San-Ji* spirit of self-mastery has long focused the company's attention on improving the world in which it operates. *San-Ji* literally refers to the "three selves" of a personal master: self-motivation to do better continuously (*jihatsu*), self-control and good character (*jichi*), and self-awareness of one's responsibilities and how to accomplish them (*jikaku*). Canon bases its evolution—toward Living Asset Stewardship, kyosei, and green procurement—on long-held traditions and beliefs.

Its green procurement objective enables it to obtain quality, cost-effective materials while returning multiple benefits: more eco-effective goods for customers, better knowledge and opportunities for society, and further global consensus on sustainable enterprise. This is the road Canon intends to take in its quest to grow soundly "forever."

Consistent with its broader social agenda of kyosei, all Canon's procurement, worldwide, is conducted openly and follows nondiscriminatory principles. A subcommittee of its Procurement Management Center works with suppliers to instruct them in Canon's standards and to create an information network. Their seven "supplier parameters" cover corporate philosophy, planning, organization, systems, evaluation, information disclosure, and education. There are also 11 product parameters, including energy and resource conservation, toxic wastes, recycling, LCA, eco-labeling, and disclosure. To help suppliers adapt to their systems, Canon hosts environmental seminars.

If suppliers want to become part of Canon's business ecosystem, they must pass two tests—one on the effectiveness of their corporate environmental policies and the other on the "greenness" of the materials being supplied. Canon's expectations are clearly stated in a "Green Procurement Standards" booklet that covers the details of a supplier's environmental management system (EMS) and its risk management procedures.

Green Products = Supplier's Environmental Activities + Products Themselves[6]
—Canon's Green Procurement approach

Canon conveys its social policy expectations under kyosei—on human rights, equal opportunity, fair labor practices, and employee health and safety—to suppliers less formally via consensus building. This method likely has more to do with the Japanese affinity for dialogue among business partners than with a lack of clarity or commitment. Canon's own ethics, which are deeply embedded in kyosei and its Code of Conduct, explicitly address "imbalances between wealthy and poor" and social justice issues.[7] Canon appears to build consensus around these issues with suppliers more by example and moral suasion than by laying out definitive guidelines as other LAMP exemplars do—yet Canon bears in mind that it cannot uphold its own ethics if it lets suppliers violate them.[8] Suppliers get the message: if they want Canon's business they must operate in congruence with kyosei principles.

In a very real sense Canon, HP, and other LAMP exemplars are LAS missionaries, striving to expand the reach of LAS for the mutual benefit of all. These companies know that traditional management practices are dysfunctional and threaten public confidence in market economies. They define success not as individual market returns (ends), but as the health of the free-market system, society, and the biosphere—the means by which their enterprises survive and thrive.

Pushing the Envelope

The notion of projecting LAS into a supply network is relatively new: few companies were engaged in this prior to the year 2000. Most LAMP companies are still experimenting with it, but those that have aggressively pushed it are laying the groundwork for future market-share gains.

I say this for two reasons. First, there are inherent synergies in LAS, as the Global LAMP Index® has shown. As more companies become proficient in LAS, the networks in which they operate become more efficient. Second, consumers—the ultimate buyers of most goods and services—are beginning to demand better corporate stewardship.

Another catalyst for projecting LAS into corporate supply networks is the recent growth of IT capacity. Until the late 1990s few companies had the wherewithal to network spontaneously with suppliers. Today, with new enterprise software and the Internet, companies find this much easier to do.

With IT accelerating the movement toward supply nets in general, and toward LAS-oriented supply nets in particular, the pace of change is so quick that traditionally managed, sequential corporate supply chains are becoming obsolete. The knowledge of a few decision makers at the top is no match for the collective wisdom of thousands of people who daily connect with customers, work on factory floors, manage distribution centers, and repair damaged goods. This is especially so when those thousands are inspired to work with their hearts as well as their minds.

LAMP companies have had an easier time exploring the networked approach to suppliers because they are more deeply immersed in LAS and more practiced in localizing authority within their organizations; consequently, they see more ways to employ the Internet in supply net management. As first movers, LAMP companies are likely to have a big advantage.

Adaptive Networks vs. Sequential Supply Chains

It is important to understand the differences between the evolving supply networks of LAMP companies and the supply chains of traditionally managed ones. As previously noted, they operate on completely different premises—one organic and adaptive, the other mechanistic and sequential. Consequently, they behave differently in critical ways, as can be seen in Table 10-1.

As in prior comparison tables, the juxtapositions noted in Table 10-1 are leanings rather than hard and fast rules. LAMP companies naturally lean toward the more-organic, networked approach; traditionally managed

Table 10-1: Organic vs. Mechanical Supply Systems

ORGANIC/ADAPTIVE NETWORKS	MECHANISTIC/SEQUENTIAL CHAINS
Purpose	
Optimize value to customer	Optimize revenue to the firm
Seek best practices	Seek best price + control
Create systemic harmony (long-term view)	Pursue what's best for us (short-term)
Improve productivity (means)	Focus solely on bottom line (ends)
Organization	
Network model (collaborative partnering)	Chain-of-command model
Distributed authority (localized)	Centralized authority
Self-organized around competency	Vertically integrated by rank
Seeks diversity of insight + skill	Seeks sameness + replaceability
United around ideals + common purposes	United by a single dominant player
Communication	
Open, spontaneous, collaborative exchange	Channeled, controlled exchange
Optimal connectivity of all stakeholders	Influence targeted stakeholders
Transparent, easy access to information	Access limited by need to know
Based on knowledge + contribution	Based on rank
Partner Qualifications	
Preference for unique know-how (synergy)	Preference for low cost
Willingness to question + innovate	Willingness to follow orders
Future growth potential	Current usefulness
LAS compatibility	Absence of legal problems

companies tend toward the more-mechanistic approach. Stewardship leaders prioritize value to the customer, LAS best practices, and systemic harmony, but this does not mean they are oblivious to the bottom line. In fact, they see these objectives as important means to a profitable end. Their view of means and ends is more holistic and process-oriented than the traditional one: they regard means as ends in the making. If the Global LAMP Index® is any indication, there can be little question which mental model works best.

Organizationally, supply networks operate more like partnerships with distributed (localized) authority than centralized chains of command.

They are quicker to collaborate, co-learn, adapt, and innovate because each partner has a vested interest in the success of the whole. They understand their interdependence. By making the most of partners' core competencies and value-added capacities, networks become more than the sum of their parts. They become synergistic.

The key to finding these synergies is open communication between network partners, which has been immensely facilitated by recent developments in enterprise software and IT networks. In open exchange, who communicates with whom tends to be based on knowledge and contribution rather than on rank. The goal of communication is to increase the capacity of the whole rather than the power of a privileged few.

Supply Net Standards

The best supply net managers meticulously model the high standards they set for their suppliers. These standards typically exceed those required by law for environment, equal opportunity, workplace health and safety, fair trade, and human rights, and are continually benchmarked to best practices. These higher standards tend to strengthen the bonds between a company and its suppliers—especially when suppliers see the workplace synergies and other benefits of LAS. As discussed previously, employees are much more likely to engage their higher thinking capacities when they believe the companies they serve are deeply committed to serving them and the larger living systems of society and Nature.

There is, of course, a risk of setting standards so high that no one can meet them. HP has reduced this risk by creating a flexible, layered approach with the following attributes:

- goals that can realistically be met;
- expectations for continual improvement and best practices;
- clear reporting guidelines that must be met quickly and accurately;
- integrated, consistent, worldwide IT-based monitoring systems; and
- partnerships with suppliers in finding better solutions.

In setting goals for suppliers, HP puts its highest priorities on reducing high-risk activities such as "chemically intensive operations" and "procurement in sensitive geographies," where suppliers may not respect human rights, fair labor practices, or acceptable employee health and safety standards. It also continually reviews these goals with suppliers and expert HP employees with a view toward raising standards at every opportunity.

To ensure access to the right people in their supplier networks, HP behaves more like a mentor than an authoritarian standard-setter. Its experts and engineers are in continual dialogue with supplier colleagues concerning environmental and social risks. Standards are reassessed periodically, based on the results of annual social and environmental questionnaires that material suppliers must complete, and on the progress these suppliers have made in meeting their own goals.[9] It is an open, interactive process based on dialogue and mutual understanding, rather than one that is rigid and vertically sequential. If there are inconsistencies in the system, HP and supplier experts are more likely to find them and deal with them because they work collaboratively; and they are less likely to ignore them for fear of "rocking the boat."

HP is clear about its expectations and consistent in applying its standards. Suppliers must commit to a "Code of Conduct" and a "General Specification for the Environment" with strong social and environmental compliance clauses. They must also sign a "Supplier Social and Environmental Responsibility Agreement" that contractually binds them to HP's standards. If HP finds that a supplier is in violation of any of these agreements, it requires the supplier to implement an immediate "corrective action plan." In other cases, it may require an independent third-party to audit and investigate complaints in order to validate adverse findings. If a supplier does not demonstrate improvement in a reasonable amount of time, HP will discontinue the business relationship. However, its preference is always to sustain the relationship and help the supplier find effective solutions.

Like Canon, HP makes its Code of Conduct and environmental specifications easily accessible via its website. This gives all potential suppliers an equal opportunity to compete and facilitates constructive feedback.

Partners in Eco-design

At HP, "product stewardship teams" help suppliers meet its high social and environmental responsibility standards. These teams oversee the development of new products from initial design through manufacture, eco-

Eight Action Items

Fundamentals of Hewlett-Packard's Supply Chain SER (social and environmental responsibility) Program

1. Secure critical management commitment. Senior executives must endorse the program if it is to cascade throughout the organization. With management commitment in place, obtaining the logistical elements to make the program a success will follow.

2. Set expectations. It is very important to set clear expectations internally with suppliers and with third parties such as nongovernmental organizations. There will likely be a phased approach to implementation, and communicating those milestones ahead of time will show to all that the course has been set.

3. Put objectives in writing. This sets out the terms and conditions of the program, although it does not need to be a legally binding document. For instance, HP's independent supplier agreement articulates what the company expects of suppliers and provides an assurance that both parties understand the importance of working toward meeting those goals.

4. Create awareness. This is important for internal audiences because it gives management and employees the context for understanding why SER is important. Among suppliers it will help gain support for the program below the top-management level.

5. Share progress. Nothing builds motivation and momentum more than success. There may be skepticism and criticism early in the process, but keeping people abreast of progress keeps it fresh and builds support.

6. Communicate and collaborate. Because people generally dislike change and resist things they don't understand, communication and an open, collaborative approach will remove many of the obstacles that arise when people smell change in the air, smoothing the fast track to success. The more sensitive the topic, the more important is collaboration.

7. Partner for success. Active partnering must take place with internal stakeholders, suppliers, industry groups, standards organizations, and governmental and nongovernmental agencies.

8. Start now. There is a building interest in, and concern about, SER programs. Don't let the window of opportunity close.

labeling, and ultimately, product take-back at the end of the product life cycle. They offer specific assistance in mission-critical areas such as design for environment (DfE), increasing energy efficiency, decreasing material use, reducing hazardous materials, extending product life cycles, improving recyclability, making products safer and easier to use, and eliminating wasteful packaging.

HP's product stewardship teams make available online product safety, environmental, and energy-efficiency information for most products. These include HP material safety data sheets (MSDS) that contain information about the physical, chemical, and toxicological properties of materials; regulatory information; and recommendations to ensure safe handling. Stewardship teams also help suppliers understand product environmental profiles dealing with specific product attributes HP wants to offer customers, including its eco-labeling standards and its certification programs.

Beyond the practical information that suppliers derive from HP product stewardship teams lies the spirit of partnership. A palpable sense of teamwork permeates the company and everyone is committed to common goals. Communication is open, spontaneous, and collaborative. Every step necessitates getting specific knowledge where it is needed as quickly as possible. Expectations are transparent. Feedback from all stakeholders—employees, suppliers, distributors, customers, regulators, and competitors—is continuous.

HP suppliers also have the confidence that they are regarded as long-term, qualitative, value-added partners rather than replaceable commodity producers who produce reliable quantities only when needed. They know that HP combines its high expectations for continual improvement and its demands for full and fast access to data with a willingness to help suppliers attain these objectives via spontaneous expert feedback. They also know that with HP, responsiveness goes both ways. HP serves its suppliers as it expects them to serve the ultimate customer by continually striving for higher quality and value-added. The whole process is integrated and ecosystemic.

Managing Transportation Impacts

Stora Enso has developed "second-generation" control systems that govern the transportation of all fiber entering its mills and all finished products it ships out to customers. Because the company moves huge amounts of bulk commodities and semi-finished goods, transportation impacts form a substantial portion of its total environmental impacts. This is not to ignore Stora's other efforts to operate a sustainable supply network—especially its "traceability" systems, which ensure that all fiber comes from certified forests—but to highlight an area in which it has demonstrated best practices.

Stora's "Base Port" system, introduced in 2000, aims to reduce fuel consumption and halve environmental emissions per unit of weight transported. The company's transport chain assessment system monitors approximately 400 transport suppliers, analyzes more than 1,500 transportation links, and then works to make each more eco-efficient. Huge savings have resulted simply by avoiding traffic congestion, shifting cargoes from trucks to rail, using more eco-efficient ships and operating them at lower speeds, and loading all carriers more scientifically. The Base Port system includes tools for calculating eco-efficiency and continuous improvement.

Base Port has already proven its worth. On the Kvarnsveden–Lille transportation line it has cut CO_2 (carbon dioxide) and NO_x (nitrogen oxides) emissions by 50 percent and 75 percent, respectively.

In Southern Finland, by channeling all container transportation through Mussalo Harbour instead of Helsinki, Stora reduced CO_2 emissions due to land haulage by 30 percent. By equipping its terminal with the latest cargo–handling equipment it made further emissions reductions of 35 percent for NO_x, 45 percent for CO (carbon monoxide), and 85 percent for particulates, while saving millions in transportation costs. A newly reopened (September 2003) rail track at its Gryksbo mill in Sweden eliminates the need for truck haulage, thereby reducing CO_2 emissions by 70 percent (or 300 tons per year), and other harmful gases by 70 to 85 percent, while also limiting product damage and cutting transportation costs. To reduce its net environmental impacts further, Stora supplies biofuel to trucks in Sweden, reducing annual CO_2 emissions by an additional 169 tons.

Novo Nordisk is also working to reduce emissions created when its goods are shipped to market. These include shippers' fossil fuel emissions plus those from transport refrigeration and heating equipment. Like Stora, Novo works with suppliers in a spirit of partnership, helping them to assess and manage emissions to reduce total impacts. The company's first priority was analyzing transport data from truckers of raw materials because that function was the source of its greatest impacts. It has now moved on to analyze data from ship and air transportation suppliers, and is working in partnership with Scandinavian Airlines to define measurement methodologies. Emissions will be calculated on the average of actual figures per route/flight, and all cargo will be taken into account.

Each step Stora and Novo have taken in optimizing their transportation supplier networks has cut costs as well as damage to the biosphere. More important, their spirit of partnership with suppliers and attention to detail send a clear message that both are deeply committed to LAS. Managing transportation impacts is a new field. By having the foresight and dedication to enter it early, Stora and Novo have inspired employees and strengthened the reinforcing cycle of LAS + OL, adding further strategic advantages.

Human and Labor Rights

Novo Nordisk has long been a forceful advocate of human and labor rights because they know such rights are inseparable from LAS. Novo's commitment to serve humanity is a matter of deep pride to employees. The company has established a committee of senior managers, supported by 100 or so employees (primarily purchasers), that directly oversees the human- and labor-rights practices of suppliers. Starting in 2002, human and labor rights have been guiding criteria for supplier evaluations. All suppliers must answer a questionnaire on: wages and benefits, working hours, health and safety, child and forced labor, freedom of association and collective bargaining, discrimination and equal opportunity, disciplinary measures, and employee privacy.

Prior to framing its questionnaire, Novo conducted workshops in 2001 with suppliers from Denmark, Germany, Sweden, France, Mexico, India, and Japan to develop a sense of issues, assessment techniques, and best practices. Its goal, which was easily attained, was to evaluate 90 percent of key raw-material suppliers and a range of key suppliers in service and engineering by the end of 2002. Because it approached suppliers in a spirit of partnership and mutual learning, Novo found "the vast majority responded very positively." Very few resisted.

When Novo discovers suppliers who are "unsure about why we are asking these questions, and what kind of information we expect to get from them," they meet and talk together until they reach mutual understanding. By transforming initial doubt into a clear position on the issues, Novo is usually able to build trust and stronger bonds with its suppliers.

All new supplier contracts include a clause stating the mutual commitment to the U.N. Universal Declaration of Human Rights, the International Labor Organization (ILO) Conventions, and the International Chamber of Commerce (ICC) Business Charter for Sustainable Development. Starting in 2003, Novo began auditing supplier performance. If suppliers find they violate any of these principles, they must notify Novo immediately and discuss remedial action. Although it is still too early to tell how these guidelines will affect performance, one thing is crystal clear: they totally affirm Novo's corporate ethics, which inspire its life sciences research.

For the first time we can now account for our suppliers' and license manufacturers' performance on basic labor rights . . . .[10]

—Novo Nordisk's Sustainability Report 2003

Synergies of Partnering

Few companies face the logistical challenges of a mobile phone manufacturer. Nokia's phones are made from a huge variety of highly specialized parts—from microprocessors to transceivers to long-life batteries—provided by a long list of suppliers. Every day, hundreds of millions of parts move through its plants. Logistics are further complicated by frequent product design changes. Nokia has further intensified its challenge by requiring that all suppliers and products that enter Nokia's system must also meet its high stewardship standards. For most companies—especially those that operate sequential supply chains—this extra requirement slows an already cumbersome decision-making process. Nokia overcomes this difficulty by making its suppliers virtual partners and connecting them into Nokia's extended enterprise network.

Nokia speeds response times within the network by being extremely transparent to its suppliers, sharing a wide spectrum of information about its goals and processes. Nokia is not concerned about the risks of such open sharing because they know transparency accelerates the pace of learning and innovation to such a degree that competitors are hard pressed to catch up. The extended enterprise network functions by connecting suppliers to expert employee teams in real time. This allows the network to address bottlenecks before they become problems and to experiment spontaneously with design changes.

Nokia learned the value of a rapid response capacity in 1995 when a parts shortage caused it to disappoint network operators and other customers expecting deliveries in time for critical Christmas sales. The next time a major parts shortage hit, following a fire at a Philips semiconductor plant in March 2000, Nokia was ready. Even before Philips informed customers about the fire, Nokia noticed the supply disruption and began to deal with it on multiple levels. CEO Jorma Ollila quickly flew to Philips headquarters and got the Dutch company to fill the supply gap from other plants. Meanwhile, Nokia engineers redesigned their chips so that producers in Japan and the U.S. could also make them. Consequently, in spite of the fire, Nokia made its production targets, took market share from slower-moving rivals, and gained economies of scale unmatched in the industry.

Nokia's extended enterprise concept succeeds because it is organized, like Toyota's factories, on principles found in Nature. It optimizes the structural principles of self-organization, interdependence, and diversity, as well as cybernetic principles of energy and information flow. Everything that occurs in the value network is highly visible, integrated, and symbiotic. Supplier-partners are authorized to self-organize as needed to meet their quality, cost, and workflow requirements. Partners are interdependent and, in effect, become one another's customers as work flows through the pipeline. Each partner is totally responsible for a specific value-added process that adds to the diversity of the finished product, and for keeping other partners informed about the flow and quality of work as it progresses. This system reduces the number of manual transactions needed to produce a finished mobile phone. Just as in the Toyota Production System, there is little wasted motion or effort.

The extended enterprise system is linked via Nokia's Global Supply Web and other emerging e-business tools. Thus, supplier-partners quickly exchange feedback on quality, demand-supply conditions, and joint targets. Materials are often merged in transit, before they get to the point of final assembly, thereby saving time, expense, and environmental impact. The entire system is energized by performance incentives, repeat business opportunities, the buzz of "killer applications," and the cachet of being a preferred partner to Nokia. It is further motivated by Nokia's transcendent sense of mission—"connecting people" in productive, sustainable ways— and the learning opportunities generated by a talented and dedicated team.

Nokia's organic, adaptive, extended enterprise system is totally congruent with its mission. Everything follows natural principles. In addition to meeting Nokia's high quality standards, all suppliers must also meet its fastidious design for environment (DfE) and ethical standards. These are periodically audited to help both Nokia and suppliers identify opportunities for improvement. The overriding objective is to broaden the scope of cooperation within Nokia's supply net so that it increasingly resembles a symbiotic ecosystem based on co-evolution.

The Adaptive Enterprise

Although state of the art today, Nokia's extended enterprise network has a long way to go in terms of what is possible. If visionary Intel chairman Andy Grove is right, the networks of the future will be, by orders of magnitude, quicker, smarter, and more adaptive. Supply net management will become more efficient by a factor of 10 or more.

Grove's vision looks to systems that move beyond electronic transactions to adaptive electronic decision-making. Networks of the future will use built-in artificial intelligence on computer data—digital data and digital intelligence working on one another—to assist supply net managers in allocating resources. Such networks will require computers that can recursively generate analyses of our economic activities, including their impacts on the larger living systems that support them. They will operate on distributed intelligence from millions and billions of local sources. Corporate networks will then behave even more like ecosystems in linking individual constituents, eliminating waste, and learning and adapting sustainably.

When we consider the magnitude of today's challenges—a world population of six billion (on its way to nine billion in 50 years) in an overstressed biosphere—we need this system *now*. It's a matter of survival. As Grove says, "we'll have to figure out how to earn profits that replace the profits that some [have] . . . sucked out of the world."[11]

Intel clearly sees the challenge. Andy Grove's commentary about needed increases in network speed and intelligence *plus* materials efficiency is clear: this is where Intel is headed. Its vision of digital convergence goes beyond the finite activity of networking between people to the infinite of "networking on behalf of people" and the living systems that support them. Intel's top engineer, Pat Gelsinger, says it's the next big thing.

What kind of culture must we have for Intel's visions and the adaptive enterprise to work? You can bet that it will be organic rather than mechanical, self-organizing rather than command-and-control, networked and interdependent rather than centralized, and systemically diverse rather than vertically integrated and sequential. That's certainly the way it works inside Intel and its supply network.

Marrying [the decision part of] order processing to the supply chain is within sight . . . . If this can be done computers-to-computers in real time, you'll see another power of ten increase in efficiency.[12]

—Andrew Grove, Chairman, Intel

Conclusion

The evolution of capitalism, like that of Nature, has been one of better and more-efficient information exchange. Networks are far better at exchanging and utilizing information than are command-and-control hierarchies. This is nowhere more apparent than in the management of corporate supply systems.

Some of the most stunning advances in the efficiency of capitalism have taken place in the past decade as corporations learned to use the Internet to improve management of their supplier relationships. Corporate networks that behave more like the living systems on which they are modeled derive the greatest benefits.

LAS-inspired supply networks are intimately connected and integral to the learning capacities of all parties. They are much faster at adaptive innovation than traditionally managed supply chains because they have more holistic vision and faster reflexes. Their speed to market is accelerated by their skillful use of IT networks that serve the whole system rather than the power of a select few.

The Internet, of course, also confers advantages on traditional command-and-control companies; but they don't get full value because their hierarchical cultures clash with the collaborative spontaneity of the web.

This disconnect is a source of growing risk for traditionalists. Given the huge leverage that now exists in supply network management, as exhibited by LAMP companies, traditionalists labor under a serious disadvantage.

Few people understand these distinctions because the Internet is such a new tool in supply network management. Furthermore, the Internet tends to be underutilized even in the realm of LAS and sustainability. As perceptions change, however, we will see LAS increasingly projected into procurement because it is one of the most fertile areas for Factor Ten efficiencies. Nokia and Intel are already demonstrating opportunities for using digital intelligence to operate on digital data, and for going beyond finite networking for people to infinite networking on behalf of people.

The most exciting part of inspired supply network management is its capacity to spread the doctrine of LAS. Success breeds success. If the old system is crumbling today against the onrush of LAMP companies, it should not be a cause for concern. It is part of a process that economist Joseph Schumpeter has famously called "creative destruction."[13] We can expect to find it at the beginning of any renaissance.

11

Financial Stewardship

"The worst crime against working people is a company which fails to operate at a profit." [1]
—Samuel Gompers, founder and first president of the American Federation of Labor (AFL)

The LAS approach looks to an infinite future rather than to finite, short-term gains. Living Asset Stewardship cannot exist without financial stewardship. Companies that behave as living systems regard and treat their financial resources as an ecosystem would view energy and food: ingredients essential for life and, therefore, not to be needlessly squandered. Samuel Gompers, founder of the American Federation of Labor (AFL), understood this well. To him, working people depended on accumulated profits to secure their jobs. No profits, no jobs. Likewise, no profits, no LAS.

One of the greatest strategic errors traditionally managed companies make is to present themselves as profit-generating machines rather than living communities or ecosystems. In doing so, they operate from false premises, blind to the adverse feedback effects they unwittingly create. The machine premise is self-destructive because it focuses too much on ends (e.g., machine output and profit) and not enough on means (i.e., maintaining the living infrastructure that supports it). The gearing premise—that profit can be accelerated by borrowing to acquire more productive assets—is perilous because it too easily ignores the liability aspect of borrowing.

The dysfunction of traditional corporate financial policy has been made worse by recent accounting abuses that enrich the machine's operators at the expense of all stakeholders, including investors. Some of the more-common abuses include misrepresenting revenues, hiding liabilities, capitalizing ordinary expenses, creating fictitious asset swaps, changing accounting rules, and underfunding employee pensions. By falsifying real corporate results—by overstating the machine's value creation—executives have made off with huge bonuses and stock option packages. According to Moody's, such misconduct has contributed to the degradation of corporate balance sheets and loss of shareholder value.[2] It also perpetuates a culture of risk-taking that degrades living systems in a desperate effort to justify the machine's existence.

Living assets are not machine parts. People and Nature are intimately bound in the biospheric web of life that sustains all, and humans are responsive to this reality both consciously and instinctively. All organisms have a genetically endowed will to live and to optimize their possibilities for growth. Corporate efforts to control people mechanistically inevitably meet resistance and backfire. This manifests in countless ways, from employee stress to global climate change and the rapid deterioration of corporate balance sheets during the past 25 years (discussion upcoming).

From a systems thinking perspective, the resistance corporations encounter when they try to exercise mechanistic control over living assets and systems, however well intended, drives the balancing cycle described in Chapter 4 and illustrated in Figure 4-1. In classical economic terms, this cycle breaks the forward momentum of a corporation and causes its trajectory to conform to the familiar "S-curve."[3]

The beauty of LAS is its capacity to reshape the S-curve by creating harmony, rather than resistance, along its edges. The natural leverage of inspired learning and adaptive innovation is far more effective than the mechanical leverage of debt. These affirming attributes of LAS replenish and energize living assets rather than mortgage and harm them. In so doing, they weaken the counterforce of the balancing cycle and enable corporations to grow more sustainably, as shown on Figure 11-1. LAS, then,

Figure 11-1: How Balancing Cycles Bend the S-curve

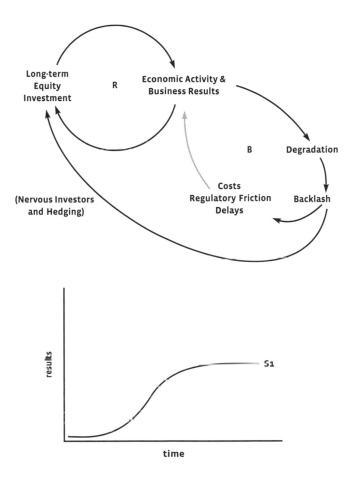

Balancing cycles occur when living systems are stressed and begin to push back. This figure describes the balancing cycles of environmental degradation and social backlash, as well as investor resistance, that have slowed the reinforcing cycle of economic activity described by the traditional business model. The slowing process is what causes the S-curve to bend over.

Figure 11-2: The Reinforcing Cycle of LAS + OL Reshapes the S-curve

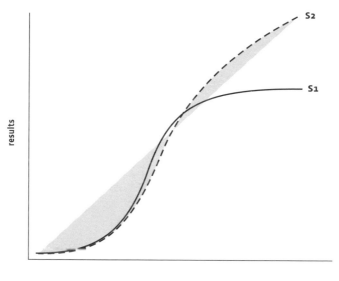

By mitigating the force of the balancing cycle, the reinforcing cycle of LAS + OL prolongs the duration of positive results as the S-curve rises to the northeast.

reshapes and extends the S-curve to the northeast as shown in Figure 11-2. Using this approach, stewardship companies get more leverage on the reinforcing cycle of profit and growth.

LAMP companies prolong this leverage by practicing good financial stewardship. It is an expression of their caring: they want to ensure the continuity of their chosen missions and their service to humanity, and know that such continuity is more likely if they are financially stable. Just as a living system conserves the food it generates, these companies conserve their cash flows, knowing that they will be sustained even in the most difficult times.

The LAS Centurions

This chapter looks at the eight oldest companies in the LAMP Focus Group: Alcoa (founded in 1888), HSBC Group (1865), Johnson & Johnson

(1886), 3M (1902), Nokia (1865), Royal Dutch Shell (1890), Stora Enso (1288), and Swiss Re (1863. I dub them LAS Centurions because each has existed for more than a century by incorporating financial stewardship into their larger visions and expressions of LAS.

These eight companies exemplify, from a variety of perspectives, the mutually reinforcing attributes of financial strength and LAS. Their financial strength offers more than food and energy for future growth. It implies a promise by each company to employees, suppliers, customers, investors, and other constituents: *we will be there, and we are committed to carrying out our mission in life.*

Conceptually, the financial stewardship that flows from LAS is the opposite of the more traditional practice of debt leveraging corporate balance sheets. An LAS firm seeks a solid inner fiscal core to support a flexible, adaptive outer self rather than using a flexible (i.e., financially engineered) core to support a more stolid and machinelike outer self. And, as affirmed by the LAS Centurions, it looks to an infinite future rather than to the finite one of the next quarter's profits.

In the final analysis, global LAMP companies succeed because their LAS cultures, operations, and finances are congruent with their purpose in life. They have *adaptive corporate cultures* and the *financial stability* to sustain those cultures. They harness life—living assets—to serve life.

Though this overview may seem at odds with most conventional financial thinking, it is supported by an impressive amount of data. The following table, which shows the balance sheet strength and bond ratings of all Focus Group companies, merely scratches the surface of that body of data. (The eight companies reviewed here are highlighted in boldface.) Theirs is a remarkable picture of strength — especially considering the general deterioration of corporate balance sheets in the past quarter-century.

A quick scan of the table shows the exceptional financial strength of the 16 Focus Group companies. The following are particularly noteworthy:

- Like the Global LAMP Index,[®] all carry investment-grade credit ratings, with the average rating in the A1–Aa3 range.
- Of the 14 nonfinancial companies, 8 (57 percent) had no net debt and 11 (79 percent) had five consecutive years of free cash flow.
- Of the 3 that lacked consistently positive cash flow, HP and Southwest had no net debt at year-end 2005.

Table 11-1: Financial Stability—Year-end 2005

	MOODY'S RATINGS ON UNSECURED DEBENTURES		DEBT/EQUITY RATIOS		
Company	Current	10-Yr. Range	LTD	Net Debt	Free Cash Flow (FCF)
Alcoa	A2	A1–A2	.40	.43	362.*
Baxter International	Baa1	A3–Baa1	.56	.58	1,094.*
Canon	Aa2	Aa2–A1	.01	None	1,733.*
Hewlett-Packard	A3	Aa2–A3	.09	None	2,747.
HSBC	Aa2	Aa2	NMF	NMF	NMF
Intel	A1	A1–A2	.06	None	7,441.*
Johnson & Johnson	Aaa	Aaa	.05	None	9,872.*
3M	Aa1	Aaa–Aa1	.14	.14	3,277.*
Nokia	A1	A1	.01	None	4,389.*
Novo Nordisk	A2	A2	.04	None	588.*
Nucor	A1	A1	.21	None	1,354.^
Royal Dutch/Shell	Aa1	Aaa–Aa1	.08	.01	14,209.*
Swiss Re	Aa2	Aaa–Aa2	NMF	NMF	NMF
Southwest Airlines	Baa1	A3–Baa3	.21	None	(144.)
Stora Enso	Baa1	Baa1–Baa2	.57	.73	(184.)*
Toyota	Aaa	Aaa–Aa1	.51	.95	4,603.*

Debt/equity ratio is stated both in terms of long-term debt (LTD) and net debt, which includes long- and short-term debt less cash and equivalents.

Free cash flow (FCF = net income + depreciation + amortization less capital spending) is stated in $U.S. millions. If FCF has been positive for each of the past five years, the number is followed by a star.

Because banks (e.g., HSBC) and insurance companies (e.g., Swiss Re) have more complex financial structures, their debt/equity ratios and FCF are considered not meaningful (NMF). Other indicators of their financial health are discussed in the text and accompanying endnotes.

The 8 nonfinancial companies that had more cash than debt carried the following net cash reserves at year-end 2005: Johnson & Johnson ($13.5 billion), Nokia ($11.7 billion), Intel ($10.4 billion); Hewlett-Packard ($8.7 billion); Canon ($8.2 billion); Nucor ($914 million); Southwest Airlines ($536 million), and Novo Nordisk ($368 million). Such reserves give them extraordinary advantages in strategic planning and new-product development relative to more-debt-burdened competitors. This is especially true in the airline and steel industries, in which debt levels have put major competitors on the edge of bankruptcy.

Significantly, 80 percent of the Focus Group companies were rated "A" or better by Moody's, and have remained in that range during the past decade when corporate debt ratings, in general, have slipped badly. Appendix 3 affirms that the same pattern holds for the larger LAMP Index. By contrast, at year-end 2005, only 45 of the world's rated corporations carried A-or-better ratings.

We should also note that all LAMP companies carry investment-grade ratings (Baa3 or better), whereas roughly one-third of the world's rated corporations are ranked below that level. Such speculative-grade bonds are the fastest-growing category of corporate debt, with most activity in the lower tiers commonly referred to as "junk." Since 1980 corporate debt downgrades have exceeded upgrades in all but two years.[4]

The two financial companies in our subject group—HSBC and Swiss Re—cannot be compared with manufacturing companies because they have different financial structures. However, both finished 2005 with excellent ratings. HSBC had the most-secure capital ratios among the world's top money-center banks,[5] and the most transparent accounting for the data included in those ratios.[6] Swiss Re, the world's largest reinsurer, has the industry's strongest reserves in relation to its underwriting risk exposure. In large part this reflects Swiss Re's expertise in evaluating risk and its unwillingness to underbid on policies for the sake of generating revenues. Such underbidding ruined many of its previous competitors after the 2005 Gulf Coast hurricane season. It also weakened Swiss Re's largest competitor, Munich Re, which was forced to take a $533 million loss in 2003.[7] Munich Re's credit rating is Aa3 (Moody's), one notch below Swiss Re's.

The two companies with the lowest credit ratings in our subject group— Alcoa and Stora Enso—both operate in cyclical industries in which bond ratings tend to be lower as a matter of course. That said, both are financially stronger than their primary competitors in terms of balance sheet strength, free cash flow, and credit ratings.[8] Beyond that, their shares typically trade at premiums to those of their competitors, as is shown in Appendix 5.

Credit Market Trends

The degradation of corporate debt has been particularly pronounced since 1999 when the stock market bubble of the 1990s began to burst. Fitch Ratings declared 2002 the worst year in a decade for global credit quality deterioration, citing debt-leveraged mergers and acquisitions, and corporate fraud as major contributing factors. Against this background, credit ratings for the Global LAMP Index® and Focus Group have been remarkably strong and stable.

A troubling aspect of the trend toward credit downgrades is the alarming lack of transparency among many of our largest corporate borrowers. According to Moody's, between 1996 and 2002 "structured finance," which consists mostly of asset-backed securities carried off corporate balance sheets, grew at a 43-percent compounded annual rate internationally, and at a 21-percent rate in the U.S.—far in excess of the growth of GDP, consumer incomes, and corporate cash flow. Yet only one in five companies surveyed by Moody's disclosed off–balance sheet liabilities in SEC filings.[9] Among the worst offenders were financial intermediaries—banks, finance companies, and the like. Within the past decade intermediaries added more than $6 trillion to their credit market exposure by "securitizing" packages of assets—such as car loans, mortgages, and credit card receivables—and then selling them as bonds to raise cash for more lending. *The Wall Street Journal* calls these bonds "an elaborate cocktail of unquantifiable credit risk" and notes that they do not always offer the financial and legal protections their issuers claim.[10]

Were financial intermediaries forced to recognize their securitized debt and adjust their balance sheets accordingly, it would shake the financial system that underpins our credit-based economy and substantially increase the cost of money to corporations that carry lower-rated debt. Such a credit tightening, in turn, would slow spending and job growth—perhaps sending the U.S. and global economies into another, deeper recession—thereby compounding the difficulty.

Although there is little that stewardship companies can do to ameliorate the risks of general financial and economic weakness, there is much they can do to insulate themselves. During the past decade, while others overborrowed, LAMP companies generally strengthened their core competencies, paid down debt, and stockpiled cash. Those core skills power the free cash flows shown in Table 11-1, and are continually strengthened by the innovative cultures of Living Asset Stewardship.

In the past 100 years, the eight companies featured in this chapter have survived worse conditions than we experience today—global economic depression and two world wars, as well as regional episodes of inflation, deflation, and financial panic. They endured and prospered because they had cultures, values, and visions of the future that inspired trust. Part of that trust was a public confidence that they had the financial stability to build on those visions. People wanted to work for them, buy from them, and invest in them because they believed these companies would deliver.

Credo

Johnson & Johnson's mission is "to alleviate pain and disease." Its credo is a promise to the people it serves about its priorities in achieving this goal— a "responsibility to doctors, nurses and patients" first, and then to employees, suppliers, distributors, communities and the environment, and finally, to stockholders. The ordering and clarity of these priorities comprise J&J's "trustmark." To uphold that trust, J&J knows it must consistently deliver on its promises; and to do that, it must maintain unquestionably strong finances.

Like all global LAMP companies, J&J sees its mission and financial integrity as inseparable. Fulfillment of mission increases financial integrity; and financial integrity enables fulfillment of mission. Putting one part of this connected whole at risk—say, by gambling financial integrity in a bid to become larger and more dominant—gambles with the entire enterprise. Employees and all other stakeholders know this. One of the surest ways to weaken a company's sense of mission and commitment to service is to weaken its financial staying power. People need to know not only where they are going, but that they can count on getting there.

Johnson & Johnson understands that its credo supports its financial power and vice versa—an interdependence like that of the reinforcing cycle of LAS + OL. It has increased sales for more than 70 consecutive years and become the world's largest integrated supplier of healthcare products because it has had the financial strength to deliver on the promises embedded in its credo. Customers have confidence that they can rely on J&J for increasing proportions of their healthcare needs. Employees have confidence that they can build long-term, productive careers at the company. Suppliers have confidence that they can develop relationships based on ethics and fair trade. Communities have confidence that J&J will be a good neighbor. Finally, investors have confidence that J&J will come through financially. Few companies anywhere can match J&J's sales and earnings growth through the last seven decades.

Johnson & Johnson's stewardship and ethical behavior have extended and reshaped the classic S-curve shown in Figure 11-2 because its culture and organization have allowed it to reinvent itself continually. Each adaptive reinvention has modified that classic curve, and represents improved outcomes. When lines are drawn to connect these overlapping S-curves, the result is a super curve that looks altogether different, as shown in Figure 11-3. This new curve, which reflects a process of continual reinvention, is conceptually closer to the evolutionary curve of Nature than to one describing the birth and death of a single entity because it describes a process of continuous learning and adaptation that allows the organization to transcend the lives of its individual members. Through the combined efforts of successive generations of connected people—employees, suppliers, customers, and others—J&J has grown into what it is today.

The likelihood of such continual self-reinvention is increased by J&J's decentralized organization: it is a "family" of more than 200 operating companies. Although individual companies vary considerably in size, the average J&J subsidiary has 540 or so employees. This scale allows people to know one another well and to develop collegial working relationships and customer intimacy. Collectively, this family arrangement works much like an ecosystem wherein the combined resources and synergies of the system support the livelihoods of its individual inhabitants, and the specialized knowledge of each inhabitant contributes to the resourcefulness and adaptability of the system. J&J's operating companies give it breadth of vision and product synergies that few companies can match. The whole company has the financial and intellectual resources of a global giant. Over time, the group has had the resources to learn, adapt, and grow in harmony with the changing world that supports it. As we step back to evaluate the larger picture, we see an energetic reinforcing cycle in which healthy financial and intellectual resources feed each other's growth.

When I tell people that Johnson & Johnson is a family of autonomous, entrepreneurial companies rather than a centrally managed monolith, they

Figure 11-3: How LAS Reshapes the S-Curve

LAS reshapes the S-curve by ameliorating the resistance of the illustrated balancing cycles. Simply put, the reinforcing cycle of LAS + OL (R-2) has two important impacts. First, it inspires innovation, which accelerates the primary reinforcing cycle of business results, profit, and long-term equity investment (R). Second, it drives a reinforcing cycle of stewardship that improves environmental and social results (R-3), which in turn lowers the resistance of the balancing cycles of systemic degradation (B) and investor caution.

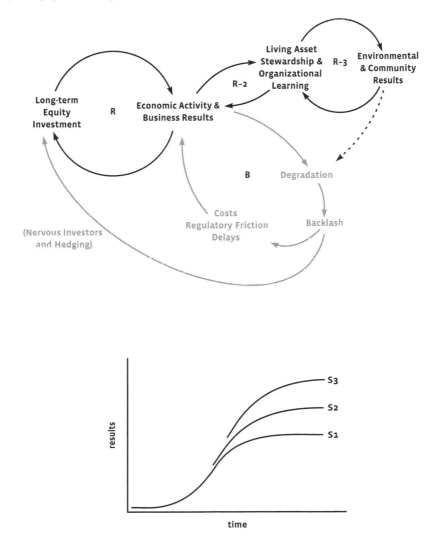

often express surprise that it could act so cohesively. Wouldn't some of the 200 member companies want to separate from the group to gain more opportunities for self-expression or to offer better rewards to executives? And wouldn't this process, over time, weaken the company to the point where no one would want to be affiliated with it? The answer to these questions is really quite simple. Like a healthy ecosystem, J&J has a purpose (its credo) and resources (financial and intellectual) that make staying within it a better option than leaving it.

If we removed from this picture J&J's credo or its financial strength, the appeal of its ecosystem—or family membership—would change altogether. Of these two strengths, the credo is arguably the stronger because it goes to the heart of enterprise. You can build a strong company on the motivating and bonding power of values; but you can't build values on the strength of a balance sheet. In the best of all worlds both are present and reinforce one another, as at Johnson & Johnson. Fewer than 1 percent of global non-financial corporations carry an Aaa/AAA credit rating. Johnson & Johnson is one of them.

A Holistic Approach

We are drawn to Johnson & Johnson for many reasons. The emotional appeal of J&J's mission, credo, and corporate ethics is strengthened by the holism of its approach. The company is committed to improving the conditions of human life and of the larger systems (Nature and society) that support human life. This commitment plays not only to our individual desires for well-being, but to our biophilic reverence for life.

Swiss Re and HSBC—both global financial powers—share with J&J this holistic approach. Swiss Re is very explicit: the company's mission is to "create a holistic approach to risk and capital management." HSBC simply calls its approach "responsible capitalism." The holistic values of these three companies impel them to adopt a decentralized structure that optimizes points of contact with the markets they seek to serve. All three see their financial integrity as part and parcel of their stewardship.

Swiss Re's normal credit rating has been Aaa, but the catastrophe of September 11, 2001 and subsequent weakness in global investment markets forced Moody's to downgrade it to Aa2. In spite of the fact that Aa2 is an excellent rating, and one most reinsurers would love to have, Swiss Re is determined to get back to Aaa. That rating is a symbol of its financial stewardship and responsibility to all constituents, and a badge of honor for employees.

In the months following its credit downgrade, Swiss Re moved quickly to rebuild its capital and reserve strength back to Aaa quality. First, it cut the dividend on its equity shares, sending a message to the markets that Swiss Re put the security of its customers ahead of shareholder returns. In an industry that lives by surety and trust, the dividend cut was as much a reaffirmation of Swiss Re's mission as it was a way to conserve capital. On the day the cut was announced, Swiss Re's shares increased in value by more than 6 percent, boosting the insurer's market value by more than $1 billion.[xi] Shareholders clearly got the message.

The more important task before Swiss Re, however, has been re-evaluating its risk management procedures and pricing its services to reflect more realistically the world in which it operates. Rather than discounting to increase the volume of insurance written, it has raised premiums in many areas, believing it to be less risky for all—insurer, insured, society, and the biosphere—to put quality of coverage ahead of premium earned.

In typical fashion, Swiss Re saw 9/11 and subsequent weakness in the global capital markets as symptoms of larger systemic risks. These risks increasingly come in the guise of global climate change, the decreasing availability of clean water, the spread of infectious disease, urban crime and terrorism, product liability claims, credit collapse due to counterparty insolvency, and financial market turmoil. As the world's largest reinsurer, whose typical customers are other insurance companies and multinational corporations, Swiss Re is very exposed and so, sensitive to these risks. To be effective at insuring and mitigating them, it must first understand their causes and the potential liabilities of ignoring them. Then it must coherently explain to customers the costs of risk coverage so they can make informed economic choices. It is a proactive, holistic process in which quality of analysis counts for more than size.

Swiss Re is effective because it not only thinks holistically—assessing and pricing large systemic risks—but also behaves holistically by partnering with its customers to reduce their risk exposures. It does this by freely sharing its expert knowledge about risk reduction and offering premium rebates for customers' loss-prevention initiatives. This partnership approach benefits customers by helping them assess and manage their systemic impacts, by deploying their capital more effectively, and by gaining public trust. It also benefits Swiss Re to have educated customers who are less likely to make large claims. The success of this partnership approach is reflected in Swiss Re's better-than-average claims experience and its typically low combined expense/claims ratio, and largely explains the enviable condition of Swiss Re's capital and reserves today.

Swiss Re's large institutional customers know that in the long run they are better served by such a holistic approach. It makes little sense to pay a lower premium to a less qualified insurer—one that offers less-informed advice, fewer performance incentives, or less surety of being there when needed.

Swiss Re's holistic stewardship approach pays because it generates so many positive feedback opportunities. By bringing customers' interests into better alignment with the long-term health of Nature and society, Swiss Re serves life, protects customers, and creates better conditions for its own business. The entire process—from its proactive risk and capital management to its excellent credit rating—is linked. In this sense, Swiss Re operates more like a symbiotic ecosystem than does any of its peers.

Sustainability—preserving social and ecological capital while producing economic value added has become ever more important . . . . If unchecked, the depletion of natural resources and growing social instability will eventually have consequences for all businesses . . . . That is why proactively analyzing and understanding any such risk, in order to develop methods of mitigating it, is a strategic task for Swiss Re.[12]

—John Coomber, CEO and Bruno Porro, Chief Risk Officer, Swiss Re

HSBC is much like Swiss Re to the extent that it is a global financial institution with exposure to multiple systemic risks and a coherent way of managing those risks. As a bank, it encounters risk whenever it lends or invests. If water scarcity, soil erosion, disease, or social unrest poses risks to HSBC and its customers, the bank must respond proactively, as Swiss Re does, and understand the business consequences of those risks. Anything less would cause them to be "working in the dark."

To help managers and customers understand the big picture of the global marketplace and its many layers of complexity, HSBC has a "holistic data modeling" team. Team members draw on the bank's huge database of loan and investment experience to help them evaluate risks and opportunities, and to know their customers better. The modeling team also works proactively with customers to identify areas of "deficiency and need."

HSBC knows that its holistic visioning capacity and its financial strength go hand in hand. If it is to lend and invest wisely, it needs knowledge and data that look beyond near-term cash flows to long-term sustainability. Customer service teams operating out of 7,000 HSBC offices in 90 countries continually gather qualitative as well as quantitative data that help the bank and its holistic modelers see emerging patterns. The process works from the bottom up and relies on a high degree of localized customer intimacy to be effective. It is more laborious and hands-on than most bankers are willing to accept, but its benefits are undeniable. The quality of HSBC's assets (principally, its customer loans) is far above that of its major global peers. The bank has more solid reserves and has hedged its risks more intelligently because it sees the market more clearly. In these and other areas, HSBC employs its capital more wisely than other global money center banks do, and it shows in the quality of its revenues and earnings. Few banks can match HSBC's growth since the early 1970s, during which time it has emerged from a mid-sized regional bank in developing Asia to a global power with a market capitalization of $182 billion at year-end 2005.

Reinvention

The mantra of all global LAMP companies is "continuous improvement"—a goal they achieve through learning and adaptive innovation. If they outlive and outperform their competitors, it is because they have repeatedly reinvented themselves as their markets change. Many of them have been through multiple transformations—both horizontally across industry sectors and vertically within their primary sectors. Each transformation has started a new S-curve; and the layering of multiple, adaptive S-curves has created the type of scenario presented in Figure 11-3.

3M, Alcoa, and Nokia all began life as basic commodity producers. Had they stayed on their original tracks, they might long ago have disappeared from the business landscape. But, by continually questioning their purpose in life, listening to and learning from their stakeholders, and pursuing adaptive innovations, they have reinvented themselves as global manufacturing and financial powers.

3M has reinvented itself both vertically in chemicals and adhesives, and horizontally by branching out into office equipment, medical supplies, and dozens of other subspecialties. Alcoa has reinvented the aluminum industry by improving its basic processes and co-creating, with customers, new applications for aluminum. The oldest of the three, Nokia, started out in the forest products industry, and then evolved into radio and electronics on its way to becoming the world's leading producer of wireless communications devices. All three companies have vibrant entrepreneurial cultures in which authority is localized and individuals are given unusual freedoms to innovate. Beyond that, these firms are deeply humanistic: they trust that employees will naturally think and act as stewards if given proper training and permission to experiment on their own.

Continual reinvention is the centerpiece of 3M's corporate strategy and the key to its financial stability. The company's "30 percent rule" holds that 30 percent of business-unit revenues must come from products introduced within the last four years. 3M consistently achieves that goal by enabling employees with good ideas to become entrepreneurs, as described in Chapter 7. To keep the cycle of invention and reinvention going, it regularly invests 6–7 percent of annual revenues in R&D— double the investment of a typical manufacturing company. The leverage 3M gets on these R&D expenditures is greatly increased by its inspiring vision of "making life easier, healthier, safer and more productive." Employees want to create in such environments because they feel they can personally make a difference. And it shows. During the past two decades, 3M has achieved more *Fortune* Magazine top-three rankings for innovation than all other companies except Rubbermaid.

3M's prodigious ability to reinvent itself has made it a financial powerhouse. In the past two decades (1985–2005), its gross profit margins have averaged nearly 50 percent and its return on equity more than 22 percent. Thanks to its perennially huge free cash flow and fiscal commitment to stewardship, 3M's credit rating has also been one of the world's strongest for decades, consistently in the top-tier, Aa1–Aaa range.

[W]e recognize that only by continuing to be a viable and successful enterprise can we continue to be a positive contributor to sustainable development.[13]

—W. James McNerney, Jr., Chairman and CEO, 3M

Alcoa launched the age of aluminum in the late 1880s when its cofounder, Charles Martin Hall, developed the first process for smelting aluminum in quantity. Alcoa is now the world's lowest-cost producer of alumina and the most innovative developer of new applications for the metal. It has largely transcended the commodity aspects of aluminum by dedicating itself to innovative *solutions*—product solutions that are strong, light, safe, corrosion resistant, nontoxic, less energy intensive (than in the past), recyclable, and embedded with advanced knowledge.[14]

Because of its intelligent reinvention of itself and the market for aluminum, Alcoa has vastly expanded its global market. Aluminum today is far more than a lightweight packaging material or an efficient conductor of heat for cookware. Smartly engineered with alloys and innovative design, it has gained market share in a host of markets, including aerospace, auto frames, precision castings, lightweight turbines, building materials, and electrical distribution systems.

A case in point is Alcoa's R&D partnership with Audi in the early 1980s, which successfully challenged the materials status quo of the auto industry and opened a vast new market. During 10 years of materials research and extensive design analysis, Alcoa and Audi co-developed the "spaceframe" body and seven new aircraft-grade alloys that set new standards in weight savings, structural integrity, safety, performance, and comfort. The effect of these developments on the auto industry was huge and transformative. Alcoa now has partnerships with Toyota, Ford, GM, Daimler-Chrysler, and other leading auto manufacturers to develop other aluminum alloy components. Because these partnerships extend toward production, Alcoa often builds dedicated mini-mills nearby customer plants to maintain close research collaboration.

Alcoa's long-standing skills at customer collaboration and inventing have coalesced into the Alcoa Business System—a set of three "overarching principles" that guides the company in its innovation. The first of these principles—*make to use*—is deeply customer intimate. It looks to provide precisely what the customer needs "on demand, defect free, and at the lowest possible cost." As in its partnerships with Audi and Mercedes Benz, Alcoa engineers work closely with their corporate customers from the design phase all the way through dedicated production. The second ABS principle is to *eliminate waste* from the production and distribution of products and to make them more eco-effective. The third is to develop a culture in which people act as *linchpins in the system*—they engage at every level to identify and solve problems, and to drive continuous improvements.

Taken together, these three principles mimic a living ecosystem—producing precisely what the system needs to thrive, generating little waste, and engaging the adaptive energy of all system constituents in the process. Alcoa's decentralized governance also mimics Nature in its capacity for spontaneous learning and adaptation. They invest authority in those who actually do the work and have contact with the customer. At corporate headquarters in Pittsburgh, only 400 employees oversee 131,000 workers located at more than 400 sites—an average of one per operating location. This system allows each unit to be a self-organizing center of entrepreneurial activity.

To maintain the spirit of entrepreneurship and customer service, the company offers all employees financial incentives for innovation. Further motivation is provided by Alcoa's determination to eliminate waste and be a sustainability leader. A bottle cap recycling plant in Holland, for example, derives all its energy needs from cap coatings. Contrary to the conventional wisdom of traditional manufacturers, this non-hierarchical system is remarkably self-organizing and efficient. Each plant becomes a learning laboratory. The best insights of each are shared throughout the system through an intranet, leadership meetings, and in-house publications. With such efficiencies, Alcoa lowered its annualized operating costs by approximately $1.0 billion in the 2001–2003 period (inclusive).

Remarkably, during three years of rolling recession throughout many of Alcoa's primary markets (2000–2002), the company maintained $2.8 billion in free cash flow while its largest direct competitors were either cash flow negative or barely positive. I believe that this superior performance arises from the natural principles of the Alcoa Business System and its ability to leverage the individual and mutual (symbiotic) learning capacities of employees. When employees feel good about themselves and their work, they naturally want to collaborate and invent. Collectively, their energy, insight, and innovation drive Alcoa forward.

At Alcoa, everyone is a potential inventor and no process or practice is immune from the question, "Isn't there a better way to do this?"[15]
—Paul O'Neill, Chairman and CEO (1987–2000), Alcoa Annual Report 1999

Nokia too has become an innovation leader by modeling itself and its supply net on natural, open, symbiotic principles. Astonishingly, at year-end 2005 its market capitalization ($84 billion) was one of the largest in the global telecom industry even though Nokia has been a telecom company only since 1981. The path of Nokia's evolution was set early on when it was a commodity producer on the remote northern frontier of Europe. To manage its logging and milling operations, Nokia had to communicate across vast tracts of wilderness. That need led it into electrical and telegraph cable and later into radio. As its proficiency in these areas grew, Nokia broadened its vision to include higher-value-added areas of electronics in which it could leverage its evolving capacities to connect, listen, and learn. It also began to think more aggressively beyond its home market. In 1981 Nokia entered the telecom market (via a co-venture) to create the world's first international mobile telephone network (NMT) in Scandinavia. The experience it gained from this venture eventually became the intellectual capital for its current status as the world's largest maker of mobile phones.

The common themes in Nokia's evolution—*connecting, listening,* and *learning*—are all key functions in innovative companies. They resonate in Nokia's strategic vision ("connecting people"), mission ("building a sustainable Mobile Information Society") and corporate culture (symbolized by annual "Listening to You" employee surveys). *Fortune* Magazine calls this culture "Nokia's Secret Code." In a feature article on the company it notes, "Nokia executives seem almost religiously committed to open standards and inter-operability in wireless . . . . They're constantly signing deals with competitors to develop shared operating systems and standards. The idea is that the easier it is to use phones and other wireless devices, and the better they work together, the more people will want to buy them."[xvi]

Extraordinary creative energy and financial stability are needed to achieve a symbiotic culture such as Nokia's. The company's energy comes from its openness to new ideas and its passion to create a more sustainable, connected world. Its stability comes from its rock-solid balance sheet. These attributes spontaneously catalyze and feed one another in a reinforcing cycle that operates much like a living ecosystem. The benefits are striking: in the past five calendar years (2001–2005) Nokia has delivered a cumulative free cash flow of $21.4 billion. Through that same period it has maintained net cash reserves (in excess of all debt) averaging more than $11 billion.

[Nokia's] real business isn't phones; it's innovation . . . . In an industry that's all about innovation, Nokia has tackled the ultimate creative act: It has installed a culture where innovation is built into the way the company operates.[17]

—*Fast Company* Magazine

Shared Responsibility

Any company that operates as an open, living system must have a sense of shared responsibility for its living assets and the larger living systems of which it is a part. This is one of the key secrets to long life and no LAMP company models this better than Stora Enso, which traces its roots back for more than seven centuries.

For most of its life Stora's sense of shared responsibility has been concerned primarily with the livelihood of employees and the communities it serves. During the past century it has also become increasingly sensitive to the natural environment in which its customers live and from which it draws forest resources. Although it has reinvented itself and its business processes countless times, Stora has never lost sight of these shared responsibilities or the importance of financial integrity to delivering on them. The good will it has earned from this approach is a primary reason it has lived and thrived longer than any company in the world.

Stora's behavior during the capital-market boom of the late 1990s offers a glimpse into the culture and strategic thinking that have sustained it for so long. While other forest companies took on massive debt to expand the quantity of their output via merger and acquisition, Stora concentrated on strengthening its balance sheet and maintaining the quality of its relationships with customers, employees, suppliers, and other constituents.

Although already the forest industry's leader in sustainability, Stora set goals in 1999 that would yield major reductions in emissions and landfill-bound waste per unit of output. As emphatically shown in its Sustainability 2003 Report, it not only achieved those goals by impressive margins, but also went on to dedicate itself to a goal of zero waste.[18] This ethic has helped Stora lower manufacturing costs and has energized employees.

Whereas traditionally managed forest companies might view Stora's balance sheet as under-leveraged and the costs of emissions control as irrecoverable, Stora sees a larger picture. It gets greater leverage through inspired employees who work with their hearts as well as their minds. The lower operating costs it achieves through waste reduction further improve operating margins. Moreover, as its largest customers seek to "green" their supply networks (see Chapter 10), Stora's market share has grown. In all these ways, Stora's strategy of continually improving its relational equity makes eminent sense.

The advantages of Stora's symbiotic strategy of shared responsibility were dramatically illustrated in the bust that followed the industry boom of the late 1990s. Competitors who had earlier pursued leveraged buyouts in hopes of eventual market domination later struggled with burdensome interest payments, cash flow deficits, credit market downgrades, large-scale layoffs, investor disgust, and general public suspicion.[19] By contrast, Stora has the financial reserves to outspend these competitors, even acquiring some of their distressed assets at knocked-down prices.

Stora's financial results have been impressive, especially given the sharp cyclicality of the forest products industry. From year-end 2000—the peak of its competitors' leveraged buyout boom—through 2005, Stora generated approximately $4.2 billion in free cash flow, with only one year (2005) of mildly negative results. During this time Stora also grew its shareholder equity by 12.5 percent, from $8.0 to $9.0 billion. By comparison, International Paper (IP) was forced to divest assets to stay afloat. Accordingly, its shareholder equity declined by 30 percent, from $12.0 billion in 2000 to $8.4 billion in 2005. The degree to which Stora has overtaken IP during this period is understated by their respective accounting methods. For example, for the past five years (2001–2005), Stora has maintained provisions for risks and charges—in effect, a rainy-day account—averaging nearly $1 billion. These provisions, which affirm its culture of shared responsibility, are not counted in its shareholder equity. By comparison, Georgia Pacific carries virtually no provisions, preferring instead to overstate its equity.

By virtually every relevant financial measure, Stora's holistic approach of shared responsibility has outperformed its traditionally managed competitors; and it has done so with less risk to employees, host communities, suppliers, and the environment.

[O]ur strengths in challenging markets are our strong balance sheet and cash flow ... [as well as] environmental and social responsibilities .... Stora Enso will continue to be developed as a sustainable forest products industry leader that creates value for its shareholders, customers and employees.[20]
—Claes Dahlback, Chairman, and Jukka Harmala, CEO, Stora Enso

Creating Legacies for Future Generations

This chapter has looked at the mutually reinforcing synergies between inspiring corporate cultures and financial stewardship. Inspiration can be found in an uplifting credo or mission, a passion for invention and continual adaptation, or a tradition of shared responsibility. These elements are present in all global LAMP companies. They inspire us because they answer a need that has driven humanity for thousands of generations: the drive to create a legacy for future generations, and to perpetuate our species and the web of life on which our existence depends.

Now consider Royal Dutch/Shell's vision: "Helping people to build a better world." On the face of it, this seems preposterous—the company produces fossil fuels whose extraction and use are harmful to the biosphere—but when we look deeper, there is much to support this claim. Shell uses a large portion of the free cash flows from its profitable oil and gas operations to build a sustainable energy infrastructure that will carry it forward for generations. The creation of that infrastructure, on a global scale, is an urgent "must." Getting there from our current, extreme dependence on fossil fuels is, of course, messy at best. But once there, the possibilities for a better world will be greatly enhanced. Shell has taken the first steps.

Shell's transition strategy is to extract, refine, and sell its mainstream products as sustainably as possible, placing increasing emphasis on clean-burning natural gas, while also aggressively investing in solar and wind power generation, co-generation, hydrogen fuel cells, and other potential energy sources. To accomplish this, in 1999 Shell created its fifth operating division—Shell International Renewables—and embarked on a mission to help Iceland become the world's first hydrogen-based economy.

Shell wants to offer customers a broad palette of future energy choices. With public pressure to combat global warming growing rapidly, Shell knows its corporate customers will increasingly need energy alternatives. In this sense, its game plan is not only the ecologically right and sustainable thing to do, but also the financially responsible one.

For Shell, hydrogen means longevity. Since 1999, Shell Hydrogen has become a global presence through use of a technology called Partial Catalytic Oxidation.[21] Its independent operating units have research joint ventures ongoing with numerous corporate giants, including Air Liquide, Ballard Power Systems, DuPont, General Motors, Siemens, and United Technologies (UTC). In 2002, Shell launched a project in Norway to explore multi-megawatt fuel cells driven by offshore natural gas, with a view to commercial production in 2010. In 2003 Shell opened its first branded retail hydrogen stations in Reykjavik (Iceland) and Tokyo.

Shell scenario planners estimate that by 2050 more than half of the world's energy needs will be met by renewables, with natural gas providing another 20 percent and petroleum 25 percent. Nuclear power might play a role, but Shell isn't counting on it and hasn't planned to spend any money on it. Of the various possible routes to this "decarbonization" process, Shell intends to concentrate on those that present the least risk and greatest future benefits to the future of life.

This is clearly "legacy thinking," and it has generated enormous enthusiasm, entrepreneurial spirit, and innovation at Shell. These attributes, more than its oil and gas fields, are the true sources of the company's energy and cash flow. Shell's credit rating (Aa1) and free cash flow are in the top tier of the energy industry, and so long as the firm remains an LAS leader, should remain so.

Shell's analysis of long term energy scenarios suggests different possible routes to decarbonisation: a direct path to renewables, supported by gas in the medium term, or an indirect path, via a global hydrogen economy that grows out of new developments in fuel cells and other technologies.[22]

—Karen de Segundo, CEO (2000–2005), Shell Renewables

The Total LAMP Experience

The eight Focus Group Centurions highlighted in this chapter, though longer-lived, fairly represent the larger 60-company Global LAMP Index.® Their sterling credit histories attest to the value they place on fulfilling their commitments to stakeholders and on sustaining their stewardship practices. The relational equity they have built as a result is largely responsible for their longevity and continuing profitability.

We learn a great deal about a company's commitment to stewardship when we look at its credit history. That is why we present credit ratings both as a single point (e.g., year-end 2005) and in the context of a 10-year range. Although all LAMP companies have credit histories that extend further back in time, we focus on the 10 years from 1995 to 2005 because it has been a particularly volatile economic period in which corporate credit ratings have undergone significant downgrades in world markets.

As shown in both Table 11-1 and Appendix 3, the 10-year credit histories of LAMP companies fall into tight channels, mainly in the A-or-better range. During this time, credit downgrades have slightly exceeded upgrades, but rarely by significant amounts. Interestingly, the Focus Group company that had the largest downgrade during the past decade (Hewlett-Packard) is today one of the most stable in terms of balance sheet strength and free cash flow. Its downgrade, along with those of some other science-based companies, reflects more the pace of innovation and obsolescence in technology today than any lack of fiscal prudence.

In the broader U.S. and world markets, as earlier noted, credit downgrades have exceeded upgrades in all but two years since 1980. And the 10 years from 1995 to 2005 have been among the most severe. The number of companies—among them former giants like Ford and GM—that have fallen to speculative-grade ratings below Baa3/BBB is alarming. According to a March 2005 Standard & Poor's report, the median industrial firm in the U.S. was then rated BB.[23] That is a full seven rating points below the LAMP median (A1/A+).

Interestingly, five of the eight Centurions (or 62 percent) maintained credit histories in the AA-or-better range during this past decade of rampant downgrades. The three that were outside this range nevertheless had credit histories that were far superior to those of their peers. A look further back in time shows that these Centurions have all survived periods of profound turmoil: world wars, depressions, and financial panics, as well as today's hyper-competitive Internet-based markets. They know what it takes to survive as well as thrive. We have much to learn from them about sustaining an enterprise for generations to come.

Conclusion

Financial stewardship is, ultimately, a declaration of intent. It tells employees, customers, suppliers, investors, and other stakeholders that a firm intends to be there for them long into the future. It also signals that this longevity will be accomplished in a professional and thoughtful manner.

LAS can't work without financial stewardship. The two are inextricable. LAMP companies continually reinforce this notion in word and deed. The interplay of Living Asset Stewardship and financial stewardship is, in fact, a reinforcing cycle that functions much like the reinforcing cycle of LAS + OL. LAS inspires learning and innovation, which in turn stimulates profit and cash flow. When LAMP companies set aside some of that cash flow as reserve money in the bank, they strengthen their capacities to learn, innovate, and pursue LAS.

The credit histories and current debt ratings of global LAMP companies are as impressive as their long-term stock market returns (see Table 5-1). They have staying power. That explains both their longevity and their ability to pick up market share when less prudent firms are in dire straits.

The LAMP Centurions, like their Roman counterparts, have a commanding sense of leadership that shows us why LAMP companies are more than heroes of history. They are likely to be heroes of the future as well.

1 2

The Unity of Systems Thinking

"What underlies the malaise of so many large and successful organizations worldwide is that their theory of the business no longer works."[1]

—Peter F. Drucker, "The Theory of the Business"

"We need paradigms to make sense of the world, yet because of these we become trapped or constrained."[2]

—Danah Zohar, *Rewiring the Corporate Brain*

Most corporations are trapped by a conceptual paradox. To realize their potentials in today's fast-paced global markets, they need mental models whose premises reflect the real world in which companies operate. Models based on false premises lead to erroneous strategies and counterproductive behaviors. The problem with the traditional model of business is not just a matter of false premises, but of premises that overtly conflict with the real, living world in which the corporation operates. Peter Drucker says that the assumptions on which the organization has been built and is being run no longer fit reality.

Many of the false assumptions inherent in the traditional model of business have been masked by time lags between actions and their consequences. It took decades of over-harvesting to produce today's declining marine and forest ecosystems. After a half-century or more of corporate pollution and consumer waste, we now have global warming and freshwater shortages. Time lags have masked the dangers within the traditional business model and allowed us to live off the natural world's accumulated capital, unaware of the damage we continue to foster. The false prosperity we achieved during this period of capital consumption, moreover, allowed the traditional model to become entrenched and accepted as an effective, even an ethical, paradigm. It has become "holy writ." Most business leaders are unwilling to abandon it even now, when they can see its shortcomings and the advantages of the emergent Living Asset Stewardship model. In part, their resistance to LAS has to do with giving up authority and rewards to which they have grown accustomed. But that would be an oversimplification. The real reason, I believe, is that they don't understand how the emergent paradigm of LAS works, and they can't make the mental leap because their minds are programmed to think in terms of linear cause and effect rather than in terms of whole systems.

The New Paradigm

The new paradigm of Living Asset Stewardship is based on whole-systems thinking. It views the corporation as a living community of people that functions much like an ecosystem. In this context, the strength and integrity of its relationships—those with its key constituent parts (living assets) and with the larger living systems that support it (global markets, society, and the biosphere)—have a direct bearing on corporate vitality. This holistic view is fundamentally different from the more linear, mechanistic view as described in Chapter 5 and elsewhere in this book.

Before turning to a functional comparison of the two models, we must understand some fundamental differences between living systems and mechanical ones that determine how they operate. These distinctions are important because they frame our thought processes and future choices.

The essential properties of living systems are properties of the whole rather than properties of their constituent parts. You can't understand the functioning of a human body by taking it apart and analyzing its various components because the body works as a total system. Its essential properties arise from the interactions and relationships among its various subsystems—nervous, circulatory, immune, etc.—which in turn are defined by the interactions and relationships of their constituent parts. If you remove or isolate one of these critical subsystems, the properties of the whole human body are compromised or completely destroyed.

Incredible as the brain is, it can't function without the heart, lungs, and other vital subsystems. Take them away and the brain is useless. Similarly, you can't understand the brain's phenomenal capacity by dissecting it and examining its parts. Instead, you must look at it contextually—as a network of billions of intricately connected cells and circuits that resides within a network of living tissue that, in turn, resides within a networked living environment. Everything is connected to everything else. Networks are embedded within networks and communication flows freely in every direction; action is a consequence of many ordered relationships between the brain and the central and autonomic nervous systems. No single cell embodies the properties of the whole system. Cells function only in relationship to one another.

When we consider the unique attributes of a system encompassing many individuals—such as an ecosystem or a company—the same principle holds. An ecosystem, for example, can feed itself and continually regenerate by recycling its own waste, which none of its constituent organisms can do. A company can operate on many fronts for 24 hours a day without stopping, something its individual executives and employees simply cannot do by themselves. By networking, both systems can perform more complex tasks because they can access the collective knowledge of all their parts.

Frijtof Capra puts it succinctly: "To understand things systemically literally means to put them into a context, to establish the nature of their relationships."[3] The *context* in which companies operate—global markets, society, and the biosphere—is a highly complex system that Capra calls the web of life. All of its key components are alive, continually changing and adapting to one another. To survive and thrive in such a system a company needs to use its full intellectual and adaptive capacities. And to do this it must operate as an open, diverse, and highly networked culture (see Chapter 7).

The advantages of such a culture can be seen in its capacity to learn spontaneously from the systems in which it operates as they change—through customer intimacy (see Chapter 8), partnering with Nature (Chapter 9), and networking with suppliers (Chapter 10)—and in its capacity to feed itself via financial staying power (Chapter 11). Companies that fail to do these things cannot possibly engage their full potential.

With machines, the case is altogether different. If you understand their individual parts, and how they are connected and programmed, you can pretty accurately predict how they will behave. A car will speed up if the driver hits the accelerator or slow down if she applies the brakes, regardless of her attitude or the environmental conditions, so long as the automobile is well maintained and safe from external harm. But corporations aren't cars. The machine example offers limited value in the context of relating to others—learning from customers, inspiring employees, brainstorming with suppliers, or getting feedback from investors.

A second major difference between living systems and machines is *the unique capacity of living organisms and systems to regenerate and reproduce themselves.* To do this, the parts of living beings must be viewed as a systemic whole. Like machine parts, they have their separate identities as cells, neurons, et al., which combine to form a complete unit. But unlike mechanical parts, which simply exist near one another in the context of a machine, our cells and neurons also exist *because of* and *for* one another.[4] Our skin, for instance, continually replenishes itself because it is part of a total system that values healthy skin. Other systems within our bodies serve this process because by serving, they replenish themselves. This self-making capacity is embedded in the DNA of all living beings. It is the means by which the web of life and all living systems exist.

The self-making capacity of corporations and other human organizations is derived from our human self-making capacities, especially our higher capacities to think, create, and adapt. This organizational self-making is a circular phenomenon: people in the organization learn to replicate principles that guide living systems in Nature, and the functioning of the organization itself improves the well-being of humanity and the biospheric web of life (i.e., Nature). In such interactive systems, the parts we individuals play continually relate to the whole that sustains us. The stuff of life for these institutions is the development of our knowledge and innovation. Thus, corporations, like universities, must necessarily be concerned with the ways in which their cultures excite or inhibit learning.

As "things in themselves," machines are defined by the sum of their parts. They function by the means of those who create and operate them—not by their own means. Absent their creators and operators, they are incapable of self-organizing, much less self-reproducing or learning. Machine parts have narrowly defined functions. They exist to support the machine until they wear out or become obsolete.

The magic of the Toyota Production System (TPS), as Johnson & Broms describe it, resides in its capacity to connect employees to the evolving needs of the system and vice versa. They call this process "management by means."[5] I have adopted the term because it so aptly describes the way LAS works: through a process of continuous feedback, learning, and adapting that's intended to improve *how effectively* work is done rather than *how fast* it is done. Plant workers have incentives to perfect quality and production methods as work flows through. TPS recognizes that people and living systems "learn as they do," and that learning is more effective when self-directed by individual employees in the process of doing rather than when it's imposed from above. This approach to innovation engages everyone, not just a select few, and utilizes relationships and information exchanges that occur spontaneously throughout the plant floor. Thus, every employee becomes a "cell" in a living system, performing a specific function while also enabling the system to regenerate (self-make) continuously through a process of ongoing feedback and learning. Understanding the value of relationships to its production system, Toyota treats its employees as valuable assets rather than as disposable parts. (See Chapter 1 for more on Toyota's production system.)

A third, and more subtle, attribute of living systems that separates them from machines is *the way their capacities for learning and innovation emerge as they become more complex.* Obviously, people have a higher capacity to learn and innovate than do single-cell organisms. A living network has a greater capacity to learn and innovate than a single organism within it does. Likewise, an integrated system of living networks has greater capacity than a single network. This *emergent* quality—an unfolding multiplication of potential—flourishes in firms that operate as open, networked living systems, and is notably lacking in firms that operate as machines. In fact, the more a company networks with the living systems in which it resides—global markets, society, and the biosphere—the more likely it is to be on the cutting edge of learning and innovation.

Companies that operate as machines subvert their capacities to learn and adapt; they dilute their capacities for learning and innovation by failing to see that they are alive. And they can't leverage those emergent capacities without becoming more integrated with other living systems. By isolating themselves from the living world that supports all humanity and human enterprise, and by treating employees like replaceable machine parts, they also deaden the human spirit.

The human spirit is, as we now know, the primary lever of global LAMP companies. When such companies think and behave systemically they engage our biophilic instincts and love of life. The reinforcing cycle of LAS + OL converts inspiration to learning and innovation, and ultimately, to profit. This is a powerful equation and so fundamentally different from what has guided the traditional model that we must call it a new paradigm.

Human Nature

Companies that care about people and the things people care about are naturally drawn to systems thinking. As E. O. Wilson points out in *Biophilia* (see note 5 to the Introduction), our brains and psyches evolved in a bio-centric world, not a mechanical one. We are biologically wired to think systemically, and to care about the web of life because it is the means of our existence. We are most creative when we think and behave in ways that enhance the quality of life. It doesn't matter whether these connections are explicitly recognized in a corporation's organization and culture, as they are at Hewlett-Packard, Nokia, Shell, and Toyota, or whether they are implicit, as they are at Nucor and Southwest. The important thing is caring. That is why LAS is "the heart of enterprise."

Abraham Maslow and others have shown that employees want to make a contribution, to do something meaningful with their lives.[6] Some psychologists say this search for meaning and purpose is actually stronger than the sex drive. When companies tap this energy, they release tremendous passion and creativity among employees. As their passion grows, so does their capacity for quantum insight and breakthrough innovation.

I know many people who have happily traded salary for meaningful employment. The CEOs of HSBC, Nucor, and Southwest Airlines are the lowest paid among the major companies in their industries. Beyond the satisfaction of reinventing their businesses, these leaders gain the spiritual fulfillment of co-creating visions of a more sustainable world, of contributing to something larger than themselves, and of engaging others in their quest.

Physicist Danah Zohar explains the emotional force of this spiritual connection between people and the web of life in cosmic terms that go beyond Wilson's biophilia. She maintains that people long to feel they are not alone, that they are more than a single atom in the endless void of the universe. People yearn to be part of a wave of continuous life and growth. We have a mental, emotional, and spiritual need to resonate with that living wave, she reasons, and we can achieve deep resonance only through our higher (quantum) minds. To Zohar, quantum thinking and quantum insight are the source of our optimal mental intelligence; our ability to handle ambiguity, uncertainty, and complexity (emotional intelligence); and our vision (spiritual intelligence).

[A]ll fundamental transformation is ultimately spiritual transformation, spiritual in the very broadest sense as issuing from the level of reflection, meaning and value.[7]

—Danah Zohar, *Rewiring the Corporate Brain*

Collins and Porras generally support Zohar's thesis. In *Built to Last*, they demonstrated the value of deeply resonant, corporate core ideologies.[8] These ideologies define the essential values and purpose (the "why we exist") of a corporation—the guiding star that helps them to navigate even the most troubled waters. When Bill Packard once claimed that The HP Way was Hewlett-Packard's greatest invention, this is what he had in mind. Johnson & Johnson has long regarded its credo as a source of competitive advantage. Both are powerful statements precisely because they spiritually resonate with people.

The strategic visions of these and other LAMP companies typically play off their core ideologies. HP's vision, shown below, is an extension of David Packard's desire, expressed almost a half-century ago, that the company's existence go beyond "making money" to "making a contribution to society." The collective wish to do something for the "common good" defines HP's soul. Talented people are drawn to HP for just this reason, and the enthusiasm of long-term HP employees is palpable. Talent and enthusiasm are a powerful mix. Like attracts like. That is human nature.

A winning e-company with a shining soul . . . to lead in an Internet age, to invent for the common good.[9]

—Hewlett-Packard: *Our Vision and Strategy*

Will to Live

The inherent purpose of all living beings and systems is to live. From this commonsense perspective, it is easy to see why systems thinking and LAS are so congruent. But it really doesn't matter which thought model one uses now. If corporate thinking and behavior fall out of synch with the living assets and systems that support enterprise, the corporation itself is ultimately threatened.

The traditional model loses coherence in its mistaken belief that we can, through science and reductive reasoning, improve on Nature and alter its courses to augment human life. In its extreme forms, this egocentric, almost God-like, view exalts humanity so far above Nature that we can do almost anything we want to the biosphere for our short-term benefit. This perspective is in sharp contrast to the biocentric view of systems thinkers, which sees humanity as an integral part of Nature, not above it. The systemic view holds that, rather than try to control or manipulate Nature, we must live in harmony with it if we want to sustain our lives on Earth and ensure the long-term success of our business institutions.

The evidence of the marketplace now suggests that companies with life-affirming cultures and processes outperform non-affirming ones by a wide margin. LAMP companies have not gained market share on traditionally managed companies by being marginally better at mechanistic management. They have a more effective business model. In addition, traditional companies self-destruct when they subvert the web of life on which we all depend.

As the traditional model falls apart, its corporate adherents have lost whatever focus and discipline they once had. Profit for them has become more and more a game of creative accounting, mergers and acquisitions, asset sales, underfunding employee pensions, layoffs, and Enron-type fraud. The deterioration of corporate balance sheets and credit ratings discussed in Chapter 11 is a symptom of this demise and loss of discipline. Traditional corporate leaders able to see the big picture now regularly change the criteria by which their bonuses are computed because simple, old-fashioned guidelines, such as shareholder returns, don't work well for them. Their excessive compensation, especially at times when their companies are losing market share and profit, is a sign of desperation rather than strength—a signal that they lack confidence in their futures.

Global LAMP companies, although affected by market conditions creat-ed by the traditional model, have gained market share during the past few decades precisely because their systemic mental models are more effective, and more congruent and harmonious with the way the real world works. Consequently, they have greater strategic clarity, consistency, and align-ment. This is a powerful base on which to build.

Every organization, whether a business or not, has a theory of the business. A valid theory that is clear, consistent and focused is extraordinarily powerful.[10]
—Peter F. Drucker, "The Theory of the Business"

Linking Theories of System and Practice

There is a strong link between the validity of a company's theory of busi-ness practice and its theory of system—namely, how it defines itself and the world in which it operates. This link gains importance as a company grows and becomes more complex. Having a viable and unified theory of system is clearly more important to large global companies, such as Shell and Canon, than to local service stations and office equipment stores because their systemic impacts are greater.

To understand these systemic impacts, and to manage the complex web of relationships that multinational corporations form to execute their busi-ness strategies, we must think in terms of whole systems. Mechanistic thinking is too simplistic—too focused on isolated parts of an issue and not enough on its contextual whole. Innovative solutions are more likely to emerge from holistic thought processes that engage the perspectives and spontaneous inputs of diverse stakeholders than from top executives work-ing through bureaucracies.

Table 12-1 is a conceptual guide to the linkages between the theories of system and of business practice. Because it draws heavily on the content of previous chapters, the table's major elements are simply summarized below. When you connect the conceptual dots, you'll see how a firm's self image and worldview affect its organization, strategic thinking, value cre-ation, and definition of efficiency.

Because the LAS model starts from the premise that the firm is a liv-ing system, comprising living assets and contained within the larger liv-

Table 12-1: Two Systemic Views of the Corporation

Systemic views of the corporation and its context (theory of system) determine how a firm is organized, how it creates value, and how it defines efficiency (theory of practice). The following distinguish the LAS model from the traditional one.

	LAS MODEL	TRADITIONAL MODEL
	Systemic View	
The company is:	A living ecosystem	A machine
Its key strengths:	Adaptive processes, flexibility	Structure, order
Its key resources:	Nature and society (biocentric)	Top managers (egocentric)
Its reason to exist:	To serve people and life (symbiotic)	To serve itself
Its vision of profit:	A means to the end of service	The end in itself
	Organization	
Archetype:	Partnership, symbiotic network	Military command
Authority:	Decentralized, localized	Highly centralized
Workplace:	Open, interactive, self-organizing	Ordered, bureaucratic
Teamwork:	Shared leadership and responsibility	Single leadership
Most valued assets:	Living assets (people and Nature)	Nonliving assets (capital)
Leverage points:	Inspired, empowered employees	Executive know-how
	Strategy	
Mission:	Improve world, quality of life	Dominate, control market
Vision:	How can we contribute?	How can we dominate?
Participation:	All people have meaningful roles	Executives run the show
Goals:	Learning, advancing long-term vision	Next quarter's profit
Execution:	Everyone accountable	Executives mainly accountable
	Value Creation	
Objective:	Customer solutions (holistic)	Products (quick turn)
Creativity:	Exists at all levels	Exists mainly at the top
Innovation:	A social, emergent process	An administrative process
Experimentation:	Exists everywhere (freedom to fail)	Controlled from top
Learning:	Individualized, intrinsic	Prescribed, extrinsic
Recognition:	Success recognized wherever it occurs	Leaders get all the credit
Driver:	Reinforcing cycle of LAS + OL	Financial reward
	Efficiency	
Goals:	Zero waste, Factor Ten, sustainability	Maximum output, profit NOW
Methods:	Local knowledge, industrial ecology	Mass production, scale
Metrics:	Balanced scorecard	Profit and loss

ing systems of society and the biosphere, it makes sense that its culture and processes would reflect a respect for life. We see that respect clearly expressed in LAMP companies' relationships with employees, customers, strategic partners, host communities, and Nature. We also see it in their missions of service, their visions of improving the quality of life, their values and strategies, and in their corporate metric systems, which reflect the importance LAMP companies place on all these aspects of their functioning.

The most important message in Table 12-1 is the ethic of unity, inclusiveness, and transcendence of the LAS model relative to the traditional one. There is nothing unifying, inclusive, or transcendent about a model that aspires only to profit—especially when that profit comes at the expense of so many people and of Nature. Comparing the two models is much like comparing the Declaration of Independence to the earlier "divine right of kings." For generations, the Declaration has inspired visions of a better world grounded in a universal respect for human rights. The other system is now virtually dead.

As with prior tables of this sort, the different theories and practices I've noted in Table 12-1 are more leanings than absolutes. No company fits perfectly in either the LAS or the traditional column. Nevertheless, a composite of leanings generally leads to a clear picture of a company's chosen path and the direction it is likely to pursue in the future.

It is also worth noting that the two systems are so fundamentally different that they cannot easily be mixed and matched. As will be discussed in Chapter 13, you cannot bolt LAS onto a traditionally managed corporation and expect it to work. Traditional theories of system and practice subvert the essential processes of LAS. It's hard to imagine how the value-creation processes of a model based on open, interactive living systems can function in an organization that is ordered, bureaucratic, and machine-like. It simply boggles the mind. When we look at the critical assumptions and elements of both models, their fundamental incompatibility becomes clear.

Theory of System: This is where everything begins. What is the fundamental nature of the firm? If we say "living ecosystem," we naturally proceed down one path; and if we say "machine," we go down another. Each path, although ostensibly guiding us toward profit and growth, asks us to think and behave in different ways as we move forward.

The LAS path asks us to think deeply about the context in which we exist, our relationships, and the centrality of Nature in everything we do. LAS regards Nature as vastly more than the air we breathe; our water, croplands, fisheries and forests; or the repository into which we dump our wastes. It sees Nature as a model of organization and efficiency whose cybernetic principles have extensive applications to business and society. The theory of Nature as a conceptual model is best articulated in the emerging field of industrial ecology. Some of its most evolved expressions today would include Intel's continual drive to surpass Factor Ten efficiencies, Nokia's value net, Novo Nordisk's co-development of the Kalundborg eco-industrial park, 3M's sustainability metrics, and Toyota's production system. Each of these companies continually raises the bar on eco-effectiveness for itself and consciously strives to define "best practices."

Beyond the practical value of Nature as a source of vital goods and services, and as a model of efficiency, LAS connects us with our deep emotional and spiritual bond with Nature as earlier described by Wilson in his biophilia concept, and by Zohar through her notion of quantum consciousness. More than half a century ago, psychologist Erich Fromm noted the wide split between people and Nature that was then being created by the industrial revolution. He, too, saw humans' very "being" as inextricably linked to Nature. Fromm's "Credo" talks of our need to experience a "unity and oneness" with our fellow humans and with Nature.[11] The LAS model recognizes this powerful psychological and spiritual drive. The traditional model does not.

Because of our emotional bonds to Nature, we become inspired when companies and the people around us respect and steward life. Conversely, we withdraw and feel stressed when they disrespect people and Nature. Stress is a form of repressed anger that is the leading cause of sickness and absenteeism in companies today.

By the very fact of his being human, [man] is asked a question by life: how to overcome the split between himself and the world outside of him in order to arrive at the experience of unity and oneness with his fellow man and with nature. Man has to answer this question every moment of his life. Not only—or even primarily—with thoughts and words, but by his mode of being and acting.[12]

—Erich Fromm, "Credo"

The alternative path of the traditional business model couldn't be more different in theory and practice. It asks us to consider the firm as an efficient moneymaking machine that is separate from Nature and society, rather than as a living ecosystem that is closely integrated in the web of life. Proponents of this model believe we need machine-like structure and order to extract value from a world that is too often disorderly and chaotic. They believe that entrepreneurs and business managers, acting rationally in their own self-interests, will create enough surplus wealth that society will come out ahead in the long run. The baser instincts that energize this process are aroused by money; and profit is the logical "end" of all enterprise because it channels those instincts to areas of greatest opportunity. The accumulation of profit—via corporate retained earnings, shareholder returns, and the economic multipliers created by corporate hiring and spending over time—generates a capital reserve that continually feeds the system and propels it forward. To traditionalists, this path has brought to the capitalist world wealth beyond our wildest dreams of a century ago.

There is much to be said for the efficiency of the capitalist model in mobilizing capital and rewarding innovation; but the traditional view of capitalism is inherently limited by its inability to price all of the resources it uses and its blindness to humanity's deep connections to Nature. Because there is relatively little immediate cost to discharging wastes into the atmosphere, watersheds, or soil, the supposed profitable thing to do is to use the biosphere as a free dumpsite. Likewise, because overharvesting fish cries, forests, and croplands maximizes near-term profit, this too is regarded as rational behavior. Designing products that wear out quickly and treating people like disposable machine parts—via layoffs, bureaucratic regimentation, or any lack of personal regard—also makes sense to traditional managers so long as those products yield a quick profit. By this reasoning, any behavior that subverts life or dehumanizes people is okay if it boosts the bottom line. It sounds crazy. But that is where the traditional path has led us.

The systemic blindness of corporations using the traditional model has been apparent for decades. Their defenders still believe these companies will self-correct under the benign guidance of a Smithian invisible hand. But that line of thinking leads to false hope. The problems of traditional companies are not set right with a bit of fine-tuning; they are the sad results of operating under false premises. The LAS model and the performance of global LAMP companies affirm that there is a lot more leverage in respecting life than in subverting it, however attractive the bottom line may be for short-term gain.

The area in which the LAS and traditional models share the most common ground concerns profit. Both models recognize that companies cannot exist without it. That said, each tends to regard profit quite differently. Under the LAS framework, profit is not the end of corporate existence, but the *means* to a higher end of serving people and life. That higher end, typically embodied in a firm's mission, vision of the future, and ideals, is a powerful driver. Alternatively, when companies consistently place ends (profit) above means (LAS), they turn people off.

In the abstract, the LAS model sounds Pollyanna-ish and "soft." Managing to serve people and life does not have the hard, mechanical precision of managing for profit or the ego-force of serving ourselves. But those perceptions are reflections of our mental conditioning rather than of the way living systems actually work. If our benchmarks for what is hard and soft are determined by business results—speed of learning and adaptation, quality of innovation, and sustainability of profit—then we have to say the weight of evidence supports the LAS model. Similarly, if our benchmark is survival, the LAS model also wins. With the average and median ages of global LAMP companies exceeding 100 years (more than double the averages for the S&P 500), there is nothing "soft" about the notion that companies learn and adapt, or they die. By this measure, trying to impose a rigid machine model on a flexible living ecosystem is soft-in-the-head thinking, because it almost certainly leads to dysfunctional behavior, eroding real profits, and premature death.

When it comes to free cash flows, balance sheet strength, or stock market returns, the LAS model is no less capitalistic than the traditional one, as shown in the Introduction, and chapters 5 and 11. Nobody would say that Alcoa, Johnson & Johnson, Nucor, or Toyota is compromised because each puts service to customers and employees ahead of profits. Few believe that Canon, Hewlett-Packard, Stora Enso, and 3M are less profitable as a result of their eco-stewardship, or that the long-term holistic visioning of Shell and Swiss Re is a waste of time. And who could say that the balanced scorecard metric systems of Baxter, Intel, and Johnson & Johnson are nonproductive? Instead, we think of these companies as forward looking and professional. What could be better for future profits than happy employees and customers, the elimination of waste from process streams, and metric systems that continually improve the means of productivity?

This holistic approach to profit is circular, not linear. We intuitively understand the merits of this approach. What goes around comes around. We reap what we sow. Do unto others as you would have them do unto you. Waste not, want not. Don't eat your seed corn. Loyalty begets loyalty. Love thy neighbor as thyself. The English language is full of rich metaphors that describe the processes of systems thinking. These metaphors express human values about life and Nature that have been with us for millennia. They apply equally to managing a business and finance and to living life because business and finance are extensions of life.

By putting our values first, business success will follow. Without these values, there is no success at all.[13]

-Paul O'Neill, Chairman and CEO (1987-2000), Alcoa

Theory of Practice: A corporation's theory of practice naturally follows from its theory of system and vision of profit. If we start with a model based on living ecosystems and symbiosis, then we are led to practices that optimize the capacities of those systems. The same is true with the traditional machine model. Anything less would be inconsistent, wasteful, and unprofitable.

Following the thought path of Table 12-1, we would expect the organization of systems thinking companies to be networked because networks are the defining attribute of all life and living systems. If we accept this proposition, we are then left with the question of how networks optimally function. The answers to this question, too, are based on universal laws of Nature. Networks must be open to attract the diverse partners they need for their collective knowledge, adaptive capacity, and long-term survival. They must allow individual members to self-organize in order to reach their full potential. And they must stimulate interdependence at every level.

Hierarchical command-and-control cultures subvert networks because they devalue diversity, distrust self-organization, and dismiss ideas of interdependence. In doing so they kill the spontaneity living systems need to realize their full creative potential.

The most important assets of living networks are—of course—alive. Because living people are the assets on which companies realize their greatest productive leverage, it is important to know how to engage these assets most productively. This brings us back to caring about people and the things people care about. Companies express their caring by nurturing people and the web of life on which they depend. Like Johnson & Johnson, they make caring an integral part of their cultures, trusting that it will inspire employees to extend that caring out to customers, and contributing to a better quality of life.

Traditional mechanistic corporate cultures are typically premised on creating order in an otherwise disorderly world. Leaders maintain tight control via centralized authority and a bureaucracy committed to maintaining orderliness. Because employees are generally considered part of the natural disorder, authority and responsibility are usually vested in individual executive leaders. Nonliving capital assets tend to be prized more than living assets because they are easier to control or manipulate. The leaders of such companies have a difficult time seeing the firms' connections to the living world or the value that world contributes to their enterprises. Because they so isolate themselves, their vision and understanding tend to be limited.

It would be wrong to imply that there is no hierarchy in companies using the LAS model. There is hierarchy in LAS companies, but it tends to be smaller and to harbor a different set of dynamics. The best LAMP companies, as we have seen, practice subsidiarity, which localizes authority and accountability by placing it with people on the front lines. As Shell and others have discovered, by shifting authority from the top to the local level, companies actually gain greater vision and control.

Corporate strategies, too, are remarkably congruent with companies' theories of system. Firms adhering to the LAS model tend to define their missions in terms of *improving the world* and *quality of life* because they understand the connectivity of all living systems. As David Packard and numerous others have done in creating such long-term visions, LAS leaders look to their core competencies and ask, "How can we contribute?" Like Nokia does, the best companies include their employees in this visioning process because such inclusion surfaces greater diversity of ideas and feedback. When LAMP companies, such as Toyota, set goals, they put relatively more weight on learning and advancing their long-term visions than do traditional companies, which put greater weight on short-term profits. And when LAS firms execute strategy, as does Shell, they hold every empowered employee accountable.

By contrast, strategic thinking at most traditionally managed companies tends to focus on domination, market control, and quick profits. Executive compensation at these companies, particularly bonuses, lavishly rewards such achievements, and in so doing, creates incentives to cut corners and take imprudent risks. It is well known, for example, that most large mergers and acquisitions today lose money for shareholders because executives are more focused on rolling up market share than on strategic synergies.[14] Such failures have, no doubt, played a significant role in declining corporate credit ratings, as noted in Chapter 11. Yet they continue because, in spite of experience, traditional thinkers remain obsessed with control and economies of scale.

Corporate methods of value creation also flow logically from firms' theories of system. Under the LAS model companies put a greater emphasis on total solutions than on simply selling products. Toyota sells cars that go beyond mere transportation. They are designed for durability, recyclability, ease of maintenance, fuel efficiency, and lower emissions—all of which add to their resale value. Toyota's goal is to maximize the value of their cars and minimize their adverse impacts from conception through end of life—the process known as life cycle assessment (LCA). That is totally congruent with LAS and an important ingredient in Toyota's exceptional employee morale and productivity.

Traditionally managed auto companies, by contrast, approach the value-added process as a machine would: produce as much as possible, then sell it as quickly as possible. It is a more linear, less holistic method and in its systemic blindness, is more error prone. The centralized, bureaucratic organizations of these companies also hinder learning and their numbers-driven strategies create employee stress—hardly a recipe for market success.

A deeper look into the methods of value creation finds that companies employing the LAS model assume that learning, creativity, and innovation are social processes that intrinsically emerge at all levels by people doing and reflecting together. This assumption is manifest in their networked organizations and inclusive cultures that engage large numbers of people in the creative process. At 3M and Hewlett-Packard, creative employees are given free time to develop their own ideas. The best LAMP companies, such as Canon, allow employees to follow their hunches and experiment. They also give employees freedom to fail—on the theory that if you're not failing, you're not reaching and trying—and quickly recognize successes wherever they occur. When such methods of value creation converge with inspiring visions of the future, companies increase the odds of generating a reinforcing cycle of LAS + OL.

Traditional companies could not be more different as regards value creation. Creativity for them exists mainly at the top, employee learning is prescribed and delivered in one-size-fits-all sessions, and innovation is bureaucratically administered. It is astonishing, for example, that the Apple Macintosh operating system was developed at Xerox's Palo Alto Research Center, and then virtually given away because Xerox executives could not see its value. As a further hindrance to innovation, recognition for any successes at traditional companies generally goes to corporate leaders who are presumed to be the prime movers of everything.

Definitions of efficiency also vary widely between the two models. Manufacturers such as Intel, Hewlett-Packard, Nokia, and 3M think beyond incremental gains in eco-efficiency to inspirational goals such as zero waste and zero injuries, Factor Ten efficiency, public health and education, and the long-term sustainability of their operations. Using principles of industrial ecology, they keep materials and manufacturing byproducts within a closed loop so little or nothing of value is wasted, and hazardous substances can be monitored and properly disposed. Companies such as Novo Nordisk and Stora Enso also learn the needs of local companies and communities that would be willing to buy reprocessed waste streams that might otherwise end up as harmful effluent. Financial intermediaries, such as HSBC and Swiss Re, share with customers their knowledge of stewardship best practices and give them incentives to be more systemic in their policies and practices. To these and other LAMP companies, efficiency means getting maximum value from the physical resources they use, inspiring employees to be more productive, coaching suppliers on the leverage in LAS, and building customer loyalty to secure a stable base of repeat business. Therefore, they look beyond traditional, backward-looking measures of efficiency, such as returns on financial equity, to more forward-looking metrics on the development of relational equity — the value of their relationships with employees, customers, suppliers, and host communities. This balanced approach, which looks to the means of efficiency, is called the balanced scorecard.

Sidebar 12-1: Toward Greater Efficiency in Value Creation

In Chapter 8 we noted that 96 percent or more of the materials and energy used in making the products and services we consume ends up as waste. This is an immense pool of potential value. For this reason, when companies sell their reprocessed wastes to one another, rather than pay to have them disposed, they can realize returns on investment that can exceed 50 percent with payback periods of two years or less.

Hewlett-Packard saves millions of dollars each year by taking back HP computers, recapturing 100 percent of their material components, and then using those materials in the manufacture of new computers at plants they co-own with Noranda in Roseville, California and Nashville, Tennessee. Nucor, the world's most-efficient steel manufacturer, derives virtually all its output from recycled steel. Alcoa, Canon, and Toyota all design their products for ultimate recycling, use large amounts of recycled materials, and are relentless in their efforts to eliminate waste from their manufacturing processes. Intel has already achieved Factor Ten and is moving on to new heights of efficiency.

Developing value from waste and/or material streams between companies that are not contiguously located is more challenging, but markets are growing to accomplish this goal. Emission credits, traded on the Chicago Board Options Exchange (CBOE), help to reduce CO_2 and SO_2 emissions by placing an economic value on them. Local and regional networks for exchanging waste/material streams have sprung up across North America since the early 1990s.[15] Although vastly underutilized, these networks will prosper as companies become more skilled at mining the value from waste streams and as laws that raise the economic costs of dumping are passed.

Efficiency at traditional companies looks more to ends—market domination, scale, maximizing output, and profit—than to means. In doing so, these companies virtually ensure that they cannot keep up with the stewardship leaders of their industries. Their metric systems, which focus mainly on profit and loss, give inadequate feedback on the key relationships that will drive their businesses forward.

Transparency

One of the best ways to tell whether a company is seriously committed to systems thinking and LAS is to see how transparent its metric systems are. How completely does it report its performance in relation to the larger living systems in which the company operates, and how openly does it discuss these "triple bottom line" results with employees and other constituents? Firms that see themselves as living communities or systems make full-disclosure reporting a priority because it invites dialogue, which in turn catalyzes learning, innovation, and profit.

The leverage in triple bottom line reporting—better yet, in triple *top line* reporting—resides in its capacity to present a more complex view of a firm and its relationships with other living systems. By seeing the firm in a more holistic context, new possibilities for meaningful learning and innovation emerge. These emergent properties create an enormous advantage for global LAMP companies.

It is significant that all 16 Focus Group companies offer information on their websites about their triple bottom line policies, objectives, and/or impacts; and 14 of the 16—88 percent—publish separate annual reports on their global environmental and/or sustainability performance. Further, 12 Focus Group companies—75 percent—adhere to demanding Global Reporting Initiative (GRI) guidelines and are certified for accuracy.[16] Fewer than 2 percent of the world's multinational companies meet these tests.

The two companies that don't publish sustainability reports—Nucor and Southwest—are renowned for caring about people and the things people care about. They, too, have processes that leverage this caring into higher levels of corporate learning and innovation, but their processes are more internal than public.

Nucor's culture is a living thing . . . . Commitment to our employees. Teamwork. Safety. Customer focus. High quality standards. Ethics and integrity. Continual improvement and risk taking. Pay for performance. Environmental focus. Decentralized divisions. Entrepreneurial spirit . . . . It's still about people—listening, keeping them motivated, and freeing them to do their jobs with corporate guidance, not interference.[17]

—Daniel R. Dimicco, President and CEO, Nucor

Going for It

As previously noted, the productivity problems of traditionally managed companies cannot be solved by imposing on them the metric systems, value creation methods, and strategic goals of LAMP companies for the simple reason that their cultures clash. Chapter 13 will follow six traditional companies that try to adopt the appearances of LAMP companies only to find they create more problems than they solve. When the desired ends of maximizing near-term output and profit conflict with the means of LAS, they quickly shed their stewardship veneers. As a result, they are left not only with the problems that originally caused the conflicts, but also with an aftermath of cynicism about their authenticity and reliability.

Employees are rarely fooled by vision statements and policies that emerge from management retreats—especially if they are incongruous with the prevailing culture of the firm. Employees quickly dismiss disingenuous "flavor of the month" window dressing. In the final analysis, superficial, market-driven vision statements only add to the separation between management and employees—a divisiveness that hampers feedback, learning, and innovation.

LAS is a complete system unto itself. Companies that want the innovation, stability, and profitability that come with stewardship best practices must adopt LAS *in its entirety*. They must learn to think systemically as well as behave systemically. They must take the learnings of Table 12-1 to heart.

This is not to say traditionally managed firms must radically transform themselves overnight into LAMP exemplars. That would be impossible in large organizations, especially those with entrenched command-and-control cultures. Realistically, transitioning from a traditional to an LAS culture is likely to take years, perhaps even generations. The starting point must be leaders who authentically care enough that they themselves will become the exemplars of the new system. And then, they must stick with the path. If leaders commit themselves to a course of LAS and then change course, for whatever reason, they will generate only cynicism and doubt.

Shell has long been migrating toward governance that operates on systems thinking. To that end, throughout the organization it began to decentralize decision-making authority in the mid-1990s by becoming more openly networked, and more committed to principles of subsidiarity and management by means. Although I think Shell's leaders would say it still has a long way to go before its networking capacity is optimized, the company has become more locally entrepreneurial, innovative, and responsive. An impressive aspect of the Shell transition was the willingness of leaders at every level to talk about their mistakes, reflect on them with diverse stakeholders, and thereby learn from them. In doing so, they opened the whole organization to constructive dialogue and learning.

Shell leaders undertook this transition because they felt they had no other choice if they wanted the company to be a long-term player in the energy industry. They had to engage everyone in their corporate group—not just those at the top—in exploring ways to produce and use energy more sustainably. And to do that they had to demonstrate, in word and deed, that they truly care about people and the things people care about. They knew there was no half-way. So they went for it.

Conclusion

Systems thinking is the core of Living Asset Stewardship because it is the attribute from which all other key attributes of LAS emerge. Whether LAMP companies engage in it by design or by simple intuition, systems thinking is a source of immense strategic advantage.

Companies that think systemically see themselves as living communities or systems that operate within the context of the larger living systems (markets, society, and the biosphere) on which they depend. They understand that all living systems are organized as networks and that one of the key advantages of networked communities is their capacity to support learning and innovation. Furthermore, the best stewards understand that new possibilities for learning and innovation emerge as living networks grow in complexity. Thus, when they approach their businesses as overlapping networks within networks, the potential for learning and strategic insight grows immensely. The reinforcing cycle of LAS + OL that drives innovation and profit affirms the importance of these emergent insights.

The failure of the traditional business model is one of vision: it fails to see the qualities of the firm that produce such results and the possibilities for leveraging these by systems thinking. This represents a huge handicap in an age in which the pace of knowledge and innovation is accelerating. We can see the effects of this handicap in the deteriorating balance sheets of traditionally managed companies and in their lagging stock market returns in comparison with those of LAMP companies. We can also see it in the desperate attempts many traditional companies now make to inflate their returns through questionable accounting practices and leveraging their balance sheets with debt.

The mechanical world view gave us a science that explained things, and a technology to exploit them as never before, but the price paid was a kind of alienation at every level of human life . . . . The mechanical world-view fails, ultimately, because it does not work towards a greater, ordered coherence. It reflects neither the intuitions nor personal needs of most people, nor the simple, quite classical fact that we live in a shrinking world, a world where technology and mass communication, industrial pollution and the threat of global extinction have made us aware as never before that in some very important sense we are all interdependent and that our human lives are inseparably intertwined with the world of Nature.[18]

—Danah Zohar, *The Quantum Self*

When Stewardship Fails

"Constraint (perceived as well as real) is a major killer of creativity
. . . . Freedom or autonomy is its major enhancer."[1]
—Warren Bennis and Patricia Biederman, *Organizing Genius*

When stewardship fails to produce desired results, it is almost always due to an inherent conflict between means and ends. Companies that adopt the rhetoric of stewardship and set stewardship agendas, and then manage in ways that egregiously exploit people and Nature, nearly always fail. More often than not, they make a bad situation worse by generating disbelief, stress, and cynicism among employees and strategic partners. When they lose stakeholder trust and loyalty, they lose relational equity, which is the foundation of their financial equity.

Simply put, you can't bolt stewardship onto an organic culture. Organic cultures must live by organic means. Companies are living, organic systems: communities of people serving other people and drawing on Nature for critical resources through a complex web of ever-changing relationships. People who try to manage such complex living systems by mechanistic means—with hierarchical, numbers-driven, linear-thinking management by objectives—dilute the synergies that naturally exist within these systems.

The most effective stewardship cultures, as we have seen, are organized and managed like living ecosystems. They are: more networked than hierarchical in structure; driven more by relationship than by numbers; more eco-centric (holistic) than egocentric (self-centered) in their mental models; and, in their strategic thinking, more focused on the infinite game of sustainability than on the finite game of next quarter's profit. When companies manage in this way—by Living Asset Stewardship—they create a symbiotic partnership between people and Nature. This is an organic means of managing a company that not only embraces complexity but also thrives on it.

This chapter focuses on six companies I call the Corporate Social Responsibility (CSR) Underachievers. These six have appeared on prominent lists of sustainability and CSR exemplars, but have failed both as businesses and as stewards. Although each has had legitimate stewardship attributes worthy of praise, they have lost significant shareholder value because their means of managing were so in conflict with their avowed goals. My purpose here is not to impugn their good intentions or the sincerity of employees committed to their stewardship efforts, but to identify the inconsistencies that led to their failures.

For perspective I will compare these six companies, during the 10-year period from 1996 through 2005, to their nearest equivalents from the LAMP Focus Group. These comparisons, summarized in Table 13-1, show the trend of their credit ratings (by Moody's) and the total returns on their common equity shares. It is important to note that each of the CSR Underachievers in this table is a one-time global leader in its industry that once had a larger market share than its LAMP comparator.

During the 10-year period identified in Table 13-1, the CSR Underachievers had the following common experiences:

- All six suffered declining returns on shareholder equity.
- Five (Bristol-Myers Squibb, Ericsson, Ford, International Paper, and Xerox) had to sell valuable assets and/or cut their dividends in order to protect their equity.
- The same five had their bond ratings reduced by Moody's, and at year-end 2005 were rated near the bottom of their ranges.

Table 13-1: Comparing Stewardship Approaches

LAS LEADERS VS. CSR UNDERACHIEVERS (1996-2005)

Companies	Moody's Bond Rating Past 10 Years (Range)			Total Investment Return Past 10 Years (as %)	
	Last	Low	High	Cum.	Annualized
HSBC Holdings	**Aa2**	**A2**	**Aa2**	**331.56**	**15.75**
JPMorgan Chase	Aa3	A1	Aa3	158.35	9.96
Johnson & Johnson	**Aaa**	**Aaa**	**Aaa**	**225.17**	**12.52**
Bristol-Myers Squibb	A1	A1	Aaa	41.13	3.51
Toyota	**Aaa**	**Aa1**	**Aaa**	**169.41**	**10.42**
Ford Motor Co.	Ba1	Ba1	A1	54.97	4.48
Canon	**Aa2**	**A1**	**Aa2**	**231.01**	**12.72**
Xerox	Ba1	B1	A2	35.88	3.11
Nokia	**A1**	**A1**	**A1**	**876.19**	**25.59**
Ericsson	Baa3	B1	Aa3	49.12	4.08
Stora Enso	**Baa2**	**Baa2**	**Baa1**	**73.69**	**5.68**
International Paper	Baa3	Baa3	A3	12.75	1.21

Comparative Returns

LAS Leaders:				**317.84**	**15.37**
CSR Underachievers:				58.69	4.73
Global LAMP Index				394.42	17.33
MSCI World Index				97.37	7.04
S&P 500 Index				138.31	9.07

LAMP companies appear in bold italics. The CSR Underachiever that most closely matches each LAMP company appears immediately below it.

- The shares of three (Ford, International Paper, and Xerox) lost value and showed positive returns only as a result of dividend payments.

Because of these difficulties, the shares of the CSR Underachiever group lagged those of their LAMP counterparts by a wide margin. For the 10-year period the LAS leaders had a cumulative average return of 318 percent—more than five times that of the CSR Underachievers. An investment of $1 million in each group would, at the end of the 10-year period, be worth $4.18 million for the LAS leaders, and $1.13 million for the CSR Underachievers—a spread of $3.05 million.

The CSR Underachievers also lagged the S&P 500 and the MSCI World indices by wide margins. This may be an unfortunate coincidence. But it is worth considering whether these results reflect the backlash of colliding cultures as described below.

Common Deficiencies of the CSR Underachievers

As previously suggested, CSR Underachievers have two common attributes that sabotage their quest for product leadership and profit:

- hierarchical cultures that stifle employee networking and initiative
- an MBO (management by objectives) fixation on creating profit and other numerical results (ends) rather than building a sustainable capacity to achieve those results (means)

Both of these attributes clash with the essential nature of firms as living systems. People are the means by which companies create value. Networking is a primary means by which people grow their learning and creative potential. People are intelligent, social animals that thrive on interaction and spontaneous collaboration. When managed as if they are profit-producing machines, they resist or become depressed. That depression is the number one occupational illness in the U.S. today, draining billions of dollars from corporate profit, and should not be assumed to be solely about workers' personal problems, temperaments, or biochemistry.

The foregoing attributes also clash with the life-affirming goals of stewardship itself. Deep stewardship requires harmony between means and ends. Companies can't effectively execute CSR agendas unless, at a minimum, they treat their employees with respect. When they avow respect for people, communities, and Nature, yet treat employees and suppliers like disposable machine parts, they lose credibility and trust. Their efforts to promote stewardship are quickly dismissed as public relations stunts.

The large gap (seen in Table 13-1) between the returns of LAMP companies and their underperforming counterparts reflects a comparable gap in employee morale. Employees who feel valued, and who are inspired by their employers' stewardship, work with greater energy and commitment than those who believe their employers are exploitive and disingenuous. One of the cardinal principles of LAS is that employees who work with their hearts as well as their minds have a greater desire to network and share information. Their spontaneous collaboration spawns inspired organizational learning (OL) and capacity building which, in turn, drive innovation and, ultimately, profit. The synergies created by this process are described by the reinforcing cycle of LAS + OL.

Before a review of what went wrong for each CSR Underachiever, it is worth noting the public persona each has projected. Five of the six are publicly committed to the triple bottom line of economic, social, and environmental return by virtue of their participation in the Global Environmental Management Initiative, the World Business Council for Sustainable Development, and other CSR organizations. JPMorgan Chase, which has the fewest credentials in this area, has been a leader in equal opportunity employment, community outreach, and philanthropy. In 2001 and 2002 *Business Ethics* Magazine named it one of the top 100 corporate citizens in the U.S.[2] *Fortune* Magazine has frequently named it "the world's most admired bank."[3] And at year-end 2005 it was one of the top 10 holdings of the Domini 400 Index of socially screened U.S. companies.

To establish their respective stewardship credentials, each of the CSR Underachievers has invested considerable effort in creating a public image of civic responsibility and transparency. All six have issued annual reports that addressed their social and environmental initiatives, and all have adopted Global Reporting Initiative guidelines. These actions are steps in the right direction because they compel a company to look at its business in a broader systemic context, which is key to acquiring the skills of LAS.

The CSR Underachievers, however, failed to create synergies because their corporate cultures deeply conflicted with their avowed stewardship agendas. To make matters worse, when they found themselves falling behind industry peers, they reacted by taking management by objectives to desperate extremes—doing "whatever it takes" to produce a sales or profit number. As the following cases attest, these methods included falsely reporting sales and profits, misleading customers, taking imprudent risks, underfunding employee pension plans, diluting product quality, and forcing layoffs.

Ericsson

In many ways Ericsson is the most tragic case among the CSR Underachievers because it has tried the hardest to be a global stewardship leader. Like the old ATT, it was considered a national economic treasure and had a well-established culture of noblesse oblige. Its hierarchical management system had enjoyed long success in a world of government-owned and -protected monopolies in which hierarchy was an established norm. But it was too bureaucratic to compete in the privatized and fast-paced telecom marketplace that emerged in the late 1990s. Compared to the open, collegial, and highly networked culture of Nokia, Ericsson entered this new competitive world fragmented by internal fiefdoms.

When its stock and credit ratings crashed in the three-year period from 2000 through 2002, Ericsson was operating under a feudal system of shareholder control, board acquiescence, and imperial management that stifled initiative and slowed response times. Its board of directors was then controlled by holders of its "A" shares, who had *1,000 times* the voting power of the "B" shareholders. This gave the two largest "A" shareholders—the Wallenberg family and Handelsbanken—disproportionate power over the company's agenda. At the time of Ericsson's demise, its board essentially served at the pleasure of a royal family. The prime minister of this hierarchy, former CEO Lars Ramqvist, was often criticized for being out of touch with subordinates and with the company's "B" shareowners.[4] Ericsson's class system flowed into the workplace, where engineers were treated as a higher-status class of employee than marketing and finance people. The whole culture was based on rank and privilege, attributes that don't inspire information sharing, much less deep stewardship.

The deficiencies of the culture became strikingly clear in March 2000 when a fire destroyed an Ericsson chip plant that served both its own and Nokia's cell phone production. The empowered frontline employees at Nokia were quick to appraise the damage and its significance to future product sales. They immediately passed their assessment up to senior executives, who, in short order, secured alternative chip supplies. Ericsson's bureaucracy, by contrast, kept the problem from senior executives, assuming that the disruption wouldn't last long. As a consequence, Ericsson virtually had to stop production of cell phone devices while Nokia increased its market share.

Ericsson has had difficulties in understanding what creates value for the consumer . . . . The result: Nokia earned US$4.5 billion on its mobile phones last year, while Ericsson lost US$2.25 billion on its handsets. Nokia's shares have doubled in the past three years, while Ericsson has added 4.3 percent . . . .[5]

—Allan T. Malm, Professor, Entrepreneurial Studies, Lund University

Hoping to recapture its handset losses, Ericsson then gambled the future of its world-class networks division by lavishing buyers of its equipment with credit. It bankrolled marginally solvent companies, allowing them to become players in a market that was quickly rushing toward excess capacity. When the inevitable economic downturn came, and the extent of that overcapacity was revealed, these marginal buyers defaulted, leaving Ericsson with a mountain of worthless paper. As a result, Moody's downgraded Ericsson's credit rating by 10 notches—from Aa3 (high grade) to B1 (junk) at year-end 2003. During the worst moments of its credit woes, its share value tumbled by 97 percent. In a more open, collegial culture, the risks of overextending credit for the sake of hitting short-term sales and profit targets would have been discussed more thoroughly than it was at Ericsson.

As Ericsson's finances and markets unraveled, it further crippled itself via deep payroll cuts. From a peak payroll of approximately 107,000 employees in 2000, it was down to 50,500 by mid-year 2005—a 53-percent reduction. These cuts eliminated many valuable employees and hurt team morale.

During 2004 and 2005 Ericsson has made a comeback by installing a new management team, reducing bureaucracy, and raising additional shareholder capital. Much of this change was due to a cyclical rebound in global demand for its superbly engineered mobile networks. However, a longer-term view would note that Ericsson is still dominated by the Wallenberg family and Handelsbanken, although the voting power of their A shares has been diluted.[6] However, the company continues to suffer from its near-fatal fall. At year-end 2005, Ericsson's credit rating was three notches below Nokia's, and in areas where the two compete head on, it lags far behind in market share. The outlook for its mobile networks, although more promising, is less secure than when Ericsson was at its competitive peak. Future customers will be hyper-aggressive, private-sector corporations rather than slower-moving government-owned ones. To compete in this market, Ericsson will have to be more open, inclusive, networked, and entrepreneurial—not hierarchical and class conscious.

Nokia's culture couldn't be more different from Ericsson's. It is one of the world's least hierarchical companies. Rather than having all major decisions emanate from a tightly controlled executive office, it uses a mixture of servant leadership and distributed decision making. Employees are coached and trained to be the best they can be, and then empowered and trusted to make decisions at the local level. As *Fortune* Magazine notes, "Almost every assignment of any importance at Nokia is given to a team, and managing the company is no exception."[7] This lively stewardship culture is one of the best examples anywhere of the synergistic reinforcing cycle of LAS + OL. Employees are enthusiastic about learning, experimenting, collaborating, and innovating. Their innovations drive a cascade of world-class products that have quickly vaulted Nokia to the top of its class. Thanks to its strong cash flow, Nokia closed out 2005 with no net debt on its balance sheet and net cash reserves of $11.2 billion.

Bristol-Myers Squibb

In 1996, CEO Charles Heimbold of Bristol-Myers Squibb (BMY) promised Wall Street that the company's earnings growth would average 12 percent per year through 2000—a clear MBO directive. At the time, BMY stock was lagging those of Johnson & Johnson (J&J) and other pharmaceutical peers due, in part, to a dearth of new products developed in-house. In Heimbold's mind, BMY had to do whatever it took to get the share price up. As with most imperial CEOs, he was quick to dismiss anyone who questioned his methods.

To compensate for BMY's deficiency in developing new products, Heimbold's management team, driven by impatience, entered into a series of ill-fated ventures. The most famous was BMY's $2 billion investment in ImClone's anti-cancer drug Erbitux, which was turned down by the FDA in December 2001. This led to a shareholder class-action lawsuit that BMY settled in August 2004 for $300 million. Following the ImClone fiasco, BMY purchased DuPont's drug unit for $7.8 billion—$2 billion more than any other bidder was willing to pay.

With time running out on Heimhold's promise, BMY's blue chip reputation at stake, and its plan to buy earnings growth faltering, the company began to manipulate its earnings in diverse, and often illegal, ways. According to a *Wall Street Journal* investigative report, BMY inflated its sales and earnings via unreported asset sales, began "channel stuffing" drugs to distributors, and adopted misleading accounting practices. It also dipped into restructuring reserves, a practice clearly forbidden by the SEC.[8] As a result of these manipulations, the U.S. Justice Department and SEC both investigated BMY in 2002 and asked the company to revise its revenues and earnings down for 2000 and 2001 by approximately $2 billion. In September 2004 BMY was ordered by a federal judge to pay $150 million to shareholders who had bought the stock during those years.

There was this constant garage sale going on. And it wasn't driven by cleaning up the portfolio—it was driven by the P&L [profit & loss statement].[9]
—Former executive of Bristol-Myers Squibb, as reported to *The Wall Street Journal*

The Wall Street Journal (WSJ) got its story from 27 executives, all of whom asked that their names not be disclosed. Most had left BMY voluntarily, but some were still at the company. Their willingness to talk suggests a culture turned recklessly deceptive and demoralizing. If BMY was promoting itself as a steward to the outside world, internally it was anything but.

The single-minded, numbers-driven dysfunction of BMY's culture was revealed in July 2001, when the company learned that Novation LLC was about to stop purchasing the anti-cancer drug Taxol for its network of client hospitals. BMY quickly unloaded its inventory of Taxol on distributors without telling them what was happening. Much of this inventory had already been labeled for Novation; BMY cleared it out by offering deep discounts. In the end, distributors were left with product that they couldn't sell and that BMY refused to take back. It is hard to overstate the relational equity destroyed by this short-term maneuver to boost BMY's sales and profits. The BMY gambit stands in direct contrast to Johnson & Johnson's $100 million recall of Tylenol in 1982, which obviously hurt short-term sales and profits, but in the end boosted its relational equity with the public, retailers, and distributors.

The Novation episode was perhaps the most egregious example of BMY's practice of channel stuffing. After a while this short-term-fix approach became a self-defeating way of life. Lacking a flow of new products to boost sales, BMY would pressure distributors to take extra product near the end of each quarter. This not only strained wholesale relationships, but also disrupted manufacturing. It caused spurts of hyperactivity, during which plants would work overtime for weeks, which were followed by long lulls—an inefficient and debilitating process for plant workers that also hurt morale.

One consequence of BMY's manipulations was a substantial boost in executive pay incentives and stock options for 2001. According to the *WSJ* investigative report, in that year approximately 94 percent of Heimbold's $18.5 million total compensation came from stock option grants, a bonus, and long-term incentive payments linked to corporate performance. His successor, Peter Donlan, received $12.9 million that year, of which 92 percent was incentive based. This is a pretty sad picture of a company that in 2001 was named the world's most sustainable pharmaceutical company by the Dow Jones Group Sustainability Index and earned an AAA rating from Innovest for triple-bottom-line transparency.

The practices BMY used to make its numbers and inflate executive compensation are, of course, symptoms of a larger problem of leadership. Executive hierarchies are not effective in the fast-paced world of commerce today. They are too out of touch with the real world, too cumbersome, and too often at odds with the creative people needed to generate company profits. CEO Donlan disavowed knowledge of the channel stuffing practices, and suggested they were the work of others. Former BMY executives, who had left the company in disgust, refuted his claim. *The Wall Street Journal* reported: "More than a dozen former employees insist that Mr. Donlan was keenly aware of [the channel stuffing]. Others point out that Bristol-Myers, since 1992, had one of the most sophisticated inventory-control systems in the industry, with countless internal reports tracking the steady increase in wholesaler stocks of company drugs."[10] If these employees are correct in their allegations, this CEO—who should most typify the ethical standards of the firm—destroyed his moral authority as a stewardship leader.

Incredibly, at year-end 2005, CEO Donlan was still at the helm in spite of subsequent ethical lapses at BMY. In August 2003 the company was ordered by the FDA, after three warnings, to stop and correct misleading advertisements for its top-selling cholesterol drug Pravachol. It also faced charges of violating federal anti-kickback rules that prohibit marketers from paying doctors in exchange for Medicare and Medicaid business.

During June 2005, BMY settled a criminal complaint, filed in New Jersey, that charged it with conspiring to commit securities fraud. As part of a deferred prosecution agreement, the company agreed to accept responsibility for its conduct and pay $300 million in restitution to victims of the fraud scheme, adopt internal compliance measures, and cooperate with the ongoing criminal investigation. That payment brings to $839 million the total the company has paid to shareholders harmed by its fraudulent conduct.[11]

The economic damage caused to BMY and its shareholders by its hierarchical, MBO culture of doing whatever it takes to show a profit extends far beyond legal costs and fines. Its ethical misconduct has severely harmed its relational equity with employees, distributors, doctors, and investors—the very people it most needs to restore its financial equity.

Xerox

The Xerox story has much in common with that of Bristol-Myers Squibb. For decades, Xerox's hierarchical culture had stifled individual initiative and innovation. Since the late 1970s Canon and other competitors gained share in Xerox's primary market for copiers and successfully migrated to new venues of information technology that were replacing photocopying.[12] Xerox products were not meeting sales and profit expectations, and there was little in the new-product pipeline to offer much hope. The company had to present a more dynamic growth image or its equity value was toast. To buy itself time, Xerox resorted to cooking the books. According to criminal charges filed by the Justice Department and SEC, the company overstated gross income for the five years through 2001 by $6.4 billion and overstated its pre-tax income by 36 percent, or $1.41 billion.

The Xerox story highlights one of the sad attributes of hierarchies under pressure. Executives, who are used to being the ultimate authorities and to having the final word, have a hard time admitting failure. As a consequence, they often are in denial about the nature and causes of their difficulties, and whitewash the truth. They have little or no tolerance for questioning of the status quo, or for searching for a better or new way.

James Bingham, former assistant treasurer at Xerox, was fired when he protested accounting irregularities to his superiors. He then filed a wrongful termination suit that alerted the SEC to the problem. This compounded the original predicament for Xerox, which was now on trial for both deceptive accounting and unfair treatment of an honest employee. In depositions for the SEC case, Bingham testified that Xerox's "culture in the late 1990s was one in which accounting trickery was routinely used to conceal deteriorating underlying results."[13] The message to employees and other constituents could not have been reassuring. Xerox's carefully cultivated public image of an open, transparent stewardship company was buried in a series of cascading negative feedbacks. The myth of executive omnipotence was exposed in the worst possible way.

The real problem at Xerox, of course, predates the ones just described. There was a long-standing clash between the traditional linear thinkers at corporate headquarters, who believed the company was in the document processing market, and the more open, innovative thinkers at its Palo Alto Research Center (PARC) who thought more expansively. Time and again, promising technologies developed at PARC failed to reach the market because they were killed by managers who couldn't see their breakthrough potential. One technology developed at PARC could have transformed Xerox—the operating system that drove the original Apple computer. After Xerox executives pushed the invention aside, Steve Jobs acquired it for a nominal sum. Another PARC invention that was ignored by Xerox management is E-paper, a flexible and cordless computer screen that looks like a sheet of paper, uses no energy for storing images or for viewing, and can be electronically written and rewritten on at least a million times. Xerox's pass on the invention enabled a startup company of MIT researchers (with support from a consortium of corporate investors that included Motorola and Philips) to replicate Xerox's experiments and become the market leader in E-paper technology.

While office copiers were becoming an endangered species, overcome by paperless IT, Xerox executives reacted like stone walls. No one at PARC could convince the proud executive hierarchy to expand beyond its shrinking market niche. It was a classic case of stasis bred by executive arrogance and fear of change.

Canon, Xerox's most powerful competitor, is the opposite of a centralized hierarchy. It is a decentralized and highly networked consortium of more than 100 quasi-independent companies. Like Nokia, Canon multiplies its points of contact with the market by carefully listening to employees, suppliers, and customers. This allows it to respond quickly to market demand for new products, and to maintain its position as one of the most prolific filers with the U.S. Patent Office. Today, Canon's overarching vision is one of making information technology (IT) available to more people for more uses, and to do it with the least environmental impact.[14] This vision has sparked a profusion of new Canon technologies, including photovoltaics, that may one day enable the company's products to operate on safe, clean, and virtually limitless energy from the sun.

The reversal of fortune between these two companies during the past 30 years has been dramatic. In 1975, Xerox was a giant compared with Canon. Since then, however, its market capitalization has stagnated while Canon's has grown by more than 15,000 percent.[15] As this performance gap widened, Xerox's leadership panicked. Having deceived themselves for decades about their products and competition, they reacted to the widening gap by trying to deceive investors. The ensuing debacle took Xerox to the edge of bankruptcy, whereupon it was forced to bring in new management and alter its operating methods.

Although Xerox is now better led and more decentralized than before, it is still burdened by restructuring costs, a weak portfolio of digital office products, and a badly damaged reputation. With a junk bond rating of Ba1 —eight notches below Canon's Aa2 rating—its borrowing costs are also significantly higher. Having fallen so far behind Canon in both its financial and relational equity, Xerox today looks more like an acquisition target than a viable stand-alone company.

JPMorgan Chase

JPMorgan Chase (JPM), more than any other CSR Underachiever, stands as a case of executive hubris. Prior to their merger at year-end 2000, both the Morgan and Chase sides of the bank were preeminent global players. Chase's area of relative strength was commercial lending and JPM's was financial assistance to large corporations and governments. Upon deregulation of the U.S. banking industry in 1999, both banks saw the opportunity to move into more lucrative areas, such as investment banking and derivatives trading. They had a vision of combining their capital and skills to become a global financial powerhouse—a one-stop shop for commercial lending, financial advice, investment banking, and risk arbitrage.

Today, JPMorgan Chase looks more like a hedge fund than a broadly based commercial bank.[16] It runs what is, by far, the largest hedge book in the country—nearly as big as those of all other domestic banks combined.[17] JPM borrows from its depositors at low cost and invests large amounts in speculative enterprises with potentially high returns. To reduce the risk of securities they underwrite or own as bank assets, they hedge their bets with options, futures, and other exotic derivatives. Although it is a risky plan for an institution that is supposed to be the guardian of other people's money, JPM executives reason that they have the skills to make this strategy work. And they demand to be paid accordingly. In 2001, the year following the JPM-Chase merger, 5 of the 10 highest-paid bankers in the U.S. were from the merged bank. For 2005, both CEO James Dimon and outgoing chairman William Harrison received $22.3 million in total compensation.

The real story of the merged JPM has been a disaster. The bank has taken too many risks for the size of its balance sheet, both in lending and in hedging. By mid-year 2002, it was obliged to write down $3.3 billion in bad loans that it had made during the prior nine months, mostly to speculative telecom and cable ventures. Its derivative book, then worth $23.5 trillion in notional terms, was a mystery to all but a few insiders. Although the bank insisted that its value at risk (VAR)—the amount of its equity capital that was at risk on any given day—was reasonable, Moody's downgraded JPM's credit rating from Aa3 to A1 in October 2002. This put JPM's rating below those of its nearest global peers, which carried ratings in the Aa vicinity.

In the face of its 2001 and 2002 problems, JPM chose not to steer the bank back to a more normal mix of commercial banking, but instead, to redouble its bets in investment banking and risk arbitrage. By year-end 2005 the size of JPM's derivative book had grown to $48.3 trillion, a doubling in only three years. If just one-half of 1 percent of this book ($238 billion) was then at risk, the bank's risk exposure would have been more than double its shareholder equity capital at the time ($107 billion).[18] Such exposure is not inconceivable, given the poor quality of bonds and other risks JPM continues to underwrite and hedge.[19]

JPM's quest to leverage its connections and expertise beyond the field of commercial banking led to its famously ill-fated investment banking relationships with Enron and WorldCom, as well as with other now-bankrupt ventures.[20] Some of these have ended in fraud charges, expensive lawsuits, and large settlements. The charges of fraud against JPM include schemes for insider self-dealing and knowingly hiding customer liabilities from public investors in offshore subsidiaries.[21] In the Enron case, JPM compounded its subterfuge by bringing other banks into the lending syndicate so that JPM's loans could be paid off.

In various settlements during 2005, JPM has paid or foregone cash claims worth $3.2 billion to settle lawsuits over its role in Enron's collapse, and $2.0 billion for its role in WorldCom's collapse. In 2006 the bank agreed to pay an additional $425 million to settle a class-action lawsuit for manipulating the market in hundreds of initial public offerings (IPOs) during the technology boom of the late 1990s. Investors, led by CalPERS and other public-employee pension funds, sued JPM and other investment banks for failure to do due diligence and for misleading investors by approving incomplete or incorrect company statements. JPM, for example, helped Enron hide $3.9 billion in debt through a company known as Mahonia Ltd., located in the Channel Islands (off the coast of England). The bank disguised approximately $5 billion in back-and-forth transactions in which Enron sold gas and oil contracts to Mahonia, but then secretly repurchased the contracts. "Instead of protecting the public from the Enron fraud, the bankers knowingly chose to become partners in deceit," said William Lerach, an attorney for the plaintiffs.[22] To put these settlements into perspective, $2 billion wipes out approximately five years' worth of underwriting fees that JPM has generated through the sale of investment-grade bonds. The cost of these settlements, of course, goes well beyond the nominal expense. The bank has trashed its prized relational equity with an industry whose services it needs to manage its oversized hedge book.

The banks weren't just at the edges of the Enron deception but central to it. Without Citi and Chase, Enron wouldn't have had enough cash to keep itself going, much less dazzle Wall Street the way it did. In the decade before Enron collapsed, the two banks helped it obtain some $9 billion, which was, in substance, actually debt. But thanks to a complicated sleight of hand known as a "prepay," Enron was able to record the proceeds on its financial statements as money generated by its operations.[23]

—*Fortune* Magazine

The picture of JPM that emerges from its recent history is not pretty: a bank that capitalizes on its "too big to fail" size in order to gamble with other people's money on increasingly risky transactions; and a bank whose culture encourages employees to cut ethical corners in pursuit of profit. Given the interlocking relationships of the banking industry—JPM is the global leader in bank loan syndications—and the centrality of banking to the health of the U.S. and world economies, government authorities are naturally reluctant to hold JPM fully accountable for its risky behaviors.

JPM's leaders maintain an image of unquestionable authority—and one therefore exempt from accountability—by presenting themselves as all-knowing, consummate dealmakers with unimpeachable connections. This image and the inflated compensation of its leadership are defining elements of the bank's hierarchical culture and approach to business. The problem with such hierarchy and unquestionable authority, however, is that it kills the inquiry, dialogue, and learning within the bank that could make it more adaptable and less susceptible to lapses in ethics and judgment. It is not surprising that JPM's average return on shareholder equity in the five years since the JPM-Chase merger (8.0 percent) is well below the *Value Line Investment Survey* composite for "Largest Banks" (13.3 percent).[24] The market understands this deficiency and its causes well enough that JPM shares have lost value since the merger while those of its major competitors, including HSBC, have gained value.

In 2004, perhaps understanding its vulnerability to being taken over by a better-run bank, JPM acquired Banc One. Though on the surface this appeared to strengthen its neglected retail base, it also made JPM a more difficult takeover target and enlarged the platform on which it can take risks. More to the point, the Banc One acquisition did little to alter the inbred corporate culture that turned JPM from a reputable bank into a hedge fund. Instead, it solidified the culture of hierarchy and outsized executive compensation. The status quo is further kept in place by a board of directors that in 2003 was rated by The Corporate Library as one of the 10 worst out of 1,700 companies in the U.S.[25]

Perhaps the greatest risks of JPM's hierarchical culture—beyond the hubris of its leadership—are its devaluation of local knowledge and its inability to think systemically. The more it places big decisions at the top and dilutes local input, the more vulnerable its risk assessments are likely to be. And the more it thinks problem loans and investments can be erased with financial derivatives, the more careless it is likely to be about managing its book of business and VAR.

HSBC Group's culture is diametrically opposite to JPM's. Although the world's third-largest money-center bank, it is the least hierarchical. Rather than being run by a small cadre of superstars who take on large deals, HSBC is decentralized, with most important decisions made by local bankers at the local level. This system solidifies the strong local relationships that have made the bank a global power. The CEO of HSBC, Sir John Bond, receives far less compensation than does his counterpart at JPM in spite of a vastly superior performance record. In 2004, Sir John Bond's total compensation was approximately half that given to William Harrison, his counterpart at JPM.[26] Bond travels to work by train. HSBC executives fly in economy class except on long trips. The bank is deeply committed to the systemic health of the communities in which it operates. Whereas JPM's public outreach tends to be showy and image conscious, HSBC quietly supports public education and environmental awareness among its customers.

Contrary to beliefs at more traditionally managed banks, HSBC's more open, unassuming, and multilocal culture produces consistently better results than does the star-studded JPM. It knows its customers better and spreads its risks more intelligently. As a result, HSBC's balance sheet and credit rating are stronger. For the past 10 years the average annual returns on its shares have been more than double those of JPM.

Another significant indicator, which has less to do with investor perception than with real management ability, is HSBC's earnings growth. During the five-year period ending December 2005, HSBC's earnings per share (EPS) grew at an average annual rate of 8.34 percent. During the same interval, JPM's EPS shrank at an average rate of 3.6 percent per year. In the same period, HSBC grew its annual dividends at an average annual rate of 7.1 percent, versus 1.2 percent for JPM. Based on these and other measures of creating shareholder value, the compensation of JPM's CEO should have been a fraction of Sir John Bond's, rather than two times greater.

Ford

Ford is another struggling hierarchy that has virtually destroyed itself financially in its pursuit of short-term sales and profit numbers. The 2002 replacement of fired CEO Jacques Nasser with Bill Ford, grandson of the company's founder, has proven more a cosmetic change than one of deep cultural substance. The board dismissed Nasser, allegedly because he tried to cover up soaring quality and safety problems, and because employee morale was plummeting. So far, the move has failed to address the real governance and cultural problems that have taken the firm down. The company that revolutionized U.S. manufacturing in the early twentieth century continues to sink because its executives have become so disconnected from the real world in which Ford operates.

Nasser's total compensation for 2001 is symptomatic of Ford's culture of executive privilege. In a year when the company lost $5.5 billion and made deep cuts in its payroll—incredibly, against a strong background of general auto sales—the outgoing CEO was awarded $17.9 million.

Current CEO Bill Ford thought he could turn the company around by creating a five-year plan with an aggressive objective of $7 billion in pre-tax profit by 2006. Instead, he has overseen a steep slide in market share and profits. The North American division has gone through four chiefs in as many years. The *Financial Times,* reflecting on the company's dysfunctional culture, has observed: "Ford's reputation as a hotbed of corporate politics remains intact . . . . I'm not sure the bad news gets up to him [i.e., Bill Ford]."[27]

One of Ford's strategic errors was management's mid-1990s abdication, to Toyota and Honda, of the market for fuel-efficient, hybrid gas-electric cars. Instead, they concentrated on mass-producing gas-guzzling SUVs and pickup trucks, and on acquiring other auto companies with luxury brand images (Jaguar, Land Rover, and Volvo). Now, troubled Ford may be forced to sell these brands at steep discounts while simultaneously playing catch-up with its Japanese rivals.

In 2005, following a spike in energy prices that sent consumers scrambling for hybrids, Ford found itself in the unenviable position of having to buy parts from Japanese companies with which Toyota had partnered in developing its hybrid engines and systems. A year earlier, Toyota had overtaken Ford as the world's second-largest automaker.

Ford's capacity to protect market share, much less regain lost share, is hampered by its weak balance sheet. Long-term debt at year-end 2005 ($94.4 billion) exceeded shareholder equity ($13 billion) by a factor of more than seven. At year-end 2005, Ford's unfunded liabilities for retiree pension and medical plans were approximately $45 billion—more than triple its shareholder equity.[28] As things stand, operating earnings from auto manufacturing can no longer cover Ford's interest expense, much less its pension and healthcare commitments to employees and retirees. On these grounds, Ford's already-low credit rating (Ba3) looks poised to fall further.

The only consistently profitable part of the company is its finance arm, Ford Motor Credit, which Ford is now tapping for extra cash. Since year-end 2001 Ford has bolstered profits by lowering its loan-loss reserves at Ford Motor Credit—from $2.75 billion to a mere $78 million at the end of the third quarter of 2005. According to *The Wall Street Journal,* this reduction in reserves boosted Ford's pre-tax profits by approximately 26 percent during that 45-month period.[29] Ford has also securitized car loans owned by its credit arm, a strategy that yields cash today at the expense of higher interest costs tomorrow.

These forms of financial engineering call into question the integrity of Ford's retained earnings and, by extension, its shareholder equity. In a survey of the global car industry published in September 2004, *The Economist* noted, "The danger in all this financial engineering is that sooner or later credit rating agencies will become worried by this pyramid of risk. They might then conclude that the underlying business model is broken, so [Ford] would get shut out of unsecured borrowing and could run out of cash."[30]

The Ford story highlights yet another unfortunate attribute of entrenched corporate hierarchies. Rather than address real systemic issues head on, executives try to buy time by mortgaging the future in order to bring more cash to the bottom line. This solves nothing. Rather, it perpetuates a vicious cycle of denial, cover-up, and eroding relational equity that eventually concludes in financial collapse.

The contrast between Ford and its LAMP Focus Group counterpart, Toyota, couldn't be more stark. Unlike Ford, Toyota's culture is decentralized, open, interactive, and inspirational. As a dedicated corporate steward, Toyota manages by qualitative means rather than by quantitative objectives, as Ford does. Its balanced scorecard accounting, for example, measures employee learning, work team skills, and morale in addition to throughput, sales, and profits. Because employees are more nurtured and respected at Toyota, and freer to self-organize, they are more productive. Toyota's commitment to operate in closer harmony with Nature and society inspires employees to come forward with ideas for product and process improvements. Its extraordinary customer loyalty has been won not by discounting, as Ford does, but by offering high quality cars on the cutting edge of eco-efficiency at prices people can afford. At Toyota, customer service and safety are paramount.

Toyota's highly networked and inspirational culture is vastly more efficient than Ford's hierarchical, numbers-driven one. Operating costs per unit of production are lower. Profit margins and free cash flow are higher. The balance sheet is stronger. At the end of its March 2005 fiscal year, Toyota's cash reserves alone ($19.5 billion) were nearly double Ford's shareholder equity.

Toyota Case Study: A Better Engine at Half the Cost

For the 2007 Camry, Toyota has developed a new V-6 engine that costs half as much to build, and offers more power and better fuel economy, compared with its predecessor. Toyota says the new engine will accelerate 40% faster than the previous model and will give 5–7% better fuel economy. This breakthrough continues a tradition of innovative product stewardship—giving customers better value and reducing the life-cycle environmental impacts of its vehicles.

The material costs of the engine are reduced by its lighter weight and simpler design. At 55 pounds, the aluminum block weighs 27% less than the previous model. The cylinder head has also been redesigned so that it requires fewer honeycomb-like passageways for fuel and air. This means that, during casting, workers need to lay fewer "cores," or clusters of sand, inside the molten aluminum to leave space for the passageways.

Assembly costs are reduced by the use of smaller, less expensive molds. The 32-foot tall casters formerly used to fabricate Camry engine blocks are being replaced with new, 19-foot-tall machines that use 40% less pressure to inject molten aluminum into molds. This design change allows air inside the molds to escape rather than being blasted back into the aluminum in the form of bubbles that can weaken the walls of the block.

The reduced injection speed means Toyota can make a V-6 engine block in a mold held together with 2,250 tons of force instead of the 3,500 tons previously needed—yet another savings of time and money. The new casters can build four-, six- and eight-cylinder engines using dies that weigh 5 tons rather than 29 tons, and so can be changed in just 60 minutes (one-sixth the time formerly required)—a benefit to other Toyota vehicles.

Toyota's new cylinder-head design replaces casters as tall as three-story buildings with 12-foot-tall casters that come complete with a furnace. Whereas casters used to be arranged in long rows, with automated lifting devices for moving unfinished cylinder heads around the factory, the new machinery now arranges them in U-shaped cells. Each cell is a mini-factory with everything needed to keep the caster operating, including machining centers and test equipment. With all of these processes located near each other, work flows more easily through the foundry, resulting in higher quality at lower cost.

Toyota's continuing goal is to simplify engine design so that more Toyota vehicles can share more parts. Among the savings realized by the Camry's new engine is an 80% reduction in the number of clamps needed to hold cylinder heads in place while they are being machined. That has helped cut machining costs by 50%. Toyota has also cut in half the length of engine assembly lines by delivering parts in kit boxes that move along the line with each engine. These are examples of the innovation that emerges when a company has a strong reinforcing cycle of LAS + OL.[31]

International Paper

International Paper (IP) stock has lost market value in the past decade (1996–2005) as a result of its obsession with quantity at the expense of quality. Because its hierarchical culture equated size and conquest with strength, it spent much of this time borrowing money to acquire other companies.[32] During its acquisition spree, its debt equity ratio dropped from a respectable 68 percent (1994) to a precarious 201 percent at year-end 2002. Subsequently, it was obliged to make a series of painful divestitures.

IP's empire building may have been good for its executive officers, but it has been bad for employees and the communities in which IP operates. CEO John Dillon received total compensation of $8.9 million in 2000, at the height of the company's acquisition surge. Total employment at IP that year was 112,900. At year-end 2005 the company's payroll was down to 68,700 people—40 percent fewer than in 2000. Tellingly, IP's annual reports make scant mention of employees other than their numbers and the costs of terminating them.[33] This leaves employees with the impression that IP views them more as costs and liabilities than as assets. This impression is reinforced by IP's deferrals of contributions to its employee pension plan—deferrals that left it with a liability of $2.4 billion at year-end 2004, the equivalent of 29 percent of shareholder equity. It is hard to maintain employee morale and productivity in such a disheartening environment. According to IP's 2002/2003 Sustainability Report, employee turnover rates ranged from 5.5 percent in its European operations to 15.3 percent in Latin America. During the same period turnover rates at Stora Enso averaged between 2.2 and 2.8 percent.[34]

In July 2005, still overburdened by debt, IP announced a further restructuring that would sell millions of acres of forestland and close more mills. According to the Associated Press, these divestitures represented nearly half the company's earnings and cash flow—a sad state of affairs for a forest products firm that once touted itself as the world's largest.[35]

As a result of its financial vulnerability, IP has chosen to cut corners environmentally. At year-end 2003, IP was responsible for 110 Superfund sites involving toxic wastes—against which liability it had a miniscule reserve of $28 million for remediation, or $393,000 per site. According to the 2004 EPA Toxics Release Inventory, more than half of IP's plants were rated among the dirtiest in the country.[36] The one bright spot on IP's horizon—its first Sustainability Report, covering 2002 and 2003—has been diluted by lack of follow-through. IP's 2004 Sustainability Report is an electronic presentation of data with little in-depth discussion of its priorities and plans for the future.

The big question concerning IP's future is whether its traditional culture has changed. The evidence is not encouraging. The company's new CEO, John Faraci, missed an opportunity to present a new strategy in the 2003 annual report and to show how IP was coalescing around it. Instead, he wrote a terse letter to shareholders praising Dillon's leadership, followed by a bland 10-K report, which the company is required to file with the SEC. Also worrisome is the fact that IP continues its practice of continually restating its results due to special restructuring charges and accounting changes. Though this tactic may put a good face on a deteriorating situation and justify large executive bonuses—CEO Faraci's total compensation for 2004 and 2005 was $14.7 million—it does not impress Wall Street.

The picture is very different at Stora Enso, the widely acknowledged stewardship leader of the global paper industry. Instead of leveraging itself to acquire other companies, Stora has been strengthening its balance sheet and buying its own stock. Its debt-equity ratio at year-end 2005 was 57 percent—less than half of IP's 132-percent ratio. Moreover, the quality of Stora Enso's shareholder equity is better because the company is better provisioned for "risks and charges" with a $751-million reserve, as compared with only $47 million for IP.

In 2000, near the height of its acquisition spree, IP was unquestionably the largest paper company in the world, with shareholder equity exceeding $12 billion—approximately 50 percent larger than Stora Enso's equity of $8 billion. Since that time the two companies' fortunes have reversed. Stora's equity at year-end 2004 was nearly $11 billion, while IP's had shrunk to $8.2 billion. The companies' contrasting approaches to acquisitions are an important factor in this reversal. Whereas IP has focused on bulking up and scale, Stora has focused on synergies.[37]

Unlike IP, Stora understands that its primary leverage lies in the commitment and enthusiasm of its employees. It optimizes that leverage by caring for employees and the things they care about—health and safety, work-life balance, professional development, community life, and environmental quality—and by transparently monitoring their progress in each area. The company has issued a detailed environment or sustainability report every year since Stora and Enso merged in December 1998. Its annual reports regularly feature employees and their contributions. The 2003 annual report elaborated on Stora's vision of "What People Can Do." Because of this caring culture, employee turnover at Stora, as previously noted, has been in the range of 2.2 to 2.8 percent—far lower than at IP. The synergies of such employee loyalty are immense: more experienced workers, better-connected teams, quicker organizational learning, and less training expense.

The message we get from the comparisons of International Paper and Stora Enso—and of the other five company pairs—is that Living Asset Stewardship produces far more synergies than does the traditional approach to management. Also, companies that adopt the language and appearances of stewardship without the deeper structures of compatible cultures and processes are likely to make a bad situation worse by overpromising and underperforming.

Mixing and Matching

Each of the CSR Underachievers analyzed in this chapter has posed as a corporate steward while maintaining a culture that undermines stewardship. I have highlighted them not because they are prototypical villains, but rather, to expose the liabilities of "mixing and matching" stewardship and traditional management practices. Living Asset Stewardship cannot be an add-on to a mechanistic culture.

Ironically, the six CSR Underachievers are on many SRI- and sustainability-approved lists. I believe the missing element in the screening process for inclusion on those lists is a systemic principle that underlies the whole of the company's organization and culture. Many ethical investors look at the variables that are important to them—human rights, environment, product safety, work-life balance, etc.—in isolation. If a company gets enough good marks on enough variables, it gets approved. The weakness of this checklist process is that it overlooks the cultural whole. It becomes a mechanistic scoring system for selected issues rather than an organic evaluation of a company's culture—especially its capacity to learn and adapt. In a world in which that capacity is crucial for survival, and the reinforcing cycle of Living Asset Stewardship and organizational learning (LAS + OL) is so potent, this oversight is dangerous.

There is now a rapidly growing industry of risk management and "incident prevention" that sells the "mechanistic checklist" approach to traditionally managed companies. Consultants do assessments of risk exposure and advise clients on fine-tuning their practices to avoid the costs of ethical and moral lapses. In too many cases, this approach is premised on the notion that companies can mix and match, and that hierarchies can be taught better stewardship—in other words, that the Titanic will not sink if the deck chairs are cleverly rearranged. These "quick fixes" perpetuate the illusion that managerial fine-tuning can overcome the problems that occur when nonliving capital assets take precedence over living assets, and MBO takes precedence over customer service and systemic harmony. Most of these consultants totally miss the cultural roots of the problems they purport to solve. They overlook the ways in which numbers-driven hierarchies cause people to become disconnected. Table 13-2 lists the risk issues addressed by one consultancy, whose website and literature are, incidentally, mute on the subject of corporate culture.

The essential attribute that underlies all LAS cultures is *respect for life*. This is what connects people in an organization to its goals, what drives the powerful reinforcing cycle of LAS + OL, and what, ultimately, enables these companies to deliver superior economic results. Hierarchy is antithetical to respect for life because it embodies lack of respect for the intelligence and self-organizing capacities of subordinates and because it isolates executives from the real world in which they operate.

Table 13-2: Typical Risk Management Checklist

- Accidental Death/Injury
- Accounting Irregularities
- Compliance Infraction
- Customer Safety
- Disability Discrimination
- Employee Theft
- Environmental Mishap
- Ethics Violation
- Industrial Espionage
- Network Intrusions
- Privacy Violations
- Race Discrimination
- Sexual Harassment
- Sweatshop Allegation
- Terrorist Threat
- Threats to Executives
- Unsafe Working Conditions
- Workplace Violence

The six CSR Underachievers explored in this chapter are all run by hierarchies whose nominal commitments to stewardship fell apart when their mechanistic approaches failed to produce the sales and profit numbers they'd identified as necessary. Fine-tuning their traditional business practices won them some public awards and recognition for stewardship but created internal confusion and dissension. In time, the vulnerabilities of their partially committed approaches became all too evident: as executive arrogance, excessive risk-taking, and profit manipulation in the bull market of the late 1990s; as executive denial, dreadful performance, and layoffs in the bear market that immediately followed; and as painful restructurings and continued loss of market share in the subsequent recovery. When executive behavior subverts respect for life, stewardship cannot survive.

By selecting these CSR Underachievers from the same general universe of approved companies used to select the LAMP Focus Group, I have made a qualitative distinction. *Stewardship divorced from corporate culture cannot work.* Companies that respond to the public's growing interest in SRI and sustainability by taking fragmentary stewardship approaches are deluding not only their constituents, but themselves, as well.

Conclusion

Management hierarchies handicap a corporation's ability to learn and adapt because they typically use only a fraction of the brainpower available to them. They get too locked into the agendas of managers whose privilege and status remove them from the real world. Failing to see how organically and qualitatively the real world is organized, and believing in the reductionist logic of classical scientific thinking, traditional executives too often reduce business to a numbers game.

Numbers are, of course, easier to understand than are the complex relationships of living systems; they may be all a small executive team can handle. But numbers are only representations of reality, not reality itself. By reducing important corporate goals to numbers—especially those that represent profit and market share—traditionally managed companies create incentives to manipulate numbers, and thereby alter the appearance of reality. This reductive approach also allows them to ignore important variables that cannot be reduced to numbers, or at least numbers that they care to see. This is clearly counter-productive.

When sickness masquerades as wellness, as we saw with the CSR Underachievers, it compounds the problems that created the sickness in the first place. Beyond the fines and legal costs the six CSR Underachievers paid for their subterfuge, they lost both opportunities for learning and faith with key stakeholders.

Although posing as stewards, these underachievers are sooner or later exposed as pretenders who can't make the grade. Their financial descent from world leadership status to their present compromised conditions has been compounded by their attempts to mix two mutually exclusive cultures. Mechanistic management systems are totally unsuited to the living world in which they operate.

Respect for life. Too often in the artificial world of traditional business management, this quality of LAS is dismissed as "soft," and as a diversion from the realities of hard numbers (especially profit). But respect for life is an effective premise for enterprise, as the six LAMP comparators have shown. A quick glance back to Table 13-1 will reconfirm just how effective the six LAMP companies have been in terms of stock market return and financial strength. It is difficult to refute such "hard" results.

The synergies of LAS arise from respect for life, which is contagious and inspiring. Companies that make LAS a strategic imperative generally outperform those that don't. When stewardship fails, it is usually because companies are too hierarchical and mechanistic. There is no getting around the fact that living, organic systems must be managed by organic means, not by mechanical means.

1 4

Changing Definitions of Value

"What must underlie successful [change], in the end, is a bedrock
belief that change is possible, that people can radically transform
their behavior or beliefs in the face of the right kind of impetus."[1]
—Malcolm Gladwell, *The Tipping Point*

L iving Asset Stewardship has long been implicitly recognized in valuing the debt and equity of publicly traded corporations. That recognition is now rapidly becoming explicit. The capital markets have
reached a tipping point—an awakening to the reality that old beliefs about
the efficiency of traditional capitalism have been invalidated by the delayed
effects of environmental destruction, global warming, mounting public
health costs, and the deterioration of community well-being.

Investors are increasingly aware that there is an alternative paradigm to
traditional capitalism. The paradigm shift started with the corporate social
responsibility (CSR) movement in the late 1960s, which, two decades later,
evolved into the sustainability movement with its focus on the triple bottom line of economic, social, and environmental return. But it didn't
become a true paradigm shift until people began to redefine the fundamental nature of the corporation itself—from a machine-like entity that

was separate from Nature and society to a living system that was totally integrated. With this conceptual shift everything changed—just as it did in the fifteenth century when people began to believe the world was round rather than flat.

Once we see the corporation as a living system we are naturally drawn to the concept of living assets (people and Nature) as distinct from nonliving (capital) assets. Living systems comprise living beings and other living systems—networks within networks—which together constitute the large, overarching web of life. Within these networks everything is ultimately connected. Caring about Nature is caring about people, because people need healthy ecosystems to survive. And caring about people is caring about business, because business is fundamentally about improving the quality of life. More to the point, living assets are the source of nonliving capital assets. Capital is supposed to serve humanity, not the reverse. In a world that seems largely to have turned that relationship upside down, is it any mystery that we, moved by our shared, human biophilia, have begun to embrace Living Asset Stewardship?

The Global LAMP Index® is powerful evidence of the ongoing paradigm shift from the mental model of traditional capitalism to LAS. It is hard to ignore a group of like-minded companies that have gained so much market share during the past few decades. In previous chapters we have seen how they have outperformed traditional peers in terms of shareholder returns, credit ratings, and longevity.

This trend toward LAS and away from traditional capitalism is now accelerating for one simple reason. It must. Otherwise, life on Earth will become a nightmare of toxic waste, disease, natural disasters, and social unrest. A critical mass of people now sees this—including a growing number of institutional investors, as we shall see in Chapter 15. In such a context, LAS is healthy, adaptive behavior, the right kind of impetus for a historic tipping point.

The Global Capital Markets

The global capital markets have immense influence over corporate decision making because they are a major source of both *investment funding* and *information feedback*. Although far from prescient in either of these functions, over time these markets tend to get things right. In the aggregate, their decisions reflect the collective wisdom of savers, investors, buyers, and sellers everywhere. If that collective wisdom leans in the direction of global stewardship leaders, as it increasingly has, those companies will enjoy preferred access to capital—even if their business models are not explicitly well articulated or understood.

Investors, bankers and financial intermediaries are supremely pragmatic. They want the best possible returns at the lowest possible risk on all their investments. To most, this entails looking beyond current rates of return to indicators of future return, such as product quality, customer loyalty, and market penetration. The best ones look further, to investigate the means by which companies achieve those results. LAS is the means by which global LAMP companies have outperformed.

Managing by means is radically different from managing by ends.[2] LAS deals with how we get from A to B most effectively, rather than focusing predominantly on the "end" of profit. This is particularly important in the context of living systems, as distinct from nonliving mechanical systems, because the means of getting from A to B necessitates a respect for life. The reinforcing cycle of LAS + OL recognizes this necessity. LAMP companies succeed because their respect for people—expressed as caring for people and the things people care about—inspires learning and innovation that ultimately generate profit.

At year-end 2005, the Global LAMP Index,® although only 60 in number, comprised more than one-third of the market capitalization of the S&P 500 Index, and approximately 20 percent of the larger MSCI World Index.[3] In part, this indicates past market share gains in the LAMP group's core businesses. But it also importantly reflects, by way of a premium price-to-earnings (P/E) multiple, the markets' confidence that these gains will continue. It is no accident that Toyota, for example, has a larger market capitalization than do its three largest competitors combined, even though it is the world's second-largest automaker.

The most stunning market share gains for LAMP companies have occurred in mature industries with long-established patterns of traditional management practice—banking, autos, airlines, office equipment, steel, and telecommunications. The old-guard leaders of all these industries have typically placed a higher value on nonliving capital assets than on living assets, and thus isolated themselves from key stakeholders. This isolation, in turn, has reduced opportunities for information feedback and organizational learning, which are critical sources of innovation. Once-proud companies such as JPMorgan Chase, General Motors, American Airlines (now AMR), Bristol-Myers Squibb, Xerox, U.S. Steel, and the old AT&T have thereby lost huge market share during the past few decades, and their equity valuations have lagged accordingly.[4] Their failures, of course, opened big opportunities for LAS companies, which have been faster learners and innovators.

Because equity valuations are a good indicator of long-term market-share trends, it is worth looking at the performances of the foregoing seven old-guard leaders compared with those of their LAMP counterparts over the past 30-year period (1975–2005). The market value of the old-guard stocks grew by less than 3 percent per year on average, which means they lost money in real, inflation-adjusted terms.[5] By contrast, the stock market values of their LAMP counterparts—HSBC, Toyota, Southwest, Johnson & Johnson, Canon, Nucor, and Nokia—grew at average annual rates ranging from 13 to 28 percent.

The market appreciation of most LAMP companies in that 30-year period has generally fallen in the range of 13–18 percent—which is far in excess of the S&P 500 Index's average annual appreciation of approximately 9 percent.[6] When dividends are added to the principal growth of both indices, LAMP companies again come out ahead. Because their earnings have grown faster, they have been able to increase their dividends at a faster rate.

Good as LAMP companies are, they don't outperform all the time. Like all vital businesses, they have downtimes due to product cycles, periods of self-reinvention, or failed ventures. Usually, these downtimes are relatively brief, but occasionally they have long-term negative effects on equity performance. Such was the case with Baxter International when a combination of increased competition in plasma products, drugs coming off patent, and a bear-market environment caused its stock to plunge by 60 percent during a six-month period in 2002. In spite of this sudden loss, Baxter's total return has been in double digits since 1975. More important, the humane way it handled its subsequent restructuring toward higher-margin BioScience products, and its commitment to remain a values-driven company, have kept employee morale and productivity high.

Based on such data, it is fair to say that the market has developed greater confidence in companies managed on LAS principles than in those managed on traditional principles. By virtually every measure, LAMP companies have delivered superior value. It is only natural that investors and analysts would be interested in the things LAMP companies themselves value.

Shifting Awareness

Since I first became interested in corporate stewardship in the late 1960s, I have watched investor focus shift from a risk-management approach (first generation) to a vision of long-term sustainability via the triple bottom line (second generation). The pioneers of both approaches have had difficulty in reforming traditional capitalism because they generally don't address its flawed mechanistic premises. In worst-case situations (as reviewed in Chapter 13), well-intended efforts to impose stewardship on traditional cultures can backfire badly.

LAS replaces the false premises of the traditional model with tenets more suited to the true nature and purpose of the corporation, i.e., a living system trying to improve the quality of life. This shift rests squarely on corporate effectiveness as described by the reinforcing cycle of LAS + OL, and understands well-executed LAS as a management best practice and a way to strengthen capitalism. I regard LAS as a third-generation approach because it looks to the integrity of processes that generate corporate results. In this sense, it is a triple top line, as distinct from a triple bottom line, approach.

Contemporary financial media and mainstream investment analysts clearly see the effects of good LAS, and frequently cover aspects of stewardship that enhance corporate performance. (This should be evident from reading the notes to the chapters in this volume.) But they have generally not been able to connect the dots—to see that *LAS is the only practical way to run a living company* that exists within living markets and a living world. That is changing, however, because, increasingly, corporate pioneers in LAS are speaking out and making it clear that stewardship is totally integral to their value added-processes. Even if LAMP companies don't frame their mental models in terms of LAS, per se, they implicitly—and often explicitly—present themselves as living communities with shared values that respect life. They think differently, talk differently, and behave differently. They also form associations with one another to discuss best practices and share success stories.

The Society for Organizational Learning (SoL), an outgrowth of the Center for Organizational Learning at MIT, is one such association. Its membership is broadly inclusive and committed to the processes of systems thinking. SoL's corporate members are some of the world's best-managed companies. Its other members have been drawn principally from management consulting, academia, and government—institutions that offer important information feedback and opportunities for co-learning. By focusing attention on the importance of mental models and the effectiveness of models premised on living systems, SoL has generated a global dialogue on the means by which companies produce value. This book is testimony to the effectiveness of this process and the insights it provides.

No one doubts the difficulty of changing the behavior of large systems such as traditional capitalism. Once established, they take on lives of their own. Yet large-scale change capable of producing planetwide results is possible if the catalyst for change deeply resonates with people and opens vast new horizons.

Once we thought our world was flat rather than round. And we once viewed companies as mechanical, rather than living, systems. If we want to understand the value of Living Asset Stewardship we must make the conceptual leap from the traditional model to the LAS model. Those who make that leap will have better success in the coming decades than those who stand pat.

Future Value

The road to creating future value is not always clear. Had Nokia, for example, not deeply listened to people and been willing to try new ideas rather than rest on past accomplishments, it might never have evolved from forest products to electronics to mobile phones. If, instead of engaging its employees in companywide visioning, it had relegated its strategic thinking to a small group of top executives, it might have ended up like AT&T, taken over by a more agile competitor.

In today's knowledge-based economy there is a close connection between a company's capacity to learn and its capacity to generate future value. Nokia's extraordinary innovation and speed to market are byproducts of its speed of learning, which in turn is a byproduct of its respectful relationships with stakeholders. This, in essence, is how the LAS model works, as shown in Figure 2-1.

To achieve quality stakeholder relationships, Nokia and other LAMP companies organize themselves in network fashion. They use the insights and perceptions of employees and partners across the entire supply net—those who most intimately know the company's products, processes, and customers—rather than relying on the judgments of a small cadre of top executives who work far from the front lines. To ensure that those frontline people have the capacity to generate useful feedback, LAMP companies create open, interactive cultures that foster learning. The logic in this approach is simple. The more eyes, ears, and minds a company can employ, the greater are its chances of learning. And the more people are invested in learning, the more likely it is the company will be an innovation leader. That is management by means.

The quality of relationships outside the company and its supply net also must not be overlooked. Beyond customers and investors, these include host communities, governments, and (increasingly) nongovernmental organizations (NGOs). The latter three give important feedback on the health of living systems impacted by company operations and products. LAMP companies make a point of connecting with all such external stakeholders and transparently sharing information with them via detailed reporting and face-to-face meetings. The quality of the information they share and their sincerity in seeking stakeholder feedback are important LAS indicators. LAMP company leaders consistently and carefully report on social and environmental impacts, as well as on their financial pictures, because they know that the better informed their stakeholders are, the better learning partners they will be. Figure 2-2 presents a visual image of the degree of companies' openness.

Emergence is a critical attribute of open, networked living systems that cannot exist in mechanical systems. It describes the processes of learning, adaptation, and evolution that occur as a system grows in complexity. Companies that mimic the behavior of machines are far too slow to compete with those modeled on open, networked systems—as is evident across the industrial spectrum from high tech to basic industries such as steel. The story of Nucor's spectacular success in steelmaking owes much to the insights of employees on the plant floor and in the field. That kind of engagement emerges as a result of good relationships between employees and managers at all levels, spontaneous networking, and team incentives that reward innovation and productivity.

If investors spent more time thinking about such *relational equity* they would better understand a firm's capacity for future growth. However interesting a firm's financial equity may be, it reflects only past history. Because the purpose of capital markets is to allocate money efficiently toward future growth opportunities, there is more forecasting strength in relational, than in financial, equity.

Forward Thinking

Investors and business managers keep score on the things they most value. As discussed in chapters 2 and 6, the balanced scorecard gives companies a method of tracking their forward-looking relational equity as well as their past performance in terms of financial equity. Measures of relational equity include employee morale and loyalty, customer satisfaction, supplier responsiveness, and company reputation.

Fred Reichheld of Bain & Company shows how employee loyalty translates to customer loyalty and profit by analyzing the net present value of customer repeat orders over a period of years.[7] James Heskett and colleagues at Harvard Business School map the chain of relationships that Reichheld describes in a technique called the service-profit chain.[8]

Using the balanced scorecard approach, a company using Reichheld's and Heskett's methods might therefore address the following questions:

- To achieve our corporate vision, what kind of employee knowledge, skills, and experience do we need?
- How can we optimize employee learning and growth so we can sustainably develop these qualities?
- How can we tell that customers are happy with the value our employees offer to them?

Some answers to these questions will be evident from objective data analysis (repeat order trends, lost customers, customer referrals, etc.), and others may require subjective analysis of employee and customer surveys or feedback sessions. Managers that have suitably distilled answers or impressions are better prepared to add value for customers than those that don't.

The intangible economy demands that you look at relationships between today's actions and their long-term impact. In other words, it requires that you do systems thinking and the analytical tools that are required to support it.[9]
—David Norton, co-inventor of the Balanced Scorecard

The following questions are not meant to be definitive, but to open some general lines of inquiry that can be extended. They comprise a systems thinking framework for achieving a more inclusive vision of a company and the quality of its stakeholder relationships. More-focused questions, including questions relating to Heskett's relationship chains and Reichheld's net present value analyses, will evolve as investors become more familiar with this framework and its relevance.

Do a company's values inspire people to learn and innovate? Are they grounded in a respect for life—as are Canon's kyosei philosophy, Johnson & Johnson's credo, and the bioethics of Novo Nordisk and Baxter International—and do they connect people to one another and to the web of life that supports them? Are they daily modeled in the behavior and communications of company leaders? Are values actively discussed by employees and regularly used as guides in decision making at all levels? And are they absolutely core to the way the company does business?

Are a company's mission and vision well aligned with its values? Does it look to expansive goals that transcend profit, such as the HP Way aim of "making a contribution" to society through technology? Does its mission give scope and urgency to its core competencies, such as Baxter International's goal of "saving and enhancing lives" or Stora Enso's goal of promoting "communications and the well-being of people"? Is its vision as clear as Toyota's *Global Vision 2010,* a vision statement that sets "concern for the Earth" as one of its top four business priorities? Are the mission and vision both transcendent and practical, as is Shell's mission of "Helping people to build a better world" through renewable energy? Does a company regularly involve its employees in the visioning process, as Hewlett-Packard, Nokia, and Shell do, so it can achieve a high level of buy-in?

How effectively does a company network? Is it an open, inclusive workplace as described in Chapter 7? Is it decentralized, multilocal, and closely connected to the communities it serves, as HSBC is? Are employees empowered to self-organize spontaneously and make decisions in their primary areas of expertise, as they are at Nokia and Southwest Airlines? Are employees treated as partners, as they are at Hewlett-Packard, Intel, and 3M? Does the firm's operating model mirror Alcoa's and Nucor's, wherein a small headquarters staff serves local business units rather than the model of local business units serving a privileged hierarchy at headquarters? Does the corporate information technology (IT) network enable organizational learning and build employee competence as happens at Swiss Re?

How effectively does a company foster learning? Do employees feel secure in their jobs as they do at Nucor, Southwest Airlines, and Toyota (which have steadfastly resisted layoffs for decades)? Does management put a high priority on building and serving employee competence, as is the case at HSBC and Swiss Re? Are employees given opportunities to connect with their customers in ways that give them deep insights into customer needs, as at Baxter International? Are employees empowered to experiment and collaborate as they are at HP? Are they openly recognized and rewarded for their contributions as they are at 3M? Do employees feel they have permission to fail when their experiments come up short, as they do at Johnson & Johnson?

How transparent is a company in its communications with stakeholders? Are its annual financial reports clear? Does it issue additional annual reports on its social and environmental impacts, its sustainability goals, and its progress toward meeting those goals? Do these reports cogently address difficult issues such as global warming and human rights? And do they do this in ways that generate useful new data (such as the CO_2 emissions generated by transporting goods to market)? Are the company's reports certified by a reputable third party and issued under GRI guidelines? Does a company use these reports, as Intel does, as a basis for stakeholder dialogue and co-learning? Is a company broadly inclusive in the stakeholders it invites into dialogue (e.g., including NGOs that will pose difficult questions)?

In researching this book, I discovered many corporate officers willing to talk, sometimes at length, about the importance of the balanced scorecard and questions that have arisen within their firms as a result of using it. One question that often came back to me is why investment analysts don't use this technique more proactively—both as a way of gaining deeper insight and as a tool for sharing their perspectives on best practices.

Counting What Counts

If living assets are more productive and valuable than nonliving capital assets, it makes sense to monitor their health and invest in their value-added capacity. By simply changing our definition of what is valuable—from nonliving capital assets to living assets—in one stroke, we become more alert to the real world in which companies operate. And it is in this real world that investors live. Companies, like the global markets they inhabit, are living systems that continually change as the resources available to them change.

Thanks to the extraordinary successes of global LAMP companies, perceptions of value are now shifting more rapidly in the direction of LAS and away from the mechanical-system approach. It is hard to ignore a small group of companies that have steadily gained market share within their industries during the past several decades and now comprise more than one-third of the market capitalization of the S&P 500.

We optimize what we most value. Of course we want a high quality of life in terms of our physical well-being and ability to make choices. For centuries we have used markets to move us in that direction and will likely continue to do so. But markets, like all living systems, have a capacity to self-destruct if they lose sight of their *interdependence* with other living systems. People created markets to serve humanity—not to threaten humanity through the destruction of our social and environmental capital in the name of profit. We know capital markets understand this very well: we can see how they price the shareholder equity and bonds of global LAMP companies compared with those of their traditionally managed competitors.

Why Most Investors Underperform

Investment analysts are notoriously poor forecasters. Few manage to beat the results of a random selection process of, for example, throwing darts at the financial pages. Most of their analytic methods and mental models are too disengaged from sustainable value-added processes to offer much insight into the future. The companies analysts work for continuously pressure them to produce short-term results. Their compensation and reward systems are also based on quick returns. With such dysfunctional mental models and incentives, they naturally become obsessed with quarter-to-quarter profit forecasts—things they can see with greater certainty.

As a result of analysts' short-term thinking and lack of future vision, investing has become progressively more oriented to trading and hedging. The turnover ratios of most equity mutual funds today exceed 100 percent. Hedge funds, the fastest-growing sector of the investment business, can do complete turnovers within hours. The trading and custody cost of such short-term tinkering is high and a significant drag on client returns. Hedging is a way of dealing with uncertainty, and there is much uncertainty in the traditional model of business. At the end of the day, these frenetic trading strategies rarely produce consistent added value and are more symptomatic of a failing system than of a vital one.

To become more efficient at adding value to client portfolios, investors must learn to identify the means of future value creation—a company's capacities for networking, forming sustainable relationships, learning, and innovation—as distinct from the short-term ends of next quarter's profit. This involves shifting their focus, by means of a balanced scorecard, toward the quality of care for living assets and away from the quantity of capital assets under their control.

The LAS model works best over long holding periods—years and decades rather than months, days, hours, or minutes—because it is intended as a long-term method of sustainable value creation. However, as the traditional model loses force, the Global LAMP Index® increasingly outperforms on a quarter-to-quarter basis, as well.

Conclusion

Through the past few decades we have felt a tectonic shift in how the capital markets perceive value. Whether consciously or unconsciously, investors invest in what works. They have rewarded companies that consistently and professionally manage by means, and have discounted companies that obsessively manage by financial objectives. Like tectonic shifts, the real causes of such market behaviors can be hard to detect without a mental model that makes sense of them. The good fortunes of LAMP companies aren't due to luck—being in the right place at the right time—but are due to disciplined, hard, forward thinking.

Living assets are the real sources of financial capital and the means of sustainable profit and growth. Because they steward those assets, LAMP companies tangibly outperform their traditionally managed peers in shareholder returns, balance sheet strength, and longevity.

Systems theorist Peter Senge says that to change a system such as capitalism, you must make the smallest changes possible that will generate the biggest effect. This is precisely what LAS does. When viewed historically, it is an adaptive change from within the capitalist system rather than one imposed from without. It delivers desired results on multiple levels. And it emerges from some of our most ancient (biophilic) instincts. In those respects, LAS is more natural to us than the mechanistic capitalism that emerged from the nineteenth-century Industrial Revolution.

Institutional investors and financial analysts are paid for their abilities to identify value for their clients and to produce consistently good returns. To do this, they need to convert knowledge the markets now implicitly understand to an explicit system of value creation. I believe we have reached a tipping point in this direction. The multiple-win benefits of LAS are plainly visible. The financial benefits of multiple wins—especially when they arise out of dire need—should continue to be exceptional.

The Value of Shareholder Stewardship

"Avoid business involving moral risk: No matter what the rate, trying
to write good contracts with bad people doesn't work."[1]
—Warren Buffett, Chairman, Berkshire Hathaway

The shareholders of a company are its legal owners. They have well-established rights to look after their property, including rights to elect directors and request changes in management policy via proxy votes. The opinions of institutional investors, who collectively manage most of the shares of large-capitalization companies, carry enormous weight because their decisions to buy or sell can radically alter a stock's valuation. Hence, many corporate CEOs spend nearly as much time romancing institutions as they do managing their companies.

With such power, institutional investors are, in effect, stewards of the corporate system. The best ones exercise this stewardship in ways that increasingly support Living Asset Stewardship. This chapter will examine two models of such institutional investor involvement. The first is based on long-term commitments to steward companies that were selected for their openness and ethics. In this instance, you might say that institutional investors are becoming *stewards of the stewards* (for example, the Berkshire Hathaway model). The second is a more ad hoc approach in which investment managers will nudge traditionally managed companies toward better stewardship practices by interceding in corporate decision making, initiating shareholder resolutions, and voting their proxies against management (e.g., the Council of Institutional Investors model).

The Berkshire Hathaway Model

Warren Buffett is one of the most successful and widely respected investors of the past half-century. For decades he has built his success, and that of Berkshire Hathaway, on partnering with portfolio companies. He has done this by buying significant stakes in a few ethical and well-managed corporations, and then holding them for long periods. He offers occasional advice and assistance to management, and may sometimes also sit as a board member, but always avoids the temptation to micromanage.

How successful has Berkshire's approach been? Consider the following. The average annual return on its portfolio, from its inception in 1965 to year-end 2005, has been 21.5 percent—more than double the 10.4-percent S&P 500 Index average return (with dividends included). Through these years, the book value of Berkshire Hathaway's portfolio has had only one calendar-year loss, as compared with 10 for the S&P 500. In those 10 years of S&P decline, Berkshire realized average annual gains of 12.8 percent while the S&P 500 lost 12.0 percent on average—a 24.8 percentage-point spread. Like the Global LAMP Index,® its exceptional long-term returns are a result of outperforming in down years. In the one calendar year when Berkshire Hathaway's portfolio lost money (2001), it lost only 6.2 percent—about half the S&P 500's loss of 11.9 percent. The main reason for Berkshire's 2001 loss was insurance claims on its reinsurance subsidiaries as a result of the 9/11 terrorist attacks against the U.S.

Although renowned as a value investor—someone who has a knack for buying good companies at discounted prices—Buffett built his success on his sense of corporate "values." Unlike most value investors, who follow a "buy low, sell high" approach with annual portfolio turnover rates approaching 100 percent, Berkshire holds its positions, on average, for decades. When asked how long he envisions holding a stock once he buys it, Buffett often responds "forever."

My message to [the CEOs of Berkshire's subsidiary companies] is simple: Run your business as if it were the only asset your family will own over the next hundred years.[2]

—Warren Buffett, Chairman, Berkshire Hathaway

What are the attributes of a corporation that would make Berkshire want to hold its shares forever? In virtually every annual and interim report to shareholders, Buffett names them. They are attributes that flow from values-based cultures, such as employee commitment and customer loyalty. Among the most frequently mentioned values are: corporate ethics, respect for people, clarity of purpose, partnership culture, honest management, financial stability, reporting transparency, and caring and trust. This is a good composite description of management by means. Like the values of the 16 Focus Group companies featured in this book, Berkshire's values inspire people to work with their hearts as well as their minds.

What makes Berkshire successful, then, is not a transitory focus on the relative value of a company's assets at a given point in time, but an enduring preoccupation with the value-generating capacity of its corporate culture—attributes that would make someone want to hold an investment *forever*. Once that distinction is understood, the Berkshire magic becomes clear.

Berkshire's extraordinary performance rests also on its ability to assess risks and help portfolio companies avoid costly systemic mistakes. The hub of its activities is a group of reinsurance companies that underwrite catastrophic risks, often for other insurance companies that lack the Berkshire group's expertise and financial integrity. Catastrophic risks include those that arise from corporate disregard for the larger living systems that support them. These larger systems incorporate three major kinds of risks: market risks, such as fraud, executive or board negligence, and product liability; societal risks, such as epidemics, war, and terrorism; and biospheric risks, such as global climate change.[3] Understanding and managing these risks demands a holistic perspective, intellectual honesty, and scenario-planning capacity that are rare in the markets today. This intelligence is a valuable intangible asset that strengthens the Berkshire group's foresight and adaptive capacity.

The partnership culture and clarity of purpose that Berkshire brings are other valuable assets because they reduce the need for costly bureaucracy.

The agenda is simple: help portfolio companies run ethical, long-lived, and profitable businesses. Once companies have been selected for Berkshire's portfolio of corporate subsidiaries, Buffett and his partner, Charlie Munger, give their managers virtually complete operational autonomy. This obviously works for managers because, since its founding in 1964, management turnover at Berkshire's subsidiaries has been almost entirely through retirement, and promotion of new talent has been from within. Such continuity, and the teamwork inspired by Berkshire's partnership culture, allows it to oversee more than 180,000 group employees with a home office of merely 17 people.

Berkshire's strength resides in its partnership model, which respects people and trusts that if they are well cared for, they will spontaneously care for the larger organization. This presumption of symbiosis permeates everything Berkshire does, from relations with investors and portfolio companies to those with employees. Within its subsidiaries, authority and trust are pushed as far as possible toward the local level. Employees are generally trusted to self-organize and to do the right thing. From a systems thinking and organizational learning perspective, Berkshire's model optimizes points of contact with the marketplace, speeds reaction times, and improves customer service. In these ways it enables and encourages portfolio companies to make the most of their intellectual resources.

Berkshire's culture of high ethical expectations, enlightened strategic guidance, and partnership leverages the biophilic learning instincts of employees. When people are given the freedom to be themselves and to self-organize according to their abilities and interests, rather than being told what to do, they tend to act with greater sensitivity to the larger living systems that support their enterprise (e.g., the free market, society, and the biosphere). When leaders design team objectives to produce real value for people, rather than numbers of sales or profit, people become more creative. The result is a dynamic akin to the reinforcing cycle of LAS + OL. The openness of Berkshire's partnership culture makes this possible. It is an implicit, rather than an explicit, feature of their organizational culture.

Berkshire's partnership model is also notable for the way it extends to its own shareholders. The company's "A" shares have never been split. Priced at $88,820 per share at year-end 2005, they do not entice traders or those with short time horizons. Rather, they are priced to attract kindred partners who can accept the risks of Berkshire's reinsurance operations, thereby allowing Berkshire to develop its managerial "circle of competence." Buffett and Munger maintain the allegiance of shareholder partners by ensuring that their economic interests are equitably aligned. These simple approaches—finding the right investment partners and treating them fairly—build extraordinary shareholder loyalty.

I cannot promise results to partners. But Charlie and I can promise that your economic result from Berkshire will parallel ours . . . . We will not take cash compensation, restricted stock or option grants that would make our results superior to yours.[4]

—Warren Buffett, Chairman, Berkshire Hathaway

Advantages of the Berkshire Model

Berkshire Hathaway has a double advantage over the managers of actively traded funds. In addition to a partnership culture that builds relational equity and long-term perspective, it has significantly lower operating costs. Such costs typically include management fees and trading costs that together constitute an "expense ratio."

Because Berkshire rarely trades and maintains low operating overhead, its expense ratio is probably less than 10 basis points (hundredths of a percent). This stands in stark contrast to the average equity mutual fund, which has an expense ratio in excess of 125 basis points, and to hedge funds, which often have expense ratios topping 1,000 basis points.[5] With such operating overhead, it is no wonder that *fewer than 10 percent* of active investment managers beat the S&P 500 in an average year, and *fewer than 1 percent* do so over a decade or longer.

This is not to say that institutions that adopt Berkshire's partnership strategy will match Berkshire's record of doubling the return of the S&P 500. Few managers have the selection skills of Buffett and Munger. Nevertheless, based on the performance of the Global LAMP Index,® institutional investors who forge constructive partnerships with ethical, well-managed stewardship companies—in effect becoming stewards of the stewards—should vastly outperform those who actively trade the stocks of traditionally managed companies in hopes of catching an earnings surprise or a takeover bid.

The role of such a partner/investor would be to provide feedback and guidance concerning LAS best practices. This would extend a portfolio company's information-gathering network further into the marketplace, thereby increasing its capacity to learn, adapt, and innovate. Furthermore, it would increase the institutional investor's probabilities of success by helping portfolio companies become more profitable.

Active trading is self-defeating because it provides no constructive feedback or learning opportunities to portfolio companies and merely adds to their instability. Traders' short time horizons pressure corporations to waste money, energy, and credibility on managing earnings via creative accounting, rather than managing their businesses. This pressure deflects corporate leaders away from productive, long-term, strategic thinking and toward meeting the demands of investment analysts for quick results. Rather than forging long-term, constructive relationships between investment and corporate managers, short-term time horizons create an adversarial atmosphere. The message to corporations is perverse: "Never mind customer service or the health of the living systems that support you; instead, produce the numbers we want now or we'll dump you." It is extremely difficult to manage a company for long-term value-added and service to customers in such circumstances.

The effects of this dysfunctional system also harm the capital markets. Share prices become more illusory than real. Stock exchanges degenerate into gambling casinos rather than organs of effective learning and adaptation. Transaction fees dilute returns on capital. Capital cannot be efficiently allocated this way. Everyone loses: shareholders, corporations, employees, customers, communities, national economies, and the biosphere that supports them all. Warren Buffett's Fourth Law of Motion sums it up well: "For investors as a whole, returns decrease as motion increases."[6]

In July 2003, following a three-year bear market that took the NASDAQ composite down 78 percent from high to low, *The Wall Street Journal* reflected on how quickly Wall Street returned to fast-money trading:

In a flashback to the days of Internet mania, stocks in money–losing companies again are doing better than those of profitable companies.... How can this be happening again?.... One explanation is that Wall Street today is populated with fast-money investors who have become more interested in short-term pops than in long-term investments.

There are 5,000 mutual funds and 6,000 hedge funds in this country [that] . . . increasingly are judged on their ability to stay ahead of competitors, month by month, quarter by quarter . . . . Even at mutual funds, money managers who fall behind competitors are under severe pressure to catch up.[7]
—The Wall Street Journal

Toward More-Efficient Capital Markets

Like corporations, the capital markets are vibrant living systems—overlapping networks of buyers, sellers, researchers, bankers, brokers, and others—dedicated to allocating capital efficiently. These, too, are intimately connected to the larger living systems in which they exist, as well as to the living assets they employ. If capital markets worked with Nature's efficiency, all these constituencies would have a mutuality of interest and investors would have built-in incentives to think and act as stewards. But today that is not the case.

Capital markets routinely reward a privileged few at the expense of the many. Expense in this context refers to damage done to the web of life that supports all humanity. Even in its purported mission of optimizing risk-adjusted financial returns for the investors and users of capital, the market leaves much to be desired over short- and intermediate-term horizons. If it were more efficient, most companies would be operating on the LAS model and very few on the traditional model.

The capital markets' failure to see more clearly the primacy of living assets over nonliving capital assets is a major shortcoming of the traditional capitalist system. That said, like any living system, the markets cannot tolerate failure for long. The rising fortunes of LAMP companies and the decline of traditionally managed companies are evidence of this. The critical issue is their speed of adaptation. If Swiss Re and other insurers of catastrophic risk are to be believed, we have little time to waste.

There is a multiple-win strategy for institutional investors willing to take the long view. They can accelerate the transition to a market system premised on LAS by becoming meta-stewards. If, like Berkshire Hathaway, they partner with portfolio companies and help these companies become better stewards, they increase their chances of success and strengthen the market economy in which they operate. If, on the other hand, they persist in high-cost trading strategies that compromise performance and put them at odds with portfolio companies, they obstruct themselves and that economy.

The Berkshire partnership model, although not specifically designed around the LAS concept, succeeds because it operates on enlightened shareholder feedback. It recognizes, as LAS does, that investors cannot succeed in the long run if their activities harm the living systems that support free enterprise. That is why Warren Buffett has been such a forceful spokesperson for corporate ethics and empowering people who work in the Berkshire Hathaway network of companies, and why he has stood so vehemently against excessive executive privilege. Good living stewards share a common vision: the health of the corporation is inextricably tied to the health of the markets in which it operates, and the health of those markets, in turn, rests on the well-being of diverse stakeholders (customers, employees, investors, host communities, etc.). The differences between this model and the Wall Street norm,[8] dominated as it is by trading, are summarized in Table 15-1.

Although few institutional managers would fit perfectly on one side of this table or the other, the distinctions are real enough. Investors generally lean in one direction or the other. The styles don't mix and match easily because they are fundamentally at odds with one another. Traders are not long-term partners and don't have the perspective or patience to be financial stewards. Managers who try to be all things to all people end up satisfying no one in the long run.

Table 15-1 is organized into three sections. The first considers a manager's *market approach* in terms of operating model, investment time horizons, vision of success, and ultimate mission. Under this section, we see that financial stewards have an integrated agenda that reaches beyond client success to a healthy economy and strong capital markets. The Wall Street norm, on the other hand, seeks quick market returns. As described in Chapter 4, the stewardship approach strives for the systemic leverage of a multiple win. Traders, by contrast, tend to go for the more-limited and systemically fragile single win: quick profit.

The second section of Table 15-1 looks to investment style. This section draws on information presented in Chapter 14, which looks at the changing definitions of values and describes the advantages of qualitative investment analysis over the more-volatile quantitative approach. The best investment stewards, exemplified by Warren Buffett, select companies that

Table 15-1: The Stewardship Difference

INVESTMENT STEWARDS	WALL STREET NORM
Market Approach	
Partnership model	Trading model
Primacy of relational equity	Primacy of financial equity
Focus on means: LAS	Focus on ends: quick returns
Strengthening capital markets (infinite vision)	Exploiting capital markets (finite vision)
Investment Style	
Qualitative emphasis	Quantitative emphasis
Serve portfolio companies	Trade portfolio companies and hedge
Catalyze effective corporate change	Follow the money
Promotion of systemic harmony, sustainability	Opportunism
Long holding periods	Short holding periods (often minutes)
Ideal Corporation	
Values- and ethics-driven	Amoral, materialistic
Triple top line approach: inspires innovation	Bottom-line approach
Decentralized, networked organization	Celebrity CEO, chain of command
Open learning culture: everyone contributes	Executives know best
Empowered, vested employees	Replaceable employees
Customer intimacy (quality relationships)	Scale, market control (quantities sold)
Eco-stewardship: striving for zero adverse impact	Agnostic stance on environment
Passion to serve, contribute to social well-being	Continual re-engineering, downsizing
Transparent earnings reports and balanced scorecard	Managed earnings growth
Financially stable	Financially leveraged

meet their qualitative criteria, then serve those companies, hoping to cat-alyze effective change that will make it profitable to hold their shares "for-ever." The ideal of promoting systemic growth is usually an implicit part of the stewardship investment style, although to many pension funds it has become an explicit part of their triple bottom line strategies.[ix] By compar-ison, traders are more opportunistic, more impatient, and as a result, more cost-constrained.[x] Consequently, they rarely produce results that match those of the S&P 500 for sustained periods.

The third section of Table 15-1 discusses the *ideal corporation* for each type of manager. Contextually, this section draws mainly on chapters 1–3, which describe the merits of living assets relative to nonliving capital assets, and the advantages of LAS over the more traditional, mechanistic approach to corporate management.

Investment stewards, such as Berkshire Hathaway, look for financially stable companies with strong ethical values, empowered employees, a com-pelling desire to serve customers, and transparent reporting. Whether implicit in their unwritten rules and practices, or explicit in their stated policies, such companies tend to be good living asset stewards. By contrast, the Wall Street norm is ethically more neutral. Its ideal company is simply one that makes money, no matter how, and as quickly as possible.

Shareholder stewardship has one main goal: to help portfolio companies be the best they can be and, in doing so, to strengthen the living systems that support those companies. The shareholder steward then becomes part of an ongoing information feedback system filled with potential synergies. Just as managers of LAMP companies are, Warren Buffett and Berkshire Hathaway are highly skilled at executing this strategy. They get involved with portfolio companies to which they can offer strategic help, but they stay away from day-to-day operations. As experts on systemic risk manage-ment, their feedback to subsidiary managers is immensely valuable.

The Council of Institutional Investors Model

Not every investment manager has the perspective and skills to employ the Berkshire approach. There are, nevertheless, other ways institutional investors can become more effective shareholder stewards, thereby improv-ing their long-term investment returns. The Council of Institutional Investors (CII), a consortium of 140 public, corporate, and union pension funds with more than \$3 trillion in assets under management, offers an alternative model that allows investors to practice shareholder stewardship on a case-by-case basis.

CII members increasingly engage corporations on a variety of fronts. These may include: informally discussing matters of concern with executives and directors; formally confronting them through shareholder resolutions; and forcibly challenging them via board shakeups and takeovers. Although rarely as effective as Berkshire's partnership approach, when these ad hoc strategies are used in a spirit of stewardship, they can produce better governance and shareholder returns.

As the dysfunction of traditional management practices weighs on the economy, the capital markets, and shareholder returns, CII policy has become more assertive. Its accountability standards are clear. "[Corporate] directors should respond to communications from shareholders and should seek shareholder views on important governance, management and performance matters."[11] Under this standard, CII members increasingly launch shareholder resolutions on policies and/or practices about which they disagree with management.

Rather than put these resolutions to a vote at corporate annual meetings, many companies simply agree to alter their behavior—usually in the direction of better stewardship practices. Those that choose to resist a resolution often end up losing significant shareholder support.

During the 2004 proxy season, a record 703 resolutions were put to shareholder votes—up from 693 in 2003. In 2005 the number dropped to 576, apparently because so many were resolved through dialogue. Issues addressed in resolutions focused mainly on the worst practices of corporate hierarchies (excessive executive compensation, anti-takeover defenses, lack of board accountability, and auditors with conflicts of interest), and on corporate conduct on human rights, consumer safety, and the environment. The issue that saw the largest increase in related proxy activity concerned majority voting for board members, action on which would typically allow investors to oppose directors who pander to management.

While another record number of resolutions was filed on issues such as human rights, consumer safety, and the environment, successful dialogue and increased corporate awareness of social issues led to the withdrawal of many proposals. Of the proposals that went to shareholder vote, the focus tended toward requests for increased disclosure, and often asked for companies to assess the financial impact that its policies and operations might have on the company . . . . [T]he level of focus placed on financial and legal risk gained sig-nificant support from mainstream investors, as evidenced by the high level of shareholder support for many of the resolutions.[12]

—Institutional Shareholder Services, *2005 Postseason Report*

What we see here is impressive. Investors are looking both to the struc-ture of corporate management and to specific stewardship issues, and increasingly seeing the linkages between the two. Hierarchies generally have poor stewardship records. By forcing boards and managers to be more open and accountable, the CII and other activist investors are tilting corpo-rations toward more responsive and responsible governance.

The importance of CII member initiatives is not so much in what they have recently done, but in where they are going. Each year, shareholder res-olutions seem to get bolder and more focused on stewardship issues. The common thread in the corporate governance resolutions discussed above is a move toward more-open, networked systems. Matters that were once deemed non-economic are now viewed more systemically, and their eco-nomic impacts are being discussed. As the linkages between LAS and finan-cial performance become more manifest, these matters will take on greater weight.

The Council supports corporate governance initiatives that promote responsi-ble business practices and good corporate citizenship. The Council believes that the promotion, adoption and effective implementation of guidelines for the responsible conduct of business and business relationships are consistent with the fiduciary responsibility of protecting long-term investment interests.[13]

—Council of Institutional Investors, *Corporate Governance Policies*

The CalPERS Effect

The California Public Employees Retirement System (CalPERS) is a found-ing member of CII and one of the most innovative in terms of corporate governance initiatives. Since 1987, it has reaped substantial rewards by annually targeting, for governance reforms, 10 poorly performing companies within the system's domestic portfolio. CalPERS does this to help those companies address the root causes of their underperformance, with the goal of enhancing shareholder returns. By choosing this partnership approach, rather than selling out, CalPERS gains economic advantages. These include lower trading costs as well as better returns from better-managed companies. It is a classic win-win and its results have been stunning.

The institutional investment consulting firm of Wilshire Associates studied the performance of 95 companies targeted for reform by CalPERS between 1987 and 1999. Results indicated that although the stocks of these companies trailed the S&P 500 by 96 percent, on average, in the five-year period before CalPERS intervened, the same stocks outperformed the index by 14 percent in the subsequent five years, adding approximately $150 million in returns to the fund each year.[14]

Although CalPERS focuses primarily on the quality, independence, and responsibilities of corporate directors, it affirms the core of institutional shareholder stewardship: making corporations more open, transparent, connected, and accountable. CalPERS has proven it can be far more effective and profitable by becoming a partner in adaptive change than it might otherwise have been by trading out of the shares of a poorly managed company.

The CalPERS approach is fundamentally different from the Berkshire approach in one key respect: it is not based on principles of partnering "forever" but on strategic damage control. That said, both approaches clearly add value because they are premised on long-term holding periods and giving constructive feedback to the managers of portfolio companies. Whether shareholder stewardship is broadly based, as in the Berkshire approach, or specifically targeted, as in the CalPERS approach, it creates a multiple win.

Individual Shareholder Leanings

Individual investors have become increasingly assertive in their demand for better stewardship. Since 2000 they have been shifting assets from traditionally managed funds to socially responsible ones at an accelerating pace. And now they have better tools with which to evaluate how responsibly a fund is acting on stewardship matters. Since August 31, 2004 all public funds must disclose their proxy votes to the Securities and Exchange Commission (SEC). In other words, they must reveal how they voted on corporate governance as well as on social and environmental issues.

In a study of mutual fund sales and redemptions for the 24-month period ending May 31, 2003 Lipper Financial Services (Lipper) reported that socially responsible investment (SRI) funds had net inflows of $2.6 billion, while the much-larger marketplace for U.S. domestic equity funds had net outflows of $17.24 billion. The fundamental issue here appears to be one of trust—a loss of faith in traditionally managed companies following the spate of corporate scandals in 2001 and 2002.

Also important is a growing perception that ethically managed companies are less risky and more profitable over the long run. This view is supported by Lipper analyst Kathryn Barland, who reports that SRI funds outperformed traditionally managed ones by more than 3 percentage points per year during the three-year period ending September 30, 2002. It is also supported by the longer-term results of the Global LAMP Index.[®]

Barland believes the increasing demand for SRI funds reflects a public perception that they "have done their homework." The negative screens of socially responsible funds generally eliminate bad behavior, thereby reducing potential market risk. Beyond that, surveys indicate that ethical companies tend to attract better and more committed employees than do traditionally managed ones—a conclusion my research on LAMP companies strongly supports.

Looking to the future, I believe investor demand will shift again once the performance advantages of LAS are better understood. The larger value-added potential of shareholder stewardship, as modeled by Berkshire Hathaway and the Global LAMP Index,[®] will motivate the next step forward. Once investors see the advantages of this approach, they will demand that their institutional advisors—those who manage the world's large mutual, pension, and endowment funds—become better stewards.

The Prudent Man Rule

The Prudent Man Rule is a common-law principle that governs risk taking by investment professionals. It states, in essence, that an investment manager should not take risks with client money that he or she would not take personally. When this rule was established in 1830 by a decision of the

Massachusetts Supreme Judicial Court, factors that today pose investment risks, such as global climate change, toxic waste, product safety, and corporate culture, were not major financial issues. They were not unimportant, but they rarely affected investors' perceptions of risk. We live in a different world.

Those with the responsibility to invest money for others should act with prudence, discretion, intelligence, and regard for the safety of capital as well as for income.[15]

—Justice Samuel Putnam, the Massachusetts Supreme Judicial Court

---

It is now fair to ask if a prudent investment manager would invest in a company whose products and manufacturing processes put his or her family at risk. If the answer is "Yes," and the investment manager remains a passive onlooker, the clients are likely to be at risk. If, on the other hand, the answer is "Yes," and the financial manager leans on corporate management to effect reforms, prudent action is the result.

The definition of "prudent" is, of course, subject to varying interpretation. Is it prudent to invest in an ethical company when its shares are overpriced in relation to its earnings momentum? Is it prudent to invest in a company, with a poor stewardship record, whose underpriced shares may be taken over by a company with a good record, or whose investor plans to do a constructive intervention? These are questions best left for investment professionals to sort out in dialogue with their clients. Their actions will likely be *prudent* if their approaches are fully disclosed and if they move corporations toward better stewardship behavior.

The SEC supports this idea, now requiring all mutual fund companies and investment advisors to disclose their proxy voting guidelines and votes. This "disclosure rule" is the backbone of SEC policy. It originated with Justice Louis Brandeis, who believed that properly informed people were the best guarantors of corporate ethics and probity.

The SEC's newest disclosure rule follows a precedent set by the United Kingdom's 1995 Pensions Act, which requires all "occupational pension funds" to disclose the extent to which they take into account social, ethical, and environmental considerations. Such rules make advisors' standards of investor prudence more transparent to the public whose money they invest.

Europe is also moving toward fuller disclosure as a guide to more-informed and prudent shareholder actions. On May 30, 2002 the European Parliament supported a requirement that companies produce independently verified annual reports on the social and environmental impacts of their activities. These reports cover all levels of a company, including its supply chain and business partners, and are now part of a European framework for promoting corporate social responsibility. France, the Netherlands, and Denmark already mandate such reporting.

These directives from the SEC, the UK Pensions Act, and the European Parliament indicate that standards of investor and corporate prudence are broadening. They carry additional weight because so many of the world's leading corporations have already adopted them as normal business practice.

Just as corporate stewardship produces superior returns, so does shareholder stewardship. Both operate from a superior mental model of the corporation. When investors become partners in stewardship we get better portfolio returns at lower risk. Whether this is done on a sustained, long-term basis, as Berkshire Hathaway does, or on an ad hoc basis, as demonstrated by the CalPERS effect, the results are consistently beneficial. *That* is prudent investing.

"Activism" reflects the simple and accepted concept that people behave and perform better if they are watched and if there are good consequences for good behavior and bad ones for bad behavior. Activism also reflects the fact that large investors can do better than to plunk money down and hope for the best—they can take steps to increase the chance that the best will actually occur.[16]

—Council of Institutional Investors, "Portfolio Risk Reduction
and Performance Enhancement"

The Freshfields Report

In October 2005, a consortium of 13 global fund managers managing more than $1.7 trillion, in collaboration with the international law firm of Freshfields, Bruckhaus, Deringer and the United Nations Environment Programme's Finance Initiative (UNEP-FI), issued a 154-page report on "a

legal framework for the integration of environmental, social and governance issues into institutional investment." The report dismissed traditional arguments that environmental, social, and governance (ESG) issues were
outside the legitimate "profit maximization" interests of investment managers. It took the opposite position: "In our view, decision-makers are
required to have regard (at some level) to ESG considerations in every decision they make. This is because there is a body of credible evidence demonstrating that such considerations often have a role to play in the proper
analysis of investment *value*. As such they cannot be ignored, because
doing so may result in investments being given an inappropriate value."[xvii]
The Freshfields report added that ESG considerations are legally required
in most major market jurisdictions—especially when requested by a client.

It is increasingly difficult for investment decision-makers to claim that ESG
[environmental, social, and governance] considerations are too difficult to
quantify when they readily quantify business goodwill and other equivalently
nebulous intangibles.[18]

—Freshfields, Bruckhouse, Deringer

The increased interest of institutional investors concerning shareholder
stewardship is impressive by the standards of the past decade, although still
constrained by conventional thinking on what is prudent. This is largely
because investment managers have yet to see a body of credible evidence
that good stewardship practices add meaningful value. The best evidence
they have so far—based on performance of the Domini social indices and
the Dow Jones Sustainability Index— is that stewardship doesn't harm
investment returns and that it may help to ameliorate portfolio risk. Such
attitudes should change once the deep stewardship characteristics of the
Global LAMP Index® are better known and differentiated from the more-
random screening methods of the leading socially responsible and sustainability indices, as illustrated in Chapter 13.

In April 2006, 32 funds with combined assets exceeding $2 trillion—
most of them public employee pension funds—signed a charter pledging
themselves to use ESG standards at the core of their investment strategies.
The signatories endorse six "Principles for Responsible Investment" that
they believe to be material to the long-term valuation of assets. These

include vows to incorporate such standards into investment analysis, active engagement with companies, demands for ESG disclosure, and cooperative action on shareholder resolutions. The importance of this voluntary agreement is not in the commitment of its signatories to specific action—the six principles are, after all, nonbinding. Rather, it is noteworthy because it continues a trend, among some of the world's largest investors, toward deeper shareholder stewardship.[19]

Conclusion

Institutional shareholders own most of the stock in the S&P 500, the MSCI World, and the Global LAMP indices. As fiduciaries for the public at large they must act prudently, both to avoid unnecessary risk and to optimize investment returns.

The corporate shares managed by institutional investors for their clients are endowed with certain property rights. Among these are the rights to elect corporate board members and to put shareholder resolutions before the board on matters of governance. These rights are powerful levers for change. Institutions can, and should, use them to promote better Living Asset Stewardship in portfolio companies. This is prudent action because consistently well-executed LAS reduces investment risk and enhances return.

This chapter has explored two different approaches to shareholder stewardship. Users of both have produced superior financial returns by thinking and acting systemically—by seeing corporations, capital markets, society, and the biosphere as closely connected living systems. In such a large network the health of the biosphere and society, which support all other systems, is crucial. As the world shrinks (metaphorically), this has become clearer to the capital markets.

The question before institutional investors today is not whether shareholder stewardship makes sense, but which version makes most sense *for them*. The systemic partnership model is the more difficult to implement because it requires the most contact with portfolio companies. However, it may be the most productive in the long run. The simpler CalPERS model offers a way to learn shareholder stewardship incrementally on a case-by-case basis. The Global LAMP Index® offers some of the benefits of both because it puts investors on the LAS track while they learn the levers and techniques of shareholder stewardship.

16

Companies That Last for Centuries

"My favorite time frame for holding a stock is forever."[1]
—Warren Buffett

"Like all organisms, the living company exists primarily for its own
survival and improvement: to fulfill its potential and to become as
great as it can be."[2]
—Arie de Geus, *The Living Company*

T he average and median ages of global LAMP companies exceed a century. Rather than being senescent and stuck in their ways, these centenarians and multi-centenarians are on the cutting edge of change in their industries. Some, such as Nokia, have reinvented themselves from within so many times that they have migrated across multiple industry sectors as they have evolved and redefined their potentials. In this final chapter I'd like to reflect on what we can learn from these companies, the mainstays of my learning laboratory.

The big lesson is not to be found in replicating, by management fiat, specific attributes of Living Assets Stewardship, such as employee friendliness, eco-efficiency, or customer intimacy. Rather, it is in creating cultures that organically develop these attributes from within, and in doing so, create virtuous feedback cycles that sustain learning, innovation, and profit far into the future.

Creating and sustaining such organic cultures is, by necessity, an ongoing process because living systems are continually in flux. The process
recursively moves in cycles of observing, planning, doing, measuring, and
reflecting—guided by a balanced scorecard that takes the organization to
deeper and deeper levels of systemic understanding. Questioning is an
essential part of the process because it guides the choices we make at every
stage. What follows is a series of six key questions that corporate leaders
can use to gain deeper insight into their firms and greater coherence in
their strategic planning.

How would we create a company that would last for centuries? This kind of
company would, in Arie de Geus's words, fulfill its potential and become as
great as it can be. It would attract and hold long-term investors like Warren
Buffet.

From an operational perspective this is a complex question because it
must be answered on so many different levels. Yet from a cultural perspective it is quite simple. An answer that does justice to both perspectives
requires a layered approach that starts holistically with the big picture, and
then progressively narrows to issues of organization, management, rules of
engagement, and leadership. Each question in the progression is premised
on the answer that precedes and shapes it. Though this formula does not
generate a specific game plan for a long-lived company, it suggests a process
that would likely yield a workable plan.

How are long-lived companies different? This conceptual question looks to
the broad outlines of corporate culture. Arie de Geus addressed it when he
was the coordinator of worldwide Group Planning at Royal Dutch/Shell in
the mid-1980s; his answer was later published as his book, *The Living
Company.* Firms, he noted, are not machines, but living communities of
people. From this premise, all else follows. Because companies are alive they
have instincts that are similar to those of all living beings and systems. They
work best when they operate in harmony with the web of life that supports
them, and they break down when they operate in disharmony. To achieve
harmony, to fulfill their potential as living entities, and ultimately, to pass
their "genes" on to successive generations, firms must "be open to the outside world." They must welcome new ideas, constructive relationships, and
the possibilities of learning. In short, they must have adaptive, life-support-
ing cultures.

If a company is indeed living, how should it be organized? Networks are the basic form of all life and living systems: Fritjof Capra says that wherever we see life we see networks. Networks allow a company to be more than the sum of its parts. By virtue of their connectivity, symbiotic exchanges, and cybernetic flows of information and energy, living networks continuously grow in retained knowledge and productive capacity. The interdependence of their constituent parts—the dynamic in which the waste of some becomes the food for others, and cycles of birth and death continuously revitalize the system from within—has kept Earth's terrestrial and marine ecosystems vital and evolving for millions of years. Stora (now Stora Enso) has continuously operated for more than seven centuries largely on these principles. Long before the Internet became widely accessible in the mid-1990s and networking became a corporate buzzword, LAMP companies operated on network principles. For them, it is not window dressing or an afterthought—it is in their genes.

How would we manage a living network to fulfill its potential? In companies, as in Nature, all life and living systems *manage by means.* Highly networked companies understand that their employees and the biospheric web of life are the means by which they create capital assets and, ultimately, value for their stakeholders. Each element within the web—whether person or microbe—has a natural urge to grow and perpetuate its kind. To build capacity, companies that manage by means empower employees to follow their natural instincts, self-organize, learn as they go, spontaneously develop relationships, and help one another as market demands shift. They do their utmost to reinforce mutually advantageous relationships and to minimize hierarchical management controls that block connectivity. Means are ends in the making. Relational equity is the means by which companies generate financial equity. In networked systems, everything is related to everything else. The system is totally integrated.

What are the rules of engagement in such an integrated system? To execute management by means effectively, companies must practice Living Asset Stewardship. The two are inextricably linked because living assets (people and Nature) are the means by which companies generate capital assets, customer value, and, ultimately, wealth. Good execution demands consistency and congruency. When companies care about people and the things people care about, they implicitly embrace LAS because people innately care about the living world and its biodiversity (*biophilia*). LAS resonates with stakeholders and motivates them to act in ways that traditional business theorists often overlook. Well-executed LAS inspires organizational learning and innovation. Caring begets caring. When employees work with their hearts as well as their minds they are more productive. When customers bond with a company, they infuse it with new energy and ideas. The reinforcing cycle of LAS + OL is a powerful catalyst to learning, innovation, and profit. It accounts, more than anything I can identify, for the extraordinary performance of the 16 Focus Group companies and the larger Global LAMP Index® from which they were extracted.

How would we lead a company toward such an innovative culture? Leaders must become what they want their companies to be. They must understand that they, their organizations, and Nature are one, and they must take personal responsibility for maintaining the vitality of the whole system. In short, they must think and act holistically. This level of insight requires a high degree of personal mastery—keeping an open, inquiring mind and a willingness to learn from anyone. When such holism is consistently and congruently modeled by those ultimately responsible for a firm's strategic thinking and development, it becomes part of the culture and is eagerly taken up by others. When people think and work in ways congruent with their inherent affinity for life, they are more likely to engage their higher thinking capacities (Danah Zohar's quantum intelligence).

If companies want to survive for centuries, they must, at a minimum, address these questions, which look to the essential qualities and strengths of their living organizations. Other questions relating to corporate mission, strategy, tactics, and such are important as well, but they are secondary. As revealed in Table 12-1, companies must have a valid theory of self and system before they can create a valid practice.

Both the company and its constituent members have basic driving forces: they want to survive, and once the conditions for survival exist, they want to reach and expand their potential.[3]

—Arie de Geus, *The Living Company*

The LAMP 60

The 60 companies in the Global LAMP Index® have collectively gained huge market share during the past 30 years by following LAS principles. Some have developed stewardship cultures from their inceptions and some by reinventing themselves, but most have done so by a process of continual learning and adaptation that has become deeply embedded in their cultures through decades and centuries. Although LAMP companies comprise only one-tenth of 1 percent of the total number of multinational companies in operation worldwide, their market capitalization today is approximately one-third that of the Standard & Poor 500 Index and one-sixth that of the larger MSCI World Index. For this fact alone they cannot be ignored.

The larger message of the LAMP 60—one that transcends their financial success—is the demonstrable superiority of LAS as a mental model. Whereas the traditional model is predicated on a singular respect for money, LAS is predicated on a systemic respect for life. People identify with this approach to business because respect for life has been wired into our genes for thousands of generations. Four or five generations of straying down the wrong path—traditional capitalism—doesn't change our wiring.

LAS also resonates with us because it is congruent with our deepest beliefs and hopes for the future. We don't want to bequeath to future generations a planet whose air, water, and soil are so contaminated that life as we know it is threatened. We do not want our children and grandchildren to grow up in a disconnected world in which: the fabric of families and communities is torn by pursuit of money for its own sake; acting on our natural altruistic instincts is devalued; and people are expected to check their ideals at the company door on their way in to work. We are already surrounded by too much of this soul-deadening reality. It has produced global stress, public health problems, and climate change.

As a result, when we discover ways to live and work that are more harmonious with our deeply embedded biophilic instincts and hopes for the future, most of us jump at them. In the words of Mark Moody-Stuart, former chairman of Royal Dutch/Shell, such harmony generates "emotional enthusiasm."

The Corporation as Catalyst

Multinational corporations today control most of the Earth's natural resources and most of its wealth. They have also developed most of the technologies we use in daily life. However and wherever they act, they have huge impacts on local economies, social systems, and ecosystems. Those impacts can simultaneously be both helpful and profoundly damaging. My purpose has been to concentrate primarily on the helpful side of the equation.

The hope corporations offer us today resides in their capacity for learning and adaptation, in their ability to mobilize human talent quickly, and in their immense financial resources. The best ones have already begun to put these resources toward reducing our demands on the Earth's biosphere and toward improving the quality of life for people everywhere. That is the spirit of Canon's kyosei philosophy and the shared direction taken by all LAMP companies. This is not to say that universities, governments, community organizations, and religious institutions must assume only minor roles in our ongoing drama. Indeed, they are crucial because they represent the interests of so many essential (interdependent) partners in creating a sustainable economy. What I envision is a collective effort with dialogue flowing in all directions.

One of the most important lessons I have learned as a student of systems thinking concerns the power of leverage. The best way to change a system is to find the simple change in thinking or acting that can produce magnified benefits. We have seen many such changes in world history. It took only a few explorers to convince us the Earth is round, not flat. Although it took many years for that discovery to become universally accepted, we cannot imagine returning to the old way of thinking today. Likewise, we cannot imagine living today without the wheel, fire, and language—Promethean developments whose ready acceptance, use, and proliferation can have been nothing short of explosive.

During the twentieth century the new sciences have revealed that the Earth, rather than being an inert mechanical system as decreed by Newtonian science, is a living system that has the capacity to renew itself continually. Building on that mind-set, de Geus took a similar conceptual leap in saying that the corporation, also, is not a machine but a living being—with a mind and a conscience. In turn, I have built on de Geus's thesis by saying that the most important assets of a living company are living assets rather than nonliving capital assets, and that Living Asset Stewardship is the only way we can assure that the corporation, as an instrument of change, will survive to serve future generations.

Once you start thinking in these terms, the possibilities of using corporations as levers for future learning and adaptation are immense. The challenge, as it has been with every paradigm shift in history, is to get a critical mass of new thinkers on board to effect real change. This can take time because people don't easily let go of traditional mind-sets. It took the sixteenth-century Age of Exploration to convince people that the Earth was round. We don't know how long it will take to achieve a major shift to LAS because the traditional system is now fighting to preserve itself and the privileges of executive hierarchy—a counter-revolution that could take years to play out. But one thing is certain: the days of the traditionally managed corporation are numbered. It has become so dysfunctional it is literally consuming itself. The evidence of this is plain: in the general decline of corporate credit ratings, in the worrying rise of unfunded pension liabilities, in strategic "re-engineerings," and in deceptive accounting practices.

The 60 companies in the Global LAMP Index® and other stewardship exemplars, although far from perfect, are the vanguard of the living company/living asset paradigm. If their evolution during the past 30 years is any indication, time is on their side. It is hard to argue with their success—especially when their records stand in such contrast to the declining fortunes of traditionally managed companies.

The appeal of this new paradigm is broad and far-reaching. It affects people of every sort, not just a select few corporate managers and privileged shareholders. As shown in Figure 16-1, stewardship is symbiotically self-reinforcing. When practiced in business, it strengthens corporations, capital markets, and the economy. The feedback effects go both ways. Stronger economies also beget stronger capital markets, stronger corporations, and stronger business conditions. The reinforcing cycle of LAS + OL is a robust catalyst. It builds success upon success, and in time will work its way up toward remediating some of the biospheric damage done in the past century. Even though that final step may be far off, people can sense its potential. Thus, at each step, LAS gains adherents.

Figure 16-1: Multi-layered Feedback Effects of LAS

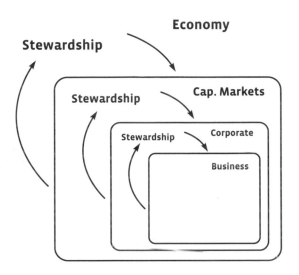

Living Asset Stewardship has reached a tipping point. The capital markets understand implicitly that LAS is more effective than the traditional model of business. We see this in the superior performance of the Global LAMP Index. As LAS becomes part of the market's explicity knowledge, it will spread up into the general economy and out into every fractal of business by the sheer force of its effectiveness. It is an evolutionary change whose time has come.

Getting It Right

Using the right mental model of the firm makes all the difference. Trying to fine-tune a flawed system to make it "less bad" is a waste of precious time and money, as we saw in Chapter 13. Living Asset Stewardship is the only way to operate a living corporation coherently, because LAS is symbiotic, and therefore harmonious, with the real world in which it operates. Living systems should behave as *living systems* rather than as static machines. They are complex, interdependent associations—networks layered within networks—in which the health of the whole depends on the health of the parts, and vice versa. That means their cultures and processes should be squarely focused on sustaining life. In terms of the living company/living asset paradigm, this is a triple top line approach because it aims to get things right from the start.

Do firms have to get it *exactly* right from the start? Certainly not. If that were the case, there would likely be no Global LAMP Index.® Without exception, every LAMP company has learned stewardship by trial and error—by making mistakes, and then having the courage and curiosity to look back and ask, "What went wrong?" They can then move forward with the benefit of profound insight. Even those companies that started with a life-affirming mission and culture, such as Johnson & Johnson, have made their fair share of mistakes. Robert W. Johnson's famous remark—that if you're not making mistakes, you're not trying—shows an acceptance of trial and error that is at the heart of every living system, and the key to J&J's longevity and success. Without such tolerance for error, corporate evolution would be constrained.

What firms have to get right from the start is not a process or even a theory, but simply, the attitude of respecting and affirming life. This doesn't have to happen on day one of their operations. Most often it comes with maturity, and only after a company has had time to reflect on its successes and failures. We can recognize such respect and affirmation by a shift in companies' essential thought processes and mental models.

Nucor did not start with a culture of servant leadership. It evolved from a process of soul-searching following the 1964 near-bankruptcy of its predecessor, Nuclear Corporation of America. Ken Iverson, whose vision guided the rebuilding of the firm, needed to win the hearts of employees in order to move ahead. He did this by respecting them, their families, and their communities. From that point forward, a miraculous process unfolded. It was spontaneous. It couldn't have been scripted. Everyone pulled together. By working together, thinking together, and sharing the rewards and burdens together, employees and management of Nucor enabled the company to evolve into the firm it is today: the nation's largest steelmaker by market capitalization. Its stewardship emerged from the hearts of its people and their care for community. Iverson's respect for life was contagious. Nucor's people hungered for it and have faithfully carried it forward.

Their faithfulness and commitment come from their hearts and spirits. Iverson understood the basic decency of people—their desires to do the right thing for their families and communities. What he did with Nucor would not have been possible had he followed the traditional model of hierarchy, command and control, and valuing nonliving assets over living ones. His leap of faith, past a conventional vision to one that emanated from his heart, and his personal mastery, which infused the company with that faith, made all the difference.

When a company deeply commits to caring about people and respecting life, the catalytic effects are much like those of the U.S. Declaration of Independence. As the founding document of U.S. democracy, its principles give us a transcendent sense of purpose and empower people to follow their dreams. Although, like individual freedom, LAS is hard to achieve perfectly, it is a goal so worth striving for that it energizes people. Because it inspires us, it sustains us through trials and multiple errors. We learn from our mistakes because we care enough to learn.

Paths to LAS

Companies have come to LAS by many paths. Like Nucor, some took a leap of faith from a state of near-bankruptcy. Others, like Johnson & Johnson, were initially founded on stewardship principles. But for most, LAS arose from a lengthy process of trial and error—continually inquiring, listening, and, above all, learning from mistakes.

The four turn-around companies in the Focus Group—3M, Nucor, Canon, and Toyota—are fascinating because they had to reinvent themselves completely in capital-intensive industries in which they faced much-larger and well-financed competitors. In every case they formed their strategies around networked cultures that enabled rapid learning and adaptation (i.e., smarts), rather than on attempts to dominate their markets via acquisition and sheer size (i.e., scale). They empowered employees, created a shared sense of mission, and then let their networks spontaneously create. Minnesota Mining, like Nucor, emerged from a failed enterprise into a spontaneously collaborative industrial firm. Now known as 3M, its culture was transformed in the 1920s by a corporate focus on ideas: giving employees the freedom to connect with customers, to engage in "experimental doodling," and then to become entrepreneurs in niche markets of their own creation. Toyota and Canon both emerged from the devastation of World War II, during which their domestic infrastructure and markets were destroyed, by modeling themselves on networked living systems and cybernetic principles that leveraged employee learning. All four of these companies are now profit leaders in their industries and continue to roll up market share wherever they operate.

The four LAMP companies that founded their ventures on stewardship ideals are also fascinating because they rejected prevailing business norms from the start. Rather than becoming centralized hierarchies managing by the numbers, they sought to create visions of the firm that were inspiring and transcendent, and would empower ordinary people to contribute their best efforts. For example, Robert Wood Johnson founded Johnson & Johnson, during the predatory Gilded Age of the late-nineteenth century, on ideals of "alleviating pain and disease" and a philosophy of putting concerns for employees and customers ahead of those of shareholders. William Hewlett and David Packard co-founded HP in 1939, on the eve of World War II, on a hopeful theme of "advancing science and the welfare of humanity." Intel was co-founded in 1968 during the Vietnam War by Gordon Moore and Robert Noyce, who envisioned technologies that would empower people to "go off and do something wonderful." A few years later, amid a global oil embargo and rising energy prices, Herb Kelleher founded Southwest to give ordinary people "the freedom to fly" by making air travel affordable, and to provide meaningful careers to employees. All four companies have built their businesses by serving employees and empowering them to self-organize in pursuit of inspiring goals—a networking strategy that has produced outstanding economic results on the road to sustainability.

If most companies have taken paths to LAS less dramatic than those just mentioned, their stories are no less compelling. The majority started as relatively open, interactive cultures and evolved into vibrant LAS networks. Such cultures were tolerant, predisposed to listening, and open to divergent opinions because they cared for employees and their host communities. These attributes gave them abilities to learn faster than their peers could, and to reinvent themselves, sometimes in astonishing ways.

During the 1980s, for example, Paul O'Neill transformed Alcoa from a commodity manufacturer to a high-value-added innovator by adopting a strategy that both served and empowered employees. The company became radically decentralized so that decisions could be made as close to the front lines as possible. Understanding that it operated in an environmentally hazardous industry, Alcoa made environmental friendliness and employee health two top-line priorities, an effort that culminated in the company's Life! program and the idealistic Alcoa Business System. Nokia's story, too, is based on an open culture of inquiring and listening that has become one of the most-integrated corporate learning networks in the world today. Since its founding in 1865 it has reinvented itself many times, moving from forest products to tires to electronics and telecommunications. Stora Enso, the world's oldest continually operating company, owes its 700-plus-year longevity, in large part, to such attributes. The same goes for HSBC, Royal Dutch/Shell, and Swiss Re, all founded in the mid-nineteenth century; these three have become the most-adaptive learning cultures in their industries. Novo Nordisk grew out of a nonprofit research company, founded in 1923, that later evolved into one of the most innovative and eco-friendly pharmaceutical firms in the world. Baxter International started as a distributor for blood transfusion therapies developed by Dr. Donald E. Baxter, who had served as a medical missionary in China during the 1920s. His ideals of public service eventually became embedded in the company's open, transparent, and collaborative learning culture.

Although these Focus Group companies have traveled different paths, they all understand this fundamental truth: people are more effective when they work with their hearts as well as their minds. If a culture that so energizes people is the goal, the only way to do it sustainably is to adopt the principles of the LAS model.

The Crisis of Traditional Capitalism

Traditional capitalism has lost its bearings and has slid into degeneracy. The capital markets, noting this slide, have become preoccupied with short-term trading and deal making. Whereas Wall Street was once a reliable source of long-term investment capital and strategic advice, its interests now lie in next quarter's earnings, the next mega-deal, and increasingly, the next rumor. Our largest banks and brokers have knowingly defrauded investors by helping corporations like Enron, WorldCom, Tyco, and Parmalat hide liabilities, overstate revenues, and sell worthless securities. Some of our largest mutual fund companies allowed hedge funds to trade their shares after hours in ways that diluted returns to individual investors. In 1998 the "mega" hedge fund Long Term Capital Management, gambling with borrowed funds willingly supplied by large banks and brokers, put the entire global financial system at risk, whereupon the U.S. Federal Reserve was obliged to orchestrate a financial rescue operation. The most egregious miscreants in these ventures rely on the perception that they are such large players in their markets—"too big to fail"—that they will be rescued from their mistakes at public expense. This is grotesquely irresponsible and uneconomic because these institutions have the capacity to do serious damage to the capital markets and the economies through which they and the rest of us ultimately make our livings.

It is astonishing that three years after passage of the Sarbannes-Oxley Act of 2002, which set higher standards on accounting ethics and transparency following the Enron and WorldCom frauds, companies continued to overstate their earnings. A recent study by Glass, Lewis & Co. tallied 1,295 earnings restatements in 2005—more than triple the number in 2002, the year the Sarbannes-Oxley legislation was passed.[4] Beyond such formal "8-K" disclosures to the SEC, the Glass, Lewis & Co. report notes "a surge of stealth restatements," whereby companies correct previous accounting errors by quietly acknowledging them in subsequent annual or quarterly reports. Of course, by the time corrections are made, investors have been misled and often company executives have received their bonus pay on inflated earnings.

The obscene compensation paid to corporate executives in cash, stock options, pensions, and other perks is a related matter. Between 1980 and 2004 the total compensation paid to CEOs vaulted from 42 times that of the average worker to 280 times that figure—even though corporate profits grew at less than the rate of growth of GDP.[5] Some of the most egregious examples are those in which compensation has gone to executives that were fired—such as the payment of $140 million to Michael Ovitz for his 14 months as the number-two man at Walt Disney. Such excess pay reflects a culture of extreme disrespect because it sets leaders so far apart from those they lead and the real living world in which their companies operate.

Bankers and brokers, who once prided themselves on maintaining the stability of the capitalist system, are today too focused on turning deals and transactions, too indebted to the corporate executives they advise, and too interested in their own bottom lines to care about the web of life. Their splendid isolation, too, is revealed in the size of their total compensation. The median remuneration of Wall Street's top CEOs in 2005 was $38.6 million.[6] For the year 2000, Sanford Weill, then CEO of Citigroup, received $330.3 million in compensation plus stock option grants.

By the latter years of the twentieth century, our business values had eroded to a remarkable extent . . . . I see far too much greed, egoism, materialism and waste to please my critical eye . . . . I see our shocking misuse of the world's natural resources, as if they were ours to waste rather than ours to preserve as a sacred trust for future generations . . . .[7]

—John C. Bogle, *The Battle for the Soul of Capitalism*

I often refer to traditional capitalism's slide into degeneracy as an endgame—a desperate attempt to maintain appearances in a system that is profoundly out of touch. However, no amount of creative accounting, hyper-trading and deal making, or record-shattering compensation can disguise the fact that it is sick and crumbling.

Say what you will about the capital markets; they are not blind. They live by the rules of all living systems, which in the long run hold that we must adapt or die. Today we live in a transitional era. As the iron grip of traditional capitalism weakens, a new form of capitalism based on Living Asset Stewardship is gaining strength. Institutional investors, who must also adapt or die, increasingly see this and are shifting their behavior.

As in all transitional periods, many early movers try to blend elements of the old and new systems together. But an amalgam of two systems so diametrically opposed is ultimately self-defeating. Just as you can't blend a political system premised on the divine right of kings with one premised on popular democracy, you cannot blend a system premised on "corporations as machines" with one premised on "corporations as living beings." The simple truth is that such antithetical systems clash. You have to make a choice. This is the fundamental issue SRI and sustainability investors must address if they want to succeed in the long run.

The Real Bottom Line

The ultimate reality is this: the biosphere and even humanity can live without corporations. They have already done so for millennia. But the reverse is not true. Whether companies accept it or not, they are part of the biospheric web of life. Although there can be no guarantees of individual survival—there never are in Nature—firms that symbiotically respect life have the best odds of future success. Those that don't will surely die.

There is no time to waste in shifting to the living company/living assets paradigm. If business is to survive and thrive into the distant future, we must abandon the traditional machine model of the firm and its destructive ways, and move with speed and intention to a deep stewardship model that respects life. We have the capacity to do so. And we need to do it now.

Epilogue: Deep Stewardship

"One piece of good sense would be more memorable than a
monument as high as the moon."[1]
—Henry David Thoreau, *Walden*

Living Asset Stewardship is premised on two fundamental truths:
1. **Profit can arise only from life.** This is a primary truth and there
are no long-term exceptions to it. Economic systems are subsystems
of biological ones. Living assets (people and Nature) are the source of nonliving (capital) assets and of profit itself.

2. **In a healthy world, profit must serve life.** This follows from the first
truth because all life in this world is connected and ultimately interdependent. Corporations cannot afford to diminish the primary sources of their
profit, whether by benign neglect or by conscious depredation. At a minimum, they must strive to do no harm, as HSBC and Swiss Re are doing in
their quests to become carbon neutral.[2] They must also contribute to the
well-being of their stakeholders—for example, by serving the professional
growth of employees and by husbanding the environments that provide
their essential resources.

Companies that nurture the web of life as they extract value from it enjoy synergies that others don't. Such firms inspire employees and strategic partners to look deeply into their value-creation processes for ways to make those processes more effective and less wasteful. This inquiry generates organizational learning (OL), which in turn increases the possibilities for innovation and profit. I have described this dynamic as the reinforcing cycle of LAS + OL. It is the driving force behind the extraordinary performance of the stewardship companies profiled in this book.

These companies, collectively called the Global Living Asset Management Performance (LAMP) Index,® not only strive to serve life, but also seek to mimic it in the nature of their organization and management. They are, for example, more interactively networked than hierarchically driven. They manage by means—building the competences of those who add value to their offers—more than by objectives such as profit. This inner consistency is immensely appealing to people. It conveys integrity, which is the foundation of trust, and inspires stakeholder commitment. People are instinctively drawn to LAS leaders. It is no accident that these companies attract the best employees, the most loyal customers, and the most patient investors.

By comparison, what passes as stewardship in most companies today is a pale imitation. Too many corporations profess allegiance to the triple bottom line of economic, social, and environmental return, only to fail because they are organized and managed in ways that fundamentally conflict with these goals. Basic attributes of these firms—excessive hierarchy, mechanistic management, and too-linear thinking—are antithetical to a genuine triple-bottom-line approach, and make impossible the consistency and congruency achieved by real LAS organizations. This basic incompatibility undermines the integrity of any efforts toward stewardship.

Like deep ecology, deep stewardship requires a fundamental shift in the way we see ourselves in relation to the rest of life. We have learned to reduce our world into component parts, but living assets are irreducible, and indivisible from one another. People do not and cannot exist separate from Nature, and the innumerable parts of the natural world likewise cannot be divided (and conquered). For better and worse, all of Nature is part of a unified whole. The best corporate stewards recognize that they, too, are part of Nature—not above it or destined to rule it. Although no company practices this ethic perfectly, highly networked cultures that manage by means are more respectful (i.e., less domineering), and therefore more open to learning about the synergies inherent in the web of life. Learning, of course, is the key to adaptation, innovation, and profit.

Humanity still has a long way to go to replicate the efficiency of Nature, in whose workings everything is recycled and nothing is wasted. If we now waste 94 percent of the energy and materials used to manufacture and deliver the things we consume, there are immense economies in closing the loop. For example, a 2-percent reduction in the waste stream yields a 33-percent return. It is within our grasp to achieve economics far more ambitious, and—for the sake of humanity's survival—we must. The companies most likely to achieve those kinds of gains are those that practice deep stewardship.

The industrial age of the nineteenth and twentieth centuries has increased the standards of living for many, but it has increased economic and civil inequities and run down the carrying capacity of the biosphere that supports us. This has happened, in large part, because of the hubristic notions that humanity ought to prevail over Nature, and that the mechanical systems we have created are superior to natural systems. As we are now seeing, this is a false and dangerous premise.

Deep stewardship is our best hope for the future. It is a journey we must make and have just begun. The leverage in it is immense. And it is profitable—highly profitable.

Appendices

Appendix 1: Focus Group Performance 1996–2000

Company	1996	1997	1998	1999	2000
Alcoa	23.07	11.96	8.11	124.77	(18.07)
Baxter International	0.73	25.80	29.80	(0.53)	42.44
Canon	19.53	6.30	(9.79)	90.30	(16.89)
HSBC	42.90	20.83	8.26	62.06	6.17
Hewlett-Packard	21.00	25.41	10.26	67.45	(43.94)
Intel	131.00	7.48	68.95	39.02	(27.24)
Johnson & Johnson	18.11	34.14	28.81	12.49	14.00
3M	27.94	0.59	(10.65)	40.76	25.49
Nokia	58.09	46.04	225.05	211.21	(8.53)
Novo Nordisk	37.02	54.75	(7.35)	(2.16)	37.72
Nucor	(10.16)	(4.49)	(9.48)	27.93	(26.49)
Royal Dutch/Shell	25.10	30.48	(8.73)	29.82	2.39
Southwest Airlines	(4.17)	69.86	39.73	7.78	108.14
Stora Enso	15.84	(7.53)	(13.28)	101.04	(32.20)
Swiss Re	(7.22)	81.62	36.15	(18.74)	18.52
Toyota	36.90	0.05	(6.64)	83.94	(34.94)

Annual Returns

Focus Group Avg. Return	27.23	25.21	24.33	54.82	2.91
LAMP 60 Avg. Return	27.72	33.91	29.23	47.66	2.02
MSCI World Index	13.47	15.76	24.31	24.94	(13.19)
S&P 500 Index	22.94	33.25	28.57	21.04	(9.10)

Focus Group Performance 2001–2005

Company	2001	2002	2003	2004	2005
Alcoa	7.45	(34.23)	69.45	(15.74)	(3.98)
Baxter International	22.77	(46.71)	11.07	15.31	10.68
Canon	4.64	5.82	30.31	14.44	9.62
HSBC	(15.61)	(3.48)	48.82	12.21	(1.37)
Hewlett Packard	(33.91)	(13.92)	33.93	(7.15)	38.05
Intel	5.54	(50.24)	106.49	(26.77)	8.08
Johnson & Johnson	13.84	(7.77)	(2.25)	25.09	(3.22)
3M	0.01	6.40	40.06	(1.79)	(3.52)
Nokia	(43.01)	(35.83)	11.61	(5.59)	19.59
Novo Nordisk	(8.65)	(27.01)	43.49	33.75	8.99
Nucor	35.15	(20.58)	37.53	88.61	30.53
Royal Dutch/Shell	(16.73)	(7.00)	23.42	13.55	12.53
Southwest Airlines	(16.40)	(24.68)	16.19	1.05	1.04
Stora Enso	8.09	(11.42)	33.56	15.72	(7.30)
Swiss Re	(13.75)	(33.83)	3.89	7.80	3.72
Toyota	(18.38)	5.18	31.28	20.49	29.07

Annual Returns

Focus Group Avg. Return	(4.31)	(18.71)	33.68	11.93	9.53
LAMP 60 Avg. Return	(6.02)	(13.80)	40.61	16.78	11.63
MSCI World Index	(16.80)	(19.88)	33.10	14.72	9.49
S&P 500 Index	(11.88)	(22.09)	28.67	10.88	4.91

Average Annualized Returns

	1 Yr.	3 Yrs.	5 Yrs.	10 Yrs.
Focus Group	9.53	17.90	4.98	14.93
Global LAMP Index	11.63	22.82	8.26	17.37
MSCI World Index	9.49	18.69	2.19	7.04
S&P 500 Index	4.91	14.38	0.54	9.07

Appendix 2: Global LAMP Index® Performance 1996–2000

Company	1996	1997	1998	1999	2000
1	51.39	40.84	3.95	25.15	(6.72)
2	23.07	11.96	8.11	124.77	(18.07)
3	(8.74)	67.65	41.70	196.78	(39.71)
4	(8.45)	(0.46)	93.19	129.76	6.45
5	38.02	60.43	15.59	63.48	1.97
6	0.73	25.80	29.80	(0.53)	42.44
7	57 37	63.47	(14.79)	31.74	14.86
8	42.66	16.47	20.34	23.25	(12.10)
9	6.23	34.90	52.17	1.43	26.56
10	19.53	6.30	(9.79)	90.30	(16.89)
11	10.53	28.97	(50.04)	151.03	(32.54)
12	44.78	23.71	46.80	46.70	(47.41)
13	20.47	37.22	46.16	(8.26)	(2.39)
14	16.64	54.68	47.72	(17.91)	3.54
15	42.90	20.83	8.26	62.06	6.17
16	5.45	77.77	108.49	70.51	(33.31)
17	38.14	36.04	35.27	(28.45)	2.89
18	21.00	25.41	10.26	67.45	(43.94)
19	66.83	39.41	77.17	17 43	(20.67)
20	51.43	25.59	52.98	0.25	36.92
21	131.00	7.48	68.95	39.02	(27.24)
22	18.11	34.14	28.81	12.49	14.00
23	(17.61)	(25.08)	15.90	405.56	(59.29)
24	65.02	21.20	68.37	8.23	11.35
25	(4.12)	69.86	39.73	7.78	108.14
26	44.44	25.34	(15.67)	9.59	34.62
27	(0.01)	(6.25)	10.00	60.11	(15.90)
28	22.41	54.51	42.50	(1.46)	66.21
29	90.48	93.71	(0.94)	(13.86)	25.65
30	27.94	0.59	(10.65)	40.76	25.49
31	30.30	(3.07)	(31.00)	25.84	0.43
32	72.47	(33.93)	4.80	23.37	13.58
33	58.09	46.04	225.05	211.21	(8.53)
34	(2.10)	42.84	43.62	(13.26)	26.25
35	(10.16)	(4.49)	(9.48)	27.93	(26.49)
36	37.02	54.75	(7.35)	(2.16)	37.72
37	31.60	49.99	15.67	21.23	(27.24)
38	14.17	53.24	13.46	101.08	8.22
39	35.22	5.29	54.69	67.27	1.37

Company	1996	1997	1998	1999	2000
40	25.10	30.48	(8.73)	29.82	2.39
41	14.85	(15.89)	(8.42)	113.96	(21.45)
42	(11.43)	157.84	33.22	45.28	(35.04)
43	36.30	34.07	46.25	(13.58)	82.47
44	15.84	(7.53)	(13.28)	101.04	(32.20)
45	(13.80)	29.02	10.51	97.68	5.04
46	32.79	(2.37)	(29.45)	39.45	15.91
47	9.83	23.59	21.32	(28.20)	11.97
48	32.80	67.27	(10.87)	40.74	24.12
49	(7.22)	81.62	36.15	(18.74)	18.52
50	69.29	34.45	50.70	76.42	(36.56)
51	59.52	73.80	61.79	36.09	(11.60)
52	36.90	0.05	(6.64)	83.94	(34.94)
53	25.18	42.30	90.81	126.11	(1.75)
54	(20.80)	68.16	8.19	(11.24)	23.39
55	18.37	44.29	32.49	(30.93)	16.83
56	41.97	11.78	51.28	20.94	22.24
57	19.65	77.82	123.51	54.26	(27.19)
58	26.10	27.03	(11.33)	10.89	(31.64)
59	35.36	58.08	87.47	0.34	42.79
60	32.09	15.37	9.18	7.58	11.39
Total	1,662.94	2,034.38	1,753.95	2,859.52	121.08
Avg. Annual	27.72	33.91	29.23	47.66	2.02
S&P 500	22.94	33.25	28.57	21.04	(9.10)
MSCI World	13.47	15.76	24.31	24.94	(13.19)

Global LAMP Index® Performance 2001–2005

Company	2001	2002	2003	2004	2005
1	(24.22)	4.42	51.05	17.74	2.67
2	7.45	(34.23)	69.45	(15.74)	(3.98)
3	5.01	(35.01)	72.21	(23.80)	4.91
4	(11.73)	(14.35)	27.82	3.82	11.93
5	(34.45)	(0.01)	37.23	17.86	(7.86)
6	22.77	(46.71)	11.07	15.31	10.68
7	7.24	(23.57)	52.15	29.27	(3.94)
8	0.14	(9.22)	25.17	21.70	13.20
9	6.48	(3.77)	15.81	4.33	1.05
10	4.64	5.82	30.31	14.44	9.62
11	41.68	(8.58)	26.69	43.10	67.52
12	17.93	12.41	44.31	7.52	16.78
13	29.83	4.51	24.86	46.21	5.27
14	(10.33)	(22.52)	27.82	4.83	9.77
15	(15.61)	(3.48)	48.82	12.21	(1.37)
16	12.02	(52.50)	48.67	21.50	4.35
17	(9.30)	11.52	32.25	15.93	14.00
18	(33.91)	(13.92)	33.93	(7.15)	38.05
19	42.91	(35.44)	20.09	7.40	(15.82)
20	(32.23)	(30.29)	45.31	33.96	19.14
21	5.54	(50.24)	106.49	(26.77)	8.08
22	13.84	(7.77)	(2.25)	25.09	(3.22)
23	(36.50)	(13.59)	18.16	16.01	(3.90)
24	(15.67)	6.91	8.87	(5.81)	(0.01)
25	(16.40)	(24.68)	16.19	1.05	1.04
26	(3.17)	(18.47)	41.47	37.03	10.15
27	(45.71)	(23.17)	46.35	16.14	21.93
28	(14.82)	(10.49)	7.19	2.81	16.65
29	(17.18)	(21.64)	32.61	14.54	2.93
30	0.01	6.40	40.06	(1.79)	(3.52)
31	2.37	9.07	42.67	29.97	35.14
32	1.63	(20.07)	55.16	35.55	(3.25)
33	(43.01)	(35.83)	11.61	(5.59)	19.59
34	(6.00)	2.01	18.91	7.34	15.67
35	35.15	(20.58)	37.53	88.61	30.53
36	(8.65)	(27.01)	43.49	33.75	8.99
37	2.67	10.49	18.17	12.15	6.95
38	(18.81)	(38.17)	66.80	(7.22)	19.28

Company	2001	2002	2003	2004	2005
39	(46.40)	(20.85)	23.64	12.13	1.32
40	(16.73)	(7.00)	23.42	13.55	12.53
41	11.90	5.07	43.00	9.47	56.14
42	4.83	(38.52)	113.80	6.79	2.49
43	(13.90)	6.98	62.71	88.06	3.75
44	8.09	(11.42)	33.56	15.72	(7.30)
45	(24.15)	(34.13)	92.14	7.52	2.94
46	(34.27)	(5.08)	55.55	44.47	24.82
47	(22.73)	14.19	25.61	19.83	25.29
48	29.56	(3.83)	61.01	42.10	78.93
49	(13.75)	(33.83)	3.89	7.80	3.72
50	(19.84)	(33.71)	69.70	29.10	(18.76)
51	27.97	(26.33)	28.66	36.23	6.59
52	(18.38)	5.18	31.28	20.49	29.07
53	(40.71)	(46.07)	96.34	(15.90)	30.71
54	(8.20)	(2.26)	42.85	26.25	17.07
55	(1.30)	17.97	1.20	8.59	5.29
56	(16.66)	(2.64)	54.71	10.25	9.90
57	(27.65)	(28.50)	39.79	10.82	(18.96)
58	3.94	1.52	90.82	33.25	22.73
59	(10.80)	(12.83)	25.18	5.96	15.90
60	14.20	0.01	63.36	31.03	14.93
Total	**(361.37)**	**(827.83)**	**2,436.72**	**1,006.81**	**698.10**
Avg. Annual	(6.02)	(13.80)	40.61	16.78	11.63
S&P 500	(11.88)	(22.09)	28.67	10.88	4.91
MSCI World	(16.80)	(19.88)	33.10	14.72	9.49

Appendix 3: Credit Ratings of Global LAMP Index® Companies

IN DESCENDING ORDER

Companies in the Global LAMP Index® were heavily concentrated in the Aa3–A1 range (as rated by Moody's) at year-end 2005. Nine LAMP companies were rated in the coveted, top-tier Aaa–Aa1 range. No LAMP companies carry junk bond ratings below Baa3. The five companies that were unrated by Moody's all have consistently positive free cash flow and hold more cash than debt on their balance sheets. Their rating equivalents are based on the cyclicality of their industries and nearest equivalent peer ratings.

	Year-end 2005 Rating	10-Year Range High	Low	Focus Group Company
1	Aaa	Aaa	Aaa	Johnson & Johnson
2	Aaa	Aaa	Aaa	
3	Aaa	Aaa	Aaa	
4	Aaa	Aaa	Aa1	Toyota
5	Aa1	Aaa	Aa1	3M
6	Aa1	Aaa	Aa1	Royal Dutch/Shell
7	Aa1	Aa1	Aa2	
8	Aa1	Aa1	Aa3	Canon
9	Aa1	Aa1	A1	
10	Aa2	Aaa	Aa2	Swiss Re
11	Aa2	Aaa	Aa2	
12	Aa2	Aa2	Aa3	HSBC
13	Aa2	Aa2	A1	
14	Aa3	Aaa	Aa3	
15	Aa3	Aa2	Aa3	
16	Aa3	Aa2	Aa3	
17	Aa3	Aa2	Aa3	
18	Aa3	Aa2	Aa3	
19	Aa3	Aa3	Aa3	
20	Aa3	Aa3	Aa3	
21	Aa3	Aa3	Aa3	
22	Aa3	Aa3	A1	
23	Aa3	Aa3	A1	
24	NR	Aa equivalent		
25	A1	Aaa	A1	
26	A1	A1	A1	Nokia
27	A1	A1	A1	Nucor
28	A1	A1	A1	
29	A1	A1	A1	

	Year-end 2005 Rating	10-Year Range High	Low	Focus Group Company
30	A1	A1	A2	
31	A1	A1	A3	
32	NR	A equivalent		
33	NR	A equivalent		
34	NR	A equivalent		
35	A2	A1	A2	Alcoa
36	A2	A1	A2	Intel
37	A2	A1	A2	
38	A2	A1	A2	
39	A2	A2	A2	Novo Nordisk
40	A2	A2	A2	
41	A2	A2	A2	
42	A2	A2	A2	
43	A2	A2	A3	
44	A2	A2	Baa1	
45	A3	Aa2	A3	Hewlett-Packard
46	A3	A2	A3	
47	A3	A3	Baa1	
48	A3	A3	Baa3	
49	Baa1	A1	Baa1	
50	Baa1	A3	Baa1	Southwest Airlines
51	Baa1	A3	Baa1	Baxter International
52	Baa1	A3	Baa1	
53	Baa1	Baa1	Baa2	
54	Baa1	Baa1	Baa2	
55	Baa1	Baa1	Baa2	
56	Baa2	A3	Baa2	
57	Baa2	Baa1	Baa2	Stora Enso
58	Baa2	Baa2	Baa2	
59	Baa2	Baa2	Baa2	
60	Baa3	Baa3	Ba3	

Appendix 4: Founding Dates of LAMP Companies

IN DESCENDING ORDER

The average and median ages of companies in the Global LAMP Index® exceed 100 years. This is more than double the age of the average exchange-listed company, which is in the range of 40 to 50 years. Focus Group companies mentioned in this book are noted.

	Date	*Focus Group Company*
1	1288	Stora Enso
2	1715	
3	1736	
4	1817	
5	1824	
6	1837	
7	1844	
8	1845	
9	1847	
10	1850	
11	1862	
12	1863	Swiss Re
13	1865	HSBC
14	1865	Nokia
15	1866	
16	1873	
17	1876	
18	1881	
19	1885	
20	1886	Johnson & Johnson
21	1887	
22	1888	Alcoa
23	1888	
24	1890	Royal Dutch/Shell
25	1891	
26	1900	
27	1901	
28	1901	
29	1901	
30	1902	3M
31	1905	
32	1906	
33	1907	

	Date	Focus Group Company
34	1911	
35	1918	
36	1919	
37	1921	Toyota
38	1923	
39	1924	Novo Nordisk
40	1924	
41	1925	
42	1927	
43	1929	
44	1930	
45	1931	Baxter International
46	1936	Hewlett-Packard
47	1937	Canon
48	1946	
49	1949	
50	1959	
51	1964	Nucor
52	1965	
53	1967	
54	1968	Intel
55	1971	Southwest Airlines
56	1971	
57	1971	
58	1972	
59	1978	
60	1980	

Looking back from 2005

Average Age:	114 years
Median Age:	104 years
Oldest:	718 years

Appendix 5: Stewardship Premiums in Mature, Cyclical Industries

The table compares the market capitalization-to-sales ratio of each LAMP company (noted in **bold**) to those of its two nearest and largest global peers. Because industry cycle and risk parameters differ between industries, minimal insight is gained by comparing numbers across industry lines. Valid comparisons can be made, however, by comparing numbers within an industry. In every case, LAMP companies enjoyed significant stewardship premiums.

Company	2005 Data in $US Millions		Market Cap/ Sales Ratio
	Sales	Market Cap	
Alcoa	**26,159**	**25,732**	**0.98**
Alcan[1] (Canada)	17,473	15,180	0.87
Nippon Light Metal[2] (Japan)	4,906	1,527	0.31
3M	**21,167**	**58,894**	**2.78**
Dow Chemical	46,307	42,292	0.91
Bayer (Germany)	32,408	30,450	0.94
Nucor	**12,701**	**10,383**	**0.82**
Mittal Steel[3] (India)	28,132	6,460	NMF
U.S. Steel	14,039	5,244	0.37
Southwest Airlines	**7,584**	**13,220**	**1.74**
American Airlines	20,712	4,218	0.20
Delta Airlines	16,191	149	0.09
Stora Enso (Sweden)	**15,607**	**12,160**	**0.78**
International Paper	24,097	16,505	0.68
Weyerhaeuser	22,629	16,136	0.71
Toyota (Japan)	**172,749**	**170,990**	**.99**
General Motors	192,604	10,982	0.06
Ford	178,101	14,398	0.08

1 In 2004, Alcan acquired Pechiney, then the world's third-largest aluminum company.

2 Data are for FY 2005 (March fiscal year).

3 In 2004, Mittal became the world's largest steel company via acquisition. The company's stock market capitalization does not fairly represent its value because most of its shares are owned by the Mittal family.

Appendix 6: Relative Industry/Sector Weightings

(DECEMBER 30, 2005)

The 60-company Global LAMP Index® has an industry/sector diversification roughly comparable to that of the MSCI World and Standard & Poor's 500 indices (its primary benchmarks). Compared to the Domini 400 Index, the LAMP is overweighted in mature, cyclical sectors (e.g., energy, materials, industrials, and consumer discretionary), and underweighted in more growth-oriented information technology. The present composition of LAMP was set in 2002, and has not changed since then. Prior to 2002 there were some minor changes in the Index's composition, designed primarily to bring its diversification into line with that of its primary benchmarks.

Industry/Sector 400	LAMP	S&P 500	MSCI-W	Domini
Energy	9.57	9.21	9.22	3.31
Materials	3.40	5.61	2.97	1.67
Industrial	10.01	10.54	11.24	6.72
Consumer Discretionary	11.31	11.77	11.45	14.77
Consumer Staples	10.31	8.21	9.50	11.94
Healthcare	13.86	10.27	13.22	13.75
Financial	19.09	25.00	21.05	21.67
Information Technology	16.71	11.21	14.96	20.14
Telecommunications Services	5.29	4.22	3.05	5.21
Utilities	0.45	3.97	3.34	0.82
Total	**100.00**	**100.00**	**100.00**	**100.00**

Appendix 7: Global LAMP Index® Performance vs. SRI/Sustainability Comparators

(IN $U.S.)

Year	Annual Investment Return (as %)			LAMP Excess (in % pts.)	
	LAMP 60	DJSI	Domini 400	DJSI	Domini 400
2005	11.83	9.12	3.00	2.72	8.83
2004	16.78	12.84	10.31	3.94	6.47
2003	40.61	36.41	28.47	4.20	12.14
2002	(13.80)	(21.26)	(20.10)	7.46	6.30
2001	(6.02)	(15.44)	(12.07)	9.42	6.05
2000	2.02	(17.50)	(14.32)	19.52	16.34
1999	47.66	29.70	24.49	17.96	23.17
1998	29.23		34.55		(5.32)
1997	33.91		38.26		(4.35)
1996	27.72		23.70		4.02
Cumulative	394.42	NMF	151.71		

Average Annualized Investment Returns

1 Year	11.63		3.00
3 Years	22.62		13.44
5 Years	8.26		0.51
10 Years	17.37	NMF	9.67

The equal-weighted Global LAMP Index® has returned more than the Dow Jones Sustainability Index (DJSI) every year since its introduction in 1999. It has returned more than the Domini 400 for 8 of the 10 years shown above. Unlike the DJSI and the Domini 400, which frequently add and delete companies to and from their indices, the LAMP has used the same 60 companies throughout this period.

LAMP returns are based on an equal-weighted back-cast with dividends not reinvested. Unlike the benchmark indices, which regularly drop laggard companies and add faster growers, there were no changes in the Global LAMP Index® for the indicated period.

Notes

Introduction

1   Frederick F. Reichheld, *The Loyalty Effect* (Boston: Harvard Business School Press, 1996), 5.

2   Ibid., 28.

3   Edward O. Wilson, *The Future of Life* (New York: Alfred A. Knopf, 2002), 42. Biologist Edward O. Wilson puts our economic dilemma bluntly: "The wealth of the world, if measured by domestic product and per-capita income, is rising. But if calculated from the condition of the biosphere, it is falling." The book goes on to explain why this is so and to make a case for better stewardship.

4   In 1972 I co-authored, with John T. Marlin, an article titled "Is Pollution Profitable?" in *Risk Management* 19 (4) (April 1972): 9–18. According to professors Joshua D. Margolis and James P. Walsh, this was "the first empirical study" linking stewardship behaviors to the bottom line. See J. Margolis and J. Walsh, *People and Profits?* (Mahwah, NJ: Lawrence Erlbaum Associates, 2001), 1.

5   Edward O. Wilson, *Biophilia* (Cambridge: Harvard University Press, 1984).

6   The term "management by means," or MBM, was introduced by H. Thomas Johnson and Anders Broms in their classic, *Profit Beyond Measure,* (New York: The Free

Press, 2000). I have adopted the term because it neatly frames my theories of system and Living Asset Stewardship.

7   I formally began the process of assembling the Global LAMP Index in 1997; the final, 60-company composition of the index was set in 2002.

8   Arie de Geus, *The Living Company* (Boston: Harvard Business School Press, 1997). The author, former director of Global Planning at Royal Dutch/Shell, convincingly argues for the proposition that corporations are living communities rather than profit-making machines.

9   Many LAMP companies metaphorically describe themselves and/or their markets as "ecosystems." Toyota's widely imitated production system is explicitly based on cybernetic principles found in Nature.

10   Industrial ecology looks to create companies that mimic Nature by aiming for "closed loop" manufacturing processes in which the wastes of one become the food for another. The *Journal of Industrial Ecology,* published by MIT Press, is an excellent resource on this subject (www.mitpress.mit.edu/JIE).

11   Reichheld, *The Loyalty Effect*, 15.

12   Robert K. Greenleaf, "The Servant as Leader," essay first published in 1979 by the Paulist Press (repr., Indianapolis, IN: The Robert K. Greenleaf Center, 1991), 30.

13   The financial stability of LAMP companies, reflected in their low debt ratios, is their first line of defense against layoffs. To protect employees' jobs, some firms, such as Nucor, will ask everyone to take a percentage pay cut, with executives taking the deepest cuts. At others, such as Toyota, employees are reassigned to new work. If layoffs cannot be avoided, LAMP companies generally give generous severance packages as well as job training and help in finding new work.

14   The Council of Institutional Investors uses shareholder proposals to effect change in corporate governance. In 2005 more than 80 majority-voting shareowner proposals were submitted for inclusion in company proxy materials. Supporting votes on these proposals averaged approximately 45 percent—a large increase from the 2004 average of 12 percent. Most institutional shareholder initiatives never get to the proxy stage because they are settled by negotiation. The trend of institutional shareholder activism is rising as investors see the benefits to shareholder return.

Chapter 1

1   Peter Senge, Art Kleiner, Charlotte Roberts, Richard Ross, George Roth, and Bryan Smith, *The Dance of Change: The Challenges to Sustaining Momentum in Learning Organizations* (New York: Currency Doubleday, 1999), 570.

2   Johnson and Broms, *Profit Beyond Measure* (see Introduction, n. 6). The authors offer an eloquent description of management by means, and demonstrate its effectiveness

through case studies of Toyota and Scania.

3   John Dalla Costa, management consultant and author of *The Ethical Imperative* (Toronto: HarperBusiness, 1998), introduced me to the term "relational equity." I believe one of the key advantages stewardship companies have over their traditional peers is the strength of such equity. They understand that living assets—people and Nature—are inextricably connected.

4   "Respect for All Life," Novo Nordisk Sustainability Report 2002, 34 (www.novonordisk.com).

5   "We are," Wilson says, "a biological species (who) find little ultimate meaning apart from the remainder of life." See Wilson, *Biophilia*, 81 (see Introduction, n. 5).

6   Edward O. Wilson, "Biophilia and the Conservation Ethic," in *The Biophilia Hypothesis*, Stephen R. Kellert and Edward O. Wilson, eds., 31–40 (Washington, D.C.: Island Press, 1993).

7   Ransom A. Myers and Boris Worm, "Net Loss: Industrialized Fishing Hits Fish Stocks," *Nature* (May 15, 2003): 280–283. According to this 10-year study, commercial fishing has wiped out 90 percent of the world's population of large predatory fish (tuna, blue marlin, swordfish and others). The study analyzed data from more than five decades of fishing in 13 sea regions that are home to large-scale industrial fishing operations. It supports earlier U.N. analyses that maintained that three-quarters of the world's fisheries had been fished to (and beyond) their sustainable limits. In addition to the damage to ocean ecology is the threat to the seafood industry and populations that depend on fish for their sustenance. In the U.S. alone this industry generates approximately $30 billion in revenue and employs 250,000 people.

8   The "Guiding Principles" at Toyota are a sweeping statement of its corporate ethics and objectives. For more, see (http://www.toyota.co.jp/en/vision/sustainability/index.html).

9   Michael Treacy and Fred Wiersema, *The Discipline of Market Leaders* (Reading, MA: Perseus Books, 1995), 188. The authors tell how this kaizen system produced "20 million ideas in 40 years, or several dozen per person annually."

10   Fujio Cho, Introduction to Toyota's 1999 Environmental Report (http://www.toyota. co.jp/en/environmental_rep/99/index.html).

11   Johnson and Broms, *Profit Beyond Measure,* 149 (see Introduction, n. 6).

12   Ibid., 150.

13   Clay Chandler, "Full Speed Ahead," *Fortune Magazine,* February 7, 2005, 1 (http:// money.cnn.com/magazines/fortune/fortune_archive/2005/02/07/8250430/index.htm).

14   de Geus, *The Living Company,* 25 (see Introduction, n. 6).

15   Bjorn Hagglund, "An Industrial Perspective on Sustainable Development," (speech to the Conference on Sustainable Development—Forum for Partnership, Malmo, Sweden, June 27, 2001).

16   Wilson, "Biophilia and the Conservation Ethic," in *The Biophilia Hypothesis,* 39.

Wilson's vision of an "expanding and unending future" is referenced several times in this volume; it is noted only here.

17   Danah Zohar, *Rewiring the Corporate Brain* (San Francisco: Berrett-Koehler, 1997).

Chapter 2

1   Letter from Debra Dunn, SVP Corporate Affairs and Global Citizenship. in HP Global Citizenship Report 2005.

2   David Packard, "A Management Code of Ethics" (speech to the American Management Association, San Francisco, CA, January 24, 1958). Quoted in Collins and Porras, *Built to Last*, 56 (see n. 7).

3   Greg Merten, "Leadership as a Commitment to Personal Development" (keynote address to the Society for Organizational Learning, Cambridge, MA, June 26, 2002)

4   David Packard, untitled remarks to an HP training group, March 8, 1960. Hewlett-Packard archives.

5   Craig R. Barrett, CEO, Intel, in the introductory letter to the Intel 1999 Environment, Health and Safety (EHS) Report, Santa Clara, CA.

6   Jennifer Hughes, "Top Tier Rating Is Losing Its Appeal," *The Financial Times*, March 9, 2005.

7   James C. Collins and Jerry I. Porras, *Built to Last* (New York: HarperCollins, 1994).

8   Ibid., 73.

9   Ryuzaburo Kaku, "Kyosei: The Guide for a New World Order in Business," *Global Virtue Ethics Review*, 1 (2): 131–148.

10   Richard Pasquale, "Grassroots Leadership—Royal Dutch/Shell: Interview with Steve Miller," *Fast Company*, April 1998): 110.

11   Robert S. Kaplan and David P. Norton, "Putting the Balanced Scorecard to Work," *Harvard Business Review* (Sept.–Oct. 1993): 134–147.

12   For background, see James L. Heskett, W. Earl Sasser, Jr., and Leonard A. Schlesinger. *The Service-Profit Chain: How Leading Companies Link Profit and Growth to Loyalty, Satisfaction, and Value* (New York: The Free Press, 1997).

13   See Humberto R. Maturana and Francisco J. Varela, *The Tree of Knowledge: The Biological Roots of Human Understanding*, rev. ed. (Boston: Shambhala Publications, 1987). The individual parts of living systems exist by means of one another because, working together, they can maintain and reproduce the system. Biologist Humberto Maturana calls this process "autopoeisis"—literally "self-making." He regards the circular organization of the nervous system as the basic organization of all living systems. He describes living systems as networks in which the function of each component is to help produce and transform other components while maintaining the overall circularity of the network. The human body exists by means of its reproductive, immune, and other systems that endow it with the capac-

ity to make and remake itself. Through their myriad food chains, forest and ocean systems, too, have a similar capacity.

Chapter 3

1   Wilson, "Biophilia and the Conservation Ethic," in *The Biophilia Hypothesis*, 39 (see Ch. 1, n. 5).

2   Erik Portanger, "No Fads Please: As Banks Regroup, HSBC Shows Why Boring Isn't Bad," *The Wall Street Journal*, page-one feature, October 28, 2002. Portanger does not include stock options in Sanford Weil's total compensation. This would have further widened the gap between the take of the Citigroup chairman and that of Sir John Bond, chairman of HSBC. The effect of stock options brought Weil's 1999 compensation to $167 million.

3   Stephen Green, *Serving God? Serving Mammon? Christians and the Financial Market* (London: Marshall Pickering, 1996).

4   Hagerty, James R., and Michael R. Sesit, "Deals & Deal Makers: New HSBC Chief Will Minister U.S.-Loan Foray," *Wall Street Journal*, March 3, 2003.

5   Kevin Hamlin, "The Greening of HSBC," *Institutional Investor*, international edition, April 22, 2003, 9.

6   "HSBC Treads Softly," *The Economist*, Finance and Economics section, April 8, 2000.

7   Stephen J. Saali, President, Republic National Bank, in a press release announcing RNB's acquisition by HSBC (October, 2000).

8   Sir John Bond, "Managing in a Complex World," (speech at University of Sheffield, UK, October 24, 2002).

9   See Reichheld, *The Loyalty Effect*, Ch. 8, for a general discussion of the net present value (NPV) approach to relational equity (see Introduction, n.1).

10   For detailed information, see J. A. Armour, "The Role of Peripheral Autonomic Neurons in Cardiac Regulation," in *Neurocardiology*, ed. J. A. Armour and J. L. Ardell, 219–244 (New York: Oxford University Press, 1994).

11   The website of the American Institute of Stress provides a continuing stream of data, drawn from a wide variety of global sources, on stress-related costs to corporations (www.stress.org).

12   Doc Childre and Howard Martin, *The HeartMath Solution* (San Francisco: HarperCollins, 1999), 59.

13   William A. Tiller, Rollin McCraty, and Mike Atkinson, "Cardiac Coherence: A New, Noninvasive Measure of Autonomic Nervous System Order," *Alternative Therapies* in Health and Medicine 2 (1) (1996): 52–65.

14   Doc Childre and Bruce Cryer, *From Chaos to Coherence: The Power to Change Performance* (Boulder Creek, CA: Planetary, 2000), 38.

15   Joseph LeDoux, a neuroscientist at New York University, was the first to map the

neural connections between the heart and the amygdala, and to show us why our emotional thinking precedes and guides our rational thinking. Although LeDoux's work applies mainly to situations in which a person or animal must respond quickly to a threat, it extends to situations wherein the threat—for example, toxic waste, a dismissive superior, a dangerous product, or a corrosive bottom-line fixation—may be more dissonant and stressful than immediately life threatening. For further background, see Joseph LeDoux, *The Emotional Brain: The Mysterious Underpinnings of Emotional Life* (New York: Simon & Schuster, 1996).

16   Daniel Goleman, *Emotional Intelligence* (New York: Bantam Books, 1995), 28. Goleman clearly explains the evolution and science of heart (emotional) intelligence in lay language, with detailed citations of medical research for those who wish to go deeper into the subject.

17   Ibid., 3–4.

18   Daniel Goleman, "What Makes a Leader?" *Harvard Business Review* (Nov.–Dec., 1998), 93.

19   Adam Ritt, Executive Editor, "Steelmaker of the Year," *New Steel* (Aug. 1998): This lengthy feature article offers excellent insight into Nucor's culture. "About ten percent of the employees at new Nucor mills come from the company's existing plants; the remaining 90 percent are local residents. The biggest lesson the ten percent teach the 90 is to trust one another. "When management says something, or another employee says something, it's trust with a capital T," Correnti says. "[The workers will] never scratch their heads and say, 'That's what Correnti told us, but what does he mean?' The ten percent also teach the new workers about how their hard work will translate into big paychecks because of the bonus plan. It's more convincing when you're slugging it out in the furnace, soaking with sweat, and the guy [next to you] says: 'I've been here with Nucor for 15 years, and what Correnti is telling you is right. I've seen it in my paycheck.' It's getting the individual's self-interest aligned with the company's self-interest," Correnti continues. "It doesn't happen the first six months or the first year, but after two years, they're Nucorized."

20   Danah Zohar, *The Quantum Self* (New York: Quill/William Morrow, 1990), 155.

21   Ibid., 236.

22   Ibid., 237.

23   Warren Bennis, in the Introduction to Ken Iverson, *Plain Talk* (New York: John Wiley & Sons, 1998), vii–viii.

24   Iverson, *Plain Talk,* 175 (see n. 23).

25   The Nokia Way is a statement of corporate philosophy that appears on Nokia's website (www.nokia.com/A402902).

26   Zohar, *Rewiring the Corporate Brain,* 19 (see Ch. 1, n. 17).

27   Zohar, *The Quantum Self,* 235 (see n. 20).

28   Wilson, *The Future of Life,* 155 (see Introduction, n. 3) Wilson agrees with Zohar's view of physics: "The central idea of the consilience world view is that all tangible phenom-

ena, from the birth of the stars, to the workings of social institutions, are based on material processes that are ultimately reducible, however long and tortuous the sequences, to the laws of physics." Source: *Consilience: The Unity of Knowledge* (New York: Alfred A. Knopf, 1998) 266.

29　Wilson, "Biophilia and the Conservation Ethic," 32 (see Ch. 1, n. 6).

30　Ibid., 39.

31　Edward O. Wilson, *Consilience: The Unity of Knowledge* (New York: Alfred A. Knopf, 1998), 297–298.

Chapter 4

1　Reichheld, *The Loyalty Effect*, 2 (see Introduction, n. 1).

2　Wilson, *Biophilia*, 140 (see Introduction, n. 5).

3　Customer net present value (NPV) is the discounted value of expected future sales and profits. As a rule, the longer customers do business with a company, the greater their worth to that company — in terms of both their own purchases and their referral of others. In *The Loyalty Effect*, 50–57 (see Introduction, n. 1), Reichheld illustrates the NPV of high customer retention rates. In one example, he shows that a 5-percentage-point increase in customer retention rate, from 90 percent to 95 percent, raises customer NPV by 75 percent.

4　Economic value-added (EVA) is net operating profit after taxes (NOPAT) minus a charge for the opportunity cost of capital. In other words, EVA = NOPAT − (capital x cost of capital). It tells us the amount by which earnings exceed or fall short of the minimum rate of return that shareholders and lenders could get by investing in other securities of comparable risk. That is considered by many analysts to be true economic profit (or loss).

5　Wilson, *Biophilia*, 140 (see Introduction, n. 5).

6　Larry D. Soderquist et al., *Corporations and Other Business Organizations*, 4th ed. (Charlottesville, VA: Michie Law Publishers, 1997), 17–18. Corporations evolved from unlimited-liability to limited-liability status in the late nineteenth century mainly through enactment of state laws. In 1875 New Jersey passed the first relatively nonrestrictive (or enabling) corporation statute. During the next two decades the New Jersey legislature amended its statute to carry the enabling philosophy further, the process culminating in the adoption of a revised and full-blown enabling statute in 1896. As these statutory developments progressed, the New Jersey corporation became the vehicle of choice for large businesses.

7　According to Swiss Re, the world's largest insurer of catastrophic risk, weather-related calamities have sharply increased since the late 1980s (see the Swiss Re 1999 annual report). The cost of damage done to the American Gulf Coast during the summer of 2005 by just one hurricane (Katrina) was more than $200 billion. The costs to companies arising from this event go far beyond the visible damages done. They include the expenses of hurricane insurance coverage, which roughly doubled following Katrina, of employee and public dissatisfaction with their climate-changing activities, and of tighter government regulation.

8   Lester R. Brown, chairman of World Watch Institute, supports this view: "I believe that there are now some clear signs that the world does seem to be approaching a kind of paradigm shift in environmental consciousness . . . a growing number of high profile CEOs have begun to sound more like spokespersons for Greenpeace than for the bastions of global capitalism of which they are a part." See his article, "Threshold—Early Signs of an Environmental Awakening," *World Watch* Magazine (March–April 1999).

9   The synergies of the Kalundborg eco-industrial park have been concisely summarized by John Ehrenfeld and Nicholas Gertler, "Industrial Ecology in Practice: The Evolution of Interdependence at Kalundborg," *Journal of Industrial Ecology 1* (Winter 1997): 67–79. See also Ch. 8 in this volume.

10   Peter M. Senge, *The Fifth Discipline* (New York: Currency Doubleday, 1990).

11   For additional background, see Paul Hawken, A. B. Lovins, and L. H. Lovins. *Natural Capitalism* (Boston: Little, Brown and Company, 1999).

Chapter 5

1   Alain Belda, Introduction to Alcoa's 2001 End-of-Year Report: Environment, Health and Safety (EHS) (http://www.alcoa.com/global/en/environment/pdf/EHS_Report_final_2001. pdf).

2   Peter M. Senge, *The Fifth Discipline* (New York: Currency Doubleday, 1990).

3   By 1996 there were, in every developed country, firms specializing in corporate social responsibility (CSR) research, plus a growing number of mutual funds that specialized in socially responsible investing (SRI). Some of these, like the Council on Economic Priorities (CEP), were already more than two decades old. By 1990, KLD Research & Analytics had launched the Domini 400 Social Index (DS 400), a capitalization-weighted index of U.S. stocks that was to track, and usually outperform, the Standard & Poor's 500 Index. In 1996, the amount of money managed with SRI guidelines was in the range of 8–12 percent of the global total, depending on how those guidelines were defined.

4   The same 60 companies were used for the entire test. In a few cases, such as that of Stora Enso, a company we know today by one name existed under another (Stora) or was spun off by another publicly traded firm with good stewardship credentials.

5   My primary source of information about companies that pioneered the field of systems thinking was the Society for Organizational Learning (SoL), of which I am a member. Through SoL's research, consulting, and corporate members, I gained a wealth of information (www.solonline.org).

6   Joseph H. Bragdon, "The Value of Living Assets," in *The Investment Research Guide to Socially Responsible Investing,* ed. Brian Bruce, 153–176 (Dallas, TX: Investment Research Forums, Inc., 1998).

7   Differences in index sector weightings are fairly common, as one can see by comparing the LAMP's two benchmarks, the S&P 500 and the MSCI World, in Appendix 6.

8   All 60 companies in the Global LAMP Index® have corporate values and codes of conduct that support human rights. More than 60 percent have also signed international conventions on human rights such as the United Nations Global Compact, the UN Universal Declaration of Human Rights, or the Global Sullivan Principles.

9   Bjorn Hagglund (deputy CEO, Stora Enso), "Taking the Longer-Term View," in Stora Enso Sustainability Report 2003 (www.storaenso.com).

10   John R. Coomber (CEO), and Bruno Porrer (Chief Risk Officer), Swiss Re, "Executive Statement," in Swiss Re Sustainability Report 2003 (www.swissre.com).

Chapter 6

1   Wilson, *Consilience*, 292 (see Ch. 3, n. 31).

2   The free market is inefficient at pricing, in the near term, "external" costs such as environmental degradation, public health hazards, community upheaval, and family stress that affect its health in the long term.

3   Wilson, *The Future of Life*, 23 (see Introduction, n. 3).

4   Ibid., 31. Data are based on projections by the U.N. Department of Economic and Social Affairs. For world population to double by 2050, the birth rate must slow. If it does not, but continues at its present rate, world population would be 14.4 billion by 2050.

5   See www.heartquotes.net/Einstein.html.

6   Peter M. Senge, "Rethinking Leadership in the Learning Organization," *The Systems Thinker* 7 (1) (February 1996).

7   From the website announcement of a brochure: Peter Zimmerli, *Natural Catastrophes and Reinsurance*, May 8, 2003 (www.swissre.com).

8   Werner Schaad, "Terrorism – Dealing With The New Spectre," Swiss Reinsurance Company brochure, 2002.

9   The Novo Nordisk Corporate Vision Statement is available on the Novo Nordisk website (http://www.novonordisk.com/about_us/about_novo_nordisk/our_vision.asp).

10   In the mid-1990s Royal Dutch/Shell undertook a radical transformation of its culture, based on two priorities: to create a more flexible, cost-effective (i.e., decentralized and localized) organization, and to maintain a business focus on the triple bottom line of financial, social, and environmental results. In 1998, following several years of internal dialogue across the entire organization, Shell published its now-famous report: "Profits and Principles: Does There Have to be a Choice?" The report covered major dilemmas facing the Shell Group, such as global warming, renewable resources, and human rights. It concluded that Shell would become healthier, more effective, more motivated, and more aligned if it became deeply committed to sustainable development. To monitor its progress in meeting its

sustainability objectives, and to facilitate public dialogue on key issues, Shell publishes its goals and performance data on a website called the "Shell Report" (www.shell.com/shellreport).

11   Excerpted from Baxter's "Shared Values," available in its Sustainability Report and in other company documents dealing with Baxter's corporate culture, and on the company website (www.baxter.com).

12   The Global Reporting Initiative (GRI) was established in 1997 to develop guidelines for reporting on corporate economic, environmental, and social performance. It was convened by the Coalition for Environmentally Responsible Economies (CERES) in partnership with the United Nations Environment Programme (UNEP) and includes the active participation of corporations and accounting firms. More than half the companies in the Global LAMP Index® use GRI reporting guidelines, compared with fewer than 1 percent of publicly traded companies worldwide.

13   The data for this table were compiled from Shell's corporate website and form a composite representation (www.shell.com).

14   Xerox continually disregarded new technologies discovered at its Palo Alto Research Center (PARC), including what was to become Apple computer's operating system. In 2002 PARC was sold to Hewlett-Packard to save Xerox from bankruptcy.

15   See Canon Science Lab, "What is Light?" (www.canon.com/technology/s_labo/light/003/05.html).

16   Wilson, *The Future of Life*, 23 (see Introduction, n. 3).

Chapter 7

1   Greenleaf, "The Servant as Leader," 30 (see Introduction, n. 12).

2   Networks are how living systems are structured. Cybernetics refers to their functioning, which might be described as spontaneous, adaptive, self-organizing, symbiotic, localized, and feedback-driven.

3   Abraham Lincoln, *Speeches and Writings*, ed. Don E. Fehrenbacher (Washington, DC: Library of Congress, 1989), 1: 717–718.

4   Alcoa's "Guide to Business Conduct" was introduced on May 11, 1999 by Alain Belda in his first major act as president and CEO. It is a clearly written statement of Alcoa's values and workplace standards that must be read and understood by all employees. In his letter introducing the guide, Belda states: "Our values are universal . . . . The test is not the legal requirement. It is beyond that; it is about what is right." (www.alcoa.com).

5   The Equator Principles, introduced in September 2003 by major international banks, are a set of voluntary guidelines that establish a common framework for addressing social and environmental issues that arise in financing projects in the developing world. See (www.equator-principles.com).

6   Baxter expects suppliers to abide by the same ethical standards that it employs. The EthicsKit, introduced in September 2003, is a web-based "ethics toolkit" to guide suppliers through the design, implementation, and maintenance of their own business ethics programs. Baxter developed the EthicsKit in collaboration with Northwestern University's Center for Learning and Organizational Change.

7   Intel's Global Citizenship Report 2002 ("Diversity and Opportunity") is referenced to other external human rights and labor performance standards, including the U.N. Global Compact and the Organisation for Economic Co-operation and Development (OEDC) Guidelines for Multinational Enterprises. The text of the report can be accessed at Intel's website (www.intel.com).

8   In 1997, Alain Belda, then president of Alcoa, introduced the *Life!* program "to analyze, predict and prevent" workplace and environmental health hazards. This grew out of a partnership with Yale's School of Occupational and Environmental Medicine. Program data systems share information on EHS best practices with all business units. *Life!* has become an integral part of the Alcoa Business System (ABS), which Belda calls "the backbone of our enterprise."

9   On October 21, 2002 Alcoa was one of 17 companies to be named "America's Safest" by Occupational Hazards (www.occupationalhazards.com). The cited statement by William J. O'Rourke was contained in a press release associated with the award.

10   Greenleaf, "Servant as Leader," 30 (see Introduction, n. 12).

11   Iverson, *Plain Talk,* 28 (see Ch. 3, n. 23).

12   Greenleaf, "The Servant as Leader," 32 (see Introduction, n. 12).

13   Further background on Intel's work/life practices is available (http://www.intel.com/ jobs/workplace/worklife/).

14   Brett Clanton, "Big Three Plan Skimpy Bonuses," *The Detroit News,* January 16, 2004.

15   For more detailed information on Hewlett-Packard's WBIRL project, see: Juanita Brown, David Isaacs, and Nancy Margulies, "Asking Big Questions," in *The Dance of Change: The Challenges to Sustaining Momentum in Learning Organizations,* 506- 509 (see Ch. 1, n. 1).

16   For more information, see the website of Appreciative Inquiry Commons (http://appreciativeinquiry.cwru.edu).

17   Charles Handy, Beyond Certainty (Boston: Harvard Business School Press, 1998), 42–43.

18   Bond, "Managing in a Complex World," (see Ch. 3, n. 8).

19   David Pringle, "Nokia Eschews Factories in Most Low-Cost Regions," *The Wall Street Journal,* January 3, 2003.

20   Johnson and Broms, *Profit Beyond Measure,* 170 (see Introduction, n. 6).

21   David B. Montgomery and Catherine A. Ramus, "Corporate Social Responsibility Reputation Effects on MBA Job Choice," May 2003 Stanford GSB Working Paper No. 1805.

Available at Social Science Research Network (http://ssrn.com/abstract=412124). In addition to the traditional lures of money and advancement, the survey covered aspects of Living Asset Stewardship such as caring about employees, environmental sustainability, community/stakeholder relations, and ethical products and services.

22   Handy, *Beyond Certainty,* 52–53 (see n. 17).

Chapter 8

1   Lars Rebien Sorensen, CEO, Novo Nordisk, in the Introduction to Novo Nordisk's 2002 Annual Environmental Report (www.novonordisk.com).

2   Estimates of the total resources that end up as final product are generally in the range of five or six percent. The six percent number used here is based on a study by R. U. Ayres, *Technology and Environment* (Washington, DC: National Academy of Sciences, 1989). The most startling estimate I have seen holds that "only one percent of the total North American materials flow ends up in, and is still being used within, products six months after their sale." See Hawken, Lovins, and Lovins, *Natural Capitalism,* 81 (see Ch. 4, n. 11).

3   Novo Nordisk has won numerous awards for its annual reports on environment and sustainability. Its 2003 sustainability Report won the European Sustainability Reporting Award for the sixth time since the award was initiated in 1996. The awards are given by the national associations of state-chartered accountants of 15 countries in Europe.

4   Marc J. Epstein and Bill Birchard, *Counting What Counts—Turning Corporate Accountability to Competitive Advantage* (Cambridge, MA: Perseus, 1999), 138.

5   Henrik Gurtler, Chairman, Novo Nordisk's Committee on Environment and Bioethics, from the Novo Nordisk Environment and Bioethics Report 1997.

6   The data presented were extracted from Hawken, Lovins and Lovins, *Natural Capitalism,* 51–53 (see Ch. 4, n. 11). In the 10 years since their data were collected, annual waste flows have grown considerably.

7   Wilson, *The Future of Life,* 23 (see Introduction, n. 3).

8   The term "Factor Ten" emerged from a conference of 16 scientists, economists, government officials, and businesspeople convened in the Fall of 1994 by Friederich Schmidt-Bleek of the Wuppertal Institute for Climate, Environment and Energy in Germany. For further background, see: Schmidt-Bleek, F. et al., "Statement to Government and Business Leaders," Wuppertal Institute, Wuppertal, Germany, 1997.

9   Wilson, *The Future of Life,* xxii (see Introduction, n. 3).

10   The 3P Program is based on the premise that environmental gains and financial savings can be achieved by eliminating pollution at the source before cleanup problems occur. This approach provided a foundation for the U.S. Pollution Prevention Act of 1990 and has fundamentally influenced legislation, regulation, and industrial practice around the world.

11   Canon Environmental Charter (original 1993; revised 2004). The charter is widely

published in Canon's print and website reporting (www.canon.com/environment/charter/charter.html).

12   Joseph J. Romm, *Lean and Clean Management: How to Increase Profits and Productivity by Reducing Pollution* (New York: Kodansha America, 1994), 53. Joseph Romm notes the prodigious scale of ideas generated by Canon's employees: "In 1985, employees submitted almost 900,000 improvement suggestions, roughly the total number of suggestions submitted by all U.S. employees to their companies. Canon received 78 suggestions per employee. One employee submitted 2,600. Canon paid out $2.2 million in prizes, but saved over $200 million as a result of the suggestions."

13   Bob Johnstone, "Canon, Lone Wolf," *Wired* magazine 2.10 (October 1994). In this 8-page feature article, Johnstone notes, "Measured by number of US patents awarded, Canon can claim to be the world's most consistently creative company . . . . Year after year, Canon has averaged more than one US patent per million dollars of R&D investment. No other company comes close to this standard of efficiency."

14   Canon's Concept on Environment, Quality, Cost, and Delivery (EQCD) is ubiquitous in company reporting (www.canon.com/ir/annual/2004/p18.html).

15   Harris Surveys conducted a "National Corporate Reputation Poll" for *The Wall Street Journal* for four years (1999–2002). In each year Johnson & Johnson was top rated.

16   "Designing for the Environment," *Healthy People, Healthy Planet Explorer* 2 (2) (Aug. 2002): 3. This is a Johnson & Johnson in-house publication (http://www.jnj.com/search/search_results.htm?criteria=design+for+environment&Find.x=0&Find.y=0&Find=Search).

17   Jeffrey T. Resnik, "A Matter of Reputation," *Pharmaceutical Executive* (June 1, 2002) (www.pharmexec.com).

18   Renee St. Denis and Holly Higgins, "HP's Innovative PRS Team Invents a Computer Recycling Solution," *Global Citizen* (March 6, 2003). *Global Citizen* is published by Hewlett-Packard to emphasize to employees its commitment to good stewardship.

19   Stora Enso Sustainability Report 2003, 30 (www.storaenso.com).

20   In January 2006, Stora Enso was named to the Global 100, a list of the 100 most sustainably operated companies in the world, for its skill in managing environmental, social, and governance risks and opportunities. The Global 100 list is maintained by Innovest (www.innovestgroup.com).

21   "Baxter Testifies Before Congress About Business Benefits of Climate Change Initiatives," from a Baxter news release, June 8, 2005.

22   "What Baxter is Doing About Global Warming," from the Baxter Sustainable Story Archive, July 2004 (http://www.baxter.com/about_baxter/sustainability/sust_stories/environment/env_chicago_climate_exchange.html).

23   In 2004 Baxter introduced Advate, a next-generation blood-clotting drug for hemophiliacs and a potential blockbuster. In 2002 and 2003 it introduced the Accura

Hemofiltration System, a new instrument for continuous renal replacement therapy (CRRT) and plasma therapies, and ARENA, a promising hemodialysis device. From its recent low in 2002, Baxter's shareholder equity grew by 42 percent to $4.2 billion at year-end 2005. These are signs of vitality.

Chapter 9

1   Frederick F. Reichheld, *Loyalty Rules! How Today's Leaders Build Lasting Relationships,* (Boston: Harvard Business School Press 2001), 9.

2   Guido M. J. de Koning, "Picture This: Your Customer," *Gallup Management Journal* (March 15, 2001), (http://gmj.gallup.com/content/default.asp?ci=802).

3   Ibid.

4   Ibid.

5   Treacy and Wiersema, *The Discipline of Market Leaders,* 131 (see Ch. 1, n. 9).

6   Baxter was an early transparency leader in its sustainability reporting. It was rated second best in a 1997 global survey of corporate annual environmental reports conducted by SustainAbility and the United Nations Environmental Programme (UNEP). The Global Reporting Initiative (GRI) today considers Baxter an exemplar for the quality of its annual sustainability report and its commitment to the triple bottom line. Baxter has been on the Global 100 list of the "Most Sustainable Corporations in the World" since that list was first published in January 2005 (see www.global100.org).

7   See RoperASW, "Green Gauge Report 2002" (November 2002). The Roper survey found that "consumers for the most part are willing to pay more for products that conserve energy or are less polluting." This would explain the success of appliances carrying the "Energy Star" label of the U.S. Environmental Protection Agency. Also significant is the annual rate of increase in sales of organic foods since the start of the millennium—approximately 20 percent, or five times the rate for conventional food sales (www.windustry.com/conferences/november2002/ nov2002_proceedings/Plenary/leinberger.htm).

8   The European Common Market adopted in 1992 a green flower "ecolabel" that indicates that a product has been judged to be the best in its class against a wide range of environmental criteria, including energy efficiency. At year-end 2003 it applied to 19 different product groups. Japan's Eco Mark was introduced in 1996 and now covers a broad spectrum of products. As a rule, these ecolabels go far beyond the prominent U.S. Energy Star label, which looks only to energy efficiency. For further background, interested readers should consult the Global Ecolabelling Network (www.gen.gr.jp).

9   Southwest Annual Report, 1999, p.4

10   Southwest has regularly been on *Fortune* Magazine's list of "The 100 Best Companies to Work for in America." Employee benefits—medical, dental, life, and disability insurance—are offered through a conventional "Regular Plan" or a pre-tax "BenefitsPlus"

plan. An employee assistance plan provides confidential, professional counseling to employees and family members in distress. The new president of Southwest, Colleen Barrett, is renowned for her personal touch with employees: sending cards and sometimes presents to those on medical leave, and notes of congratulations upon graduations, for example.

11   This part of Southwest's mission statement is found frequently on Southwest's website and in company reports (www.southwest.com/about_swa/mission.html).

12   The survey, called the Customer Service Index, was conducted between August and September, 2002 by Market Facts of Canada, now known as Synovate (www.synovate.com).

13   Johnson and Broms, *Profit Beyond Measure*, 30 (see Introduction, n. 6).

14   Veli Sundback, Senior Vice President, Corporate Relations and Responsibility, in "Letter to Stakeholders," Nokia Corporate Responsibility Report 2004, 6 (www.nokia.com/NOKIA_COM_1/About_Nokia/crr2004en.pdf).

15   The 1995 Insurance Industry Initiative, under the United Nations Environment Programme (UNEP), was launched to foster greater industry awareness of environmental risk in insurance decisions. It is a forum in which practitioners share experiences across lines of business and national boundaries, and develop a better understanding of environmental issues. Insurers participating in the initiative want to be proactively involved when strategies for dealing with new risks are debated and when regulatory frameworks are defined. Swiss Re was one of the architects of the initiative.

16   Ulrich Bremi's remarks were made during an August 1, 1999 interview with Dr. Walter Gunthardt, Economics Editor of the *Neue Zurcher Zeitung*. The interview, which also included Walter B. Kielholz, CEO of Swiss Re, was later published in a Swiss Re brochure titled *The Art of Taking Risks* (1999).

17   RoperASW, "Green Gauge Report 2002," (see n. 7).

18   Government purchasing agents in most developed countries have approved lists of vendors that meet specified stewardship standards, The Environmentally Preferable Purchasing guidelines of the U.S. Environmental Protection Agency (EPA), for example, include "Tips for Buying 'Green' with the Government Credit Card." For additional perspective, see (www.greenseal.org/greeninggov.htm).

19   Dalla Costa, *The Ethical Imperative*, 185 (see Ch. 1, n. 3).

20   Ibid., 178.

21   Michael Treacy and Fred Wiersema, "Customer Intimacy and Other Value Disciplines," *Harvard Business Review* (Jan.–Feb. 1993). Copies of the article (HBR reprint 93107) can be ordered via (www.hbsp.harvard.edu).

Chapter 10

1   William C. Capacino et al., "A Global Study of Supply Chain Leadership and its Impact on Business Performance," an Accenture, Stanford and INSEAD research report,

October 2003. The study analyzed financial data from more than 600 global companies and applied statistical models to assess supply chain performance relative to market-capitalization growth. The report analyzed the operating strategies of more than 20 leading companies, including Nokia.

2   HP's Supplier Code of Conduct Questionnaire (question 4) asks all tier-one suppliers: "Does your company have a code of conduct or similar standards to which you expect your suppliers (including temporary labor agencies) to adhere?" HP asks this question because it wants all suppliers to have, eventually, codes of conduct that adhere to its standards on environment, and worker health and safety, as well as fair labor and employment policies.

3   The U.N. Global Compact has become a model for procurement practices of the best corporate stewards. These corporate leaders expect suppliers to adopt environmental best practices, to honor the Universal Declaration of Human Rights, to treat employees fairly in accordance with the conventions of the International Labor Organization (ILO) and to contribute to the social well-being of the communities in which they operate.

4   Although HP may be the most advanced company in the computer industry in terms of implementing social and environmental standards for suppliers, others are moving ahead briskly. Lindsey Ridgeway, program coordinator of HP's Supply Chain Social and Environmental Responsibility (SER) Program, told me in an August 4, 2004 email message that "IBM and Dell have just released Supplier Codes of Conduct and they, too, are starting to have these requirements of suppliers. Between the three companies, most suppliers in the IT industry will know about the requirements." If HP's leadership in setting SER standards for suppliers sets a pattern for the IT industry, as it appears to be doing, the multiplier effect will be huge. Lower-tier suppliers, many operating in developing economies with lower SER standards, will have to raise their standards if they want to do business with the major global IT players.

5   Economic value-added (EVA) is a commonly used measure in financial analysis. It is defined as net operating after-tax profit minus a charge for the opportunity cost of capital. Information on how to calculate EVA and how companies use it is available at (www.valuebasedmanagement.net).

6   Canon's definition of green products makes a distinction between the environmental qualities of the products themselves and the environmental quality of the processes by which they are produced. This is consistent with their internal design for environment (DfE) and life cycle assessment (LCA) programs.

7   Canon frames its social and environmental ethics in terms of a company's maturity. Mature companies, like mature individuals, understand they are organic parts of larger social and environmental systems and are morally obliged to "play a larger role" by correcting systemic imbalances. Ryuzaburo Kaku, who first articulated kyosei within Canon, explains the philosophy in "The Path of *Kyosei*," *Harvard Business Review* (July–Aug. 1997).

8   Canon's humanistic Code of Conduct and ethics are integral to its kyosei philosophy and are frequently referenced in corporate communications, including the company
website (www.canon.com). To the individualistic Western mind, these may seem general and
lacking in definition; but to the more-consensual Eastern mind they honor a person's natural affinity for the common good. Canon calls this *ji-kaku*, which means "self-awareness of
one's working environment and responsibilities."

9   HP supports the objectives of ISO 14001 on environmental performance and gives
preference to suppliers that have achieved ISO 14001 certification. To help suppliers reduce
paperwork and duplication, HP accepts ISO 14001 conformance in lieu of completing a portion of the HP Supplier Environmental Performance Review Questionnaire.

10   Novo Nordisk's Sustainability Report 2003 contains 22 sections on specific stewardship commitments. "Responsibility in the supply chain" is one of them. Working with con-
tractors and suppliers to support human rights is cited as one of the company's top goals in
this area.

11   David Hamilton, "Inflection Point: Intel Chairman Andrew Grove Talks About How
E-commerce Will Transform Just About Everything," *The Wall Street Journal,* April 17, 2000,
R48.

12   Ibid.

13   For a more precise definition of "creative destruction" see Joseph A. Schumpeter,
Capitalism, Socialism and Democracy, rev. ed. (1942; repr., New York: Harper, 1975) 82–85.

Chapter 11

1   Samuel Gompers, founder and first president of the American Federation of Labor
(AFL), in 1908, according to (www.quotationspage.com).

2   Moody's Investors Service sees a linkage between excessive executive compensation
and the probabilities of corporate credit problems. In a June 2005 report titled "CEO
Compensation and Credit Risk," Moody's VP, Christopher Mann found that companies that
sweeten CEO compensation packages with unusually large bonuses or option grants have
experienced historically higher default rates and more-frequent and larger rating downgrades than have their peers.

3   The "bending over" of the S curve—the slowing and ending of the growth that it
describes—can have many causes. A benign cause may be the introduction of better products or processes. When the cause is life destructive—the abuse of people and/or nature—
the forces of resistance become more intense and the bending over more predictable.

4   Hughes, "Top Tier Rating Is Losing Its Appeal," *The Financial Times* (see Ch. 2, n. 6).

5   The Bank for International Settlements (BIS), known as the world's central bank, in
1988 set minimum capital requirements for member banks in terms of three measures: (1)
tier one capital, which consists primarily of common stock and certain preferred stock; (2)

total capital, which includes tier one plus loss reserves and subordinated debt; and (3) the leverage ratio which is tier one capital divided by risk-adjusted total assets (mainly bank loans). Risk-adjustments cover perceived credit risk and include certain off–balance sheet exposures, such as unfunded loan commitments, letters of credit, and derivative and foreign exchange contracts. To meet minimum capital requirements, bank holding companies must maintain tier one capital ratios exceeding 4 percent, total capital ratios (tier one + tier two) exceeding 8 percent, and leverage ratios exceeding 3 percent. The following shows how HSBC compares to its three largest global money-center bank peers. It has the soundest ratios in all three categories, and the highest quality of earnings (in large part because of its more-conservative use of derivatives). It has also had the highest net income growth and strongest stock market performance for the 10 years ending December 30, 2005.

Year-end 2005 Capital Ratios

Bank Holding Company	Tier One	Total Capital	Leverage
BIS Minimum 4.0%	*8.0%*	*3.0%*	
Well Capitalized Minimum 6.0	*10.0*	*5.0*	
HSBC Group **9.0**	**12.8**	**9.0**	
Bank of America 8.3	11.1	5.9	
Citigroup 8.8	12.0	5.4	
JPMorgan Chase 8.1	11.2	6.1	

6   Accounting for capital ratios is often more art than science. Citigroup and JPMorgan Chase are both more aggressive in their accounting practices than is HSBC. Each carries hundreds of billions of dollars in potential liabilities off their balance sheets in the forms of "securitized" loans and bonds, and option contracts. Were they required to disclose these fully, their capital ratios would likely fall below the "well-capitalized minimum" shown in note 4, and possibly also below the global standards set by the Bank for International Settlements (BIS).

7   One indicator of a company's skill in bidding for insurance contracts is its "combined ratio" of claims and expenses to premium income. High ratios indicate trouble. In 2002, a difficult year for reinsurers, Munich Re's combined ratio was 123, versus 104 for Swiss Re. Since 2002 both reinsurers have held their combined ratios in the vicinity of 98.

8   Moody's bond rating on Alcoa (A2) is strong for a metals company. Its largest competitor, Alcan, is rated two notches lower at Baa1. Alcoa has generated consistently strong and positive free cash flow in the past five years (2000–2004), whereas Alcan has had a cumulative negative free cash flow for this period. Moody's bond rating on Stora Enso (Baa1) is better than that of its nearest competitors, International Paper (Baa2), Louisiana Pacific (Baa3), and Georgia Pacific (Ba3). Stora has also had consistently positive free cash flow during the five-year period from 2000 to 2004, whereas the others have not.

9   Moody's Corporation Annual Report 2002, 15 (http://ccbn19.mobular.net/ccbn/7/

191/199/).

10   Henny Sender, "Market Fears are Spreading to Asset Backed Securities," *The Wall Street Journal*, May 29, 2003. Sender cites John Olert, a managing director of Fitch Ratings: "The trends are significantly worse than our expectations. We are downgrading both the companies and the deals in this sector."

11   Ulrike Dauer and Anita Greli, "Swiss Re Narrows 2002 Loss; Write-Down Hits Munich Re," *The Wall Street Journal*, March 28, 2003. The article compared Swiss Re's "steps to preserve its capital" to those of Munich Re, the world's largest reinsurer. Although both had large casualty and investment losses in 2001 and 2002, Swiss Re had the better plan for restoring its financial strength. By cutting its dividend, working internally to preserve its equity capital, and improving its risk management, the company told investors it saw no need to raise fresh funds in the global capital markets. Munich Re, by contrast, reported it was selling assets and planned to raise additional capital through a subordinated bond issue. On March 27, 2003, while Swiss Re shares jumped 6.3 percent in value, those of Munich Re dropped 11 percent—a huge, 17.3-percent performance gap. The following week Moody's put Munich Re on watch for a credit rating downgrade.

12   John R. Coomber, CEO and Bruno Porro, Chief Risk Officer, "Executive Statement," in Swiss Re Sustainability Report 2002 (www.swissre.com).

13   W. James McNerney, Jr., Chairman and CEO, 3M, Environmental, Social & Economic Sustainability Report 2002.

14   Alcoa estimates that approximately two-thirds of beverage cans and 85–90 percent of the aluminum in cars are returned for recycling. Recycling saves 95 percent of the energy it takes to make new metal from ore and it lessens the need for solid waste disposal.

15   Paul O'Neill, Chairman and CEO, Alcoa, 1999 Alcoa Annual Report (www.alcoa.com).

16   Justin Fox, "Nokia's Secret Code," Fortune Magazine (May 1, 2000) (http://money.cnn.com/magazines/fortune/fortune_archive/2000/05/01/278948/index.htm)

17   Ian Wylie, "Calling for a Renewable Future," Fast Company 70 (May 2003): 46.

18   Stora Enso "Sustainability 2003 Report," 17 (www.storaenso.com).

19   International Paper (IP) and Georgia Pacific (GP) are examples of forest companies that over-leveraged themselves during the late 1990s in a bid to dominate their markets through acquiring other companies. From this period to year-end 2005, Moody's lowered IP's credit rating from A3 to Baa3 and GP's from Baa2 to Ba2. By year-end 2005, GP was so weakened that it was taken over by Koch Industries, and IP, in spite of selling important assets, still had a debt-equity ratio (132 percent) that was more than double that of steward-ship leader Stora Enso (57 percent),

20   Claes Dahlback, Chairman, and Jukka Harmala, CEO, Stora Enso, "Letter to Shareholders," in the Stora Enso Annual Report 2002 (www.storaenso.com).

21   Shell Hydrogen was established in 1999 to pursue and develop business opportuni-

ties related to hydrogen and fuel cells. Based in The Hague, Houston, and Tokyo, its goal is to "bring hydrogen into a retail setting." Shell expects that substantial markets for hydrogen-powered vehicles will begin to develop between 2015 and 2025 (and perhaps sooner), considering remaining technical hurdles to be readily surmountable. Its Partial Catalytic Oxidation technology allows a vehicle to run on hydrocarbon mixtures such as LPG as well as hydrogen fuel cells. (www.shell.com/hydrogen).

22   "About Shell Renewables," on the Shell website (www.shell.com/home/Framework? siteId=rw-br&FC2=/rw-br/html/iwgen/leftnavs/zzz_lhn2_0_0.html&FC3=/rw-br/html/ iwgen/about_shell/who_we_are_0729.html).

23   Nicholas Riccio and Giovanni Galeotafiore, "The Decline and Fall of the 'AAA' Rated Company," research report in Standard & Poor's Ratings Direct, March 8, 2005.

Chapter 12

1   Peter F Drucker, "The Theory of the Business," *Harvard Business Review: Business Classics* (orig. Sept.–Oct. 1994): 32–41 (HBR reprint #94506). This article is about building, implementing, and continually testing a valid theory of business. All quotations from Drucker in this chapter are from the cited article.

2   Zohar, *Rewiring the Corporate Brain,* 24 (see Ch. 1, n. 17).

3   Fritjof Capra, *The Web of Life* (New York: Anchor Books, 1996), 27. Capra credits Heinz von Foerster for this observation.

4 See Maturana and Varela, *The Tree of Knowledge* (see Ch. 2, n. 13).

5   The self-making capacity of management by means (MBM) is described by Johnson and Broms in *Profit Beyond Measure* (see Introduction, n. 6).

6   Abraham Maslow's hierarchy of human needs differentiates between basic needs (survival, safety, and security) and growth needs (belonging, self-esteem, and self-actualization). LAMP companies address these latter needs with their LAS practices. The LAS model links the emotional, mental, and spiritual needs of employees to the creative process.

7   Zohar, *Rewiring the Corporate Brain,* 18 (see Ch. 1, n. 17).

8   Collins and Porras, *Built to Last,* Ch. 3 (see Ch. 2, n. 7, this volume). In Chapter 3, the authors define "core ideologies" as ideals that transcend profits.

9   See the HP website (http://www.hp.com/hpinfo/abouthp/diversity/vision.html").

10   Drucker, "The Theory of the Business," (see n. 1).

11   Erich Fromm, *Beyond the Chains of Illusion* (New York: Simon & Schuster, 1962), 174.

12   Ibid.

13   Paul O'Neill, Chairman and CEO, Alcoa, "1997 Alcoa Environment, Health & Safety Annual Report" (www.alcoa.com).

14   Mark Sirower, *The Synergy Trap* (New York: Free Press, 1997). Sirower found that

approximately two-thirds of mergers and acquisitions actually destroy value for shareholders.

15   There are two approaches to effluent trading—tradable credits and waste exchange programs. The tradable credit system is the more advanced and operates worldwide. The most actively traded credits are currently SO_2 and CO_2 offsets. For more information on effluent trading, see Environmental Financial Products, LLC (www.envifi.com), the Effluent Marketing Exchange (www.emissions.org), and the Environmental Resources Trust (www.ert.net). Waste exchange programs operate more locally because the costs of shipping waste/material streams over long distances can be prohibitive. The U.S. Environmental Protection Agency (EPA) lists dozens of local waste/materials exchanges (www.epa.gov/jtr). The Northeast Recycling Council (www.nerc.org) is a model regional exchange. The National Center for Remanufacturing and Resource Recovery at the Rochester Institute of Technology (RIT) (www.reman.rit.edu) consults with corporations and government on converting waste streams into useful materials.

16   The Global Reporting Initiative (GRI) is a multi-stakeholder process for developing and disseminating sustainability reporting guidelines that look to the economic, environmental, and social dimensions of a company's activities, products, and services. GRI guidelines incorporate the perspectives of representatives from business, accountancy, investment, environmental, human rights, research, and labor organizations from around the world. At year-end 2005, approximately 800 companies were reporting under GRI guidelines out of roughly 64,000 multinational companies then in existence—a ratio of less than two percent. If we were to count only parent companies, and not their subsidiaries, as we do in the LAMP Index, the GRI membership list would be considerably smaller. For example, GRI counts 23 subsidiaries of British American Tobacco and 10 of Telefonica among its member companies. For more information on GRI and its membership companies see www.globalreporting.org.

17   Daniel Dimicro, President and CEO, Nucor, Nucor 2002 Annual Report, 4 (www.nucor.com/indexinner.aspx?finpage=investorinfo).

18   Zohar, *The Quantum Self,* 234-235 (see Ch. 3, n. 20).

Chapter 13

1   Warren Bennis and Patricia W. Biederman, *Organizing Genius: The Secrets of Creative Collaboration* (Reading, MA: Addison-Wesley, 1998), 20.

2   JPMorgan Chase was rated #21 in 2001 and #27 in 2002 on *Business Ethics* Magazine's list of the Top 100 Corporate Citizens. The Center for Corporate Citizenship at Boston College, which compiles the list in collaboration with *Business Ethics,* is quoted in JPMorgan Chase's Community Partnership Report (2003) as saying: "Relative to other organizations, JPMorgan Chase has developed a model that clearly places it among the leaders in corporate involvement in terms of vision, organization and impact. It is a model that demonstrates value to both the corporation and . . . the lives it touches."

3   *Fortune* Magazine has at various times rated JPMorgan Chase as one of "The 100

Best Companies to Work for in America" and "The World's Most Admired Bank." *Fortune*'s archives can be searched (http://money.cnn.com/magazines/fortune/fortune_archive).

4   "Best & Worst 2001," *Fortune* Magazine, December 13, 2001. *Fortune* named Ramqvist one of Europe's 10 worst executives for his inability to pick an "adequate successor." An earlier article (Richard Tomlinson, "Trouble on the Bottom Line," Fortune Magazine, April 18, 2001) described Ramqvist's management style as "dictatorial."

5   Allan T. Malm, Professor, Entrepreneurial Studies, Lund University. Professor Malm's remarks were excerpted from an article titled "Some Say Sony, Ericsson May Be Aiming Too High," published by Bloomberg, Stockholm (October 2, 2001) (www.bloomberg.com).

6   In July 2004 the voting power of Ericsson's A shares was diluted. The voting power of the A shares was reduced from 1,000 times the voting power of the B shares to 10 times the power. This dilution still left the Wallenberg family and Handelsbanken in effective control, but with a softening of their iron grip on the company.

7   Justin Fox, "Nokia's Secret Code," *Fortune* Magazine (see Ch. 11, n. 15). The gist of this feature article was that Nokia's culture is its secret code. Fox notes that the attractions of this kind of hands-off management are obvious—it encourages creativity, entrepreneurship, personal responsibility.

8   Gardner Harris, "Ex-Executives Tell How Bristol Burnished Its Financial Results," *The Wall Street Journal,* front page, December 12, 2002.

9   Ibid.

10   Ibid.

11   Stephen Taub, "Bristol's Former CFO Indicted," CFO.com, June 16, 2005, 1. In the article Taub notes, "The $300 million payment brings the total that the company has paid to shareholders harmed by the fraudulent conduct to $839 million."

12   In the mid-1970s Canon entered the office equipment market with an array of new technologies: the laser beam printer (1975), fax machines (1976), the world's first retention-type copying machine (1977), color copying services (1978), a mini–floppy disk drive (1979), and the NP-8500 ultra-high-speed copying machine (1980). From these early product introductions, Canon has expanded its technology into office networking and multimedia applications.

13   James Bandler and Mark Maremont, "How Ex-Accountant Added Up to Trouble for Humbled Xerox," *The Wall Street Journal,* front page, June 28, 2001.

14   Canon's "Mission" under its current Five Year Plan is on "eco-friendly technologies . . . to benefit people . . . [and] maximize resource efficiency . . . [by] employees that are enthusiastically committed to achieving their ideals." See the Canon website (www.canon.com).

15   Bob Johnstone, "Canon, Lone Wolf," *Wired* magazine (see Ch. 8, n. 13). Johnstone explains how Canon's open, entrepreneurial culture rapidly overtook the more hierarchical, complacent Xerox. He notes "Breaking the Xerox monopoly is the defining event in Canon's corporate history . . . . Copiers were notorious for breaking down, a propensity Xerox exploit-

ed by charging for service calls. [Canon] realized that to be successful, a personal copier would not only have to be cheap, it would also have to be virtually service free. Canon's revolutionary solution was to include all the key components—drum, charger, toner, and cleaner—in a replaceable cartridge. As it turned out, this was not just a good idea for copiers, it was also a great one for laser printers, where "service free" was even more of a priority."

16   Andy Kessler, "JP Hedgie," *The Wall Street Journal,* guest editorial, September 28, 2004. Author and money manager Kessler noted that "JPMorgan is buying its way into the wild hedge fund circus" for the fees and in order to enhance its corporate image.

17   According to the U.S. Comptroller of the Currency, the notional value of derivative contracts of JPMorgan Chase on December 31, 2005 was $48.3 trillion—approximately four times the size of the U.S. economy. That is nearly as much as that for all other major U.S. banks combined. For details see OCC Bank Derivatives Report, Fourth Quarter 2005, Table 1, 18 (www.occ.treas.gov/ftp/deriv/dq405.pdf).

18   In a speech to the Global Association of Risk Professionals (GARP), delivered in New York City (February 28, 2006), Timothy F. Geithner, president of the New York Federal Reserve Bank, said: "The ten largest U.S. bank holding companies, for example, report about $600 billion of potential credit exposure from their entire derivatives positions, the total gross notional values of which are about $95 trillion. This 'credit equivalent amount' is approximately 175 percent of tier-one capital . . . . This is a relatively conservative measure of the credit risk in total derivatives positions, but, for credit derivatives and some other instruments, it still may not adequately capture the scale of losses in the event of default in the underlying credits or the consequences of a prolonged disruption to market liquidity. The complexity of many new instruments and the relative immaturity of the various approaches used to measure the risks in those exposures magnify the uncertainty involved."

19   The growth of JPM's derivative business is tied, in part, to the growth of high-risk debt instruments. The $17 billion bankruptcy of Parmalat is a case in point. Parmalat's poor credit was temporarily disguised from investors by JPM, Citigroup, and Bank of America, which helped the firm generate revenues from offshore shell corporations that the banks helped create. On the supposed strength of that falsely created liquidity, they brokered derivatives based on virtually worthless Parmalat bonds, which they rated as sound financial investments by way of credit default swaps, asset swaps, total return swaps, credit spread options, credit spread forwards, and other exotic derivatives sold by the banks. If JPM and other banks are held accountable for investors' losses on Parmalat bonds, the bank's capital could be further impaired. Parmalat has claimed that the fraud was primarily the banks' doing.

20   In addition to the losses related to Enron and WorldCom, JPM has lost billions through bad loans and derivatives connected with K-Mart, Global Crossing, Tyco, the Argentine government, and Parmalat. In August 2004 it was sued by institutional investors for misleading them on similar investments connected to National Century Financial Enterprises.

21   *The Wall Street Journal,* editorial, July 29, 2003. Referring to emails that detailed the

accounting subterfuge, the WSJ alleged that JPM bankers "knew precisely what they were doing." It concluded, "This is hardly reassuring about the bank's sense of responsibility . . . . Morgan's board of directors and shareholders might ask themselves what kind of a message CEO William Harrison has sent to his troops with his handling of this Enron mess."

22   Eric Dash, "Who Runs Morgan?" *The New York Times* (October 20, 2005), sec. C, 1.

23   Bethany McLean and Peter Elkind, "Enron Banks Dodge a Bullet," *Fortune* Magazine 148 (4) (Sept. 1, 2003) (http://money.cnn.com/magazines/fortune/fortune_archive/ 2003/ 09/01/348180/index.htm).

24   Theresa Brophy, *Value Line Investment Survey,* 13 (Feb. 24, 2005): 2101–2111.

25   The board of directors of JPMorgan Chase was rated by The Corporate Library in June 2003 as one of the 10 worst, out of 1,700 companies in the U.S. The Corporate Library is an independent research group that has been involved in shareholder advocacy. Its concerns about JPM centered on "governance risk," in particular, the board's ability to keep executive compensation under control and in alignment with performance.

26   Total compensation is here defined as salary plus bonus and shares or options. The compensation gap between executives at underperforming JPM and top-performing HSBC is not a one-off event. In the year of the Chase merger, total compensation for William Harrison, CEO of JPM was $17.2 million—more than six times higher than that of Sir John Bond, CEO of HSBC, at $2.8 million.

27   Bernard Simon, "Spotlight on Bill Ford," *The Financial Times UK,* October 17, 2005, 38. Further to Simon's point, see Doron Levin, "Bill Ford Enters Fifth Year Searching for Leaders," Bloomberg (Nov. 8, 2005). Levin reports, "In the four years since Bill Ford took over as CEO of the No. 2 U.S. automaker . . . [Ford] has been beset by executive hiring, firing, resigning, reassigning and headhunting . . . [and] waging combat against rivals for the next promotion."

28   At year-end 2004 Ford's net debt was $138.8 billion and its shareholder equity was $16 billion.

29   Jeffrey McCracken, "General Motors, Ford Offset Losses by Dipping into Cookie-Jar Funds," *The Wall Street Journal,* November 22, 2005.

30   *The Economist,* "Perpetual Motion: A Survey of the Car Industry," September 4, 2004, 8.

31   All information in this sidebar was verified by the author through personal communication with Bill Kwong (Product Communications, Toyota Motor Sales, Torrance, CA), February 22–24, 2006.

32   International Paper made many acquisitions between 1994 and 2000, the peak period of its expansion. Its larger takeovers include: Federal Paperboard (1996), Union Camp (1999), and Shorewood Packaging and Champion International (2000).

33   International Paper's annual reports make little mention of employees and show little concern for their health, safety, work-life balance, or professional development. Except for

a one-page statement in the 2001 annual report on how important good employees are, the annual reports for 2000–2004 mention employees only as raw numbers or in the context of terminations and the associated costs.

34   Data on employee turnover rates were obtained from International Paper's 2002/2003 Sustainability Report (http://www.internationalpaper.com/our%20company/environment/ehs/MenuMain.aspx).

35   John Christoferson, "International Paper Plans Spin off Units," *Associated Press,* July 19, 2005. The article was picked up by various newspapers in the U.S., including the *Kansas City Star,* which titled it "Paper Giant Takes Axe to Its Tree," C3.

36   Source: EPA Toxic Release Inventory (TRI) Program (www.epa.gov/tri/).

37   In September 2004 Stora Enso acquired, from International Paper, Scaldia Papier, a Dutch merchant paper company that has synergies with Stora's Papyrus merchant operations. This sale is noteworthy both for the fact that IP was forced to sell Scaldia to strengthen its balance sheet and for the fact that Stora could buy it because it had a healthy balance sheet. LAMP companies are often able to buy business units of traditionally managed companies at bargain prices because of the latter's failed acquisition strategies.

Chapter 14

1   Malcolm Gladwell, *The Tipping Point* (Boston: Little, Brown and Co.), 258.

2   The case for management by means is best stated in the classic by Johnson and Broms, *Profit Beyond Measure* (see Introduction, n. 6). The authors build their case by analyzing the extraordinary productivity of the Toyota Production System (TPS).

3   At year-end 2005, the market capitalization of the 60 Global LAMP Index™ companies was $3.87 trillion, as compared with $11.26 trillion for the S&P 500 Index and $17.9 trillion for the MSCI World Index. The latter comprises more than 1,500 companies from 23 major market countries.

4   In January 2005 the old ATT was taken over by its former offspring, SBC. The newly merged company will keep the venerable ATT name, which dates back to the company's founding in 1875. However, it will be managed by a new team. SBC was spun out of ATT in 1984 as part of an antitrust action. At the time of the January 2005 takeover, SBC's market value ($80 billion) was more than five times that of its former parent ($15 billion).

5   During this 30-year period (1975–2005), four of the seven old-guard stocks (ATT, GM, U.S. Steel, and Xerox) lost principal value for investors. The three that made money posted compound annual growth rates between approximately 5 percent (AMR and JPMorgan Chase) and 8 percent (Bristol-Myers Squibb). The original ATT was taken over by SBC in 2005, and has re-emerged under new management as ATT, as described in the previous endnote. U.S. Steel went through a series of downsizings and restructurings in the 1980s, a recapitalization in 1991, and a reorganization in 2001.

6   It would be interesting to compare total returns for the Global LAMP Index® relative to other benchmarks for that period (1975–2005). However, the further back in time we go, the more difficult the data become because of mergers and acquisitions, spin-offs, and other events that complicate performance accounting. For this reason, I rest my case for the long-term performance of LAMP companies on professional chart services, such as that found at www.BigCharts.com. These analyses amply support the evidence of our more-detailed, 10-year performance comparisons.

7   In Chapter 8 of his book, *The Loyalty Effect,* Frederick F. Reichheld, chairman emeritus of Bain & Company, describes how employee loyalty translates to customer loyalty and, ultimately, to net present value (see Introduction, n. 1).

8   Heskett, Sasser, and Schlesinger, *The Service Profit Chain* (see Ch. 2, n. 12).

9   Juergen Daum, "Intangible Assets and the Balanced Scorecard," an interview with David P. Norton in "The new New Economy Analyst Report," July 18, 2001 (www.juergen-daum. com/news/07_18_2001.htm).

Chapter 15

1   Warren Buffett, "Chairman's Letter to Shareholders," Berkshire Hathaway 2001 Annual Report (http://www.berkshirehathaway.com/letters/letters.html).

2   Warren Buffett, "Chairman's Letter to Shareholders," Berkshire Hathaway 2004 Annual Report (http://www.berkshirehathaway.com/letters/letters.html).

3   Warren Buffett, "Chairman's Letter to Shareholders," Berkshire Hathaway 2005 Annual Report (http://www.berkshirehathaway.com/letters/letters.html). In his 2005 letter, Buffett referred to the risks of global climate change, explaining that Berkshire's insurance subsidiaries cut back on their coverage of such risks in 2004 because coverage premiums were too low. He then added, "Now our caution has intensified."

4   Buffett, Berkshire Hathaway 2001 Annual Report (see n. 1).

5   According to The Vanguard Group, the average mutual fund had an expense ratio of 132 basis points (1.32 percent) in 2001 (www.vanguard.com). The base management fees and trading costs of most hedge funds exceed 500 basis points. When incentive fees that typically take 20 percent of profits are added in, expense ratios can easily top 1,000 basis points.

6   Buffett, Berkshire Hathaway 2005 Annual Report (see n. 3).

7   E. S. Browning, "Stock Rally Seems Like Déjà Vu," *The Wall Street Journal,* July 14, 2003.

8   John C. Bogle, *The Battle for the Soul of Capitalism* (New Haven: Yale University Press, 2005), 122. Bogle, founder of the Vanguard group of mutual funds, describes the culture of excessive trading that dominates Wall Street in his book, telling how "combined NYSE/NASDAQ volume leaped from 15 million shares a day in 1970, to 80 million in 1980, to 300 million in 1990, to nearly 3 billion in 2000 . . . and 3.3 billion in 2004." Such volume

increases far exceed the growth of economic activity over this 35-year period.

9   In the U.S., pension funds operated by the states of California and Connecticut actively engage corporate managers on social, environmental, and governance issues. Many other states offer "social choice" options in their pension plans. Among these are: Alaska, Colorado, Massachusetts, Illinois, Indiana, Tennessee, Vermont, and Washington. In addition, the cities of New York, Chicago, and San Francisco have social-choice options, as does the giant College Retirement Equity Fund (CREF).

10   According to Securities & Exchange Commission annual reports, revenues to broker-dealers have dramatically increased as a result of hyper-trading activity. Such revenues have grown from $20 billion in 1980, to $76 billion in 1990, to $325 billion in 2000—rates of growth that far exceed those of economic activity.

11   Each year, the Council of Institutional Investors publishes, on its website, brief descriptions of the corporate resolutions put before its members and the shareholder support they generate. During the 2004 proxy season there were 467 resolutions posted on the Council's website, organized by subject, proponent, and voting outcome (www.cii.org).

12   Institutional Shareholder Services (ISS), "2005 Postseason Report: Corporate Governance at a Crossroads," 41 (www.issproxy.com/pfd/2005PostSeasonReport FINAL.pdf.).

13   The Council of Institutional Investor's corporate governance policies are published on its website (www.cii.org).

14   Steven L. Nesbitt, "Long Term Rewards from Shareholder Activism: A Study of the CalPERS Effect," *Journal of Applied Corporate Finance* 4 (4) (Winter 1994): 8–17.

15   Justice Samuel Putnam, writing in a decision of the Massachusetts Supreme Judicial Court in 1830, established The Prudent Man Rule.

16   Council of Institutional Investors, "Portfolio Risk Reduction and Performance Enhancement: A Spectrum of Activism Practices," August 5, 2005, 1–9 (www.cii.org).

17   Freshfields, Bruckhouse, Deringer, "A Legal Framework for the Integration of Environmental, Social and Governance Issues into Institutional Investment," produced for the Asset Management Working Group of the UNEP Finance Initiative, October 2005, 10–11.

18   Ibid., 11.

19   Investment funds that endorsed the six "Principle for Responsible Investment" include: ABP Netherlands with $248 billion in assets, British Telecom's pension scheme ($52 billion), the Caisse des Depots et Consignations of France ($232 billion), the Government Employees Pension Fund of South Africa ($69 billion), and the Norwegian Government Pension Fund ($221 billion).

Chapter 16

1   Warren Buffett, "Chairman's Letter to Shareholders," Berkshire Hathaway 1999

Annual Report (http://www.berkshirehathaway.com/letters/letters.html).

2   Arie de Geus, *The Living Company,* 11 (see Introduction, n. 8).

3   Ibid, 200.

4   Mark Grothe, "Getting It Wrong the First Time," a Glass, Lewis & Co. Restatements Trend Alert, March 2, 2006.

5   John C. Bogle, *The Battle for the Soul of Capitalism,* 25 (see Ch. 15, n. 8). According to Bogle, founder of the Vanguard group of mutual funds, corporate profits grew at an average annual rate of 6 percent between 1980 and 2004, slightly less than the 6.2-percent growth rate of nominal GDP.

6   Graef Crystal, "Wall Street Chiefs Cruising on Pay Gravy Train," Bloomberg (March 14, 2006).

7   Bogle, *The Battle for the Soul of Capitalism,* xvi–xvii (see Ch. 15, n. 8).

Epilogue

1   Henry David Thoreau, *Walden; Or, Life in the Woods*

2   In October 2003 Swiss Re announced a plan to become carbon neutral by 2013 through reducing its energy consumption and buying carbon offset credits. Swiss Re also offers commercial solutions to client companies through its risk assessment, mitigation strategies, and transfer know-how. In December 2004 HSBC pledged to become carbon neutral by 2006 through a combination of reducing energy use, buying green energy, trading carbon credits, and planting trees.

Index

Acknowledgments

The idea of writing a book on corporate stewardship began percolating in my mind during the early 1970s, when I was writing reports on the subject at the investment research firm H.C. Wainwright & Co. At the time I could make a coherent economic case for environmental stewardship as a means of conserving resources and reducing the costs of employee health care. But I was too schooled in linear cause-and-effect thinking to see the broader economic case.

Then, in the mid-1990s, while reflecting on three systems thinking classics—Peter Senge's *The Fifth Discipline*, Arie de Geus's *The Living Company*, and Fritjof Capra's *Web of Life*—I got an insight on how to proceed. Good stewardship was not reducible to checklists of desirable or undesirable corporate behavior. Quite the opposite. It was a systemic way of being, a realization that companies are living entities that are part of a larger social and biospheric web of life. You could not understand good stewardship by stripping it apart into finite segments. You had to see it as a whole, as an expression of a larger respect for life. In fact, it soon became clear that the best corporate stewards mimicked life in virtually everything they did—from the ways they were organized and managed to their processes of creating value.

The title and central theme of *Profit for Life* was inspired by two other authors who helped me see important connections between the ways companies operate and their results: Edward O. Wilson and Danah Zohar. Wilson's "biophilia" explains our deep reverence for life, which is universally expressed in humanity's beliefs and values. Zohar shows how we access our higher thinking capacities when we work in ways that affirm these beliefs and values. Companies that competently respect and mimic life in the ways they operate are therefore predisposed toward innovation. By continually learning, adapting, and reinventing themselves, they extend their opportunities for profit and life expectancies.

I stand on the shoulders of these five authors in particular. Others who have inspired my thinking include (in alphabetical order): Warren Bennis, Anders Broms, Lester Brown, Warren Buffett, James C. Collins, John Dalla Costa, Daniel Goleman, Robert Greenleaf, Charles Handy, Paul Hawken, H. Thomas Johnson, Amory Lovins, Thomas H. Peters, Jerry I. Porras, Frederick Reichheld, and Fred Wiersema.

Beyond these renowned authors and exemplars, I owe a great deal to thinking partners and manuscript readers from the Society for Organizational Learning (SoL). Foremost among these is Rick Karash, who did all the conceptual diagrams in this book and who has continually challenged me toward greater clarity. Chapter 4 is a distillation of an article we coauthored for SoL's journal *Reflections* (Fall, 1993). Nina Kruschwitz, SoL's director of publishing, and Bettye Pruitt, cochair of the SoL Council, have both generously supported me with advice and critical feedback. Sherry Immediato, SoL's executive director, has given me voice in various SoL publications, including most importantly this book.

Other important thinking partners and manuscript readers include: W. Michael Brown, former CEO of The Thomson Corporation; John Budden, director of SoundVest Capital Management and senior business editor of Ottawa's "Business at Night" radio talk show; Mark McElroy, chairman of Knowledge Management Consortium International (KMCI); Ezra Levine, partner, Arrowstreet Capital, LLC; and Frank Peabody, cochair of the Merton Foundation and former CEO of the Meidinger consultancy.

For six of the 10 years I spent researching and writing *Profit for Life*, I have had the guidance of my friend and neighbor Karen Speerstra, who is both an author and a consulting editor. A former director of publishing at Butterworth Heinemann, she helped me envision the book's audience and write to their interests. Debra Simes, another consulting editor to SoL, was brilliant at distilling complex thoughts into simple prose.

The corporate leaders, NGO representatives, journalists, and independent researchers I have interviewed in the course of my research are far too numerous to mention. Some of them are cited in the book's endnotes. The rest will know who they are.

And finally, to my family, how can I ever say how much I have thrived on your love and inspiration? The notion of stewardship was planted in me at an early age, first by my mother, Marjorie, and later by her brother, Robert Saltonstall, who was the very model of a thoughtful corporate steward. My wife, Jeanne, was my most constant thinking partner. She urged me to continually think as an ecologist, especially in understanding the bonds companies develop with employees and other important stakeholders. She also coined the phrase "deep stewardship," which brilliantly distills the mental model I present here. Our children—Caroline, Molly, Josiah, Jordan, and Josh—embody the future we both so passionately care for.

About SoL

SoL, The Society for Organizational Learning, Inc., is a nonprofit membership organization that connects researchers, organizations, and consultants around the world. Founded in 1997, SoL's purpose is to create and implement knowledge for fundamental innovation and change. By providing a variety of forums, projects, courses, and publications, SoL enables individuals and institutions to expand their capacity for inspired performance, creating results together that they could not create alone.

SoL publishes an e-journal, *Reflections*, that is available by subscription or as a benefit of membership. A portion of the net proceeds from SoL publishing sales are reinvested in basic research, leading-edge applied learning projects, and building a global network of learning communities.

More information about projects, resources, membership,
and publications can be found at
www.solonline.org.